Corpus Approaches to Contemporary British Speech

Featuring contributions from an international team of leading and up-and-coming scholars, this innovative volume provides a comprehensive sociolinguistic picture of current spoken British English based on the Spoken BNC2014, a brand new corpus of British speech. The book begins with short introductions highlighting the state of the art in three major areas of corpus-based sociolinguistics, while the remaining chapters feature empirical studies based on the Spoken BNC2014 data. These analyses focus on English spoken in everyday situations in the UK, with brief summaries reflecting on the sociolinguistic implications of this research included at the end of each chapter. The Spoken BNC2014 as a robust dataset allows this team of researchers the unique opportunity to focus on speaker characteristics such as gender, age, dialect and socio-economic status, to examine a range of sociolinguistic dimensions, including grammar, pragmatics and discourse, and to reflect on the major changes that have occurred in British society since the last corpus was compiled in the 1990s. This dynamic new contribution to the burgeoning field of corpus-based sociolinguistics is key reading for students and scholars in sociolinguistics, corpus linguistics, pragmatics, grammar and British English.

Vaclav Brezina is a Lecturer at the Department of Linguistics and English Language, Lancaster University. His research interests are in the areas of corpus design and methodology, sociolinguistics and statistics. He is an author of *Statistics in Corpus Linguistics: A Practical Guide* (CUP, 2018). He also designed a number of different tools for corpus analysis such as #LancsBox, BNC64, Lancaster Vocab Tool and Lancaster Stats Tool online. He has been involved in the development of corpora such as the Spoken BNC2014, Trinity Lancaster Corpus and Guangwai-Lancaster Corpus.

Robbie Love is a Research Fellow at the School of Education, University of Leeds, with research interests in applied and corpus linguistics. He completed his PhD at Lancaster University in 2017, where he was lead researcher in the development of the Spoken BNC2014. Before moving to Leeds, he held a post-doctoral position at Cambridge Assessment English, where he worked on the development of the Cambridge Learner Corpus.

Karin Aijmer is Professor Emerita in English Linguistics at the University of Gothenburg, Sweden. Her research interests focus on pragmatics, discourse analysis, modality, corpus linguistics and contrastive analysis. Her books include *Conversational Routines in English: Convention and Creativity* (1996), *English Discourse Particles: Evidence from a Corpus* (2002), *The Semantic Field of Modal Certainty: A Study of Adverbs in English* (with co-author) (2007) and *Understanding Pragmatic Markers: A Variational Pragmatic Analysis* (2013). She is co-editor of *Pragmatics of Society* (Handbooks of Pragmatics, Mouton de Gruyter, 2011) and of *A Handbook of Corpus Pragmatics* (CUP, 2014), and co-author of *Pragmatics: An Advanced Resource Book for Students* (Routledge, 2012).

Routledge Advances in Corpus Linguistics

Edited by Tony McEnery
Lancaster University, UK
Michael Hoey, *Liverpool University, UK*

15 Spoken Corpus Linguistics
From Monomodal to Multimodal
Svenja Adolphs and Ronald Carter

16 Digital Literary Studies
Corpus Approaches to Poetry, Prose, and Drama
David L. Hoover, Jonathan Culpeper, and Kieran O'Halloran

17 Triangulating Methodological Approaches in Corpus Linguistics Research
Edited by Paul Baker and Jesse Egbert

18 The Language of Hate
A Corpus Linguistic Analysis of White Supremacist Language
Andrew Brindle

19 Metaphor, Cancer and the End of Life
A Corpus-Based Study
Elena Semino, Zsófia Demjén, Andrew Hardie, Sheila Payne and Paul Rayson

19 Understanding Metaphor through Corpora
A Case Study of Metaphors in Nineteenth Century Writing
Katie J. Patterson

20 TESOL Student Teacher Discourse
A Corpus-Based Analysis of Online and Face-to-Face Interactions
Elaine Riordan

21 Corpus Approaches to Contemporary British Speech
Sociolinguistic Studies of the Spoken BNC2014
Edited by Vaclav Brezina, Robbie Love and Karin Aijmer

For a full list of titles in this series, please visit www.routledge.com

Corpus Approaches to Contemporary British Speech

Sociolinguistic Studies of the Spoken BNC2014

Edited by
Vaclav Brezina, Robbie Love
and Karin Aijmer

Routledge
Taylor & Francis Group

NEW YORK AND LONDON

First published 2018
by Routledge
711 Third Avenue, New York, NY 10017

and by Routledge
2 Park Square, Milton Park, Abingdon, Oxon OX14 4RN

Routledge is an imprint of the Taylor & Francis Group, an informa business

© 2018 Taylor & Francis

Library of Congress Cataloging-in-Publication Data
A catalog record for this book has been requested

ISBN: 978-1-138-28727-3 (hbk)
ISBN: 978-1-315-26832-3 (ebk)

Typeset in Sabon
by Apex CoVantage, LLC

MIX
Paper from
responsible sources
FSC
www.fsc.org   FSC® C013056

Printed and bound in Great Britain by
TJ International Ltd, Padstow, Cornwall

Contents

Preface   vii
Acknowledgements   viii

PART I
**Short Introductions to Corpus-Based Sociolinguistics
and the BNC2014**   1

1 Corpus Linguistics and Sociolinguistics: Introducing
   the Spoken BNC2014   3
   VACLAV BREZINA, ROBBIE LOVE AND KARIN AIJMER

2 The Spoken BNC2014: The Corpus Linguistic Perspective   10
   TONY MCENERY

3 Current British English: The Sociolinguistic Perspective   16
   BEATRIX BUSSE

4 Using the Spoken BNC2014 in CQPweb   27
   ANDREW HARDIE

PART II
Discourse, Pragmatics and Interaction   31

5 Politeness Variation in England: A North-South Divide?   33
   JONATHAN CULPEPER AND MATHEW GILLINGS

6 *'That's Well Bad'*: Some New Intensifiers in Spoken
   British English   60
   KARIN AIJMER

 7 Canonical Tag Questions in Contemporary British English 96
    KARIN AXELSSON

 8 *Yeah, Yeah Yeah* or *Yeah No That's Right*: A
    Multifactorial Analysis of the Selection of Backchannel
    Structures in British English 120
    DEANNA WONG AND HAIDEE KRUGER

PART III
Morphosyntax 157

 9 Variation in the Productivity of Adjective Comparison in
    Present-Day English 159
    TANJA SÄILY, VICTORINA GONZÁLEZ-DÍAZ
    AND JUKKA SUOMELA

10 The Dative Alternation Revisited: Fresh Insights From
    Contemporary British Spoken Data 185
    GARD B. JENSET, BARBARA MCGILLIVRAY
    AND MICHAEL RUNDELL

11 *'You Still Talking to Me?'*: The Zero Auxiliary
    Progressive in Spoken British English Twenty Years On 209
    ANDREW CAINES, MICHAEL MCCARTHY
    AND PAULA BUTTERY

12 *'You Can Just Give Those Documents to Myself'*:
    Untriggered Reflexive Pronouns in 21st-Century Spoken
    British English 235
    LAURA L. PATERSON

    Contributors 256
    Index 261

Preface

The volume is a contribution to the area of corpus-based sociolinguistics. Its main aim is to provide new insights into current spoken British English based on the Spoken British National Corpus 2014 (Spoken BNC2014), a brand new corpus of British speech (collected around 2014). The Spoken BNC2014 is a subset of the new British National Corpus (BNC2014), which is currently being compiled at Lancaster University. The Spoken BNC2014 samples English used in everyday situations across the UK, with a particular focus on speaker characteristics such as gender, age, region and socio-economic status. It therefore allows an in-depth exploration of social factors that play a crucial role in the use of language in current British society.

The idea for this book started in December 2015, when we received an overwhelmingly positive response to our call for applications for early data access to the Spoken BNC2014. The Spoken BNC2014 Sample was made available to the authors of twelve successful proposals. These were selected based on their innovative use of the data and the significance of the topic. Eight of the resulting research papers are featured in the current volume, while the remaining ones can be found in a special issue of the *International Journal of Corpus Linguistics* (IJCL, 22(3), 2017). The publication of both this volume and the special issue of IJCL are intended to celebrate the public launch of the Spoken BNC2014 in September 2017 and demonstrate its potential for research on current British speech. Our hope is that the readers will find the exploration of current British speech and the changes that have taken place over the period of the last twenty years as exciting as we did when we were reading through the chapters and preparing the volume.

Acknowledgements

We wish to thank the authors of the chapters for their contributions bringing unique insight into current British speech. The chapters in this volume were externally reviewed; we are greatly indebted to the external reviewers for their time and helpful comments on the submissions. We would like to thank Mercedes Durham, Signe Oksefjell Ebeling, Jesse Egbert, Robert Fuchs, Sandra Goetz, Stefan Gries, Andrew Hardie, Sebastian Hoffmann, Susan Hunston, Christian Mair, Heike Pichler, Maria Stubbe, Charlotte Taylor, Gunnel Tottie and Deanna Wong. We also extend our thanks to the collaborators from CUP, Claire Dembry, Olivia Goodman, Laura Grimes, Sarah Grieves and Imogen Dickens, and the Routledge editors. Finally, we are very grateful to Sam Armstrong for assistance with formatting of the chapters.

The work on the book was supported by ESRC grants no. EP/P001559/1 and ES/K002155/1.

Vaclav Brezina
Robbie Love
Karin Aijmer

Part I

Short Introductions to Corpus-Based Sociolinguistics and the BNC2014

1 Corpus Linguistics and Sociolinguistics

Introducing the Spoken BNC2014

Vaclav Brezina, Robbie Love and Karin Aijmer

1.1 Sociolinguistics Meets Corpus Linguistics

Systematic, large-scale exploration of sociolinguistic features in everyday language use has been made possible by the availability of corpora representing informal speech, such as the demographically sampled spoken component of the British National Corpus (the Spoken BNC1994DS) and indeed the new Spoken BNC2014 (see Section 1.2). These corpora include rich metadata about social characteristics of the speakers and a large volume of data, which can be analysed using different techniques. Sociolinguistic exploration of large corpus data is, however, not without its challenges (e.g., Brezina & Meyerhoff, 2014). Language represents a dynamic system with variation occurring simultaneously at multiple levels, reflecting both conscious and unconscious choices by speakers as well as the requirements of the mode of communication, genre and a specific linguistic context (see Chapter 3 in this volume). Capturing socially meaningful variation is therefore a difficult task, requiring a good understanding of social and linguistic processes as well as familiarity with the dataset. The analysis often needs to shift between showing general patterns in the data and providing specific examples of language use to arrive at an interpretation that does justice to the complexity of the data. Bringing corpus linguistics and sociolinguistics together (cf. Baker, 2010) to investigate current spoken British English creates a unique opportunity to gain insight into everyday language use of people from different parts of the UK and different 'corners' of society. It is a fascinating exploration to which this volume intends to contribute.

1.2 The Spoken BNC2014: Full Dataset and Sample

For over twenty years, the British National Corpus (BNC) has been one of the most widely known corpora used as a representative sample of current British English. Focusing on the five-million-token Spoken BNC1994DS, Love, Dembry, Hardie, Brezina, and McEnery (2017) show that no other orthographically transcribed spoken corpus compiled since its release has matched it in its size, representativeness or usefulness. However, as Love, Dembry, Hardie, Brezina, and McEnery (2017) argue, a new dataset reflecting current usage is needed to better serve the requirements of the research community than the aging Spoken BNC1994DS.

The Spoken BNC2014 is a response to this need. Publicly released in September 2017, initially via CQPweb (Hardie, 2012), the corpus is a result of collaboration between the ESRC Centre for Corpus Approaches to Social Science (CASS)[1] at Lancaster University and Cambridge University Press (CUP).) Love, Dembry, Hardie, Brezina, and McEnery (2017) describe in greater detail how the Spoken BNC2014 was designed and built within the Lancaster/Cambridge partnership; the BNC2014 user guide (Love, Hawtin, and Hardie 2017) includes information about the structure of the full 11.5-million-word corpus.

The studies in this volume are based on a five-million-token sample of the Spoken BNC2014 data, referred to as the Spoken BNC2014 Sample (Spoken BNC2014S), which contains transcripts from conversations recorded between 2012 and 2015. The Spoken BNC2014S was made available on a competitive basis to the authors of this volume, who focused on a variety of sociolinguistic applications (see Section 1.3). The Spoken BNC2014S consists of 4,784,691 tokens (including punctuation), approximately 60% of which were produced by female speakers and 40% by male speakers. A wide range of age groups are represented in the dataset, with the largest proportion (41%) in the data being produced by speakers between 19 and 29. Information is also available about the speaker's socio-economic status and region. A detailed break-down of these categories is provided in the Appendix at the end of this chapter.

1.3 Sociolinguistic studies of the Spoken BNC2014

This volume offers four short theoretical/methodological pieces and eight empirical studies. It demonstrates a corpus-based sociolinguistic approach to the Spoken BNC2014 and provides a snapshot of sociolinguistic variation in spoken British English in the 2010s, often contrasted with the situation in the 1990s. The volume is divided into three broad sections: (i) Introductions, (ii) Discourse, Pragmatics and Interaction, and (iii) Morphosyntax.

I Introductions to Corpus-Based Sociolinguistics and the Spoken BNC2014

In addition to this introduction, the first section of this volume comprises three short contributions, which offer a reflection about the state of the art in corpus linguistics and sociolinguistics and provide context to the empirical chapters that follow. McEnery offers a compelling account of the major design decisions when building the Spoken BNC2014; this chapter lays out principles of spoken corpus design and highlights the importance of data in corpus linguistics. Busse's contribution outlines different sociolinguistic perspectives on British English with the focus on the current debates in the field. Finally, Hardie highlights some of the main features to be found in CQPweb—the online corpus analysis system which hosts the Spoken BNC2014.

II Discourse, Pragmatics and Interaction

This section is devoted to studies dealing with language use in context and the dynamics of discourse. In Chapter 5, Culpeper and Gillings focus on a well-known stereotype about British politeness. Whilst politeness in Britain is often thought of as a monolithic phenomenon characterised by indirectness, there is an assumption in lay discourse that northerners are perceived as having very different politeness practices from southerners, practices which, broadly, are characterized by friendliness. The authors put this assumption to the test by selecting fourteen key British formulaic politeness expressions, each belonging to one of three different types of politeness (tentativeness, deference or solidarity), and then examining their frequencies in the combined north and south components of the Spoken BNC2014S and the Spoken BNC1994DS.

In Chapter 6, Aijmer draws attention to new and unusual intensifiers in present-day English which appear to be in the process of undergoing delexicalisation and grammaticalisation. The following intensifiers fit into this category of intensifiers: *fucking, super, dead, real, well (good)* and *so(+NP)*, in their roles as intensifiers before adjectives. Aijmer's method involves a comparison of the intensifiers in the Spoken BNC1994DS and Spoken BNC2014S.

The aim of Axelsson's contribution (Chapter 7) is to provide an in-depth analysis of the frequencies and formal features of tag questions (including instances with *innit*) as well as their distribution across gender, age, dialect and socio-economic status. This study complements the evidence in her previous work, which is based on the BNC1994DS. The study thus explores diachronic change in informal discourse and its dynamics.

In Chapter 8, the final chapter in this section, Wong and Kruger examine structural categories derived from the number of words, non-words and partial forms that contribute to a backchannel. They seek to establish the factors that condition the selection of various backchannel structures in British English, using a multifactorial method. With the help of corpus annotation, they identify backchannel structures, and then use grammatical and speaker metadata associated with each utterance as predictors of backchannel choice.

III Morphosyntax

The final section in this volume is concerned with morphosyntactic features in British speech. Säily, González-Díaz and Suomela's chapter (Chapter 9) is a contribution which investigates the use of adjective comparison. It focuses on the productivity of two comparative strategies in English: the inflectional -*er* and the periphrastic *more* strategy. The study builds on recent research using novel methodologies that shows sociolinguistic variation in the productivity of extremely productive derivational suffixes.

Jenset, McGillivray and Rundell's contribution (Chapter 10) investigates English verbs whose argument structure preferences include the dative alternation (*Give me the money/Give the money to me*). Although this is a well-researched topic, most published work draws either on introspection or on data from written sources. Using contemporary unscripted spoken data will therefore take the research into fresh territory and will bring new insights about the dative alternation in spoken English with attention being paid to sociolinguistic variation.

Caines, McCarthy and Buttery (Chapter 11) investigate zero auxiliary use in progressive aspect interrogatives in spoken British English, e.g., *You talking to me? Where we going? What you been doing?* The authors outline the situation of the progressive aspect in English, including the zero auxiliary, and offer two comparable empirical studies on the use of zero auxiliary in British speech, one dealing with data from the 1990s, the other with 2010s data.

Finally, Paterson (Chapter 12) explores the use of untriggered reflexives in current British English from the sociolinguistic perspective, i.e., the use of untriggered reflexives by particular demographic groups (defined by age, gender, etc.). The analysis provides a snapshot of current usage of untriggered reflexives and facilitates comparison with the existing corpus-based research of this grammatical phenomenon.

Note

1 The Spoken BNC2014 compilation project was supported by the ESRC Centre for Corpus Approaches to Social Science, ESRC grant reference ES/K002155/1.

References

Baker, P. (2010). *Sociolinguistics and corpus linguistics*. Edinburgh: Edinburgh University Press.

Brezina, V., & Meyerhoff, M. (2014). Significant or random? A critical review of sociolinguistic generalisations based on large corpora. *International Journal of Corpus Linguistics*, 19(1), 1–28.

Hardie, A. (2012). CQPweb—combining power, flexibility and usability in a corpus analysis tool. *International Journal of Corpus Linguistics*, 173, 380–409.

Love, R., Dembry, C., Hardie, A., Brezina, V., & McEnery, T. (2017). The spoken BNC2014: Designing and building a spoken corpus of everyday conversations. *International Journal of Corpus Linguistics*, 22(3), 319–344.

Love, R., Hawtin, A., & Hardie, A. (2017). *The British national corpus 2014: User manual and reference guide (version 1.0)*. Lancaster: ESRC Centre for Corpus Approaches to Social Science.

Appendix: Population of the Main Speaker Demographic Categories in the Spoken BNC2014 Sample (BNC2014S)

Gender

Gender	No. Words
Female	2,872,758
Male	1,911,836
Unknown	97
Total	4,784,691

Age

Age	No. Words
0–10	1,281
11–18	191,987
19–29	1,961,779
30–39	834,379
40–49	463,022
50–59	375,368
60–69	625,013
70–79	254,263
80–89	45,066
90–99	3,812
Unknown	28,271
Total	4,784,241

Socio-Economic Status: NS-SEC

NS-SEC	Description	No. Words
1.1	Higher managerial, administrative and professional occupations:	81,728
1.2	Large employers and higher managerial and administrative occupations	106,0691
2	Higher professional occupations	1,498,777

NS-SEC	Description	No. Words
3	Lower managerial, administrative and professional occupations	527,335
4	Intermediate occupations	95,523
5	Small employers and own account workers	93,004
6	Lower supervisory and technical occupations	78,227
7	Semi-routine occupations	40,390
8	Routine occupations	668,608
Uncategorised	Students/unclassifiable	614,721
Unknown		25,687
Total		4,784,691

Socio-Economic Status: Social Grade

SG		No. Words
A	Higher managerial, administrative and professional	1,142,419
B	Intermediate managerial, administrative and professional	1,498,777
C1	Supervisory, clerical and junior managerial, administrative and professional	622,858
C2	Skilled manual workers	93,004
D	Semi-skilled and unskilled manual workers	118,617
E	State pensioners, casual and lowest grade workers, unemployed with state benefits only	1,283,329
Unknown		25,687
Total		4,784,691

Region

Global	Country	Supra-Region	Region
UK (4,419,193)	English (4,358,132)	North (1,158,231)	North East (320,464)
			Yorkshire & Humberside (478,268)
			North West (not Merseyside) (155,552)
			Merseyside (116,420)
		Midlands (375,259)	East Midlands (28,178)
			West Midlands (58,880)
			Eastern (378,065)

Global	Country	Supra-Region	Region
		South (2,470,535)	South West (33,104) South East (not London) (215,420) London (188,188)
	Scottish (10,440)	Scottish (10,440)	Scottish (10,440)
	Welsh (40,843)	Welsh (40,843)	Welsh (40,843)
	Northern Irish (0)	Northern Irish (0)	Northern Irish (0)
Non-UK (74,214)	Irish (12,462)	Irish (12,462)	Irish (12,462)
	Non-UK (61,752)	Non-UK (61,752)	Non-UK (61,752)
Unspecified (291,284)	Unspecified (301,062)	Unspecified (655,169)	Unspecified (2,686,655)

2   The Spoken BNC2014

The Corpus Linguistic Perspective

Tony McEnery

In this brief chapter, I thought it would be helpful to explain the major obstacles we had to overcome in order to construct the Spoken BNC2014. In part it is useful simply as a brief historical account of some of these issues, but there is also a very important methodological purpose to the overview—it both explains some of the important design decisions that shaped the corpus, and makes us reflect on what it means to build and use a model of language.

When the possibility of building a new spoken BNC corpus arose, it raised in my mind a number of very serious questions. How could it be afforded? How might it be collected? Last, but far from least, we had to think of who would use it. Each of these questions represented a barrier to completing the project. Breaking through these barriers shaped the project.

The question of the affordability of the corpus was a serious one. When it was constructed, the first spoken BNC (the Spoken BNC1994) was a very expensive venture by the standards of the time. The BNC1994 was constructed with two large grants from a UK research council (the Science and Engineering Research Council, later renamed the Engineering and Physical Sciences Research Council), direct funding from a government department (the Department for Trade and Industry), substantial contributions from publishers (Chambers, Longman and Oxford University Press) and with further support from the British Academy and the British Library. To give an idea of how substantial the funding needed was, the two research council grants alone, which were focused solely on the part of speech tagging of the corpus, amounted to £471,000 pounds.[1] The project also benefited from the input of Norwegian researchers—indeed, the Spoken BNC1994 would not have been completed without a substantial contribution of data from Norwegian researchers working on a Corpus of London Teenage English (Stenström, Andersen, & Hasund, 2002).

The effort put into the BNC1994 was remarkable both in its scale and in the degree to which the project was a leap of faith—unlike many research projects in the UK today, the output of the project aimed to produce a dataset that enabled a range of possible applications and research projects. It was not a research project *per se*. Yet it was based on a fundamental realisation that the research bottleneck that funding could clear was not related to algorithm development or the pursuit of a specific research question, for example. The bottleneck was the availability of data in the first place which could be used to explore a wide range of research questions. That is the insight that led to such a substantial, yet apparently aimless, project. The team knew, and the funders knew, that if the data was provided much would be possible, and so it proved to be.

Moving on through time, it was very unlikely that a similar argument could be made today. Data now seems to have taken a back seat to the algorithm—there is much talk of machine learning and all that it is believed it may achieve. Data seems at times to be almost taken for granted—it is captured from online or other sources and exploited very rapidly to come to apparently swift and ground-breaking conclusions. In a context like this it was difficult to see how a large-scale project could be put together to build a new BNC. Even when we had started the project, we came across people who—with almost evangelical zeal—would tell us that transcribing material using human transcribers, as we were doing, was quite unnecessary as a machine could do it, and if they could not today they would be able to tomorrow. Every time we heard of some wonder package that could apparently help us or negate our efforts we tried it—and every time we came to the same conclusion: people were wrong. For the type of messy conversational data that we wanted to collect, the doubtless impressive advances in the machine understanding of speech were not at all helpful. This in itself was a reminder to us throughout the project that what we were doing probably represented a bottleneck that still had to be broken—the provision of data to help those wishing to work on such data. If the machines were not modelling it yet, it was probably a sign that there was not appropriate data, or that this material defied the abilities of the machines to analyse it—so we went on.

But let me return to the question in hand—how did we get our work on the corpus funded? Four factors combined to let us achieve this. Firstly, we were fortunate to be within a centre, Corpus Approaches to Social Science (CASS) funded by the UK Economic and Social Research Council.[2] This gave us the flexibility and time to devote some resources to getting the project running—but it was not enough. Secondly, as part of its commitment to CASS, the University of Lancaster gave us a modest research budget each year to allow us to pursue new lines of work. That, combined with the resources from CASS, really helped. Yet we were still short of the resources we needed to complete the project. So we sought additional help and that was provided by an industrial partner, Cambridge University Press, who wished to build a corpus of conversational English to refresh a corpus of spoken English they had developed in the past, Cancode (Carter, 1997). While Cancode had not been made publicly available, we made an agreement with CUP—if they joined forces with us to build the new spoken BNC they could have access to the data, on the understanding that the whole corpus would be made freely available for use in non-profit-making research. They agreed to this and we were almost ready to begin the project. Yet the last point on affordability leads, into the next question—how was it to be done?

Some options for building the corpus were rejected out of hand. We had considered recording pairs of speakers in laboratory settings to get very clean, high-quality recordings. While this may have produced very clean data that may well have been susceptible to automated analysis, we rejected this because it represented the negation of what we wanted—we wanted recordings of spoken interactions that were as natural as possible, produced between social groups that naturally formed and reformed as the events within which speech were occurring unfolded and, crucially, we were interested in language in intimate settings, e.g., in the home. We wanted to study the type of language we experience every day but which, because of its nature, is hard to access and is therefore only analysed at scale if a project such as this one goes to the trouble of collecting the data. So, tempting as the laboratory approach was, we rejected the option.

This left us with the problem faced by the original spoken BNC (Spoken BNC1994)—how were we to record what was said in such a context as unobtrusively as possible? Like the Spoken BNC1994, we would pay due regard to ethics, but before we got to that issue we had the basic mechanical issue of getting people to record conversations to solve. In the early 1990s this was done by distributing and collecting back recording equipment. This was an expensive exercise—equipment had to be purchased and dispatched, users had to be trained, equipment had to be collected, breakages had to be made good and recordings undertaken again if recordings failed for some reason. Yet technology has moved on from the early 1990s, and in 2011 we had noted that rather than having to provide people with recording equipment, an alternative might be to exploit the recording equipment that people commonly carry around with them nowadays—their smartphone. We carried out some field tests with smartphones to see to what extent they could be relied upon to provide fair recordings of conversations suitable for undertaking orthographic transcriptions. The results were compared to what could be achieved with high-quality portable digital voice recorders, and smartphone recordings were found, for our purposes, to be broadly comparable. Hence in working out how the corpus was to be gathered, we also solved the last part of the puzzle of how we were to afford the costs of building the corpus—relying on our contributors to provide the equipment to be used to record their conversations removed a substantial financial burden from the project, making the whole undertaking—just—affordable!

This leaves the last question—who would use it? This, to the people engaged in the project, was very obvious indeed. At the very least, linguists interested in everyday conversation would use this corpus. Some, we were sure, would venture to compare the data we collected with that collected in the early 1990s and look for diachronic change. While that was never going to be easy, it was clearly one of the potential uses of the data that we were collecting. For the first time, we believe, linguists would be able to look at large volumes of conversational English, gathered twenty years apart, and explore changes in spoken English. But we were also sure that some linguists would focus solely on the present—and quite reasonably so, for there is much to say about contemporary spoken English, as this book shows. In due course we are also very sure that researchers interested in computational linguistics and the like will want to use this dataset also, just as they used the Spoken BNC1994. So, the problem for us in thinking of users of the data was not imagining who might use the data; it was, rather, considering which users we excluded by virtue of some of our design decisions. For example, we knew that when we decided to use smartphones for the collection of our data, we were excluding, to all intents and purposes, the great bulk of phoneticians from finding our corpus useful. However, even if we set considerations of affordability to one side, we were centrally focused on other research questions, and in excluding phoneticians as users we were doing no more than the Spoken BNC1994 release did, which did not impact unduly on the use of that data. So when excluding potential groups of users we were driven by pragmatic, but also by more principled, considerations.

So this, in very abstract terms, was how the Spoken BNC2014 was created. We found a way of funding it, we found a means of collecting the data and we were quite sure there was a need for the data. Before concluding, I would like to draw a few lessons from this experience that corpus linguists may wish to reflect on.

Firstly, and most importantly, while technological advances can lead to new approaches to collecting data, we should not always wait for the tide of technology to wash our problems away. It had been assumed in the past that speech technology would ensure that a transcription effort like that which produced the Spoken BNC1994 would not be necessary again and that "the availability of transcribed material online . . . and automatic transcription" would mean that the model of corpus production embodied in the BNC1994 was 'past its sell-by'.[3] Yet such claims have proved premature—there are no large archives of contemporary spontaneous conversations in the home appearing spontaneously on the web from which we could have built our corpus. Also, while it may have appeared in 2007 that speech recognition software would soon conquer messy data such as that we gathered, it has not. Time has moved along and the BNC1994 model of corpus production for spontaneous conversational material gathered in situ has far from passed its sell-by date. So my first word of advice to corpus linguists would be this—if you need to collect and process data for your research, get on with it. If technology overtakes you, so be it. However, if it does not, the research insights you gain will be a rich reward for your efforts. Once reaped, you should ensure that such the reward is shared with as many researchers as possible.

Secondly, a related point is that if, when you are building a corpus, someone tells you to stop because there is a better, automated way of doing it, do not take the statement at face value. Check if it is true by all means, but if it is not, carry on. While we did not succumb to the temptation, it is clearly appealing to think that, but for a little investment of time and money in a technological solution, you might be able to proceed much faster. However, we approached such a temptation with simple British pragmatism. We had a choice—we could invest our money in maybe building our corpus faster by investing in developing technology, or we could use the resource we had, which was sufficient for the purpose, to build the corpus we needed. When trading a hope against a certainty, we plumped for the certainty every time. Had we come across the certainty that technology could have helped us we would have taken it, of course. Yet in spite of trying various tools presented to us as working solutions, none of them were, in fact, solutions when we tried them. So we set them aside and continued with our task. If our principal goal had been the development of speech processing tools, we might have made different decisions—but it was not. Our goal was to clear a research bottleneck by providing a new corpus of spontaneous spoken English conversations in intimate settings, and that is what we made sure we produced.

Finally, never, to use an English idiom, be afraid to cut the cloth to fit. With much more money and infinite time we could have produced a corpus on a grander scale, with a better balance and with all sorts of other desirable attributes. However, we did not let the perfect plan deflect us from a good plan. We used the resources we had to produce the best corpus we could within the limits that those resources set. Given that in many ways the dataset we produced is an improvement on the Spoken BNC1994, the compromises we made in producing a resource that will have a wide range of uses are ones that we are entirely comfortable with and which are entirely justifiable. As with all scientific endeavours, we engage with approximation when we engage with modelling. The UK Office of National Statistics (ONS) articulates our philosophy well—on page twelve of their new Code of Practice, they say one should use statistics and numerical information that "represent the best available estimate of what they aim to measure" and further, that data are "approximations to what the statistics aim to measure". It is important, therefore that the "using and understanding" of those data sources go hand in hand.[4] So it is with a corpus, just as it is with all other data—one needs not merely to use data, but to understand it. In that way the observations based on that data can be best nuanced and understood and points relating, potentially, to design decisions can be identified and considered. So while this brief chapter may have seemed to the casual reader to be an amiable trip down memory lane for the author, there is an important point to what is written here—in presenting the pragmatic and principled design decisions that shaped the corpus I am highlighting, quite consciously and without apology, some of the factors that make the corpus the necessary approximation of reality that any such dataset is bound to be. This is what we should expect, as the ONS notes, and what should lie at the root of a sensible and critical interpretation of any statistical or other analysis arising from such a dataset.

Notes

1 Grant reference GR/F 99847 granted in 1991 and grant GR/K14223/01 awarded in 1994.
2 Grant reference ES/K002155/1.
3 These quotes are from a document produced in 2007 available at www.kilgarriff.co.uk/Publications/2007-KilgAtkinsRundell-CL-Sellby.pdf
4 See the Office for Statistics Regulation's Code of Practice for Statistics: www.statisticsauthority.gov.uk/wp-content/uploads/2017/07/DRAFT-Code-2.pdf

Bibliography

Carter, R. A. (1997). Speaking Englishes, speaking cultures, using CANCODE. *Prospect*, *12*(2), 4–11.
Stenström, A-B., Andersen, G., & Hasund, I. K. (2002). *Trends in teenage talk: Corpus compilation, analysis and findings*. Amsterdam: John Benjamins.

3 Current British English
The Sociolinguistic Perspective

Beatrix Busse

3.1 Introduction

In his famous New York study, Labov (1966) showed a regular pattern of fixed socio-economic stratification of linguistic form, with greater than expected regional and ethnic as well as non-standard differentiation at the lower end of the socio-economic hierarchy. His study marked the *urban turn* in sociolinguistic research and triggered a vast number of follow-up investigations in British cities (Trudgill, 1974; Milroy, 1980; Eberhardt & Downs, 2013). These studies based linguistic meaning in the socio-economic hierarchy or attributed agency to the use of the vernacular or the standard when getting closer to the local dynamics of variation.

More or less fifty years after Labov's seminal work, this chapter aims at looking at the state of the art of current sociolinguistic research of British English; that is, the English language spoken and written on the British Isles and its more specific linguistic variations complexly associated with and created by the interplay between so-called primary societal variables. These include social, geographical, situational, attitudinal and relational variables and also aspects which capture "uncommon" or new emerging phenomena particularly influenced by human and non-human technological variables (Friginal & Bristow, 2018, p. 3). Hence, sociolinguistics is mainly the study of variation in linguistic form and use in interplay with societal influences, and underlying the sociolinguistic model of language is that everybody's language usage is varied for a number of purposes and in varied contexts. In turn, linguistic variation in interplay with societal variables relies on and is constructive of various language norms or characteristic linguistic features of, for example, a language variety or a community's language practices in space and time.

Recent sociolinguistic investigations of Eckert's (2012) "third wave" have highlighted both how linguistic features are indexically endowed with social meaning over time, and how these may serve the functions of social positioning and styling which are dynamic and mutable in context. Hence, a second aim of this chapter is to briefly discuss if and how the "third wave" has also influenced sociolinguistic investigations of British English. This chapter will then end with a brief discussion of future perspectives. I will focus on the observation that in everyday representations, space cannot only be theorised as a fixed geographical coordinate, but rather that through linguistic and other semiotic practices—singular and iterative, material or immaterial—human beings (often declaratively) create places and position themselves so that social meanings may be multidimensionally competing with one another, all the while being in constant transition (Britain, 2009; Busse & Warnke, 2014, and Busse, 2018).

3.2 State of the Art of Current Research

Sociolinguistic investigations of current British English (BE) abound. BE and its varieties often represent the bases of comparison, if not the norms, for studies of languages, dialects, and varieties of global Englishes, most certainly still because BE is the variety of English in Kachru's (1992) inner circle that spread across the world through imperial expansion and colonisation. When the complex relations between language usage and social demographics, register, gender, sexuality, race, nation, workplace, urban space, communities of practice (Lave & Wenger, 1991) and role-relations, as well as power structures, social media or diachrony are studied, linguistic and semiotic data frequently originate in Britain as a geographical space.

So, what are specific features of current British English? In order to answer this question, many (socio)linguists have turned to large corpora and to comparison with other varieties. Baker's (2017) corpus-based investigation of British and American English in the set of eight corpora of the Brown family is a case in point. He discusses the dominance of American English (AE) in triggering language change and leading to the partial 'Americanisation' of BE, which also indicates a 'British English lag' of about thirty years behind some linguistic trends in AE.[1] AE is at the forefront of language change on the grammatical level. For example, BE lags behind AE with regard to the declining use of modal verbs (all examples taken from Baker, 2017). While *who* is increasing in AE, it is decreasing in BE. There is also an increase of apostrophe forms in both varieties—marking a case of densification. For example, *didn't* is increasing in BE and AE, but BE marks the 'follow-my-leader' pattern. As another example of densification can serve the increase of the lexeme *UK*, which in the British corpora becomes a keyword from 1961 onwards. With regard to the use of swear words AE is in the lead, while BE tends to have more discourse markers which are also finding their way into writing.

Generally speaking, empirical studies of linguistic variation on all levels of language profit very much from the growing number of corpus tools, written corpora and the growing body of meticulously compiled spoken corpora of British English and their varieties, which are also register-specific. Outstanding resources for further corpus-assisted sociolinguistic investigations are the Helsinki Dialect Corpus, The Corpus of Global Web-Based English, the British part of the International Corpus of English (which comprises data from different written and spoken genres) or the Brown family of corpora and, of course, the very recently released Spoken BNC2014, which will be followed by the Written BNC2014 in autumn 2018.

Some studies attest to the versatility of these corpus resources. For example, on the basis of the BNC1994, Leech, Rayson, and Wilson (2016 [2001]) provide a word frequency book for both written and spoken British English, including informal dialogues or task-oriented dialogues, which can now be used as a reference guide for further genre studies and studies of sociolinguistic change. At the interface between pragmatics and sociolinguistics, Aijmer (2013) compares the use of *well* between EFL speakers and native English speakers. Beltrama (2015) investigates the strategy of intensification in different genres and for different communicative purposes using the Corpus of Contemporary English, while Tottie (2015) investigates *uh* and *um* as sociolinguistic markers in Spoken British English. Register characteristics are investigated by Johnson and Partington (2018) who explore the representation of "underclass" in the English-speaking press of different political persuasions in various countries.

It comes as no surprise, then, that methodological considerations and discussions of advantages and disadvantages in using corpus methodology have become more frequent (Anderson & Corbett, 2009; Baker, 2010, 2012; Kendall, 2011; Ruhi, Haugh, Schmidt, & Wörner, 2014; Kirk & Andersen, 2016). The complex interplay between linguistic and social variables, on the one hand, and the strive for quantification, which assumes that the correlation between language usage and social variables can be measured, and linguistic distribution as well as (high) frequency data provide patterns of usage that can be further inspected qualitatively, on the other hand, demand a careful consideration of methods and, ideally, a combination of qualitative and quantitative approaches. Using BNC32, a one-million-word corpus of informal speech, Brezina and Meyerhoff (2014) illustrate, for instance, the effect of data skewing if within-group variation is ignored and—following aggregate data—a focus is on inter-group variation only.

Quantitative methods cannot replace qualitative research, but must complement it. One reason for mixed-methods approaches lies in the re-evaluation of certain variables, e.g., gender and, perhaps more recently, also age have been understood as personal, situation-dependent and "performed" (Friginal & Hardy, 2014). Hence, corpus methodology and tools can only be seen as a way into the linguistic data in studies of how groups (defining themselves, e.g., by their gender) employ language across situations and contexts. Clancy (2011), for example, uses a small-scale spoken corpus of two Irish families (middle-class and ethnic minority travellers) to investigate research questions pertaining to variational pragmatics, i.e., "the effect of macro-social pragmatic variation on language in action" (Schneider & Barron, 2008, p. 1). Torgersen, Gabrielatos, and Hoffmann (2018) use the "Linguistic Innovators Project Corpus" (Cheshire, Fox, Kerswill, & Torgersen, 2008 and Cheshire, Fox, Kerswill, & Torgersen, 2013) to study the distribution and function of the pragmatic marker *you get me* among young speakers in inner London.

There can be no doubt that, for BE, the classic variationist agenda, which focuses on regional dialectology and variation in language, is still one of the most important topics in sociolinguistic research. Beal (2010) illustrates the various features of regional dialect variation in England, and Tagliamonte, Durham, and Smith (2014) investigate the future BE GOING TO construction in so-called conservative British dialects. Britain (2011, 2017a) has revised our understanding of dialect formation, reallocation and dialect contact for British dialects.

What Eckert (2012) has termed the "third wave of variationist sociolinguistic research" has influenced sociolinguistic research of BE, too. These studies highlight the stylistic *practices* and the various semiotic repertoires speakers use to position themselves in the social landscape (Bucholtz, 2010). In this view, language use in general and specific linguistic constructions on all levels of linguistic analysis, including (but not limited to) dialectal and pragmatic features, correlate with other semiotic resources and are seen as part of a social semiotic system (developed to be) capable of expressing the full range of a community's or an individual's social concern, attitudes and values. As an example, Moore and Carter (2015), using the speech of individuals living on the Isles of Scilly, investigate the linguistic variables of the vowels in the TRAP and BATH lexical sets. In their speakers' language usage, they find contact features between standard English and the Cornish variety and variation between the speakers due to their different educational backgrounds. Furthermore, they detect phonological deviations which are not in tune with the speakers' "education types" (Moore & Carter, 2015) and which have to be explained by their need to position themselves in interactionally dynamic ways. In a similar vein, Kirkham and Moore (2016) analyse /t/-glottaling and the types of verb processes that occur with the pronouns *we* and *you* in two political speeches by the former UK Labour Party Leader Ed Miliband and correlate these with the ways in which he positions himself in relation to different audiences.

The construction of social meaning through language usage in communities of practice were also starting points for research carried out by Cheshire et al. (2008, 2013) in their long-term project "Linguistic Innovators: The English of Adolescents on London" and "Multicultural London English". On the basis of a corpus of young people aged 16 to 19 from the inner and outer London area, they have illustrated that different ways of speaking can be distinguished in their spoken English based on ethnicity. In addition, they observe group and friendship dynamics influencing phonological and grammatical linguistic innovation. Kerswill (2014) analyses how, why and since when exactly this specific speech style—labelled as "Multicultural London English" by sociolinguistic scholars—came to be stigmatised by the British press, usually alongside usage of the term 'Jafaican'.

Researchers have become critical of ideological discourses that either dominate specific sociolinguistic research trends or bring others in that field to a standstill, on the one hand, and they have become critical of metalinguistic practices of *language criticism* (cf. Busse, Vit, & Möhlig-Falke, 2017) that are rather ideologically overpowering to prescribe good and proper English, on the other. Schwyter (2016), using a vast amount of BBC archival resources, documents the prescriptive BBC broadcasting practices which show conceptualisations of the "correct" or "best" English speaker.

Britain (2017a) shows that the fixed *urban/rural* distinction in traditional and variationist sociolinguistic research has prevented scholars from explaining the complexity of language variation and change in rural areas and has led to a purely geographical conceptualisation of space. Even more pointedly, Britain (2017b) criticises that the sociolinguistic "gaze" has been circular for a very long time because there has been a prevalent sociolinguistic research focus on elite accents and a guiding equation of the ideological view that the BE standard or norm pronunciation is "Received Pronunciation" spoken by exactly that elite (resulting from social and economic considerations of what "the elite" and "the gentry" stand for).

I would like to further follow the path of a sociolinguistics that addresses the constructive potential of linguistic and semiotic practices and show how current sociolinguistic research (of BE) also has to converse with societal challenges such as mobilities, internationalisation, multilingualism, superdiversity (Vertovec, 2007), urbanisation, gentrification and counter-urbanisation, or digitisation—to name but a few. Future sociolinguistic investigations of British English must more prominently than before consider and track the sociolinguistic bricolage, its liminality and "turbulent" character (Brosius & Wenzlhuemer, 2011) and therewith re- and de-centre the current sociolinguistic "gaze" (Britain, 2017c) to the complexity of everyday (sociolinguistic) encounters. These may be momentary, simultaneous and consist of semiotically multivariate data in which, for example, multi- or metrolingualism (Pennycook & Otsuji, 2015) are partly the norm and not (simply) a deviation from a standard. Therefore, sociolinguistic data to be investigated are not only classic sociolinguistic resources, such as interviews, speech samples or language corpora. To do justice to the complexities of linguistic practices in urban space, Busse (forthcoming) includes data from social media outlets (such as Twitter) as well as the names of Wireless Lan Access points (SSIDs), which can only then be made visible, recorded and compiled in a corpus when particular technical tools and software are applied and developed (Busse, forthcoming). At the same time, data must also be more ethnographic in style and include, for example, semiotic landscapes (Jaworski & Thurlow, 2010; Smith, forthcoming), artefacts, street art or graffiti. Methodologically speaking, this demands not only a kind of resilience of the sociolinguist to cope and bear with the heterogeneous and often contradictory semiotic data and their social meanings in context. It demands a triangulation of methods (Busse & Warnke, 2015; Busse, 2018) from disciplines such as ethnography, sociolinguistics, stylistics and corpus linguistics, at least, and a belief in grounded theory (e.g., Strübing, 2004).

The photograph below (Figure 3.1) should be used to briefly illustrate my point.[2] It was taken on 139 Commercial St, London E1 6EB, UK. The coffee shop is directly located next to Spitalfields Market and Liverpool Street Station, which can be defined as gentrification 'hubs' in Shoreditch, London.

The noun phrase 'Brooklyn Coffee' designates the name of this coffee shop and is also part of the semiotic landscape on Commercial Street. It is a discursive place-making strategy with a global dimension. Based on the model of urbanity in Busse and Warnke (2015), Busse (2018) argues that through a number of linguistic and semiotic practices visible in selected gentrified neighbourhoods of Brooklyn, NY, such as Williamsburg, DUMBO or Park Slope, Brooklyn as one of New York's largest boroughs

Figure 3.1 139 Commercial St., London

is created as a brand which is frequently—and by means of different linguistic and semiotic data types—generically referred to by the toponym *Brooklyn*. This generic reference comprises not only direct associations with hipster, artist and coffee cultures and with "how Brooklyn became cool" (Zukin, 2010), but also evaluative comparisons with Manhattan which enregister through language (Johnstone, 2009) Brooklyn to be more 'authentic' (e.g., Coupland, 2003) and 'homegrown' than Manhattan. As the website of Brooklyn Coffee illustrates (see www.brooklyncoffee.co.uk/) the naming practice, its interior design and its philosophy are discursive declarative positionings both as actions and representations within a tradition of global urban place-making, branding and commodification in gentrified neighbourhoods. Hence, the notion of practices and representations of/in the city may even go beyond the discipline of (socio) linguistics. In reality, of course, they encompass all "living experiences of real people in real places" (Wortham-Galvin, 2012, p. 233).

3.3 Conclusion

Current sociolinguistic research of BE is marked by quantitative corpus-assisted investigations that highlight patterns and distributions of sociolinguistic usage paving the way for qualitative interpretations. At the same time, next to classic variationist sociolinguistic investigations, the constructive potential of sociolinguistic variation for social styling has been studied from two angles: a) from that of the sociolinguistic researcher who has both been trapped by and is critical of the empirical and theoretical sociolinguistic bias; and b) from the need to study multivariate data of everyday practices which root discourses about and of particular places or people and function to multimodally declare, construct and make their positions or places. It seems to me that in this vein to further translational research, including the participation of the public in the approach called *citizen science* is inevitable. Cheshire and Fox (2016) and Cheshire, Adger, and Hall (2017) use their corpus of London multicultural English of adolescents to illustrate its potential for the teaching of varieties of English in the UK secondary school curriculum. Mention should also be made of Bell et al.'s (2016) smartphone app which enables the user to discover English dialects and, by means of linguistic crowd-sourcing and citizen science, to document linguistic data in real time, but also to illustrate the ethical and social value of linguistic variation and regional dialects. Following citizens' (local) sociolinguistic paths and their creative processes, as well as how these are represented and practiced, is the task of future sociolinguistic studies of BE.

Notes

1 Corpus-assisted comparisons of BE with AE as well as other varieties have been and are current research trends with a variety of exemplary studies. In chronological order, I would like to refer to: Hoffmann and Lehmann (2000),

Hunston (2002), Leech (2004), Finegan (2004), Leech & Smith, 2005; McEnery and Xiao (2005), Fuster Márquez and Pennock Speck (2008), Dahlmann and Adolphs (2009), Leech, Hundt, Mair, and Smith (2009), Rühlemann (2009), Juola (2012), Baker and Potts (2012), Szmrecsanyi, Grafmiller, Heller, and Röthlisberger (2016) and Bell, Sharma, and Britain (2016).

2 I am grateful to Jennifer Smith for sharing this photograph with me, which is part of her doctoral project on Place-Making Activities in Shoreditch, London. It also belongs to the larger corpus-based research study heiURBAN and comprises a comparison of discursive urban place-making between selected neighbourhoods in Brooklyn and London, UK.

References

Aijmer, K. (2013). Well I'm not sure I think. . .: The use of well by non-native speakers. In G. Gilquin (Ed.), *Errors and disfluencies in spoken corpora* (pp. 93–116). Amsterdam: John Benjamins.

Anderson, W., & Corbett, J. (2009). *Exploring English with online Corpora: An introduction*. Basingstoke: Palgrave MacMillan.

Baker, P. (2010). *Sociolinguistics and corpus linguistics*. Edinburgh: Edinburgh University Press.

Baker, P. (2012). Acceptable bias? Using corpus linguistics methods with critical discourse analysis. *Critical Discourse Studies*, 9(3), 247–256.

Baker, P. (2017). *American and British English: Divided by a common language?* Cambridge: Cambridge University Press.

Baker, P., & Potts, A. (2012). Does semantic tagging identify cultural change in British and American English? *International Journal of Corpus Linguistics*, 17(3), 295–324.

Beal, J. (2010). *An introduction to regional Englishes: Dialect variation in England*. Edinburgh: Edinburgh University Press.

Bell, A., Sharma, D., & Britain, D. (2016). Labov in Sociolinguistics: An introduction. *Journal of Sociolinguistics*, 20, 399–408.

Beltrama, A. (2015). Intensification and sociolinguistic variation: A corpus study. *Proceedings of the 41st Annual Meeting of the Berkeley Linguistics Society*, 41, 15–30.

Brezina, V., & Meyerhoff, M. (2014). Significant or random? A critical review of sociolinguistic generalisations based on large corpora. *International Journal of Corpus Linguistics*, 19(1), 1–28.

Britain, D. (2009). Language and space: The variationist approach. In P. Auer & J. Schmidt (Eds.), *Language and space: An international handbook of linguistic variation* (pp. 315–347). Berlin: De Gruyter.

Britain, D. (2011). The heterogenous homogenisation of dialects in England. *Taal en Tongval*, 63(1), 43–60.

Britain, D. (2017a). Which way to look? Perspectives on 'Urban' and 'Rural' in dialectology. In C. Montgomery & E. Moore (Eds.), *A sense of place: Studies in language and region* (pp. 171–188). Cambridge: Cambridge University Press.

Britain, D. (2017b). Language, mobility and scale in South and Central Asia: A commentary. *International Journal of the Sociology of Language*, 247, 127–137.

Britain, D. (2017c). Beyond the 'gentry aesthetic': Elites, received pronunciation and the dialectological gaze in England. *Social Semiotics*, 27, 288–298.

Brosius, C., & Wenzlhuemer, R. (2011). Transcultural turbulences: Flows of images and media. In C. Brosius & R. Wenzlhuemer (Eds.), *Transcultural turbulences: Interdisciplinary explorations of flows of images and media* (pp. 3–26). Vienna, Heidelberg: Springer-Verlag.

Bucholtz, M. (2010). *White kids: Language and white youth identities.* Cambridge: Cambridge University Press.

Busse, B. (2018). Patterns of discursive urban place-making. In V. Wiegand & M. Mahlberg (Eds.), *Corpus linguistics, context and culture.* Berlin: De Gruyter.

Busse, B. (forthcoming). Digital Discursive Place-Making Practices in Brooklyn, New York. Book project in preparation.

Busse, B., Vit, B., & Möhlig-Falke, R. (2017). Critique of language norms in English. In E. Felder, H. Schwinn, B. Busse, L. M. Eichinger, S. Grosse, J. Gvozdanovic, K. Jacob & E. Radtke (Eds.), *Handbuch Europäische Sprachkritik online—handbook of language criticism in European perspective.* Vol. 1 *Sprachnormierung und Sprachkritik—Standardisation and language criticism* (pp. 109–116). Heidelberg: Universitätsbibliothek Heidelberg.

Busse, B., & Warnke, I. H. (2014). *Place-making in urbanen Diskursen.* Berlin, Boston: De Gruyter.

Busse, B., & Warnke, I. H. (2015). Sprache im urbanen Raum. In E. Felder & A. Gardt (Eds.), *Handbuch Sprache und Wissen* (pp. 519–538). Berlin, Boston: De Gruyter.

Cheshire, J., Fox, S., Kerswill, P., & Torgersen, E. (2008). Ethnicity as the motor of dialect change: Innovation and levelling in London. *Sociolinguistica, 22,* 1–23.

Cheshire, J., Fox, S., Kerswill, P., & Torgersen, E. (2013). Language contact and language change in the multicultural metropolis. *Revue Française de Linguistique Appliquée, 18*(2), 63–76.

Cheshire, J., & Fox, S. (2016). From sociolinguistic research to English language teaching. In K. P. Corrigan & A. Mearns (Eds.), *Creating and digitizing language corpora. Vol. 3. Databases for public engagement* (pp. 265–290). Basingstoke: Palgrave Macmillan.

Cheshire, J., Hall, D., & Adger, D. (2017). Multicultural London English and social and educational policies. *Languages, Society & Policy,* available at: http://www.meits.org/policy-papers/paper/multicultural-london-english-and-social-and-educational-policies [accessed 1/05/18].

Clancy, B. (2011). Do you want to do it yourself like? Hedging in Irish traveler and Settled family discourse. In B. L. Davies, M. Haugh, & A. J. Merrisen (Eds.), *Situated politeness* (pp. 129–146). London: Continuum.

Coupland, N. (2003). Sociolinguistic authenticities. *Journal of Sociolinguistics,* 7(3), 417–431.

Dahlmann, I., & Adolphs, S. (2009). Spoken corpus analysis: Multimodal approaches to language description. In P. Baker (Ed.), *Contemporary corpus linguistics* (pp. 123–139). London: Continuum.

Eberhardt, M., & Downs, C. (2013). A department store study for the 21st century: /r/ vocalization on TLC's *Say Yes to the Dress. University of Pennsylvania Working Papers in Linguistics, 19*(2), 50–60.

Eckert, P. (2012). Three waves of variation study: The emergence of meaning in the study of sociolinguistic variation. *Annual Review of Anthropology, 41,* 87–100.

Finegan, E. (2004). The distinctiveness of American English. In E. Finegan & J. R. Rickford (Eds.), *Language in the USA* (pp. 18–38.). Cambridge: Cambridge University Press.

Friginal, E., & Bristow, M. (2018). Corpus approaches to sociolinguistics: Introduction and chapter overviews. In E. Friginal (Ed.), *Studies in corpus-based sociolinguistics* (pp. 1–15). Oxford: Routledge.

Friginal, E., & Hardy, J. (2014). *Corpus-based sociolinguistics: A guide for students*. London: Routledge.

Fuster Marquez, M., & Pennock Speck, B. (2008). The spoken core of British English: A diachronic analysis based on the BNC. *Miscelánea A Journal of English and American Studies, 37*, 53–74.

Hoffmann, S., & Lehmann, H. M. (2000). Collocational evidence from the British national corpus. *Language and Computers, 30*, 17–32.

Hunston, S. (2002). *Corpora in applied linguistics*. Cambridge: Cambridge University Press.

Jaworski, A., & Thurlow, C. (Eds.). (2010). *Semiotic landscapes: Language, image, space*. London: Continuum.

Johnson, J. H., & Partington, A. S. (2018). Representations of the 'underclass' in the English-language press: Who are they, how do they behave and who is to blame for them? In E. Friginal (Ed.), *Studies in corpus-based sociolinguistics* (pp. 293–318). Oxford: Routledge.

Johnstone, B. (2009). Pittsburghese shirts: Commodification and the enregisterment of an urban dialect. *American Speech, 84*(2), 157–175.

Juola, P. (2012). Large-scale experiments in authorship attribution. *English Studies, 93*, 275–283.

Kachru, B. (1992). *The other tongue: English across cultures*. Champaign: University of Illinois Press.

Kendall, T. (2011). Corpora from a sociolinguistic perspective. *Revista Brasileira de Linguística Aplicada, 11*(2), 361–389.

Kerswill, P. (2014). The objectification of 'Jafaican': the discoursal embedding of Multicultural London English in the British media. In J. Androutsopoulos (Ed.), *The media and sociolinguistic change* (pp. 428–455). Berlin: Walter de Gruyter.

Kirk, J. M., & Andersen, G. (2016). *Compilation, transcription, markup and annotation of spoken corpora*. Amsterdam: John Benjamins.

Kirkham, S., & Moore, E. (2016). Constructing social meaning in political discourse: Phonetic variation and verb processes in Ed Miliband's speeches. *Language in Society, 45*(1), 87–111.

Labov, W. (1966). *The social stratification of English in New York City*. Washington, DC: Center for Applied Linguistics.

Lave, J., & Wenger, E. (1991). *Situated learning: Legitimate peripheral participation*. Cambridge: Cambridge University Press.

Leech, G. (2004). Recent grammatical change in English: Data, description, theory. In K. Aijmer & B. Altenberg (Eds.), *Advances in corpus linguistics: Papers from the 23rd international conference on English language research on computerised corpora (ICAME 23)* (pp. 61–81). Amsterdam: Rodopi.

Leech, G., Hundt, M., Mair, C., & Smith, N. (2009). *Change in contemporary English: A grammatical study*. Cambridge: Cambridge University Press.

Leech, G., Rayson, P., & Wilson, A. (2016 [2001]). *Word frequencies in written and spoken English: Based on the British national corpus*. London: Routledge.

Leech, G., & Smith, N. (2005). Extending the possibilities of corpus-based research on English in the twentieth century: A prequel to LOB and FLOB. *ICAME Journal, 29*, 83–98.

McEnery, A. M., & Xiao, R. Z. (2005). Two approaches to genre analysis: Three genres in modern American English. *Journal of English Linguistics*, *33*(1), 62–82.

Milroy, L. (1980). *Language and social networks*. Oxford, New York, NY: Wiley-Blackwell.

Moore, E., & Carter, P. (2015). Dialect contact and distinctiveness: The social meaning of language variation in an island community. *Journal of Sociolinguistics*, *19*(1), 3–36.

Pennycook, A., & Otsuji, E. (2015). *Metrolingualism: Language in the city*. New York, NY: Routledge.

Ruhi, S., Haugh, M., Schmidt, T., & Wörner, K. (2014). *Best practices for spoken corpora in linguistic research*. Cambridge: Cambridge Scholars Publishing.

Rühlemann, C. (2009). Exploring the BNC jungle with BNCweb. *International Journal of Corpus Linguistics*, *14*(4), 557–560.

Schneider, K. P., & Barron, A. (2008). Where pragmatics and dialectology meet: Introducing variational pragmatics. In K. P. Schneider & A. Barron (Eds.), *Variational pragmatics: A focus on regional varieties in pluricentric languages*. Amsterdam: John Benjamins.

Schwyter, J. (2016). Dictating to the mob: The history of the BBC Advisory Committee on Spoken English. Oxford: Oxford University Press.

Smith, J. (forthcoming). Semiotic landscapes. In B. Busse & I. H. Warnke (Eds.), *Handbook language in urban space*. Berlin: de Gruyter.

Strübing, J. (2004). *Grounded theory*. Wiesbaden: VS Verlag.

Szmrecsanyi, B., Grafmiller, J., Heller, B., & Röthlisberger, M. (2016). Around the world in three alternations: Modeling syntactic variation in varieties of English. *English World-Wide*, *37*(2), 109–137.

Tagliamonte, S. A., Durham, M., & Smith, J. (2014). Grammaticalization an at early stage: Future 'be going to' in conservative British dialects. *English Language and Linguistics*, *18*(1), 75–108.

Torgersen, E., Gabrielatos, C., & Hoffmann, S. (2018). Corpus-based analysis of the pragmatic marker 'You Get Me'. In E. Friginal (Ed.), *Studies in corpus-based sociolinguistics* (pp. 176–198). Oxford: Routledge.

Tottie, G. (2015). Turn management and 'filled pauses,' uh and um. In K. Aijmer & C. Rühlemann (Eds.), *Corpus pragmatics: A handbook* (pp. 448–483). Cambridge: Cambridge University Press.

Trudgill, P. (1974). *The social differentiation of English in Norwich*. Cambridge: Cambridge University Press.

Vertovec, S. (2007). Super-diversity and its implications. *Ethnic and Racial Studies*, *30*(6), 1024–1054.

Wortham-Galvin, B. D. (2012). Making the familiar strange: Understanding design practice as cultural practice. In S. Hirt & D. Zahm (Eds.), *The urban wisdom of Jane Jacobs* (pp. 229–224). London: Routledge.

Zukin, S. (2010). *Naked city: The death and life of authentic urban places*. Oxford: Oxford University Press.

4 Using the Spoken BNC2014 in CQPweb

Andrew Hardie

CQPweb (Hardie, 2012) is an online corpus analysis system that acts as an interface to the Corpus Workbench software (CWB) and its powerful Corpus Query Processor (CQP) search utility. The architecture of CQPweb was based closely on that of an earlier tool, BNCweb (Hoffmann, Evert, Smith, Lee, & Berglund-Prytz, 2008), which provided much of the same functionality, but only for the original BNC1994. By releasing the BNC2014 initially through Lancaster University's CQPweb server, we have, therefore, made it available first in a form which many or most of the scholars who have worked on the earlier corpus will be familiar with. In this short chapter, I will outline some of the main affordances to be found in CQPweb, and how they are usable alongside the data design of the Spoken BNC2014.

4.1 Concordance

Once you have logged in to the CQPweb server and entered into the interface of a particular corpus, the first thing you see is always a query entry screen. This is because CQPweb is organised around the assumption that most analyses will begin with a query of the corpus and the *concordance* display of the results found for that query. CQPweb supports two different query languages: the Simple query (which is the default), and CQP syntax (a more powerful and more formal query language which is also used in other software such as Sketch Engine). Most users will begin with the Simple query language and many never need to go beyond it.

When you run a query, the results are presented as a concordance— the classic search display also known as *Key Word In Context* (KWIC), showing a little of the text before and a little of the text after each hit (result) for the query. As well as the immediate co-text, the location of each hit in the corpus is shown (on the left of the display): the ID code for the text where the result occurs is shown as a clickable link which leads through to a full view of all the metadata available for that text. In the Spoken BNC2014, moreover, an utterance number is given alongside the text ID, indicating how far into the text the utterance is in which the hit occurs.

4.1.1 Extra Information in the Concordance

Corpora in CQPweb sometimes consist only of plain text—and in that case, that is all which appears in the concordance. However, when a corpus contains XML markup, CQPweb can display representations of the extra information that the XML encodes—making for a richer concordance. Since the Spoken BNC2014 contains several different types of XML markup, CQPweb is configured to make use of this in the concordance. For instance, utterance breaks are marked up in the corpus—and are shown in CQPweb by placing the speaker ID code of the person who is speaking at the start of their utterance. Many other features of the underlying corpus markup are also made visible in this way. For instance, the transcribers of the Spoken BNC2014 were able to flag up utterances where they were less than usually sure of who was speaking. In the XML of the corpus, this is represented as *whoConfidence*="*low*". When we set up the corpus in CQPweb, we opted for a rather more compact marker to visualise this: a superscript *[??]* placed next to the uncertain speaker IDs. Over time, and in light of user feedback, we will continue to enhance and refine the concordance representation of XML features to make them easily readable for CQPweb users.

4.2 Restrictions and Metadata

In the process of compiling the Spoken BNC2014, we collected a substantial amount of metadata about both the speakers in the corpus and the texts in the corpus (that is, the individual transcriptions and the recorded conversations from which they arise). As explained, this metadata can be viewed via the concordance display. However, often you would want to actually use the metadata at the outset of the analysis, to limit the part of the corpus that is included in the initial query. For instance, you might be interested in the usage of a word specifically in the language of younger people (say, under-30s). Or you might wish to search only within texts with just two or three speakers. The way to do this is via a Restricted Query, which is available as an alternative option to the default Standard Query at the corpus's entry page in CQPweb.

The Restricted Query presents the same basic search tool as the Standard Query, but in addition, there are several extra tables laying out different categories of texts or speakers. The categories that restrict a query to certain types of text are directly below the query controls; the categories concerning types of speaker are found further down on the page. If you select a category before running a query, then CQPweb will only search within that category. You can select more than one type of restriction at once (e.g., you could combine restrictions based on number of speakers in the text, year of recording and age of speaker). If you don't select any categories of a particular type, then that criterion is simply not used: e.g., if you select neither *Male* nor *Female* nor *N/A* from the list of gender categories, then the query will retrieve results from utterances by speakers of any gender.

4.3 Collocation

Once you have run an initial query, you will in many cases want to apply further analyses to reorganise or summarise the concordance data. CQPweb has several tools for follow-up analysis of a concordance—all accessed from the concordance display's control menu. There is not space to deal with all of them here, so we will focus on just the Collocation and Distribution tools.

Generally speaking, a collocation analysis looks for items (words or tags) in the co-text of some node item. Items which are highly frequent, or more frequent than expected, in the vicinity of the node are described as that node's *collocates*. In CQPweb, the collocation system builds a list of nearby items from the results in the concordance—the 'node' is simply whatever you searched for, whether that's an individual word, a phrase, or something more complicated. CQPweb then allows you to explore this data using different statistical measures and other tweaks to the method.

In practical terms, this means that when you enter the Collocation tool the first thing you have to do is choose the settings for the database of nearby items around the node. For all but advanced uses, the default settings are normally fine. Once the data is collected, you are shown the Collocation display. At the top of this display are controls that allow you to adjust how the collocates are calculated, with the actual table of collocates, ordered by their statistical score and presented with additional quantitative information, shown in the rest of the display below the controls.

4.4 Distribution

The Distribution tool makes use of the corpus's metadata, just like a Restricted Query does. The difference is that the Distribution display shows you differences in the frequency—both absolute and relative—of the word or phrase you have searched for across different sections of the corpus.

By default, you are shown the distribution of your results across categories of texts. However, since the Spoken BNC2014 also contains speaker metadata—as we've already seen—you can switch to viewing distribution across the categories of speaker (age, gender and so on). Both can be displayed either as tables or as bar charts. An interesting additional function is the tool to look at text-frequency or speaker-frequency extremes. This means that, once you have searched for a word, you can find out the ID codes of the speakers who use that word (relatively) most or least often.

4.5 Keywords and Subcorpora

An alternative 'way in' to a corpus, rather than starting with a query for a word or phrase that you already know is of interest to you, is to use quantitative techniques to identify words that are likely to be of interest because of their unusually high frequency—relative to some comparison point. This technique is called a *keywords* analysis (or more generally, *key items*, since it can be run on tags as well as words) and can be seen as a more exploratory, or bottom-up, approach than beginning with a single search. The Keywords tool in CQPweb is another option accessible from the corpus entry screen. Once you access it, you can select two corpus frequency lists to compare, for instance, the Spoken BNC2014 itself as corpus 1, and some other English dataset as corpus 2.

As with Collocation, CQPweb's Keywords system offers many options to tweak the details of the statistical procedure that will be used. Whatever you choose, running the analysis will lead to a list of words that are distinctive of corpus 1 versus corpus 2 (and/or vice versa)—ordered by their statistical score. However, CQPweb is still designed to emphasise the importance of looking at, and interpreting, words and other items in their actual context—so each entry in the Keywords table is actually a link through to a query for that word.

You can also use the Keywords tool to compare different sections of the Spoken BNC2014 to one another. To do this, you first have to define the sections for use in the comparison as subcorpora. This is yet another option accessible from the corpus entry screen. There are various methods for creating a subcorpus, but the most common is defining a subcorpus using corpus metadata—that is, using the same category-selection controls as in the Restricted Query function. Once you have created a subcorpus and compiled its frequency list, it will be available in the Keywords tool for use in comparisons.

4.6 Advanced Features

CQPweb also supports many more specialised analyses and procedures—including annotation of saved concordances, exploratory statistical analysis and visualisation as well as thinning, randomisation and reduction of query result sets. While there is no space here to explore all these functions, many of them are explained by CQPweb's built-in video help files. We hope you find these systems valuable and a source of insight in your exploration of the Spoken BNC2014.

References

Hardie, A. (2012). CQPweb—combining power, flexibility and usability in a corpus analysis tool. *International Journal of Corpus Linguistics*, 17(3), 380–409.
Hoffmann, S., Evert, S., Smith, N., Lee, D., & Berglund-Prytz, Y. (2008). *Corpus linguistics with BNCweb-a practical guide*. Frankfurt am Main: Peter Lang.

Part II
Discourse, Pragmatics and Interaction

5 Politeness Variation in England

A North-South Divide?

Jonathan Culpeper and Mathew Gillings

5.1 Introduction

One of the newest sub-fields of linguistic pragmatics is variational pragmatics, combining pragmatics and dialectology. The foundational work,
Barron and Schneider (2005), focused on the pragmatics of Irish English. British English awaits comprehensive study. Our study will focus on
politeness variation in England. As we will elaborate in Section 5.2, the
stereotype of British English politeness is focused on indirectness. The
notion of indirectness, usually conceived of in terms of pragmatic frame-
works such as indirect speech acts (Searle, 1975) or conversational impli-
cature (Grice, 1975), has provided the theoretical backbone of the classic
works on politeness, including Brown and Levinson (1987) and Leech
(1983). It is not surprising, therefore, that those works on politeness have
been accused of being Anglo-centric (e.g., Matsumoto, 1988; Ide, 1989;
Gu, 1990; Mao, 1994; Nwoye, 1992; Wierzbicka, 2003 [1991]).

However, for anybody living in the north of England, the idea of
British indirectness does not seem to be the whole story. Indirectness is
somewhat stand-offish and cold, not reflective of the much-proclaimed
northern warmth and friendliness. One way of squaring this is to suggest that these politeness studies may simply be orienting to a cultural
stereotype of English politeness, one based on a middle class (cf. Allen,
2015; Grainger & Mills, 2016) and, pertinently for our study, a southern
perspective. This chapter seeks evidence of the empirical facts regarding a
divide between the north and south of England in terms of different types
of politeness practices.

In the following section, we will briefly elaborate on the English politeness stereotype, and in particular the notion of a north-south divide. We
will focus on the articulation of relevant beliefs by non-academics, not least
because nothing has been written on north-south politeness variation by
academics, though we will point out tangentially relevant discussions in
perceptual dialectology. In Section 5.3, an extensive section, we discuss the
background to and the nature of the politeness expressions which constitute diagnostics in this study. At the end of this section, we briefly outline

the hypotheses we will be testing in our study. In Section 5.4, we will turn to our data, the Spoken BNC1994 and Spoken BNC2014S, and our corpus method. In Section 5.5, we present quantitative results regarding a north-south division. Finally, we conclude and reflect on our findings.

5.2 British Politeness Stereotypes and the North-South Divide

The stereotype of British—by which is almost always meant the inhabitants of England—politeness is pervasive, and, moreover, it is usually linked to what people say. Take, as an example, this advice on British stereotypes for study abroad students:

[5.1]

> The way that British people speak and the language that we use is also considered quite polite. The language that many people use, including lots of phrases like 'please', 'thank you', 'pardon' or 'excuse me' and 'would you mind. . .' certainly back this up. (www.your-study-abroad.com/2011/04/stereotypes-about-british-culture-%E2%80%93-how-true-are-they/)

In fact, the first item in the list, *please*, seems to be elevated by many English parents to the supernatural—the 'magic word' for achieving successful requests. In the example, the expressions "would you mind", "pardon me" and "excuse me" all readily fit "off-record" or "negative politeness" (Brown & Levinson, 1987), categories that represent non-conventional and conventional indirectness respectively. The stereotype of British indirectness is often fuel for humour. Witness, for example, the "Anglo-EU translation guide", which has been widely circulated on the internet (e.g., http://twitpic.com/4xha23). Here, the joke is that the British are so indirect that people in continental Europe need help in translating what they actually mean. For instance, one of their examples is "could we consider some other options", which is translated as meaning "I don't like your idea".

A significant number of academic studies have found evidence that present-day British English politeness is often characterised by off-record or negative politeness (e.g., Blum-Kulka, 1987; Stewart, 2005; Ogiermann, 2009). Indeed, Brown and Levinson's (1987) politeness model is said to reflect characteristics of English politeness, notably, an emphasis on individualism (e.g., Matsumoto, 1988; Ide, 1989). Politeness in England, then, is about such things as not imposing upon other individuals, not violating their privacy, being respectful. The popular social anthropologist, Kate Fox, reinforces the point:

> The identification of England as a predominantly 'negative-politeness' culture—concerned mainly with the avoidance of imposition and intrusion—seems to me quite helpful. The important point here

is that politeness and courtesy, as practised by the English, have very little to do with friendliness or good nature.

(2004, p. 173)

There is little doubt that at least some people in England favour indirectness in their politeness practices. However, no study has actually examined whether that is generally true of all.

Certainly, there is no shortage of commentary from non-academics on the varying practices in England, and notably the idea that what happens in the north of England is different from the south:

[5.2]

> I have a northern perspective on things and by that I mean that I think we're maybe a bit more friendly, a bit more down to earth than the South. (www.theguardian.com/uk/2007/oct/28/britishidentity.society)

[5.3]

> As for my daughter's experience of unfriendliness, this arose from her visit to a prospective British university. And yes, you've guessed it, the university was on the south coast. (www.usabuyingguide.com/content/usa-different-kinds-politeness-britain-vs-america)

[5.4]

> There is definitely a North/South divide when it comes to politeness. Having lived on the South coast of England and then Scotland, it is very noticeable that people are more friendly and polite the further North you go in Britain. (http://news.bbc.co.uk/1/hi/talking_point/759276.stm)

Lists of supposed north-south differences, often slightly tongue-in-cheek and sometimes the purported products of surveys, are fairly regular features of newspapers. For example, the *Mirror* newspaper published a list of "18 things only Northerners living down south will understand" (29/9/16). The fifth and sixth relate to politeness issues, and so we quote them here (each point in the list appears above a photograph, which we describe in square brackets, and most of the photographs are followed by a short additional comment, which we represent in round brackets):

[5.5]

> 5. Down here, if you call a woman "duck" or "love" she might accuse you of being sexist [A picture of three ducks, one

with the caption "Ey up, duck"] (Southerners don't understand that, up north, even the manliest of men will address
each other that way)
6. People are just generally friendlier back home [A picture
of the people on a London Underground platform; all the
people are looking away from each other] (You miss being
able to say hello to strangers at the bus stop without causing them to back away in alarm) (www.mirror.co.uk/news/
weird-news/18-things-only-northerners-living-8687457)

As these quotations show, politeness in the north is often connected to
friendliness. Of course, the idea of "northern friendliness" could be said
to be yet another stereotype. Does it have a basis in what people actually
do in the north of England?

Although no academic studies have examined north-south politeness
variation in England, there have been a number of dialectology studies
about a linguistic north-south divide which we should briefly mention,
especially those in the area of perceptual dialectology. Wales (2000) writes
specifically on the north-south divide, arguing that there is a "regionism"
(bias against a region) in the form of a negative bias against the north.
Wales suggests that "Northerners, especially from Scotland and Yorkshire, are perceived as miserly; but also friendly and down-to-earth". An
important issue concerns where exactly the north-south divide is thought
to be. Montgomery's (2012, 2015) empirical work showed that there is a
large geographical variation, especially amongst northerners, as to where
the north-south divide is. Northern informants tended to put the line just
south of where they happened to be, even when they were located in Car-
lisle, not so far from the Scottish border. Clearly, issues of identity play a
role. However, Upton (2012) reminds us that the north-south dichotomy
ignores the Midlands. Contrary to suggestions of the Midlands as a transition zone, Upton (2012, p. 262) argues that it "might warrant attention
in its own right rather than being thought of as a mere junction between
contrasting varieties". Our study will also ignore the Midlands, but for
methodological reasons, as we will elaborate in Section 5.4.

5.3 Formulaic Politeness Expressions in England:
Diagnostics for the Study

The key for our method is that particular formulaic expressions can be
considered strongly diagnostic of politeness. Such expressions are often
mentioned in politeness metadiscourse, where their mediation often
helps cement or challenge their status as politeness formulae (see the
first quotation in Section 5.2). Of course, one might object that politeness always involves a contextual judgement—how else would we know,
for example, if the expression *thank you* were a genuine expression

of politeness or sarcasm? This objection is valid. However, almost no account of politeness would deny that some expressions become at least semi-conventionalised for politeness. We follow Terkourafi's (e.g., 2001, 2002, 2005a) frame-based approach to politeness, which argues that we should analyse the concrete linguistic realisations (i.e., linguistic expressions) and particular contexts of use which co-constitute "frames". Terkourafi suggests that it is through that regularity of co-occurrence that we acquire "a knowledge of which expressions to use in which situations" (2002, p. 197), that is, "experientially acquired structures of anticipated 'default' behaviour" (2002, p. 197). It is worth noting that a precursor to Terkourafi's approach appears in Aijmer's (1996) corpus-based work on pragmatic speech acts. There we find the "pragmatic frame", a notion that is very similar. However, thus far, we arrive at expressions that are pragmatically conventionalised in some way, but not necessarily for politeness. Terkourafi solves this problem by adding: "[i]t is the regular co-occurrence of particular types of context and particular linguistic expressions as the unchallenged realisations of particular acts that create the perception of politeness" (2005a, p. 248; see also 2005b, p. 213). The fact that the formulae are not only associated with a particular context but go unchallenged is the important point (this feature is also echoed in Haugh, 2007, p. 312).

Our study is not designed to investigate variation in overall degree of politeness but variation in type of politeness. There is a multitude of different classifications of politeness. We will deploy a slightly modified version of that proposed in the most cited politeness framework of all, namely, Brown and Levinson (1987). Brown and Levinson's conception of face consists of two related components. One component is labelled positive face, and is defined as: "the want of every member that his wants be desirable to at least some others . . . in particular, it includes the desire to be ratified, understood, approved of, liked or admired" (1987, p. 62). Positive politeness typically comes about when, for example, somebody acknowledges your existence (e.g., *Hello*), approves of your opinions (e.g., *You're right about that student*), or expresses admiration (e.g., *I thought you did a good job*). Note that the technique here is to strengthen social relationships by expressing solidarity, sympathy, approval and so on, and thereby counterbalance, often indirectly, a face-threatening act. The other component, negative face, is defined as, "the want of every 'competent adult member' that his actions be unimpeded by others" (1987, p. 62). Negative politeness typically comes about when, for example, somebody acknowledges that you want to attend to what you want, do what you want and say what you want. Thus, requests that inconvenience somebody are softened through indirectness, hedging and the like. However, Brown and Levinson (1987) placed two different politeness phenomena in the category of negative politeness: non-imposition politeness and deference. Whilst non-imposition politeness is to do with the softening that we mentioned, deference works by emphasising the addressee's superior power and thus rights to immunity from imposition, something which might be achieved, for example, through the use of the vocative *sir*. Following Jucker (e.g., 2012), we will treat these separately. The terms "positive" and "negative" are not transparent labels for types of politeness (indeed, they are misleading as they might be taken to suggest "good" versus "bad"). Therefore, we will refer to our three types of politeness as: solidarity, tentativeness and deference. Although we have anchored these types of politeness in Brown and Levinson (1987), they are pervasive through much of the politeness literature (see Section 5.2 of Culpeper et al., forthcoming).

Three constraints shaped our selection of formulaic politeness expressions. The first two relate to methodological issues: the expressions had to have a searchable form and occur with reasonable frequency across our northern and southern groups of data (for further discussion, see Section 5.4). The third constraint was that our selection of formulaic politeness expressions had to reflect a range of diverse types of politeness. Candidates for selection were suggested by non-academic commentaries, as illustrated by the quotations in Section 5.2. This led relatively straightforwardly to the selection of *please, sir, madam, thank you/thanks/ta, love, mate* and *hello*. The quotation in [5.1] mentions the conventionally indirect requestive expression *would you mind*. This did not meet our frequency constraints, so we exchanged it for the most frequent conventionally indirect requestive expression in British English, *could you V* (cf. Aijmer, 1996, p. 157). *Cheers* is not usually mentioned in commentaries on politeness, whether academic or non-academic. Given that we encompassed other thanking expressions, we decided that this should be included. Unlike the greeting *hello* (as in [5.5]), *goodbye/bye* is not often mentioned in non-academic commentaries, but so-called greeting-at-partings are obviously very closely related to greetings. Our final choice of formulaic politeness expressions are displayed in Table 5.1.

We have included what might be considered variants, namely, *thanks, ta, hi* and *bye*, in the same group as their fuller forms. However, it is possible that particular variants have developed politeness profiles that do not match the fuller forms. This is one of the reasons why we also examine the frequencies of every form individually. It is also worth noting that we avoided any word or expression that is known to be purely a matter of dialectal lexical variation (e.g., *hinny*), and thus might interfere with our claims about pragmatic variation. None of our items are listed as dialectal terms of address in, for example, Dunkling (1990); all of our items occur frequently and widely across Britain.

Below, each expression is discussed and illustrated with our Spoken BNC2014 data. We include notes on the development of these expressions in English, not only to more clearly show how their politeness value emerged, but also to give a sense of their entrenchment. We should stress that our brief overview does not aim to capture every single function

Table 5.1 Formulaic Politeness Expressions and Their Corresponding Politeness
Types

Formulaic Politeness Expressions	*Politeness Type*
could you *please*	tentativeness
sir, madam *thank you, thanks, ta*	deference
love, mate *cheers* *hello, hi* *goodbye, bye*	solidarity

these expressions might achieve. For example, many can be used ironi-
cally (this is often the case for *sir* and *madam*). Such functions are not
relevant to this study, and, as we point out in the following section, are
excluded from our counts. We would acknowledge that not every usage
of each expression is equally strong as an expression of politeness. Sometimes, for example, *thank you* is more about closing a conversational
sequence than politely acknowledging a debt. However, we would argue
that even examples like this at least pay weak lip-service to politeness.

Tentativeness Politeness

The term "tentative" is used by Leech (1983, e.g., 108) and occasionally
by Brown and Levinson (1987, e.g., 164) for softened requests, requests
that in Leech's case abide by his Tact politeness maxim, and in Brown
and Levinson's case express negative politeness. Beeching (2002, p. 27)
elaborates that tentativeness is associated with a style whereby "speakers modestly and/or conventionally signal respect for the opinion of the
interlocutor and downtone their own opinion"; it "may be implemented
through the use of hedging mechanisms of various linguistic types including expressions of epistemic modality (modal verbs and modalising adverbials) as well as question forms (including rising intonation) and (phrases
including) the pragmatic particles" of her study (e.g., *you know*).

Conventionally indirect requests are the output strategy that Brown
and Levinson (1987, pp. 132–142) discuss first under the heading of negative politeness, and they are a notable feature of Leech's (1983, pp. 107–
123) Tact Maxim. The most common way of delivering a conventional
indirect request in British English is to use the structure *could you* V
(Aijmer, 1996, 157), as illustrated in [5.6].

[5.6]

> 0199: yeah **could you** erm shut that toilet door for me please?
> 0192: yeah certainly (BNC2014 SRYY)

This structure seems to have evolved in the second quarter of the 19th century, probably driven by the emerging Victorian values of individualism, self-sufficiency and privacy, all of which meant an indirect approach was likely to be highly valued (Culpeper & Demmen, 2011). *Could you* in [5.6] clearly signals tentativeness, something which the hesitation suggested by the filled pause "erm" further reinforces. It fits non-imposition negative politeness.

Recently, Leech (2014, p. 76), observing that formulae such as *Could you V* or *Would you mind Ving* are "virtually specialized to the pragmatic function of a directive, although there there polite origin is apparent", notes that the formulaic politeness expression *please* is "similar" (see [5.6] for a use of this expression). Yet despite its popularity in lay discourse—note its appearance in the first quotation in Section 5.2—it is little discussed in the classic academic politeness literature. There is no doubt that historically it fits non-imposition negative politeness or tentativeness. The single word *please* dates back to the 19th century, but before that it was part of expressions such as "if it please you" with the sense of "if it be your will or pleasure", a usage that is analogous to similar expressions in other European languages, such as French *s'il vous plaît*, which most likely influenced its development in English (cf. Allen, 1995). However, that original conditional sense has been now largely bleached away. Nevertheless, although little attention is paid to *please*, occasional mentions in Brown and Levinson (1987, p. 101) or notes about how it might be translated (1987, p. 291) support the idea that it has to do with softening or minimising. Wichmann (2004), discussing the treatment of *please* in the politeness literature, comments that the "addition of *please* is considered to be a further way of softening the force of requests, particularly if they are in the form of imperatives, in which case the force of command is thought to be reduced to that of a request". Similarly, Aijmer (1996, p. 165) treats at least some cases of *please* as a downtoner. Interestingly, she notes a study by Holmes (1983) which found that it was never used where social distance between participants was reduced, and observes that *please* can be "experienced as unfriendly". Clearly, then, *please* has little to do with solidarity politeness.

Deference Politeness

The expressions *sir* and *madam* are amongst the very few honorific vocatives or terms of address in British English. In Leech's (1999) corpus-based study, they are the first two listed examples for that category of vocative, and the only examples he illustrates or discusses in his paper. Both evolved from respectful terms of address. *Madam*, from Old French *madame* (*ma + dame*), has been in use from the 14th century onwards as a polite form of address to women of higher rank (Oxford English

Dictionary *madam, n.,* 1a). *Madam's* approximate male counterpart, *sir,* possibly also from Old French, is first recorded at the end of 13th century as a title placed before a first name to denote the rank knight or baronet, but within decades seems to have been used on its own "as a respectful term of address to a superior or, in later use, an equal" (Oxford English Dictionary *sir, n.,* 7a). Today, with the democratisation of British society, "the relation of respect towards an addressee is rarely marked by such vocatives" (Leech, 1999, p. 112). Nevertheless, Leech (1999, p. 112) notes that there are "exceptional cases such as formal service encounters characterised by a markedly asymmetrical relation between the speakers" where they do occur with greater frequency. Our examples of *sir* and *madam* from the Spoken BNC2014 are typical, both pertaining to asymmetric situations, one being an airport service encounter, and the other a school pupil-teacher interaction[1]:

[5.7]

> 0262: and he said n- let let's see about that and so I was like because I'm a bit worried I've lost him and we've got this connecting flight so he said okay calm down **madam** calm down and er he said yeah okay he's been detained (BNC2014 SYHP)

[5.8]

> 0325: with this well he really likes well cos—ANON-name-f's a complete suck up
> 0324: yeah I know
> 0325: and she's like by- did you hear her today? she was like bye **sir** bye (BNC2014 S7WY)

We should note here that the very fact that *sir* and *madam* are largely restricted to particular situations, notably schools and to some extent public service encounters, where their occurrence is a norm, makes them somewhat less suited to determining regional variation, as their occurrence in a corpus might in part be a reflection of how often recordings were made in those situations. Honorific vocatives can be related to Brown and Gilman's (1972 [1960]) famous investigation of pronominal address forms in terms of two complimentary dimensions, power and solidarity. Honorific vocatives clearly index an asymmetrical relationship between the speaker and addressee based on a difference in power. They also normally express formality, as noted by Leech (1999, p. 112), and distance. From the point of view of mainstream models of politeness, they clearly belong to the domain of deference. According to Brown and Levinson (1987, p. 178), deference consists of two sides, "one in which S humbles and abases himself, and another where S raises H", and this "serves to defuse potential face-threatening acts are indicating that the addressee's rights to relative immunity from imposition are recognised". Note that in [5.8] the use of *sir* is equated with a "sucking up" strategy—it still is deployed as a politeness strategy to achieve one's goals.

In lay discourse in England, *thank you* is often treated, just like *please*, as emblematic of politeness (see the first quotation in Section 5.2). We will also take into consideration the derivative gratitude expressions *thanks* and *ta*. Just as with *please*, the classic academic politeness literature has little to say on these. Recently, interest in thanking and thanking formulae has been increasing, as evidenced by, for example, Jautz's (2013) monograph, though even here there is no discussion of *ta* in British English. Historically, and again like *please*, *thank you* began life as part of a longer expression, specifically, *I thank you*, which dates from at least as far back as the 13th century, and expressed "gratitude or obligation to" somebody (Oxford English dictionary, *thanks*, v., 3a). An example in the Spoken BNC2014 data, which expresses gratitude for compliance with a request, is as follows:

[5.9]

> 0207: can I be annoying and ask for my bacon to be crispy?
> 0204: yeah
> 0207: **thank you** (BNC2014 SMC2)

The nominal expression *thanks*, with a similar sense of gratitude for a favour rendered, seems to be derived from longer expressions to do with giving, offering returning or receiving thanks, and was established by the 17th century (Oxford English dictionary, *thank*, n., 3, 5a). Example [5.10] is a typical use.

[5.10]

> 0421: basically just carry on and don't bear left
> 0423: yeah just keep going straight
> 0421: **thanks** for that (BNC2014 S3AC)

Ta seems to be completely neglected by research. It gets short shrift from the Oxford English Dictionary, which briefly defines it as "an infantile form of 'thank-you', now also commonly in colloq. adult use" (*ta*, int.). We would agree that it is reasonably common in colloquial, and also informal, adult use, and also that in some respects it is functionally similar to *thank you/thanks*. Example [5.11] provides an illustration.

[5.11]

>0142: Yeah well yeah I only had a little taste of it but I did like it
>0143: That's why he bought it
>0144: Oh
>0142: That's why I bought it so
>0144: Oh nice one
>0142: Yeah
>0143: **Ta**
>0144: Thanks (BNC2014 SP6E)

In Brown and Levinson (1987, p. 67) we do get a clue about the type of politeness achieved by all these thanking expressions, when they write "expressing thanks (S accepts a debt, humbles his own face)". "Go on record as incurring debt" is listed as a negative politeness strategy (1987, pp. 210–211). Moreover, it is deference negative politeness, as it fits the way that they conceive of deference as the humbling of the self or the "raising" of the other, as noted in the previous paragraph. Other comments in the literature on the social functions of thanking expressions have echoed this general sense that it is an acknowledgement of some benefit derived from another person (see Aijmer, 1996, p. 52, and references therein).

Solidarity Politeness

Love and *mate* in some ways contrast with *sir* and *madam*. Rather than being characterised by Brown and Gilman's (1972 [1960]) power dimension, they reflect solidarity. Leech (1999) treats *love* as a term of endearment, and *mate* as a familiariser. Regarding endearments, Leech (1999, p. 112) states that they are "typically used in address to close family members (but not usually male-to-male), social partners and other 'favourite' people". Example [5.12] illustrates such usage.

[5.12]

>0167: yes dad yes oh I need some need some water **love** does anyone want some water?
>0110: did you like your pie last night? (BNC2014 S6MQ)

However, in a footnote, Leech adds that "visitors to the UK often note with some surprise (if not some discomfort) that strangers can be addressed by endearments such as *love* and *dear*, especially in the speech of older women", but notes that this kind of usage was not found in his data (1999, p. 111). Leech's data comprised a total of 99,566 words, and thus was many times smaller than the data we will be taking into consideration. We should also recollect here that the use of *love* as a term of address even for strangers is popularly associated with the north of England (see Section 5.2). Regarding familiarisers, Leech (1999, p. 112) states that they "mark the relationship between speaker and addressee as a familiar one [. . .] rather than a more distant and respectful one. It can also be argued that they are in complimentary distribution to endearments, being chiefly used for male-to-male address, in establishing or maintaining solidarity". With regard to *mate*, the features of indexing familiarity, solidarity or maleness have been noted by other researchers, especially those working on the term in Australian English (e.g., Rendle-Short, 2010). A hint of teasing camaraderie can be seen in [5.13] (both participants are male):

[5.13]

> 0384: pot belly
> 0351: it's all them takeaways you're eating **mate** (BNC2014 SA6W)

In Brown and Levinson (1987), *love* and *mate* clearly fit positive politeness, and more specifically the output strategy "use in-group identity markers", where they are both mentioned amongst others as possible examples. By claiming in-group solidarity, Brown and Levinson (1987, pp. 108–109) suggest that they reduce a face threat by emphasising the lack of power difference, as well as emotional agreement.

The formulaic expression *cheers* is notable for the complete lack of research attention it has attracted. *Cheers* is a development from the singular noun *cheer*, which indicates a state of joy, gladness, happiness, cheerfulness and so on. Its plural usage is first recorded in the early 20th century, when it was used as "an expression of encouragement, approval, or enthusiasm" (Oxford English Dictionary, *cheers*, int., 1), and then its more "usual sense" as "as a toast or salutation before drinking" developed (Oxford English Dictionary, *cheers*, int.). However, this usage is not the specific one that concerns us here. That is a highly restricted conversational routine—thus it is not likely to be of much use in diagnosing politeness variation. What does concern us is a more recent development. The final sense of *cheers* listed in the Oxford English Dictionary concerns its use to "express gratitude or acknowledgement for something: 'thanks' ". Functionally, then, this usage of *cheers* seems to be more of a thanking expression. We deliberately did not, however, list it amongst our earlier thanking expressions. This is because, in our view, it performs a different kind of politeness, one that is related to solidarity and emotional connection. *Cheers* is clearly associated with the expression of happiness and conviviality; it is a very common drinking salutation, is

imbued with good wishes and positive emotion and is normally recipro-
cally expressed by all in the drinking group. Thus, it is easy to see how
the expression of cheers is not an acknowledgement of indebtedness, but
more a reciprocation of good wishes and the reinforcement of emotional
connection. It is more a matter of solidarity. In [5.14], the speaker recip-
rocates the politeness of a complimentary comment:

[5.14]

> 0084: Aw that's so cute
> 0041: **Cheers** dad (BNC2014 STSS)

Our final two sets of expressions, *hello* and *hi* and *goodbye* and *bye*,
are symmetrical in that the first set usually involves greeting, whereas
the second involves greeting-at-parting. One reason for including such
items in our study is that the friendly greeting of strangers is something
that is popularly assumed to be much more likely in the north of England than the south (see Section 5.2). *Hello*, according to the Oxford
English Dictionary, is a relatively recent interjection, first cited in 1826,
though it seems to be a variant of the older interjection *hallo*. Like *hallo*,
hello started life as a cry to attract attention. Its use as a greeting is first
recorded in 1853 (Oxford English Dictionary, *hello*, int. 3). An example
of a typical use is given in [5.15].

[5.15]

> 0428: **hello**
> 0505: **hello**
> 0428: how are you?
> 0505: alright (BNC2014 SM6J)

Hi follows a similar development route to *hello*. Its first citation in
the Oxford English Dictionary is dated 1475, where it is used as an
"exclamation used to call attention (Oxford English Dictionary, *hi*, 1).
By 1862, it is recorded as a greeting, but is also labelled "colloq. (chiefly
N. Amer.)" (Oxford English Dictionary, *hi*, 2). It is clearly now a general term in British English and not marked as American English, but
it is still colloquial and informal. An example of a typical use is given
in [5.16].

[5.16]

> UNKFEMALE: **Hi**
> 0041: **Hi**
> 0084: **Hi**—ANONnameF

UNKFEMALE: Are you going to have dinner now or?
0041: No no (BNC2014 SEGU)

Neither *hello* nor *hi* are discussed in Brown and Levinson (1987), and greetings attract but a few fleeting comments. One probable reason for this is that Brown and Levinson orientate their work solely to mitigating face threats. Freely given face support or enhancement, a compliment for example, does not fit their overall theory. Other studies have touched on these items and noted their politeness potential. Farese (2015) investigates *hi* and Italian *ciao*, partly through corpus data. He concludes that "saying *hi* counts as saying 'something good' (i.e. something 'nice') to the interlocutor, signalling that one is friendly and has good intentions towards the other person" (2015, p. 6). Clearly then, it ties in with solidarity politeness. Interestingly, he suggests that the point of distinction from *hello* is that *hi* also includes the following meaning component: "when people say *hi* to someone they profess to think about this person as 'someone like me'" (2015, p. 7). In other words, *hi* is imbued with a certain egalitarianism that *hello* is not.

Goodbye is a relatively well-known example of language change in historical linguistics circles, evolving from a speech act of blessing, *God be with you/ye* (see Arnovick, 1999, for details). In its contracted form, the form one would recognise today, it seems to have been in use since the late 16th century, functioning as a "farewell gesture" or expressing "good wishes when parting or at the end of the conversation" (Oxford English dictionary, goodbye, A.1 and B.1). Most of the examples from the Spoken BNC2014 are metalinguistic ones such as [5.17]:

[5.17]

0266: >> so when did you say **goodbye** to these people?
0271: I said **goodbye** to them at er erm Strasbourg but I kept in tou- I moved back to London after that and I kept in touch with them (BNC2014 S7KK)

Partly reflecting differences in the data (as we will discuss in Section 5.4.1), there are many more non-metalinguistic examples in the original BNC, as in [5.18] (each line of the transcription represents a different speaker):

[5.18]

I'd better go.
I know, I'd better go, she'll be needing money.
Goodbye then.
Goodbye. (BNC1994 KBE)

The presence of so many metalinguistic examples hints at the fact that *goodbye* has expanded its functional repertoire beyond a straightforward greeting-at-parting. Examples such as "I have to say goodbye to this jumper" (BNC2014 SJLT) are not uncommon. *Bye* evolved as a shortened form of *goodbye*, and like *hi* has a more colloquial and informal flavour. It is first recorded in 1618 (Oxford English Dictionary, bye, *int.* and *n.*). An example of a typical use is given in [5.19].

[5.19]

      0447: alright I think I'm gonna go
      0448: okay
      0447: I've got to get up early
      0448: I know
      0447:—UNCLEARWORD but well I'll text you before I go to sleep
      0448: okay
      0447: okay night night
      0448: **bye**
      0447: **bye** (BNC2014 SAG4)

As with *hello* and *hi*, neither *goodbye* nor *bye* are discussed in Brown and Levinson (1987), and probably for the same reasons. Where greeting-at-partings or closings have more generally attracted research attention is in Conversation Analysis, as exemplified by Schlegloff and Sacks' (1973) famous paper. Nevertheless, such CA studies frequently observe the ramifications for politeness. For example, Pojanapunya and Jaroenkitboworn (2011, p. 3593), examining saying "goodbye" in the virtual world of Second Life, comment that "ending a conversation abruptly can be regarded as an act of disrespect or rudeness [. . .] If you can close the conversation appropriately, you not only establish grounds for a current good relationship with your interlocutor but also guarantee an ongoing relationship". Forms of *goodbye* (including *bye*) were the most frequent closing strategy in their data. Establishing and reinforcing good relationships is very much the business of solidarity politeness.

This section and the previous have prepared the ground for the hypotheses we will test in this chapter. We hypothesise that:

(1) tentativeness politeness occurs less frequently in the northern data compared with the southern,
(2) deference politeness occurs more frequently in the northern data compared with the southern, and
(3) solidarity politeness occurs more frequently in the northern data compared with the southern.

The basis of the first and third hypotheses will be evident from our comments in Section 5.2. But what of the second hypothesis? Deference politeness, despite the fact that Brown and Levinson (1987) classified it as part of negative politeness, works rather differently from either negative politeness—by which we mean non-imposition politeness—and positive politeness (solidarity). It has much to do with meeting particular social expectations in a situation, notably those connected to an accepted hierarchy, and only indirectly orientates to matters of face. It is a core part of what Watts (2003) would refer to as "politic behaviour", rather than politeness. Moreover, deference politeness does not preclude solidarity. Many Mediterranean cultures have deference systems that are alive and well, yet are often identified as positive politeness cultures (e.g., Sifianou, 1992). In fact, one of the best illustrations of a culture (strictly speaking, a set of cultures) mixing deference politeness and solidarity politeness relates to earlier stages of English in England. For example, Raumolin-Brunberg (1996, p. 168), studying terms of address in 15th-century correspondence, cites examples such as "Reverent and worshipful sir and my special friend and gossip", which clearly mix deference (the first half) with solidarity (the second half). Nevertheless, we would admit that the basis of the second hypothesis is less certain than the first or third.

5.4 Data and Method

5.4.1 Data

In this study, we use data in the Spoken British National Corpus 2014 (Love, Dembry, Hardie, Brezina, & McEnery, 2017), or, more precisely, the early-access Sample of the Spoken BNC2014 (hereafter Spoken BNC2014S). This is described elsewhere in this volume (see Chapter 1). The Spoken BNC2014S amounts to some five million words transcribed from informal conversations between speakers whose first language is British English, produced between 2012 and 2015. Speakers vary widely according to age, socio-economic status and—importantly for our purposes—region. At the heart of our study is a comparison between speakers designated as "south", and those designated as "north". We deliberately did not include the Midlands in order to make a clear distinction between our two target groups.

A design feature of the Spoken BNC2014S is that its contents are similar to those of the demographically sampled subset of the original BNC's spoken component (hereafter Spoken BNC1994DS). This is crucial for us, as neither the Spoken BNC2014S nor Spoken BNC1994DS offers sufficient data for us to retrieve robust patterns. Together, they not only provide a larger dataset, but also provide a more contextually varied

one. The majority of speakers in the Spoken BNC2014S are very familiar with each other (often family members or friends). Recordings were
conducted in a range of settings, but typically in the home or workplace
of one or more of the speakers. This is not a surprise, given the particular recording constraints. Contributors recorded conversations on
their phones, and were required to elicit the written consent of anybody
recorded for use in the Spoken BNC2014. In contrast, informants for the
Spoken BNC1994DS had carried portable recording devices around with
them recording all their conversations, including those with strangers in
public settings, over a period of up to a week. Also, commensurate with
ethics policies in the early 1990s, they were not required to elicit consent from participants before recording and consents did not have to
be written. What this means is that public interactions, and especially
fleeting public interactions, such as service encounters, are not so likely
to be recorded in the Spoken BNC2014S data. From a pragmatic point
of view, the mix of speech acts in a body of language data and how they
are realised is strongly influenced by the context of usage. For example,
transactional speech acts, such as requests to order a cup of coffee, are
much more likely to be a feature of public service encounters. In addition, such encounters are likely to be with strangers, and it is well-known
that interlocutor social relations strongly influence how speech acts are
realised. In sum, combining the north and south components of both the
Spoken BNC2014S and the original BNC's spoken demographic component was the obvious thing to do.

The numbers of words involved in the datasets for the north and the
south is displayed in Table 5.2.

To give an idea of the number of different recordings this represents,
and hence also the number of different speech events, and to some extent
the number of different speakers,[2] Table 5.3 displays the numbers of text
files from which the instances of formulaic politeness expressions are
drawn. One text file corresponds to one recording submitted for inclu-
sion in the BNC2014.

As is transparent from Table 5.3, the occurrences of *madam* in particular, but also *sir*, *ta* and *goodbye* are dispersed across relatively few files,
especially with respect to the northern data. This needs to be borne in
mind when considering the results.

Table 5.2 The Numbers of Words in the North and South Components of the
Spoken BNC2014S and Spoken BNC1994DS

	Spoken BNC2014S	*Spoken BNC1994DS*	*Total*
North	1,158,231	1,231,110	2,389,341
South	2,470,535	2,736,206	5,206,741

Table 5.3 The Numbers of Text Files in the Formulaic Politeness Expressions Data for the North and South Components of the Spoken BNC2014S and Spoken BNC1994DS Combined

	North	South
Could you	125	139
Please	123	260
Sir	14	45
Madam	5	25
Thank you	132	280
Thanks	105	195
Ta	18	22
Love	56	122
Mate	44	106
Cheers	37	51
Hello	95	216
Hi	57	108
Goodbye	13	39
Bye	67	119

5.4.2 Method

An important criterion affecting our selection of politeness formulae is that the politeness expression had to be retrievable through a combination of qualitative and quantitative methods without putting an unreasonable burden upon the researchers. What this means is that frequent expressions had to be reasonably strongly associated with politeness. For example, a frequent way of doing polite requests in English is to use the structure *can you X*? In fact, Searle (1975), who did more than anybody else to establish the notion of indirect speech acts, used the expression *can you pass the salt?* as his paradigm example. However, this expression is actually frequently used in its literal sense of a question about ability, rather than as a polite indirect way of asking somebody to do something. Scrutinising a random sample of one hundred instances from the Spoken BNC2014S, we discovered that only twenty-one clearly performed politeness. In tune with the criteria for identifying conventionalised impoliteness expressions used in Culpeper (2011, Chapter 4), we decided that at least 50% of the occurrences of the item had to clearly belong to politeness contexts for us to consider it. Of course, even the items that pass this threshold would contain a lot of irrelevant items. We therefore manually screened all the occurrences retrieved when searching for a particular formulaic politeness expression, removing any that were met with a challenge (recollect the point in the first paragraph of Section 5.3 that politeness is not challenged). Consequently, and importantly, frequency counts in this chapter represent not simply the occurrence of a form in the data but the occurrence of a form *and* an interpretation that it was being used to do politeness.

Retrieving concordances and frequency counts was straightforward in cases where the numbers of unscreened items were relatively few (e.g., *sir, madam, cheers*), as they could fairly easily be manually scrutinised and cleared on non-politeness uses. In some cases where there were many hits (*could you, thank you, thanks*), we had no choice but to manually scrutinise all results. In other cases (*love, mate, ta, please*), we elicited the help of part of speech tagging. These cases are briefly noted here:

> *Love*: To avoid instances where *love* was being used as a verb, we searched on love_NN1, thereby limiting the query to singular common nouns, the grammatical category in the data associated with the vocative politeness expression.
>
> *Mate*: Some instances of *mate* in the BNC2014 were tagged incorrectly. For example, in "look at your fucking trainers mate you big bad baby" (BNC2014 S5EM), *mate* was tagged VV0. So we ran a search for everything rather than limiting it to mate_NN1, and then manually sifted the data. In the BNC1994, we did not find the same tagging errors, so we searched on mate_NN1.
>
> *Ta*: Running a query for *ta* alone produces instances of *gotta*, which is split, with the second morpheme tagged as ta_TO (infinitive marker *to*). Limiting the query to ta_UH or ta_ITJ retrieved instances where they are being used as interjections, which is the grammatical category in the data associated with the relevant politeness expression. The BNC2014 tagged these interjections as _UH, whilst the BNC1994 tags interjections as _ITJ.
>
> *Please*: To avoid instances where *please* was being used as a verb, we searched on please_ RR (general adverb) in the BNC2014, and please_AV0 (adverb, unmarked) in the BNC1994.

5.5 Politeness in the North and South Components of the Spoken BNC2014S and the Spoken BNC1994DS: Results

Table 5.4 displays the frequency differences within types of politeness between the north and south components of the Spoken BNC2014S

Table 5.4 Frequency Differences Within Types of Politeness Between the North and South Components of the Spoken BNC2014S and Spoken BNC1994DS Combined (Relative Frequencies per Million Words Are in Brackets)

	North	*South*	*North/South Difference (Fisher Exact Test p Values)*
Tentativeness	807 (337.8)	1671 (320.9)	0.234
Deference	1062 (444.5)	2744 (527.0)	0.000
Solidarity	1161 (485.91)	3037 (583.3)	0.000

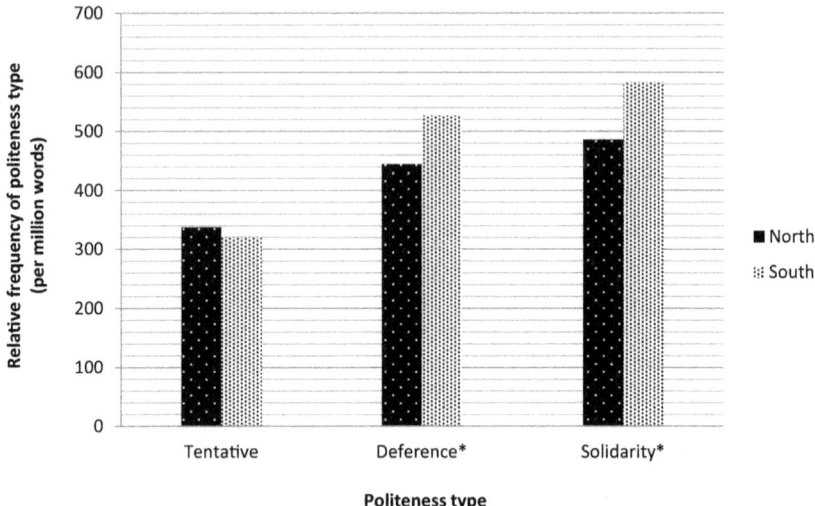

Figure 5.1 Relative Frequency Differences (per Million Words) Within Types of Politeness Between the North and South Components of the Spoken BNC2014S and Spoken BNC1994DS Combined (Politeness Types Displaying a Statistically Significant North/South Difference Are Asterisked)

and Spoken BNC1994DS combined, and Figure 5.1 is a visualisation of the relative frequencies (per million words) displayed in brackets in Table 5.4. It should be noted that it makes little sense to compare the overall scores for politeness types against each other, as their contents are not balanced (e.g., they contain differing numbers of expressions). The focus here is on north-south differences *within* politeness types.

In short, none of our hypotheses are supported. Our first hypothesis, that tentativeness politeness occurs more frequently in the northern data compared with the southern, is not supported: no significant difference between north and south was found for tentativeness politeness. Our second hypothesis, that deference politeness occurs more frequently in our northern data compared with the southern, is not supported either. There is a statistically significant difference between them, but the preponderance is in favour of the southern data. Finally, our third hypothesis, that solidarity politeness occurs more frequently in our northern data compared with the southern, is not supported either. Like deference politeness, a statistically significant difference is evidenced, but the preponderance is in favour of the southern data.

Clearly, we need to inspect the detail, not least because Table 5.4 and Figure 5.1 represent the accumulative scores of groups of expressions, with some of those expressions being more numerous than others and thus playing a disproportionate role in determining the overall result. Table 5.5 displays the frequency differences of each formulaic politeness expression between the north and south components of the Spoken BNC2014S and Spoken BNC1994DS combined, and Figure 5.2 is a visualisation of the relative frequencies (per million words) displayed in brackets in Table 5.5.

The expressions that comprise tentativeness politeness, *could you* and *please*, are distributed similarly: neither show a significant difference between north and south. Three of the five expressions comprising deference politeness, namely, *sir*, *madam* and *thank you*, show a significant difference between north and south, but with the preponderance occurring in the southern data. One of the expressions, *thanks*, shows no significant difference. The final expression, *ta*, shows a significant difference and one that is in favour of the northern data. However, it should be remembered that *ta* is one of our least frequent expressions overall, and so this finding does not carry much weight. Only two of the seven solidarity politeness expressions, *mate* and *hello*, show a significant difference, but in favour of the southern data. In sum, at the micro level of individual expressions, there is no evidence of skewing such that we should disbelieve the rejection of all hypotheses, as suggested earlier in the light of the results displayed in Table 5.5 and Figure 5.2.

Table 5.5 Frequency Differences in Formulaic Politeness Expressions Between the North and South Components of the Spoken BNC2014S and Spoken BNC1994DS Combined (Relative Frequencies per Million Words in Brackets)

	North	*South*	*North/South Difference (Fisher Exact Test p Values)*
Could you	38 (15.90)	102 (19.58)	0.317
Please	769 (321.85)	1569 (301.34)	0.136
Sir	18 (7.53)	289 (55.50)	0.000
Madam	4 (1.67)	35 (6.72)	0.003
Thank you	632 (264.50)	1670 (320.73)	0.000
Thanks	343 (143.55)	704 (135.21)	0.369
Ta	65 (27.20)	46 (8.83)	0.000
Love	82 (34.31)	186 (35.72)	0.793
Mate	51 (21.34)	201 (38.60)	0.000
Cheers	54 (22.60)	105 (20.16)	0.495
Hello	407 (170.34)	1378 (264.66)	0.000
Hi	150 (62.79)	337 (64.72)	0.770
Goodbye	29 (12.14)	77 (14.79)	0.404
Bye	388 (162.39)	753 (144.62)	0.064

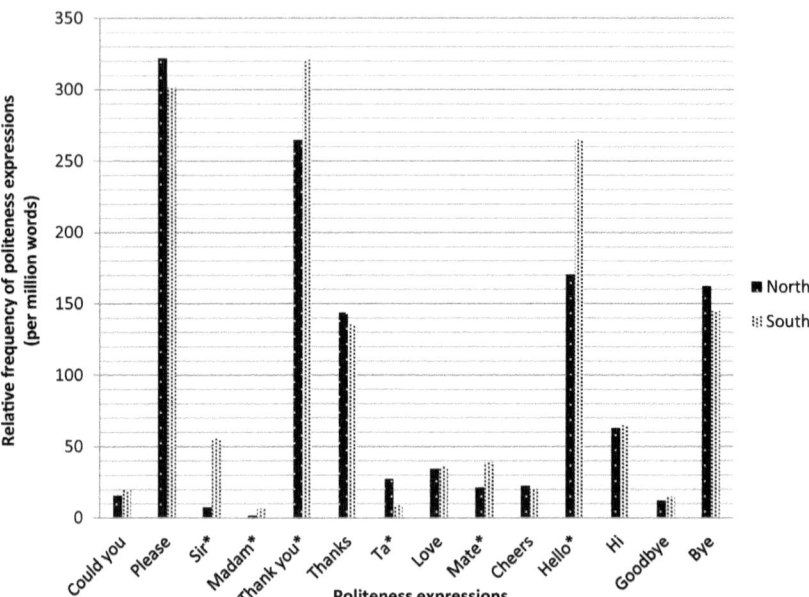

Figure 5.2 Relative Frequency Differences (Per Million Words) in Formulaic
Politeness Expressions Between the North and South Components of
the Spoken BNC2014S and Spoken BNC1994DS Combined (Politeness Expressions Displaying a Statistically Significant North/South
Difference Are Asterisked)

5.6 Conclusions

The results of our study were not expected. They do not provide evidence for the popularly assumed north-south England divide in terms
of preferences for different types of politeness. It would be somewhat
premature, however, to declare that a myth. We have, after all, only
examined a limited number of formulaic politeness expressions. Having
said that, those expressions are amongst the most emblematic of British politeness expressions, looming large in people's metadiscourse, and
include some of the most frequently occurring politeness expressions
in British English—it would be odd if these were all patterning against
the grain of other politeness practices. One might observe that the stereotype of tentativeness politeness associated with the British English
as a whole by academics and non-academics alike is indeed supported:
no significant north-south differences in tentativeness politeness were
detected—it seems to be a general feature of polite discourse in England.
Having said that, we should bear in mind that the way indirectness is
evaluated is not necessarily the same across all social groups. Indeed,

some research hints that it need not always be associated with social distance (see, e.g., Britain, 1992; White, & Watson-Gegeo, 1990).

Nevertheless, inspection of the north-south distributions for individual politeness expressions also hints at a different kind of variation: the northern data tends to avoid more formal and/or elaborate expressions or variants and favour the opposite. Regarding deference politeness, the frequencies of *sir* and *madam* are weighted towards the southern data. Also, the set comprising *thank you*, *thanks* and *ta* has the elaborate variant *thank you* weighted towards the south, whilst the relatively colloquial and informal *ta* is weighted towards the north (*thanks* is similar for both north and south). Regarding solidarity politeness, the evidence displayed in the *hello*, *hi* and *goodbye*, *bye* sets also seems to lend some support to this pattern. Whilst the relatively formal and less egalitarian *hello* is weighted towards the south, *hi* is about the same in the south and north; whilst the more elaborate *goodbye* is slightly weighted towards the south, the relatively informal *bye* is slightly weighted towards the north. Not all these tendencies, it should be remembered, achieved statistical significance. Nevertheless, there seems to be sufficient evidence here to suggest a general tendency. (In)formality is not, of course, unrelated to politeness; it is often considered to be manifested through different types of politeness behaviour. However, detailed discussion of the relationship between the two is lacking. Occasional remarks by Brown and Levinson (1987, e.g., 129, 207) link formality to negative politeness and informality to positive politeness, and other scholars have drawn similar parallels. Holmes (1995, p. 20) comments that "[i]n general negative politeness strategies will occur more often in formal settings and interactions, while positive politeness tends to characterise more intimate and less formal situations". Intuitively, this makes sense. However, whilst there is overlap between these types of politeness and (in)formality, the two are not exactly parallel. Aggressive or insulting behaviour does not usually involve formal language, and yet could not be considered friendly (obviously, this statement encompasses genuinely impolite behaviours, and not banter, jocular mockery, etc.). Similarly, the use of honorifics is often seen as formal, but choosing not to use them may be considered rude, rather than simply informal or friendly. It is intriguing to ponder whether it is in fact the construction and evaluation of (in)formality that best captures varying practices that constitute a north-south England divide rather than the politeness types suggested in the academic literature. One way of squaring the conclusion in this paragraph (about apparent northern informality) with that of the previous paragraph (about the seeming north and south English universal of tentative politeness) is to suggest that northerners may be working to construct a blended identity—a friendly northern, but also polite English, person.

Needless to say, we are under no illusions that our findings are at this stage more than suggestive. Aside from increasing the number of

politeness diagnostic expressions, future work could benefit from qualitative analyses of the use of those expressions, along with complementary
explorations into their perception. Also, a study specifically designed to
investigate (in)formality, its relationship with politeness and how it varies
would be invaluable.

Acknowledgement

The research presented in this article was supported by the UK's Economic
and Social Research Council (ESRC) Centre for Corpus Approaches to
Social Science, ESRC grant reference ES/K002155/1. This publication is
based on datasets which in due course will be publicly available. We
would like to thank the two anonymous reviewers of this chapter for
providing thoughtful and thought-provoking feedback. Remaining inad-
equacies are, of course, ours.

Notes

1 Both examples involve reported discourse. We include examples in our study
   irrespective of discourse level. What matters is that they are/were performing
   politeness in some way. The reason for choosing examples involving reported
   discourse in this particular case is simply that they were the clearest amongst
   the few examples that appear in the Spoken BNC2014. The original BNC contains many more instances, for reasons which we will explain in Section 5.4.
2 At the time of writing, we are not able to extract precise figures for the numbers of speakers involved in our data. However, we are not aware of any cases
   where the same set of speakers appears in in more than one recording (file).
   Thus the number of text files gives at least some sense of the numbers of different speakers involved.

References

Aijmer, K. (1996). *Conversational routines in English*. London: Longman.
Allen, C. L. (1995). On doing as you please. In A. H. Jucker (Ed.), *Historical
pragmatics* (pp. 275–308). Amsterdam: John Benjamins.
Allen, K. (2015). A benchmark of for politeness. In A. Capone & J. L. Mey
(Eds.), *Interdisciplinary studies in pragmatics, culture and society, perspec-
tives in pragmatics, philosophy and psychology 4* (pp. 397–420). Heidelberg:
Springer.
Arnovick, L. (1999). *Diachronic pragmatics: Seven case studies in English illocu-
tionary development*. Amsterdam and Philadelphia: John Benjamins Publish-
ing Company,
Barron, A., & Schneider, K. P. (2005). The pragmatics of Irish English. *Trends
in linguistics: Studies and monographs 164*. Berlin, New York, NY: Mouton
de Gruyter.
Beeching, K. (2002). *Gender, politeness and pragmatic particles in French*.
Amsterdam: John Benjamins.

Blum-Kulka, S. (1987). Indirectness and politeness in requests: Same or different? *Journal of Pragmatics, 11*, 131–146.

Britain, D. (1992). Linguistic change in intonation: The use of high rising terminals in New Zealand English. *Language Variation and Change, 4*, 77–104.

Brown, P., & Levinson, S. C. (1987 [1978]). *Politeness: Some universals in language usage*. Cambridge: Cambridge University Press.

Brown, R., & Gilman, A. (1972 [1960]). The pronouns of power and solidarity. In P. P. Giglioli (Eds.), *Language and social context* (pp. 252–282). Penguin: Harmondsworth.

Culpeper, J. (2011). *Impoliteness: Using language to cause offence*. Cambridge: Cambridge University Press.

Culpeper, J., & Demmen, J. (2011). Nineteenth-century English politeness: Negative politeness, conventional indirect requests and the rise of the individual self. *Journal of Historical Pragmatics, 12*(1/2), 49–81.

Culpeper, J., O'Driscoll, J., & Hardaker, C. (forthcoming). The neglected west: Notions of politeness in Britain and America. In E. Ogiermann & P. Garcés-Conejos Blitvich (Eds.), *From speech acts to lay concepts of politeness: A multilingual and multicultural perspective*. Cambridge: Cambridge University Press.

Dunkling, L. (1990). *A dictionary of epithets and terms of address*. London, New York, NY: Routledge.

Farese, G. M. (2015). *Hi* vs. *Ciao*: NSM as a tool for cross-linguistic pragmatics. *Journal of Pragmatics, 85*, 1–17.

Fox, K. (2004). *Watching the English: The hidden rules of English behaviour* ([Revised edition]. ed.). London: Hodder & Stoughton.

Grainger, K., & Mills, S. (2016). *Directness and indirectness across cultures*. Basingstoke: Palgrave Macmillan.

Grice, H. P. (1975). Logic and conversation. In P. Cole & J. L. Morgan (Eds.), *Syntax and semantics, Vol. 3: Speech acts* (pp. 41–58). London, New York, NY: Academic Press.

Gu, Y. (1990). Politeness phenomena in modern Chinese. *Journal of Pragmatics, 14*(2), 237–257.

Haugh, M. (2007). The discursive challenge to politeness theory: An interactional alternative. *Journal of Politeness Research, 3*(2), 295–317.

Holmes, J. (1983). The structure of teachers' directives. In J. Richards & R. W. Schmidt (Eds.), *Language and communication* (Applied linguistics and language study) (pp. 89–117). London, New York, NY: Longman.

Holmes, J. (1995). *Women, men and politeness*. London: Longman.

Ide, S. (1989). Formal forms and discernment: Two neglected aspects of linguistic politeness. *Multilingua, 8*(2/3), 223–248.

Jautz, S. (2013). *Thanking formulae in English*. Amsterdam: John Benjamins.

Jucker, A. H. (2012). Changes in politeness cultures. In T. Nevalainen & E. C. Traugott (Eds.), *The Oxford handbook of the history of English* (pp. 422–433). Oxford: Oxford University Press.

Leech, G. N. (1983). *Principles of pragmatics*. London: Longman.

Leech, G. N. (1999). The distribution and function of vocatives in American and British English conversation. In H. Hasselgard, S. Johansson, & S. Oksefjell (Eds.), *Out of corpora: Studies in honour of Stig Johansson* (pp. 107–118). Amsterdam: Rodopi.

Leech, G. N. (2014). *The pragmatics of politeness*. Oxford: Oxford University Press.

Love, R., Dembry, C., Hardie, A., Brezina, V., & McEnery, T. (2017). The spoken BNC2014: Designing and building a spoken corpus of everyday conversations. *International Journal of Corpus Linguistics*, 22(3), 319–344.

Mao, L. (1994). Beyond politeness theory: 'Face' revisited and renewed. *Journal of Pragmatics*, 21(5), 451–486.

Matsumoto, Y. (1988). Reexamination of the universality of face: Politeness phenomena in Japanese. *Journal of Pragmatics*, 12(4), 403–426.

Montgomery, C. (2012). The effect of proximity in perceptual dialectology. *Journal of Sociolinguistics*, 16(5), 638–668.

Montgomery, C. (2015). Perceptions of borders and boundaries in the North of England. In R. Hickey (Ed.), *Researching Northern English* (pp. 345–368). Amsterdam: John Benjamins.

Nwoye, O. G. (1992). Linguistic politeness and socio-cultural variations of the notion of face. *Journal of Pragmatics*, 18(4), 309–328.

Ogiermann, E. (2009). Politeness and in-directness across cultures: A comparison of English, German, polish and Russian requests. *Journal of Politeness Research*, 5(2), 189–216.

Pojanapunya, P., & Jaroenkitboworn, K. (2011). How to say "good-bye" in Second Life. *Journal of Pragmatics*, 43(14), 3591–3602.

Raumolin-Brunberg, H. (1996). Forms of address in early English correspondence. In T. Nevalainen & H. Raumolin-Brunberg (Eds.), *Sociolinguistics and language history: Studies based on the corpus of early English correspondence* (pp. 167–181). Amsterdam: Rodopi.

Rendle-Short, J. (2010). 'Mate' as a term of address in ordinary interaction. *Journal of Pragmatics*, 42(5), 1201–1218.

Schlegloff, E., & Sacks, H. (1973). Opening up closings. *Semiotica*, 8, 289–327.

Searle, J. (1975). Indirect speech acts. In P. Cole & Jerry Morgan (Eds.), *Syntax and semantics, Volume 3: Speech acts* (pp. 59–82). New York, NY: Academic Press.

Sifianou, M. (1992). *Politeness phenomena in England and Greece: A cross-cultural perspective*. Oxford: Clarendon.

Stewart, M. (2005). Politeness in Britain: It's only a suggestion. In L. Hickey & M. Stewart (Eds.), *Politeness in Europe* (pp. 116–130). Clevedon: Multilingual Matters.

Terkourafi, M. (2001). *Politeness in Cypriot Greek: A frame-based approach*. Unpublished Ph.D dissertation. Cambridge: University of Cambridge.

Terkourafi, M. (2002). Politeness and formulaicity: Evidence from Cypriot Greek. *Journal of Greek Linguistics*, 3, 179–201.

Terkourafi, M. (2005a). Beyond the micro-level in politeness research. *Journal of Politeness Research: Language, Behaviour, Culture*, 1(2), 237–262.

Terkourafi, M. (2005b). Pragmatic correlates of frequency of use: The case for a notion of 'minimal context'. In S. Marmaridou, K. Nikiforidou, & E. Antonopoulou (Eds.), *Reviewing linguistic thought: Converging trends for the 21st century* (pp. 209–233). Berlin: Mouton de Gruyter.

Upton, C. (2012). The importance of being Janus. In M. Markus, Y. Iyeiri, R. Henberger, & E. Chamson (Eds.), *Middle and modern English corpus linguistics* (pp. 257–268). Amsterdam: John Benjamins.

Wales, K. (2000). North and South: An English linguistic divide? *English Today*, 16(1), 4–15.

Watts, R. J. (2003). *Politeness*. Cambridge: Cambridge University Press.

White, G. M., & Watson-Gegeo, K. A. (1990). Disentangling discourse. In K. Watson-Gegeo & G. M. White (Eds.), *Disentangling: Conflict discourse in Pacific societies* (pp. 3–52). Stanford, CA: Stanford University Press.

Wichmann, A. (2004). The intonation of Please-requests: A corpus-based study. *Journal of Pragmatics*, 36(9), 1521–1549.

Wierzbicka, A. (2003 [1991]). *Cross-cultural pragmatics: The semantics of human interaction*. (2nd ed.). Berlin, London: Mouton de Gruyter.

6 'That's Well Bad'

Some New Intensifiers in Spoken British English

Karin Aijmer

6.1 Introduction

Intensifiers hold a great fascination for scholars because of their variability and the changes they undergo (Bolinger, 1972). In Bolinger's words (1972, p. 247), intensifiers "are the chief means of emphasis for speakers for whom all means of emphasis quickly grow stale and need to be replaced". Their analysis has generally focused on variation and changes taking place over a long period of time. However, new methods of data collection now make it possible to start from the assumption that language change can also be witnessed while still in progress (Murphy, 2010, p. 5). The approach in this work draws attention to new and unusual intensifiers in present-day English which seem to be in the process of undergoing delexicalisation and grammaticalisation signalled by changes in frequency and their association with sociolinguistic factors. The following intensifiers fit into this category of intensifiers: *fucking, super, dead, real, well (good)* and *so(+NP)*:

(1) it's a *fucking* amazing book (BNC2014 SA6W)
(2) but don't worry you know we'll be s- like *super nice* to you (BNC2014 SKGU)
(3) there's some really nice dresses that this other woman does and she's called Jenny Packham and she actually she supplies some stuff for Debenhams but no wedding dresses they're *real nice* as well (BNC2014 STXT)
(4) she's not actually in it at any point it's just Joaquin Phoenix but erm yeah it's *dead weird* what was it telling him to do the other day (BNC2014 S4YQ)
(5) that's *well good* (BNC2014 S5SJ)
(6) I'm gonna be *so crap*. I haven't played computer games in ages (BNC2014 S682)

The research questions have to do with the short-term changes the intensifiers undergo and how these should be explained. By analysing the changes of intensifiers over a short time period, we can study if a change is fast and dramatic, and if the changes are visible in the contexts where the intensifiers are found. Why, for example, is it that *well* suddenly (and just now) appears in new combinations with adjectives (*well good*)?

The research questions are:

- How has the frequency of a particular intensifier changed in relation to (some) other competing intensifiers over time?
- How are the variation and changes reflected in the syntactic, semantic and pragmatic features of the intensifiers?
- How are the developments of the intensifiers with different adjectives related to the gender and age of the speakers and the speakers' norms and values? What conclusions can we draw about the speakers spearheading the changes?
- What are the mechanisms of intensification characterising the processes of change taking place over time?

Intensifiers lend themselves to discussing the popular issues of delexicalisation (and how it leads to lexical replacement) and grammaticalisation. The study is therefore also of theoretical interest. By analysing intensifiers from a syntactic, semantic and pragmatic perspective in successive corpora we can, for example, account for ongoing changes and the mechanisms underlying these changes.

The chapter is structured as follows. In Section 6.2, I give a short overview of previous work dealing with ongoing changes in the area of intensification. Section 6.3 discusses methodology and introduces the corpora. Section 6.4 presents the frequencies of selected intensifiers. Section 6.5 consists of case studies of the intensifiers with adjectival heads on the basis of their description in the corpora.

In Section 6.6, I will summarise the sociolinguistic implications of the analyses and come back to what is characteristic of the changes undergone by the intensifiers in connection with their delexicalisation and grammaticalisation.

6.2 Previous Work

Intensifiers have a potential for rapid changes. These may involve both the growth in popularity and their decrease in frequency or disappearance. *Really* and *so* are, for example, characterised by a steep rise in frequency, while *very* is experienced as old-fashioned and is used less.

Previous studies of intensifiers have generally focused on the most frequent intensifiers such as *very, really* and *so*. Until recently not much attention has been given to new and unusual intensifiers such as *well* (*weird*), but their existence has been hidden under headings such as 'all other items' in studies of intensifiers and their study has been taken less seriously (cf. Ito & Tagliamonte, 2003). The newcomers taking up the competition with more established intensifiers may be associated with non-standard grammar; they have an emergent character and tend to be age-related. *Really* (and *so*), for example, have had to compete with 'upstarts' such as 'the new *well*' or other intensifiers in adolescent speech.

Several articles by Sali Tagliamonte and her colleagues have drawn attention to ongoing changes and variation in the area of intensification in a variationist perspective (Tagliamonte & Ito, 2002; Ito & Tagliamonte, 2003; Tagliamonte & Roberts, 2005; Tagliamonte, 2008). Recently there has also been a great deal of interest in studying intensifiers quantitatively and qualitatively on the basis of corpora and corpus-linguistic methods. We can, for example, take advantage of new data collections of spoken language which can be used for sociolinguistic purposes. Stenström, Andersen, and Hasund (2002, p. 141) have opened up a discussion about teenagers' use of intensifiers on the basis of the Bergen Corpus of London Teenage Language (COLT). The authors observed that "teenagers and adults do not use exactly the same set of intensifier; nor do they use the ones they have in common to the same extent". For example, teenagers used the 'emphasiser' *really* but also *bloody* and *fucking* more than adults (see also Stenström, 1999). Other teenage-specific intensifiers that they noted were *enough, right* and *well* (cf. also Paradis, 2000). Following up Stenström et al.'s study, Palacios-Martínez and Núñez-Pertejo (2014) showed that *really* was frequent in several corpora of adolescent speech and that *bloody* and *fucking* were also widely attested.

Other specific intensifier variants have a regional origin. Macaulay (2006) studied *pure*, "an unusual intensifier in the speech of adolescents in Glasgow", in samples of speech representing working-class adolescents in 1997 and then again in 2003 (and 2004). According to Barnfield and Buchstaller (2010), young speakers in Tyneside in North-East England create their own trends using *pure, proper* and *canny* as intensifiers. The authors studied what happens when these new intensifiers enter into the system and the footprints they leave when they become more frequent. It is, for example, possible to trace the developments or 'incremental growth' of the intensifier across examples with adjectives having a positive and negative effect (cf. also Macaulay, 2006, p. 271).

It is also important to consider mechanisms or patterns of intensification going beyond the function to specify degree. Waksler (2012, p. 17) has argued that the intensifiers *super, uber, so* and *totally* can be associated with "over-the-top intensification" which indicates that the intensifier calls attention to the speaker's point of view "by surpassing the usual syntactic, semantic, or pragmatic limits on a particular intensifier's domain".

To sum up, the results from previous work give fuel to the discussion of the ongoing grammaticalisation of intensifiers and how adolescents develop their own preferences for certain intensifiers and use them in innovative ways. In order to explain what new or re-emerging intensifiers are doing in conversation, we also need to consider the role of such factors as expressivity and exaggeration.

6.3 Method and Data

The study of intensifiers raises a number of methodological issues. How should we analyse the variation and semantic changes undergone by intensifiers over time? The new Spoken BNC2014 should be seen as a challenge and an opportunity for sociolinguistic studies of variation and change, since it pays attention to social factors at the speaker level such as age and gender. This raises the question of what sociolinguists and corpus linguists have in common and, more generally, the methodology to study variation and change. Sociolinguists have used a variationist approach to study phonological variation. Variationist methods have also been used to study grammatical or discourse phenomena quantitatively although there are obvious problems of what it means to say the same thing. This methodological approach involves determining (circumscribing) the context in which the intensifier occurs and then analysing the influence and strength of linguistic and social factors. As shown by recent research (see, e.g., work by Sali Tagliamonte and her colleagues) a sociolinguistic variable can be[1] conceptualised by grouping together intensifiers which share position and function and then further investigated.

The methods used in this study have corpora as the starting point. The corpus-linguistic approach characteristically starts with linguistic forms and investigates their frequency and functions in different syntactic and semantic contexts. Corpora can also be used for studying the relationship between function and extra-linguistic or social factors. This approach imposes special demands on the corpora used for the analysis. In order to study the variation and ongoing changes of intensifiers we need corpora which represent up-to-date language. Moreover, it is important to have access to corpora which are suitable for comparative purposes. According to Pichler (2010), comparable research has generally been difficult because the existing corpora tend to be of different sizes; they were compiled for different purposes, use different principles of word count, etc. (Buchstaller, 2009; Pichler, 2010).

The spoken component of the 'new' British National corpus (the Spoken BNC2014; Love, Dembry, Hardie, Brezina, & McEnery, 2017) was initiated as a project to make studies of sociolinguistic variation and change possible. The corpus represents data from the early part of the 21st century. The role model is the spoken component of the 'traditional' British National Corpus, compiled twenty years earlier in the 1990s. The present study uses a sample of spoken data consisting of about five million words (representing 376 speakers)—the Spoken BNC2014S. This corpus is parallel to, although slightly smaller than, the demographic component of the original BNC (the Spoken BNC1994DS) which is used for comparative purposes. The comparability of the Spoken BNC1994DS and the Spoken BNC2014S allows us to study the frequencies of selected intensifiers at different times, to observe how changes come about and how they spread across syntactic and semantic contexts at different speeds.

The corpus data consists of informal conversations between two or more speakers who are mostly friends or family members and covers a large number of different topics. The metadata give information at the speaker level about region, nationality, social class, age and gender differentiation. The topic for this study is the parameters of age and gender of the speakers and their influence on the speakers' use of intensifiers.

As a starting point I extracted all the individual intensifiers and their collocating adjectives from the corpus in order to analyse their frequencies. The context was restricted to intensifiers followed by an adjective even when the intensifier could be used in other grammatical contexts, for example a verb or an adverb.[2] Their variation is discussed from a syntactic, semantic and pragmatic perspective. The adjectives are described syntactically as predicative or attributive and analysed semantically with regard to the frequency and semantic type of adjective, semantic prosody, style ('trendiness') and subjective force. From a pragmatic perspective, the intensifiers express degrees of expressive or subjective force and they can vary with regard to whether they have scope over the speech act. In the type of data I have studied, they are also used rhetorically for different pragmatic effects. Finally, the intensifiers were compared across the corpora in order to investigate the effect of age and gender on the intensifier over time.

6.4 Frequencies of Some Selected Intensifiers in the Spoken BNC2014S

The intensifiers (upgraders or amplifiers)[3] in Figure 6.1. have in common that they were significantly more frequent in speech than in writing in the Spoken BNC1994DS according to Xiao and Tao (2007). *Fucking*, which was not studied by Xiao and Tao, has been added. The examples only include the intensifiers followed by an adjectival head. The frequencies have been normalised to one million words.

The figure gives a picture of ongoing changes in the intensification paradigm based on some individual intensifiers followed by an adjective in the Spoken BNC1994DS and Spoken BNC2014S.[4] Certain changes have a landslide quality. The rise of *really* in the Spoken BNC2014S, for example, is striking. In the old Spoken BNC *really* was used with an adjective in 406.81 examples per million words, to be compared with 1,579 examples per million words in its more recent 'sister corpus'. However, the same rise in frequency is not found with *real*, which has

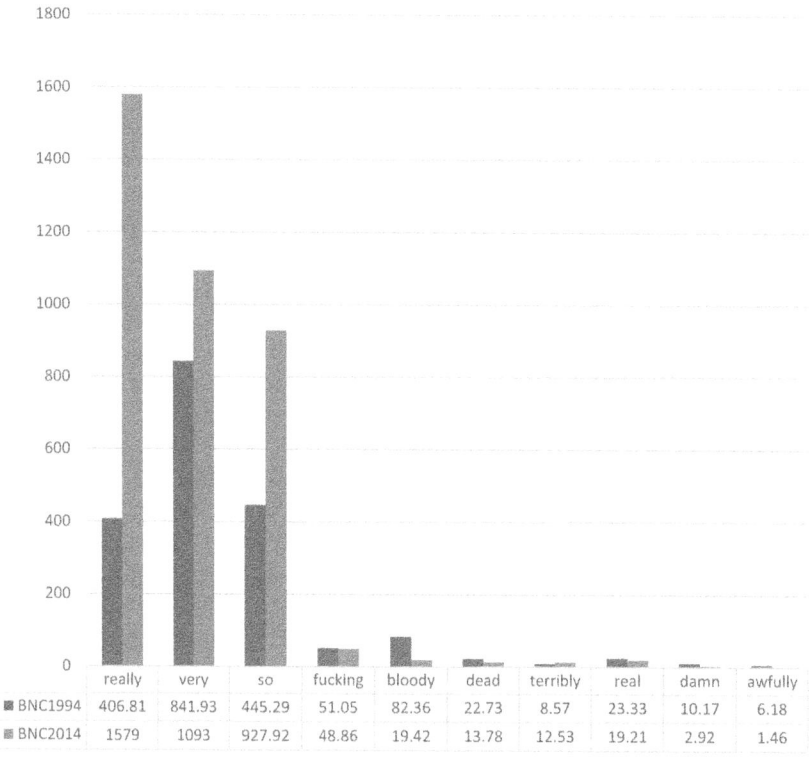

	really	very	so	fucking	bloody	dead	terribly	real	damn	awfully
■ BNC1994	406.81	841.93	445.29	51.05	82.36	22.73	8.57	23.33	10.17	6.18
■ BNC2014	1579	1093	927.92	48.86	19.42	13.78	12.53	19.21	2.92	1.46

Figure 6.1 The Frequencies of Selected Intensifiers With Adjectival Heads in the Spoken BNC1994DS and Spoken BNC2014S

become less frequent in the Spoken BNC2014S. *So* has continued on its upwards rise.[5]

We can see from the table that the intensifiers *dead*, *bloody* and *damn* have decreased in frequency. The expressive *fucking*, on the other hand, has become slightly more frequent and is used instead of *bloody* and other taboo intensifiers.[6] *Terribly* and *awfully* are probably regarded as old-fashioned and seem to have been replaced by other more expressive intensifiers.[7]

The quantitative generalisations provide the groundwork analysis only. We need to go beyond frequencies and study the intensifiers in their syntactic and semantic contexts in order to get a more detailed picture of the changes. This qualitative study will be combined with a description of the users and a discussion of why they pick up a particular innovation and why an intensifier loses in popularity.

6.5 Case Studies

6.5.1 Introduction

A first observation is that *fucking* is untypical as an intensifier, since it is derived from a verb rather than an adjective (Stoffel, 1901; Macaulay, 2006, p. 276). Its position is before adjectives although other, less proto-typical, syntactic distributions are also found. In the example *I fucking love digging holes* (BNC2014 S4T3) it has, for example, the function to reinforce the predicate. According to the OED, it was first mentioned in a handbook of slang in 1893. The first example of *fucking* as an intensifier recorded by OED is from 1948.

Fucking was the most frequent intensifier after *very, really* and *so* in the Spoken BNC2014S and has increased its frequency over a twenty-year period in competition both with more prototypical intensifiers and other taboo intensifiers (see Section 6.4).

Fucking can be described as expressive and subjective. This raises questions about its relationship to ordinary degree-modifying intensifiers. Another issue has to do with the semantic types of adjectives it co-occurs with and their evaluative prosody. From a diachronic perspective, the syntactic and semantic properties of *fucking* also bring up questions about its ongoing grammaticalisation and delexicalisation. Finally, we need to consider who the users are and how the speakers' age and gender can be evidence of ongoing change.

6.5.2 The Expressive Fucking

Fucking and (the near-synonymous) *bloody* are strongly emotional and expressive, as can be expected from their origins as taboo words and swearing. *Fucking* has been described as "a kind of hyperbolic stereo-type" (Altenberg, 1999, p. 140) determined by the speaker's needs to express strong emotions towards persons or things. The expressive use is illustrated in (7) where it co-occurs with *oh my god* for extra emphasis.

(7) oh my god it's *fucking horrible* (BNC2014 SAR5)

  As a general conceptual notion, expressivity also reveals the perspective from which the utterance is made ("perspective dependence") (Potts, 2007, p. 173). *Fucking* is, for example, subjective and typically adopts and emphasises the speaker's perspective. Moreover, expressive items such as *fucking* have an immediate quality (like performatives, they achieve their effect by being uttered) (Potts, 2007, p. 180). Finally, they are "separate from the regular descriptive content" and can be deleted without any change to the content (Potts, 2007, p. 166). In other words, *fucking* does not vary in relation to other intensifiers (only), but with regard to the unmodified proposition.

Cacchiani (2005, p. 414) groups *fucking* (and *bloody*) among modal adverbials because it expresses the speaker's commitment to the truth of what is asserted:

> Crucially, taboo-intensifiers may be grouped among the "epistemic" stance adverbials in Conrad and Biber (2000). They might be assigned to the category of "evidentiality" (specifically the "certainly group") in Biber and Finegan's (1989, p. 98) classification, or fit into the "surely" and the "amazingly" stance adverbials of Biber and Finegan (1988).

However, what makes *fucking* special is that it combines the speaker's commitment to the truth of what is said with the meaning to express the speaker's emotions here and now.

Under certain circumstances, *fucking* can be regarded as a degree modifier before adjectives indicating that it is becoming more grammatical (and more like prototypical intensifiers). The interesting examples are those where *fucking* precedes an attributive adjective.

(8) you have to be *a fucking good skier* to do that. (BNC2014 STGP)
(9) and when you come out on to the main road at—ANON-place between that connect to—ANON-place and you know the other end the other side it's you're this close to *fucking great big lorries* (BNC2014 S8LS)

The examples raise questions about the scope of *fucking*. When it is followed by an attributive adjective (especially if it is a gradable adjective),[8] *fucking* seems to have two possible interpretations, depending on the scope it is assumed to have. In one situation, *fucking* is expressive and has scope over the proposition. However, in (8) *fucking* could also be taken to emphasise 'the quality of good' (on a scale of goodness) and in (9) the speaker may be understood to draw attention to the fact that the lorries are big to a very high degree. The distinction between expressive intensifiers with the function of emphasising the speech act and degree modifiers does not seem to be watertight in such examples. Moreover, ambiguous structures exist where either or both meanings may be present:

(10) yes I enjoyed it tr- tremendously I thought it was *fucking good* (BNC2014 SZPS)

Is *fucking* a modifier of the adjective which can be considered a variant of *very* or does it express the speaker's emotions of satisfaction or approval?[9]

The context is important: if *fucking* follows another intensifier, it can only be interpreted as speaker-oriented and expressive with an emphatic effect on the following adjective (see Section 6.1.4).

(11) I like rea- I was reading all their policies and they sound *pretty fucking good* (BNC2014 SMC2)

To sum up, diachronically, *fucking* as an adjectival intensifier raises questions about ongoing grammaticalisation and the degree to which it can be said to have been grammaticalised. There is some evidence that *fucking* can shift into a strong emphasiser of an adjective in certain contexts, for example when the adjective is attributive or if it gets the focus by being placed after other intensifiers.

6.5.3 Semantic Properties of Fucking

The collocational range of adjectives is closely associated with the expressive meaning of *fucking* in both the Spoken BNC1994DS and Spoken BNC2014S. Hence we find collocations such as *fucking funny* and *fucking awful*, where the adjective has subjective and evaluative meaning and the speaker expresses his or her involvement with what is said. The meaning is illustrated in (12) where the verb is *be*, and *fucking+adjective* emphasises the speaker's attitudes or emotions to the proposition ('that's funny').

(12) did you see that? oh no that's so *fucking funny* (BNC2014 S5EM)

With evaluative predicates, the speaker expresses his or her emotional state or judgements of persons or things in the here-and-now of the speech situation. Non-evaluative adjectives appear later in the grammatical development of *fucking* (e.g., *fucking long, fucking big*) and result in its becoming more delexicalised.

In the Spoken BNC2014S, *fucking* collocates with adjectives expressing evaluation or feelings (81%) to be compared with only 72.6% in the Spoken BNC1994DS. In other words, *fucking* is 'alive and kicking' and even rising in frequency in its function to express the speaker's generally negative attitude to persons and things. This suggests that we must also consider the users and their motivations for using *fucking*.

Another issue is whether *fucking* is followed by adjectives with positive or negative connotations. Speakers generally evaluate things in a consistent way and select intensifier + adjective with a suitable semantic polarity to signal the speaker's approval or disapproval, abhorrence, frustration, admiration, etc. (Partington, 2015, p. 285). Because of its etymological taboo meaning, *fucking* can be expected to be combine mainly with negatively coloured adjectives. The broadening of the collocational range

of *fucking* to adjectives with positive connotations can therefore be interpreted as a sign of delexicalisation and ongoing grammaticalisation.
When the speaker chooses to say *fucking fine* the negative connotations
of *fucking* have disappeared and *fucking* expresses emphasis mixed with
approval (admiration). The positive adjectives include *funny, fine, amazing, good, awesome, massive, brilliant, great* and *cool*.

The number of adjectives with positive connotations is slightly larger
in the Spoken BNC2014S, but so is the number of negative adjectives (see
Table 6.1 and Figure 6.2).

When we compare the frequencies of the collocating adjectives with
positive and negative polarity over time, it is shown that the number
of adjectives with negative polarity slightly increases. Moreover, when
the intensified adjective is neutral (not clearly positive or negative) the
default meaning of *fucking* is negative affect (*fucking long flight, I'm*

Table 6.1 The Frequencies of *Fucking* With Negative, Positive and Neutral Prosody (Raw Numbers and Percentages)

	Spoken BNC1994DS	%	Spoken BNC2014S	%
Negative	114	47.30%	129	52.65%
Positive	68	28.22%	70	28.57%
Neutral	59	24.48%	46	18.78%
Total	241	100%	245	100%

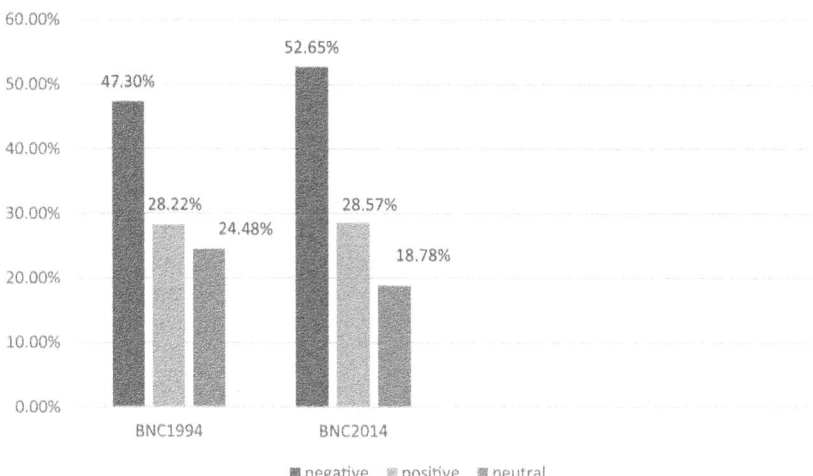

Figure 6.2 Distribution of *Fucking* With Adjectives With Negative, Positive
or Neutral Connotation in the Spoken BNC1994DS and Spoken
BNC2014S.

fucking poor) indicating that the original negative meaning persists and that delexicalisation is only partial or has stopped on the way.

We can conclude that the main function of *fucking*+adjective is to express the speaker's negative feelings of anger, irritation, etc. and that this use may be on the rise. In this case, sociolinguistic factors appear to have overruled the expected results of delexicalisation. Young speakers favour *fucking* to express negative feelings and may even increase their use of *fucking* in negative contexts in spite of the fact that its effect may be weakened.

A more striking scenario of change, in line with sociolinguistic factors, is provided by the use of linguistic strategies for increasing the expressivity and emotionality of *fucking*. The changes undergone by *fucking* in the Spoken BNC2014S have less to do with the spread to new semantic types of adjectives but are associated with a certain generational style and hyperbole.

6.5.4 Fucking and Conversational Hyperbole

Fucking (and *bloody*) are non-prototypical intensifiers because they have pragmatic expressive function rather than degree-modifying function (Cacchiani, 2005, p. 414). However, expressivity and subjectivity are not only a property of *fucking* itself, but a result of the way it is used in discourse to express the speaker's emotions or attitudes together with an adjective. From a discourse-pragmatic perspective, intensifier constructions can, for example, be selected for exaggeration and to express a higher degree of intensification than expected. Let us consider some of the ways in which the use of *fucking* is associated with hyperbole and rhetorical strengthening (emphasising an assertion in the most extreme way).

Expressivity and evaluation are closely connected to the newness and connotations of the adjective. According to Lorenz (2002, p. 143), "crudely speaking. the more 'novel' or 'unusual' a linguistic item in a given function, the more expressive it will be perceived to be". *Fucking*, for example, collocates with *weird, awesome, brilliant, cool, mental, retarded, massive, gross, mad, insane, vile, cheesy* and *mardy*. *Fucking mental* was the most frequent combination (9 examples) followed by *fucking great* (7 examples), *fucking ridiculous* (7 examples), *fucking weird* (6 examples), *fucking awesome* (5 examples), and *fucking brilliant* (5 examples).

New adjectives like *weird* or *brilliant* convey a different social or indexical meaning than the more conservative or common-place *strange* and *nice* (none of which co-occurred with *fucking*). Combinations such as *fucking weird* or *fucking mental* therefore lend themselves to being used as 'shibboleths' or linguistic clues to the identity of the speaker and signal group membership.

In (13) the speakers, who are both in their twenties, are close friends talking 'their funniest episodes':

(13) S0187: the head of McPoil dribbles

S0188: it's fucking weird isn't it?
S0187: oh god (BNC2014 S5EM)

By using the slangy and extreme *weird* the speaker (a 21-year-old male) shows that he fits the picture of a tough and modern adolescent and disaffiliates himself from the social values held by the adult community. The tag question in the same example is another device with the interpersonal function to build a relationship to the hearer and affirm values shared by the peer group.

Adolescents can be assumed to be especially creative in their uses of intensifying constructions. The speaker can refer to herself as *fucking livid* rather than 'angry'; people are said to be *fucking loopy* instead of 'crazy'. The young female student in example (14) imagines what her reactions would be if someone had put her laptop in a bowl of water:

(14) S0205: like I don't think I would even go to the extent of putting somebody's like iPad and laptop in a bowl of water

S0207: no
S0205: >> cos if somebody had done that to me I'd be *fucking livid like beyond livid like* (BNC2014 SAR5)

In (15) the conversation is about a couple who will miss the Titanic celebrations because of their wedding and this is making them 'fucking loopy'. The speaker is a young male:

(15) yeah it's driving em *fucking loopy* must be really bad it's like you'd think that it would have sailed from Belfast (BNC2014 SLDB)

Hyperbole can also be achieved by metaphor. The metaphorical adjective in (16) helps the speaker to give voice to her emotions and to achieve the strongest possible rhetorical effects. The speaker is a young university graduate who has received a letter from her solicitor employed by the National Accident Help and is annoyed because he has got her statements all wrong. *Fucking thick as pig shit* expresses the speaker's anger and annoyance further reinforced by *oh my god*. The intensifier partakes in the push towards exaggeration and an increase in subjectivity.

(16) well it's Gould Solicitors oh my god they're *fucking thick as pig shit* (BNC2014 S8X7)

Fucking is also used in extended discourse patterns where it represents a step-up in emotional force and subjectivity. The speaker repeats 'it's messy' reinforcing the adjective by means of 'really fucking':

(17) it's it's messy it *really fucking messy* (BNC2014 SMME)

The pattern with an intensifier is used for reinforcement (a case of 'climax constructions'; Cacchiani, 2009, p. 242).

The following example (also containing repetition) is on the surface a 'mismatch' since *fucking* is followed by a noun which is by its nature non-gradable:

(18) enjoyed it *yeah fucking ace fucking ace* (BNC2014 SEPP)

Fucking ace has the meaning of 'fucking cool' but is more creative and new and therefore more likely to attract attention.

There are also examples of *fucking* in conjunction with other intensifiers (fifty-five examples in all) including collocations with *so* (thirty-nine examples), *really, pretty, absolutely, just, very (very), a bit, well, all* and *proper* ('complex collocations'; Cacchiani, 2009, p. 236).

(19) stop being selfish stop being *so fucking selfish* (BNC2014 SU82)

Fucking functions as an emphatic discourse marker with a fixed position before the adjective. It is clear that the function of *fucking* to emphasise the adjective is in the foreground. The additional intensifier is not redundant but has the function to increase the expressive force (and subjectivity) signalled by *fucking*:

(20) yeah but it'll be *all fucking gross and shit* man we—UNCLEAR-WORD (BNC2014 SDJA)

In (21) the cluster of different intensifiers additionally reflects the unplanned character of the informal conversation:

(21) we have like a barbecue sometimes for supper and she's *like proper just ah just really fucking* irritates me (BNC2014 S8RY)

6.5.5 Fucking and the Social Context

Who uses *fucking*? Can the variation in its use be related to the age and gender of the speakers? Both *fucking* and the adjectives it co-occurs with may, for example, have a 'generational' ring. Table 6.2 compares the speakers in the corpora using the BNC1994 age bands. The speakers in the Spoken BNC2014S include only those who have specified their exact age (thirty-one speakers out of thirty-seven). See also Figure 6.3:

Table 6.2 *Fucking* as an Adjectival Intensifier in BNC1994 and BNC2014 in Different Age Groups (Raw Numbers and Percentages)

Age	Spoken BNC1994DS		Spoken BNC2014S	
0–14	19	7.88%	–	–
15–24	80	33.20%	89	51.45%
25–34	93	38.59%	46	26.59%
35–44	19	7.88%	25	14.45%
45–59	28	11.62%	8	4.62%
60+	2	0.83%	5	2.89%
	241	100%	173[10]	100%

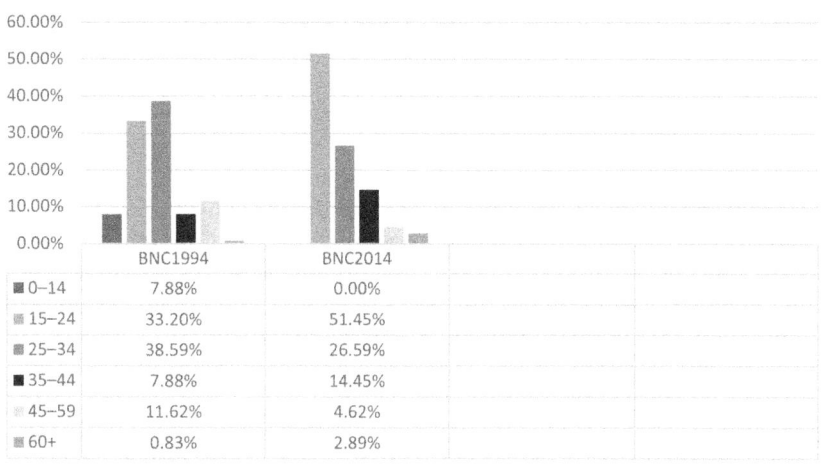

Figure 6.3 *Fucking* as an Adjectival Intensifier in the Spoken BNC1994DS and Spoken BNC2014S in Different Age Groups

The reason why we find so many examples of *fucking* among 15- to 24-year-olds may be that the young speakers use *very* or other more common-place intensifiers less frequently than adults, or that adolescents in general make more frequent use of intensifiers. Another reason may be that the use of *fucking* is popular among younger speakers because it fulfils a need or desire to be linguistically different from adults.

Murphy, for example, stresses the linguistic freedom associated with a particular life stage and the need or desire by young people to fit in with their peers (Murphy, 2010, p. 207). By exaggerating, being creative and innovative young people establish a distinct, youthful identity. There is a striking decrease in the frequency of use in the 'middle-age' speakers (35- to 44-year-olds). According to Murphy (2010, p. 130), this decrease "may have to do with conservatism setting in due to professional lives and the discourse that is expected and required in such settings or perhaps it is associated with parenthood and the responsibility that comes with that in terms of linguistic politeness".

Also, the gender aspect is important. The data in the Spoken BNC2014S stand out because of the frequency of *fucking* used by (young) women (57% females vs. 43% males). This is a larger number of female speakers than what has been reported on the basis of other corpora and a larger number than we find in the Spoken BNC1994DS. In the BNC1994, about three-quarters of the speakers were male (73% male vs. 27% female). In COLT (Stenström et al., 2002) *fucking* was mostly used boys (78% vs. 22% girls)[11] and Murphy (2010) also found that males tended to use *fucking* more than females in a corpus study comparing intensifiers (amplifiers) in comparable corpora of female and male speech across different age groups. The data from earlier corpora seem to suggest that males have been the leaders in the rise of frequency of *fucking* and that the pattern has been usurped by females in a fairly short period.[12]

Why do women use *fucking* so frequently? Murphy (2010, p. 129) quotes Bailey and Timm's observation (1976) that younger women "tend to engage in the use of strong expletives such as *'fucking'* and the like because they view them more as stylistic devices which seem to be relatively free of moral or ethical overtones". The young females in the data from the Spoken BNC2014S bond with each other by using *fucking* together with adjectives for mock insults to show their verbal skills. They may, for example, describe people as "you big fucking fat turkey", "you fucking upright bitch", "a fucking massive knobhead", or "fucking smart-arse big fuck".

Bloody is a near-synonym of *fucking*. The two intensifiers can therefore be regarded as competing forms. *Bloody* occurred 19.42 times per million words, to be compared with *fucking*'s 48.86 times per million words (Section 6.4). In COLT, *bloody* was however more frequent than *fucking*, and the popularity of *fucking* in the 1990s is when we look at the whole of the BNC1994. We can speculate that *bloody* is experienced as being outdated by many young speakers since it was used so often by older speakers in the Spoken BNC2014S (about 23% of the examples represent 60+ speakers).

6.5.6 *Concluding Discussion of Fucking*

Fucking is unusual as an intensifier, since it is not degree-modifying. It has expressive or subjective meaning in addition to signalling the speaker's commitment to the truth of the proposition or what is asserted. However, in some contexts it has developed into an emphatic intensifier (or discourse marker) and there are many examples of ambiguity. In a short-time perspective the changes undergone by *fucking* are above all sociolinguistic and difficult to explain in a grammaticalisation perspective. It was, for example, increasingly used by female speakers who used *fucking* to signal a young female identity.

Summing up the results of the corpus investigation:

- *fucking* was the most frequent intensifier (after *very, really* and *so*) although a close competitor is *bloody*.
- *fucking* was used with many semantic types of adjective including non-evaluative ones.
- *fucking* was used with positively coloured adjectives which suggests that has expanded its collocation range.
- in a short-time perspective, subjective *fucking* expands its expressive territory by being used with fashionable adjectives and for hyperbole and exaggeration.
- *fucking* was popular primarily by younger speakers. Over a short time period it was increasingly used by speakers in the age band 15–24.
- *fucking* was used more frequently by (young) women than by males.

Will the popularity of *fucking* last? As we have seen, young people nowadays use it overwhelmingly to signal a 'youthful' speaker identity. However, it is well-known that linguistic variation or change which is linked to age are not without problems. *Fucking* is not used uniformly by speakers in different age groups but the results may be interpreted in terms of age-grading rather than change; in other words, the high frequency of *fucking* is correlated with a particular phase of life and this tendency is repeated in successive generations. Speakers in the young age group, for example, use *fucking* a lot, but it is used much less by older speakers.

6.5.7 Super

Super is a new or emerging intensifier which is quickly and dramatically increasing in frequency in American English. The comments on its use are mostly anecdotal, as in the following extract from the internet:

> The adverbial *super* has usurped "really" (really!) and "pretty," and has left "very" so far in the dust that the latter has acquired a kind of anachronistic charm. And no, we are not super tired of "super." We are exhausted, worn out, bored and annoyed. Our ears wince.[13]

It is also pointed out that in COCA (the Corpus of American Contemporary English) *super* was five times more common during 2010–2012 than 1990–1994. To judge from the quotation, *super* may have reached its peak in American English where speakers have started finding it annoying and are looking for new 'strong' words. In British English, on the other hand, *super* is still on its way upwards in frequency and popularity.

Super occurred 129 times in the Spoken BNC2014S (26.94 tokens per million words [pmw]), to be compared with only seven examples in the Spoken BNC1994DS (1.40 tokens pmw). With regard to the type or mechanism of intensification it belongs to the conceptual domain of intensifiers expressing a 'telic' evaluation. Telic intensifiers presuppose a norm that has to be fulfilled (Lorenz, 2002, p. 149). Likewise, telic evaluation concerns cases where a given norm is not reached or over-reached (Lorenz, ibid.). The new *super* would be an example success-fully competing with old-fashioned telic intensifiers such as *excessively* or *unbelievably*. Something which is *super brilliant* is not just brilliant but exceeds expectations or norms associated with what it usually means to be brilliant. According to Waksler, the function of *super* is to indicate subjectivity by surpassing "the usual syntactic, semantic and pragmatic limits" (Waksler, 2012, p. 18).

Super expresses an evaluative judgement on things and people which can be positively or negatively coloured (cf. Waksler, 2012, p. 25). Not surprisingly, considering its literal meaning 'excellent', *super* harmonises with adjectives having a positive effect. However, its gradual delexicalisa-tion has also made it compatible with adjectives associated with a nega-tive aspect to express that a property is present to an unexpected degree. The Spoken BNC2014S contains the following examples of *super* char-acterised by negative semantic prosody: *super annoying, super inconven-ient, super hungover* and *super hammered*. In the Spoken BNC1994DS, where *super* appeared eight times, the adjectives were mostly positive (e.g., *efficient, elegant, fantastic*).

The collocations with fashionable adjectives can be regarded as a pre-phase of spread and change. In the Spoken BNC2014S, things were not only *super nice* but also *super brilliant, super geeky, super cute, super posh, super weird,* or *super hyper* (twelve examples in all of trendy adjectives).

Hyperbole and exaggeration seem to be the rule with *super*. As a result of 'surpassing limits', *super* can come to be used in more subjective and emo-tional ways. In (22) the speaker (a 29-year-old woman) describes in a very dramatic way how she went on an expensive fishing trip and got seasick:

(22) that's like when we went on that fishing trip it was like really expen-sive it was like four hundred dollars or something like US in—ANON-place got up in the morning was *like super hungover* got seasick for the first time in my life like vomming (BNC2014 SXCB)

Super hungover is an innovative formation adding colour and drama to the speaker's narrative of how seasick she felt. Such highly emotional and subjective uses of intensifiers may highlight the emotive content of the narrative "specifically emphasising the character or self-portrayal of the speaker" (Brown & Tagliamonte, 2012, p. 8).

In (23) the speaker works at an office where they have acquired a new printer which is not only very good but surpasses "the pragmatic limits of the target's placement of the values continuum" (Waksler, 2012, p. 18):

(23) they can you know they can do whatever they like and then bring it into the w- into the office and print them out cos *we've got a super duper whizzy lovely one printer* um and they can actually keep copies so she said she's gonna volunteer and do that cos they're one of they're one of our registered charities (BNC2014 SK3B)

There are several ways in which more expressivity can be achieved. In example (23), *super* occurs in a complex collocation "extending to the right in the form of multiple collocates" (Cacchiani, 2009, p. 230). The speaker uses the extended pattern "super duper whizzy lovely" to further increase her enthusiasm and praise of the advantages of the printer.

Repetition of *super* was used in eight examples for more emphasis. In (24) the speaker describes his feelings visiting the basement of the Science museum:

(24) but it's it's it's feels like some sort of train station in from Tokyo in the nineties or something *it's like it's super super weird* and there's like I mean it's hard to explain you have to see it (BNC2014 SP2X)

Super could combine with other intensifiers (*so super excited, just super geeky, really super shiny*). However, most frequently, it collocated with *like* (fifteen examples). In (25) the reference is to Polish workers who were packing boxes and doing really hard work:

(25) and sort of like they were like always sweating with the effort of what they were doing and they were *like super super strong* (BNC2014 SP2X)

The speaker was not content to say *super strong* or *strong* but uses repetition and a reinforcing *like* to dramatize what was going on.

Super was mainly used by young speakers (with no great difference between the age bands 15–24 and 25–34) (see Table 6.3 and Figure 6.4):

By choosing *super* rather than a more old-fashioned intensifier, speakers "place themselves in the social landscape through stylistic practice" (Eckert, 2012, p. 94). *Super* was chosen primarily by young women to achieve a special feminine style characterised by a great deal of emotionality. There were, for example, fifty-six female compared with only five male speakers using *super* in the Spoken BNC2014S.

Table 6.3 Frequency of *Super* in Relation to Speaker Age in the Spoken BNC2014S

Age Range	Number of Examples	%
0–14	–	–
15–24	22	32.84%
25–34	24	35.82%
35–44	15	22.39%
45–59	2	2.99%
60+	4	5.97%
Total	67[14]	100%

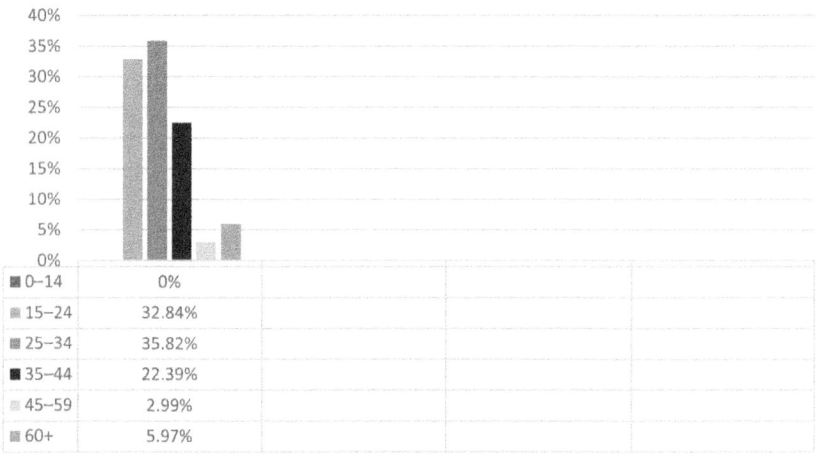

Figure 6.4 Super as an Adjectival Intensifier in the Spoken BNC2014S in Different Age Groups

When an intensifier is more frequent in the Spoken BNC2014S than in its predecessor, this raises the question of linguistic innovation and how this happens. *Super* spreads to more and more contexts (number and type of adjectives) and at the same time it is used by new groups of speakers. The rapid spread of *super* in present-day British English may be due to influence from American English television and social media. The types of examples in the Spoken BNC2014S are hardly likely to spread into writing and may be replaced by other more up-to-date items in young people's speech.

6.5.8 Real as an Intensifier

Really was one of the most frequent intensifiers in the Spoken BNC2014S, reflecting what seems to be a recent development in present-day British English (see Section 6.4). In addition, *really* has the variant *real* with zero affixation. While *really* changes its frequency dramatically from 1994 to 2014, this is not the case for the zero adverb *real*. In fact, the historical trend in a short perspective is that *real* has become less frequent. In the Spoken BNC2014S, there were ninety-two examples[15] of *real* (21.92 examples pmw) to be compared with 117 examples in the Spoken BNC1994DS (22.73 examples pmw). In a longer perspective, *real* is not a newcomer in English but is recorded from 1658 (Tagliamonte & Ito, 2002, p. 257). However, the present-day use of the zero adverb *real* in British English can be explained as due to American influence from television and other media rather than as a long-term development. Biber, Johansson, Leech, Conrad, and Finegan (1999, p. 564) describe *real* as an informal amplifier (in American English) which is generally not used in academic prose. Stenström et al. (2002) found 10 examples of the intensifier *real* in COLT used primarily by middle-class girls and boys who maybe are "more exposed to American influence than lower class boys and girls" (Stenström et al., 2002, p. 151).

The most common collocates of *real* in Biber et al.'s American data (occurring over five times per million words) were the adjectives *good, nice, hard, bad, big* and *easy* (Biber et al., 1999, p. 564). In the Spoken BNC2014S, *real* was used both with frequent adjectives (*good, nice, bad* and *big*) and more fashionable ones (*cool, cute, brilliant, classy,* and *weird*). Positive evaluations dominated (twenty-seven examples including the adjectives *good, nice, happy, classy*). The negative examples (nineteen examples) were, for example, *bad, weird, shocking, evil, troublesome, obnoxious,* and *nasty*.

The speakers use *real* before adjectives to make judgements about their peers or about things. In (26) four friends are talking about an episode where one of them happened to fall over another:

(26) S0330: what have you done?

    S0328:it was your fault babes
    Unknown female[??]: yeah
    S0330: that 's really funny it's
    S0331: *real funny* (BNC2014 SUWR)

Real funny is used interchangeably with "that's really funny" to evaluate the episode as amusing.

Real has a distinct sociolinguistic profile with regard to age and gender. Table 6.4 compares the relative frequencies of *real* in the Spoken BNC1994DS and Spoken BNC2014S. (The speakers in BNC2014 have been regrouped on the basis of the indication of their exact age.) See also Figure 6.5.

Real is more informal than *really*, which fits in well with the picture that young people use non-standard grammar and vocabulary. Young people may also *real* because it sounds American and therefore modern.

Table 6.4 The Relative Frequencies of *Real* in the Spoken BNC1994DS and Spoken BNC2014S

Age Range	Spoken BNC1994DS		Spoken BNC2014S	
0–14	6	5.13%	2	3.33%
15–24	30	25.64%	10	16.67%
25–34	21	17.95%	6	10%
35–44	17	14.53%	14	23.33%
45–59	28	23.93%	9	15%
60+	15	12.82%	19	31.67%
Total	117	100%	60	100%

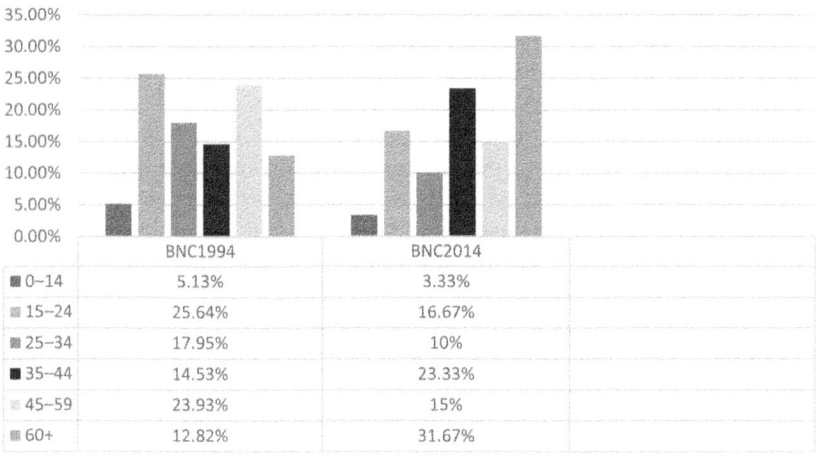

	BNC1994	BNC2014
0–14	5.13%	3.33%
15–24	25.64%	16.67%
25–34	17.95%	10%
35–44	14.53%	23.33%
45–59	23.93%	15%
60+	12.82%	31.67%

0–14   15–24   25–34   35–44   45–59   60+

Figure 6.5 *Real* as an Adjectival Intensifier in the Spoken BNC1994DS and Spoken BNC2014S in Different Age Groups

However, in the diachronic perspective, *real* has become less frequent in the 15- to 24-year-old age group and in the 25–34 group, suggesting that it has lost its newness and attraction among the young speakers. On the other hand, *real* has increased among speakers 35–44 years old and among the older speakers.

Another tendency was that *real* was generally favoured by females in the Spoken BNC2014S (sixty examples to be compared with twenty-eight examples with male speakers). In the Spoken BNC1994DS, on the other hand, both males and females used *real* with the same frequency.

In other spoken corpora, the zero intensifier *real* has generally been associated with male speakers. D'Arcy (2015) found that *real* was consistently more frequent among males than females over different time periods in the ONZE Corpus (Origins of New Zealand English Corpus

1860–1977) which she took to be indicative of a male-led change. Yagu-cchi et al. (2010, p. 594) found that the ratio of *real* uttered by female speakers was lower compared to male speakers in professional speech, suggesting that females avoided *real* because it is a stigmatised intensifier and experienced as casual. However, the appearance of *real* in predicative position was more frequent in female than in male speech where its function was to help speakers to sound affective and listener-oriented (Yagucchi et al., 2010, p. 594).[16]

6.5.9 Dead

Dead is not a true innovation since it occurs as an intensifier in older English.[17] According to Blanco-Suárez (2014, p. 118), it emerged in early Middle English but only became grammaticalised as an intensifier in Early Modern English. It has attracted the attention of researchers because it has as undergone a rapid process of rise and fall in several British dialects. Barnfield and Buchstaller (2010, p. 266) refer to the 'rise of fame' of *dead* in Tyneside English in the 1990s with female speakers leading the way to change. By 1994 *dead* was reported to be the most frequent intensifier used by young speakers in that dialect (Barnfield & Buchstaller, 2010, p. 269). In 2007/2008 the frequency of *dead* had dropped. In fact, many of the older users reverted to using *very* as an intensifier as they got older. A similar trend was observed in the speech of Glasgow teenagers where *dead* is seen to decrease in frequency since 1967 (Macaulay, 2006, p. 270).

The intensifier *dead* is not restricted to dialects. Claridge (2011) traced 'the new *dead*' back at least to the 1960s (Claridge, 2011, p. 1998). However, Paradis (2000, p. 154) found only few examples of *dead* in the London-Lund Corpus and only as a 'maximiser' similar to *absolutely*. The COLT Corpus, which was compiled in the early 1990s, contained only three examples of the intensifier *dead* (*dead easy, dead funny* and *dead upset*).

According to Claridge (2011, p. 200), who reviewed *dead* in many different corpora, there seemed to be no evidence that the intensifying *dead* was expanding. However, in the Spoken BNC1994DS it is becoming popular, especially among young speakers (107 examples or 22.73 tokens pmw). *Dead* thus seems to have gone from being practically unused to a dramatic rise in a very short time, paralleling its development in a fairly short period of time in Barnfield and Buchstaller's study. In the Spoken BNC2014S, on the other hand, there were only sixty-six examples (13.78 tokens pmw) indicating that its frequency is on its way down again, perhaps because of competition with *fucking* and parallel to its decline in regional dialects.

Dead seems to be a forceful intensifier item which can be explained by its association with death. Claridge (2011, p. 198) gives it the meaning 'extremely', 'totally', or 'absolutely' as an intensifier. *Dead* can also be compared with *very* since it seems to have proceeded most of the way to grammaticalisation. In the Spoken BNC2014S, it combined both with evaluative (43%) and non-evaluative adjectives (57%) and it is used for both positive and negative evaluation. *Dead* expresses either positive (sixteen examples) or negative evaluation (fourteen examples) depending on the positive or negative aspect of the collocating adjective. In (27) the speaker describes a trapeze bar thing that you swing on:

(27) S0246:and that was really good but—ANON-name-m was too short for it and—ANON-name-m was too big and erm so only me and—ANON-name-n went round and played on it *dead good*

S0245: *dead good*
S0246: really good I miss my I miss my swing (BNC2014 S5LP)

Dead was preferred in predicative position in both the Spoken BNC1994DS and Spoken BNC214S. The BNC1994 also had examples such as *dead hard work,* and *a dead nice bloke* which were not represented in the more recent data from the BNC2014, where there were no attributive uses. In the Spoken BNC1994DS, it is also used with predicative adjectives. However, in the Spoken BNC2014S, speakers are using *dead* less than in the BNC1994, although it was used in the same contexts. As mentioned, there were no examples with attributive adjectives. However, with the rise in frequency we also find a development to use *dead* with adjectives having attributive function.

Although *dead* has become less frequent in the Spoken BNC2014S, it was still used with fashionable adjectives or participles (*geeky, mad, comfy, chuffed*) to suggest a youthful style. *Dead geeky* is strongly evaluative and fashionable. In (28) it receives extra emphasis by being repeated in a new clause strengthened by *just*:

(28) yeah he does—UNCLEARWORD he's *dead geeky* no he's *just dead geeky* (BNC2014 S5LP)

In (29) *dead* was used in an innovative way with a noun instead of an adjective:

(29) I mean it's my dad's family were *dead working class* and er his gran- my my grandfather he used to be a livery painter he used to paint trams and stuff and he was also a song and dance man and my dad always fucks up this story so I'm gonna fuck it up as well (BNC2014 SEPP)

Dead working class has been used because it is colourful and creative. *Working class* is reanalysed by the hearer as conveying certain properties commonly associated with an adjective. By using the unusual combination, the speaker emphasises subjectivity and expressivity.

Interestingly, *dead* was more frequently used by female speakers in the Spoken BNC1994DS (68.22% female vs. 31.77% male) suggesting that it started out as a change led by women. The tendency that females are leading the change is also found in Barnfield and Buchstaller's (2010) study of Tyneside users where 57% of the (young) speakers were female. Moving on to the more recent data in the Spoken BNC2014S, *dead* is, however, becoming more frequent among the male speakers. *Dead* was used by males (60%) and females (40%).

Table 6.5 compares the ages of the speakers using the BNC1994 age grouping as the base-line. See also Figure 6.6.

Table 6.5 The Frequencies of *Dead* as an Adjectival Intensifier in Different Age Cohorts in Raw Numbers and Percentages

Age Range	Spoken BNC1994DS		Spoken BNC2014S	
0–14	2	1.87%	–	–
15–24	49	45.79%	21	41.18%
25–34	21	19.62%	12	23.53%
35–44	15	14.02%	10	19.61%
45–59	14	13.08%	2	3.92%
60+	6	5.61%	6	11.76%
Total	107	100%	51	100%

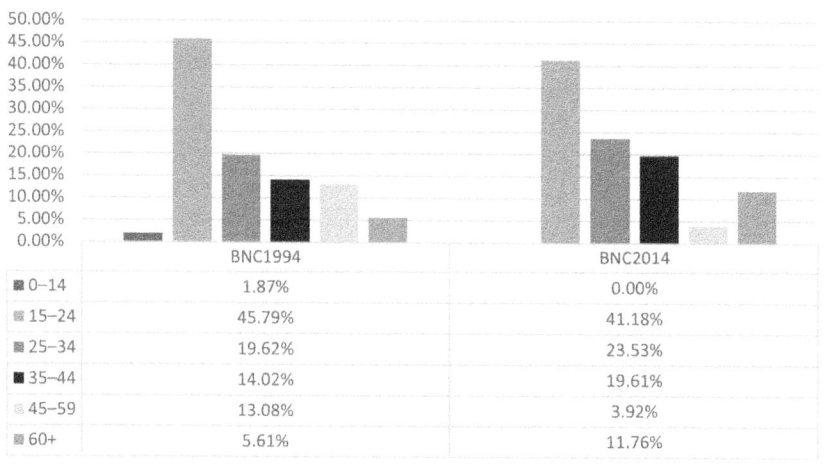

	BNC1994	BNC2014
0–14	1.87%	0.00%
15–24	45.79%	41.18%
25–34	19.62%	23.53%
35–44	14.02%	19.61%
45–59	13.08%	3.92%
60+	5.61%	11.76%

■ 0–14   ▩ 15–24   ▨ 25–34   ■ 35–44   ░ 45–59   ▩ 60+

Figure 6.6 *Dead* as an Adjectival Intensifier in the Spoken BNC1994DS and Spoken BNC2014S in Different Age Groups

In the Spoken BNC2014S, *dead* is still used by young speakers (15- to 24-year-olds) but less frequently than in the Spoken BNC1994DS and slightly more among more middle-aged speakers. In the Spoken BNC1994DS it is also fairly frequent in the age-band of 45- to 59-year-olds. However, in the Spoken BNC2014S it has instead become more frequent among those in their sixties or older.

Dead was primarily used by young speakers in both corpora indicating that it functioned to mark group identity. It was more frequent with female speakers in the Spoken BNC1994DS, indicating that the high frequency is the result of a change led by females. In the Spoken BNC2014S, *dead* was used less often by females than by males.

To sum up, the intensifier *dead* is not a newcomer in the Spoken BNC2014S, but its rise in frequency from a modest beginning can be witnessed in the BNC1994. The drop in frequency in 2014 indicates that it is losing its popularity, perhaps in competition with other strong intensifiers. *Dead* was primarily used by young speakers in both corpora indicating that it functioned to mark group identity. It was more frequent with female speakers in the Spoken BNC1994DS, indicating that the high frequency is the result of a change led by females. However, the trend does not continue. In the Spoken BNC2014S, the shrinkage of the popularity of *dead* is accompanied by its adoption by male speakers, while female speakers use it less.

6.5.10 *The New Well*

(30) my mum says I go yeah that's well nice and she goes erm goes well nice I said [unclear] and I say well and I'm well cool and I keep on saying that I've said it like about so many things when we're at home and she goes what is this you always saying well [unclear] with everything. (BNC1994 KPF)

Interestingly, we may be witnessing a new use of *well* in adolescent speech as in *that's well nice, I'm well cool*. This is a phenomenon which attracts attention as when the mother says: "what is this you're always saying *well* with everything". Ito and Tagliamonte give further evidence for the intensifier use of *well* based on personal observation (Ito & Tagliamonte, 2003, p. 279) and several examples can be found on television and other media. In a popular Catherine Tate comic show on BBC the main character Lauren uses *well* instead of the commonplace *very* or some other intensifier before an adjective: *that is well bad, that's well good cheerleading, well impressive, well shameful, it's well funny*. Against the background of these anecdotal observations it should be interesting to study the usage and progress of the intensifying *well* on the basis of the Spoken BNC2014S.

Well as an intensifier is not of new origin, and the historical sources indicate that it was in use already in old English. Ito and Tagliamonte (2003, p. 239) observe that *well* became the most common intensifier after the middle of the 13th century and then gave way to other variants by the middle of the 14th century.

The re-emergence of *well* as an intensifier may come as no surprise since it already collocates with adjectives as in *well aware* and can therefore easily be extended to other contexts. The distribution of the new *well* with different adjectives and participles in the Spoken BNC2014S is shown in Table 6.6:[18]

Well as an intensifier occurred in seventy-eight examples with thirty-four different adjectives or adjectival participles (16.28 tokens pmw). It

Table 6.6 The New *Well* with Different Adjectives in the Spoken BNC2014S

1	amazing
2	annoyed
3	annoying
4	bad (2 examples)
5	big
6	cheap
7	chuffed (3)
8	cool (2)
9	crazy (2)
10	different
11	dodgy
12	easy
13	full
14	funny (5)
15	geeky
16	good (24)
17	great
18	grumpy
19	gutted (3)
20	happy (3)
21	hard
22	harsh
23	hot
24	irritating
25	long
26	lovely (2)
27	lucky
28	nice (8)
29	pissed
30	posh
31	scary
32	strange
33	weird
34	wicked

was also attested in the Spoken BNC1994DS (fifty-six examples or 11.16 tokens pmw)[19] and some speakers used it frequently.

The new *well* was infrequent in attributive constructions, which may be a characteristic feature of the 'newer and encroaching' intensifiers (cf. Barnfield & Buchstaller, 2010, p. 276). The Spoken BNC2014S contained seven examples (e.g., *a well good talk, well nice burgers, a well crazy year*). The Spoken BNC1994DS contained a single example (*a well famous composer*) which can be taken to indicate that the attributive construction develops later.

The collocating adjectives were both frequent ones like *good, nice* and *bad* and newer more fashionable ones such as *geeky, cool, weird, dodgy* and *wicked*.[20] In addition, *well* could be followed by participles (*gutted, chuffed, pissed, warped*). 68% of the adjectives had a positive connotation as can be expected from the association with the manner adverb (56% in the Spoken BNC1994DS).

A comparison can also be made with other corpora. Stenström et al. (2002) noticed the use of the newcomer *well* in the COLT corpus. In COLT there were thirty-eight examples, only a few of which contained trendy adjectives, suggesting variation and change (Stenström et al., 2002, p. 155). Moreover, "due to the relatively few instances, it is difficult to arrive at a conclusion as to whether premodification of *well* is more or less restricted to very common adjectives such as *good* and *nice* or trendy adjectives such as *cool* and *wicked*" (Stenström et al., 2002, pp. 156–157). The data in the Spoken BNC2014S suggest both a spread of *well* to trendy adjectives and a leap in frequency of the construction, due to the large number of occurrences of *well* with adjectives such as *good* (twenty-three examples) and *nice* (eight examples).

The frequency of *it's well good* seems to be a recent phenomenon. Stenström et al. (2002) found only a single example of *well* collocating with *good* (although there were seven examples with *nice*) and BNC1994 contained two examples.

The speakers were generally young both in the Spoken BNC1994 and BNC2014 data. The teenagers seem to use *well* as a modern equivalent of the degree modifier *very* or *really*. There is a dip in frequency with fewer speakers aged 35–44, reflecting the transition to a new life-stage in society. See Table 6.7 and Figure 6.7.

The speakers in the younger age bands (15–24, 25–34) use *well* to mark themselves off linguistically from the adults by choosing newer and more popular intensifiers.

There is also a gender aspect. In Stenström et al.'s (2002) study of *well*, only three out of the ten speakers were girls, indicating that it was mainly boys who had adopted the intensifier. In the Spoken BNC1994DS, *well* was used mainly by males (65% male; 35% female). In the BNC2014 data, *well* had spread and there were mostly female speakers (55% female; 45% male).

Table 6.7 The Frequency of the Intensifier *Well* in Different Age Groups in the Spoken BNC1994DS and Spoken BNC2014S (the Examples in the BNC2014 Have Been Regrouped on the Basis of Exact Age)

Age Range	Spoken BNC1994DS		Spoken BNC2014S	
0–14	5	8.62%	–	–
15–24	22	37.93%	34	57.63%
25–34	18	31.03%	18	30.51%
35–44	6	10.34%	4	6.78%
45–59	5	8.62%	3	5.08%
60+	2	3.45%	–	–
Total	58	100%	59[21]	100%

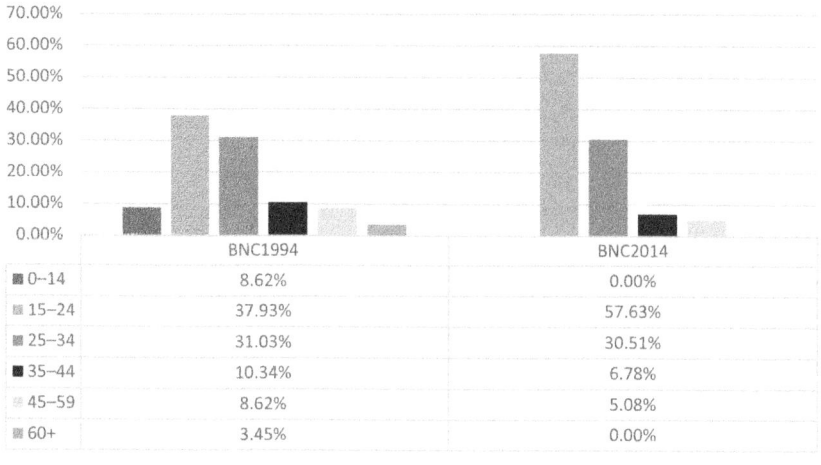

Figure 6.7 *Well* as an Adjectival Intensifier in the Spoken BNC1994DS and Spoken BNC2014S in Different Age Groups

5.6 The Pragmatic *So*

Over the last decades, *so* has become a favourite intensifier, especially for young speakers in the US (Tagliamonte & Roberts, 2005; Kuha, 2004) and in Canada (Tagliamonte, 2008). Tagliamonte and Roberts (2005) focused on its canonical uses before an adjective. However, *so* can also be present in syntactic and semantic contexts where intensifiers are normally not permitted.[22]

(31) illustrates an example of *so* modifying a noun. Three flat-mates (young males in their twenties) are talking about going out. It has been suggested that they should visit a particular glass bar which looks cool with water coming down. However, one of the young men objects that "it's just so cocktail party". The others understand what is meant because

they share assumptions or experience about what a cocktail party is like and whether it is something good or bad. The collocation with *just* makes *so* more prosodically prominent. As a result, it functions as hyperbole to convey that a certain norm is surpassed. Moreover, *so* can be associated with positive or negative evaluation prosody depending on the speakers' shared experiences and assumptions. In (31) the *so*-construction is associated with negative evaluation and has a dismissive discourse function (Wee & Ying, 2008, p. 2106).

(31) S0080: There's a massive like glass bar

    S0072: Yeah
    S0080: With like water coming down I don't know if it's water or whether it's just light but it looks cool—UNCLEARWORD
    S0072: Well good
    S0134: Mm
    S0080: *It's just so cocktail party*
    S0072: That's well good (BNC2014 S5SJ)

Similar, unusual, examples of *so*[23] have been referred to as 'Gen X *so*' (Zwicky, 2011), 'speech act *so*' (Potts, 2004) or 'Drama SO' (Irwin, 2014). Generation X *so* refers to the appearance of *so* in the speech of members of 'generation X' (usually associated with American English) in contexts where it does not modify an adjective or adverb phrase. Speech act *so* emphasises the fact that the construction with *so* involves a high degree of commitment to the proposition. According to Irwin (2014), 'Drama SO' is prosodically prominent and has polarity properties. Semantically, Drama SO is "generally uttered with a high degree of emotion" (Irwin, 2014, p. 2).

I will use the term 'the pragmatic (or interpersonal) *so*' with reference to its function in discourse. Since the speakers are acquainted and can be supposed to share social norms, the current speaker can use *so* plus noun to refer to a familiar scenario or a shared experience. The effect is to strengthen the bonds between the speakers.

Gonzalvez-García describes 'it is so N' as a 'construction' (2014, p. 373) drawing on usage-based strands of CxG [construction grammar] understood as follows:

> Any linguistic pattern is recognized as a construction as long as some aspect of its form or function is not strictly predictable from its component parts or from other constructions recognized to exist. In addition, patterns are stored as constructions even if they are fully predictable as long as they occur with sufficient frequency.
>
> (Goldberg, 2006, p. 5)

'It is so N' can be regarded as a construction, but so can patterns with *be* as a verb followed by *so* and other unexpected expressions. The pattern or construction is typically associated with evaluation and expressivity; it can be exploited by speakers to establish a harmonious relationship by referring to what is shared. Gonzalvez-García (2014) did not find any examples in established corpora such as the BNC1994 or COCA (The Corpus of Contemporary American English). On the other hand, both Spoken BNC1994DS and Spoken BNC2014S contain examples of *so* before nouns meaning 'worthless' (*it's so rubbish, it's so shit, it's so crap (crop), it's so yada yada, so yolo*). What these examples with *so* have in common is that the noun can be coerced into an adjectival interpretation. They are therefore different from the pragmatic *so*, where the link between the construction and its interpretation may be found in the larger cultural context.

Other examples are less generational. In example (32) two female nurses are discussing what clothes to wear if you want to be really cool. They are both aware of the importance of a 'designer label' to mark quality and fashion. The speaker is a 53-year-old woman:

(32) S0104: if you've got Hollister clothes then you're really cool

    S0379: oh right
    S0104: erm
    S0167: yeah
    S0379: >> *so designer label?*
    S0104: yeah
    (BNC2014 SBKM)

So is followed by a noun which has to be interpreted in a non-literal way to refer to certain positive qualities.

So can also be followed by a locational noun as in (33). The example is taken from a conversation among university colleagues. The speakers are sharing their memories about special 'beer-offs' where they used to get a beer by referring to this as being 'so Yorkshire'.

(33) S0147: but in—ANON-place em they're not actually call them outdoorsy

    S0063: oh
    S0147: they are called them beer-offs
    S0063: veers offs? So is that a—UNCLEARWORD?
    S0147: so *so Yorkshire* I know I know
    S0147: so you always used to say em things like I'm going to the beer off to get em I don't know a bottle of beer or a bottle of pop or something like that but oh my goodness (BNC2014 S5HH)

So has often been considered feminine (Tagliamonte, 2008, p. 183). However, the examples which have been illustrated here have both male and female speakers. A larger material would be needed to establish if the innovative uses of *so* are associated with females. However, when I looked at other uses with '(it is) so noun' (*it is so shit; it is so rubbish*) they were used by both males and females and of different ages.[24]

6.6 Conclusion

The intensifiers discussed in this study have in common that they seem to be undergoing changes, either rising in frequency or becoming less frequent; they vary syntactically and semantically across time; and they are interesting from a sociolinguistic perspective. On the one hand, intensifiers are undergoing long-term changes associated with delexicalisation and grammaticalisation. These processes can be studied in the collocation of the intensifier with new adjective types and a wider range of adjectives with both positive and negative prosody. Diachronically, these processes are associated with delexicalisation or semantic bleaching and their grammaticalisation as intensifiers (see D'Arcy, 2015 for a discussion of the relationship between the two types of process).

When we take a corpus snapshot of the uses of intensifiers at a particular period of time, we find both intensifiers undergoing developments in terms of frequency and intensifiers characterised by a shrinkage in popularity. New forms can be illustrated by *super*, which can be assumed to have come into the language as a result of influence from American television shows or other media. Most typically, there are intensifier forms that come, disappear and then come again—such as *well* and *dead*—which existed already in older English but then disappeared in their intensifier use.

Comparing intensifiers across a time span of two decades, we can only draw limited conclusions about the mechanisms of change and the trajectories characteristic of delexicalisation and grammaticalisation. In the words of Tagliamonte, "delexicalization processes appear to stop and start again" (Tagliamonte, 2008, p. 391). *Fucking*, for example, did not show traces of a stepwise development to new contexts, although we would expect such processes to be ongoing. What we can observe is, above all, changes associated with the sociolinguistic status of the intensifier.

In a shorter perspective we can, however, consider the effects of the mechanisms of intensification or exaggeration (hyperbole). Intensifiers seem to be in a constant process of change, driven by speakers' needs to be creative, trendy and to capture attention. By means of hyperbole, linguistic creativity and innovation young people establish a 'modern' identity for themselves and screen themselves off from the adult community. The speaker's gender is also important. Female speakers use intensifier constructions to parade their independence linguistically, both in relation to the adult community and to males. An interesting tendency in the data was, for example, that female speakers from 1994 onwards have changed their linguistic behaviour and use stronger intensifiers such as *fucking* more than males. Comparing how intensifiers are used at different time periods also draws attention to how 'life stage' impacts on the frequency and use of intensifiers (cf. Murphy, 2010). The frequency curve of a particular intensifier may peak in adolescent speech and then turn downwards, mirroring how middle-age speakers now prioritise a professional identity and have adopted the norms of adult society.

We can sum up the sociolinguistic observations about the selected intensifiers in terms of the speakers' age and gender in the Spoken BNC2014S:

- *fucking* has slightly increased its frequency in the BNC2014 and is one of the most popular intensifiers among young speakers. It was used primarily by young female speakers to mark their linguistic independence.
- *super* can be regarded as a recent importation from the US. It was found especially in the speech of young females to express a higher degree than usual of emotionality.
- *real* as a zero intensifier was shown to increase its frequency among middle-aged speakers (35- to 44-year-olds) and was also fairly frequent in the group of 60+ speakers in the BNC2014. The most noticeable change undergone by *real* was that it was used more by females than by males in the BNC2014.
- *dead* has decreased in frequency in the BNC2014. It illustrates a grammaticalisation path where an intensifier enjoys a peak of popularity and then rapidly decreases in frequency. Like *well*, it has been present in the early history of English but disappeared. It was used by both males and females and primarily by the younger groups of speakers.
- *well* was primarily used by young speakers, the majority of whom were female. It increased in frequency in the BNC2014 in comparison with the BNC1994, especially in combination with frequent adjectives (*well good*). *Well* represents a change led by females. However, it is becoming more frequent in male speech in the BNC2014.

What will happen to intensifiers such as *fucking* or the new *well* in the future? The outcome may have less to do with delexicalisation and grammaticalisation and more to do with sociolinguistic factors such as their popularity among young speakers. Intensifiers which are primarily used by young speakers may turn out to be a transient phenomenon or a fad, if it can be shown that their frequency in the corpus is related to the speaker's age and gender. The system is continuously changing and speakers pick up new 'stronger' intensifiers, deserting the older ones as they get exhausted of meaning.

Notes

1 See Buchstaller (2009), Pichler (2010) and in particular D'Arcy (2015) for a discussion of different traditions for carrying out quantitative studies of intensifiers in sociolinguistics.
2 An exception is *so* which is analysed when it is followed by a noun.
3 According to Quirk et al. (1985, p. 590), amplifiers function semantically to increase intensification, or "scale upwards from an assumed norm".
4 *Super* and *well* have not been included in the graph. The frequencies of *real* have have been manually checked in order to exclude examples such as a *real English gentleman* or *real live yoghurt*.
5 However, I am interested only in its non-prototypical uses modifying a noun (not represented in the table).
6 The more polite *fecking* was found in a single example. According to Murphy (2010, p. 180) *fecking* is particular to Irish English. However, the person using it in the Spoken BNC2014S is a 23-year-old British speaker.
7 In addition, *awful* with zero affixation was used as an intensifier (e.g., *awful long time*) in BNC1994 (nine examples) and BNC2014 (six examples).
8 The positive connotations of the adjective (*good*, *great*) may be another factor favouring the degree-modifying interpretation.
9 Cf. Swales and Burke's (2003, p. 14) discussion on the ambiguity of *it's really wonderful*.
10 In seventy-two examples (omitted) the speakers' exact age was not specified.
11 The large number of males in COLT may, of course, also explain the high frequency of male speakers in the BNC1994.
12 In the Spoken BNC1994, McEnery and Xiao (2004, p. 240) found that *fucking* was used significantly more frequently by male than by female speakers (at the < 0.001 significance level). However, they did not restrict their study to *fucking* followed by adjectives.
13 See article by Pooja Bhatia "Let's abolish the word 'super'": www.ozy.com/immodest-proposal/lets-abolish-the-word-super/40226 accessed 16 August 2017.
14 See article by Pooja Bhatia "Let's abolish the word 'super'": www.ozy.com/immodest-proposal/lets-abolish-the-word-super/40226 accessed 16 August 2017.
15 In addition, for sixty-two examples the exact age of the speaker was unknown.
16 Examples such as *real New Yorker, real Italian ones*, or *real inverted commas* were not included.
17 In the context-governed part of the Spoken BNC1994 there were twenty-one examples of *real* before adjectives, suggesting that it is not restricted to informal conversation.
18 Claridge (2011, p. 198) traces it back to the late 16th century on the basis of OED evidence.
19 Examples like *well aware* or *well mannered* where *well* is not an intensifier have been omitted. Furthermore. the examples *sort of well partridgy, well Christmassy*, where *well* functions as a hedge, have been left out.
20 The adjectives in the Spoken BNC1994DS were *afraid, angry, annoyed, bad, busy, clever, cool* (three examples), *crafty, crazy, cute, dirty, disappointed, drunk, famous, fluky, funny, glad, good* (two examples), *happy, hard* (two examples), *hot, impressed, keen on, knackered, mad, mucky, nice* (seven examples), *pleased, powerful, proud, rough, skillful, slim, tasty* (two examples), *unhappy, upset, weird*, and *whippy*. The examples include the complex intensifiers *bleeding well glad, flipping well angry*, and *fucking well mad*.
21 The BNC2014 also provided the example 'well fucking great' (BNC2014 SK3B) where *well* premodifies 'great'. However, such examples with *well* are difficult to search for and have not been included.

22 In nineteen examples the speakers' exact age had not been indicated.
23 The contexts also include dates, time expressions, pronouns and negatives (cf. Gonzalvez-García, 2014).
24 Some other contexts for Gen X so would be:
Before a determiner followed by a noun phrase:

(i) she said have you seen my new car there? and it's *so a bright yellow fiat* (BNC2014 SXDQ)

Before a negation:

(ii) erm it's *so not true* (BNC2014 SDJA)

Before a verb phrase:

(iii) I think he's got a massive task I *so couldn't* be him and we've got a lot of new faces I'm trying to introduce myself to them (BNC2014 S7KK)

25 *So shit* was only used by males (all in the age range 19–29). On the other hand, *so rubbish* was only used by females but with a wider range of ages (75% of the speakers were between 19–29 years old).

References

Altenberg, B. (1999). Amplifier collocation in spoken English. In S. Johansson & A-B. Stenström (Eds.), *English computer corpora: Selected papers and research guide* (pp. 127–147). Berlin: de Gruyter.

Bailey, L. A., & Timm, L. A. (1976). More on men's and women's expletives. *Anthropological Linguistics, 18*, 438–449.

Barnfield, K., & Buchstaller, I. (2010). Intensification on Tyneside: Longitudinal developments and new trends. *English World-Wide, 31*, 252–287.

Biber, D., & Finegan, E. (1988). Adverbial stance types in English. *Discourse Processes, 11*, 1–34.

Biber, D., & Finegan, E. (1989). Styles of stance in English: Lexical and grammatical marking of evidentiality and affect. *Text, 9*, 93–124.

Biber, D., Johansson, S., Leech, G., Conrad, S., & Finegan, E. (1999). *The Longman grammar of spoken and written English*. London: Longman.

Blanco-Suárez, Z. (2014). *Oh he is olde dogge at expounding* deade *sure at a Catechisme: Some considerations on the history of the intensifying adverb in English*. Acta Linguistica Hafniensia, 46(1), 117–136.

Bolinger, D. (1972). *Degree words*. The Hague: Mouton.

Brown, L. A., & Tagliamonte, S. A. (2012). A *really* interesting story: The influence of narrative in linguistic change. *University of Pennsylvania Working Papers in Linguistics, 18*(2). Article 2.

Buchstaller, I. (2009). The quantitative analysis of morphosyntactic variation. *The Linguistic Compass, 3/4*, 10101–11033.

Cacchiani, S. (2005). Local vehicles for intensification and involvement: The case of English intensifiers. In P. Cap (Ed.), *Pragmatics today* (pp. 401–419). Frankfurt am Main: Peter Lang.

Cacchiani, S. (2009). Lexico-functional categories and complex collocations: The case of intensifiers. In U. Römer & R. Schulze (Eds.), *Exploring the lexis-grammar interface* (pp. 229–246). Amsterdam: John Benjamins.

Claridge, C. (2011). *Hyperbole in English. A corpus study of exaggeration*. Cambridge: Cambridge University Press.

Conrad, S., & Biber, D. (2000). Adverbial marking of stance in speech and writing. In S. Hunston & G. Thompson (Eds.), *Evaluation in text* (pp. 56–73). Oxford: Oxford University Press.

D'Arcy, A. (2015). Stability, stasis and change: The longue durée of intensification. *Diachronica*, 32(4), 449–493.

Eckert, P. (2012). Three waves of variation study: The emergence of meaning in the study of sociolinguistic variation. *Annual Review of Anthropology*, 41, 87–100.

Goldberg, A. E. (2006). *Constructions at work: The nature of generalization in language.* New York, NY: Oxford University Press.

Gonzálvez García, F. (2014). 'That's so a construction!' : Some reflections on innovative uses of 'so' in Present-day English. In M. A. Gómez González, F. J. Ruiz de Mendoza Ibáñez, F. Gonzálvez-García, & A. Downing (Eds.), *Theory and practice in functional-cognitive space* (pp. 271–294). Amsterdam, Philadelphia: John Benjamins.

Irwin, P. X. (2014). SO [TOTALLY]. Speaker-oriented: "An analysis of drama SO". In R. Zanuttini & L. R. Horn (Eds.), *Micro-syntactic variation in North American English* (pp. 29–70). Oxford: Oxford University Press.

Ito, R., & Tagliamonte, S. (2003). *Well* weird. *right* dodgy. *very* strange. *really* cool: Layering and recycling in English intensifiers. *Language in Society*, 32, 257–279.

Kuha, M. (2004). *Investigating the spread of "so" as an intensifier: Social and structural factors.* Retrieved from http://salsa-tx.org/proceedings/2004/Kuha.pdf

Lorenz, G. (2002). *Really worthwhile* or *not really significant*: A corpus-based approach to the delexicalization and grammaticalisation of intensifiers in modern English. In I. Wischer & G. Diewald (Eds.), *New reflections on grammaticalization* (pp. 143–161). Amsterdam: John Benjamins.

Love, R., Dembry, C., Hardie, A., Brezina, V., & McEnery, T. (2017). The spoken BNC2014: Designing and building a spoken corpus of everyday conversations. *International Journal of Corpus Linguistics*, 22(3), 319–344.

Macaulay, R. (2006). *Pure* grammaticalization: The development of a teenage intensifier. *Language Variation and Change*, 18, 267–283.

McEnery, T., & Xiao, R. (2004). Swearing in modern British English: The case of *fuck* in the BNC. *Language and Literature*, 13(3), 235–268.

Murphy, B. (2010). *Corpus and sociolinguistics: Investigating age and gender in female talk.* Amsterdam, Philadelphia: John Benjamins.

OED: Oxford English Dictionary Online. Accessed 16 August 2017. http://oed.com/view/Entry/270263?rskey=pH0h0I&result=3&isAdvanced=false#eid

Palacios Martínez, I. M., & Núñez-Pertejo, P. (2014). That's absolutely crap. totally rubbish: The use of the intensifiers *absolutely* and *totally* in the spoken language of British adults and teenagers. *Functions of Language*, 21(2), 210–237.

Paradis, C. (2000). *It's well weird.* Degree modifiers of adjectives revisited: The nineties. In J. Kirk (Ed.), *Corpus galore: Analysis and techniques in describing English* (pp. 147–160). Amsterdam: Rodopi.

Partington, A. (2015). Evaluative prosody. In K. Aijmer & C. Rühlemann (Eds.), *Corpus pragmatics: A handbook* (pp. 279–303). Cambridge: Cambridge University Press.

Pichler, H. (2010). Introduction: Discourse-pragmatic variation and change. In H. Pichler (Ed.), *Discourse-pragmatic variation and change in English: New methods and insights* (pp. 1–18). Cambridge: Cambridge University Press.

Potts, C. (2004). Lexicalized intonational meaning. In S. Kawahara (Ed.), *UMOP 30: Papers on prosody* (pp. 129–146). Amherst, MA: GLSA.

Potts, C. (2007). The expressive dimension. *Theoretical Linguistics*, *33*(2), 165–197.

Quirk, R., Greenbaum, S., Leech, G., & Svartvik, J. (1985). *A comprehensive grammar of the English language*. London: Longman.

Stenström, A-B. (1999). He was really gormless-she's bloody crap: Girls, boys and intensifiers. In H. Hasselgård & S. Oksefjell (Eds), *Out of corpora: Studies in honour of Stig Johansson* (pp. 69–78). Amsterdam: Rodopi.

Stenström, A-B., Andersen, G., & Hasund, K. (2002). *Trends in teenage talk: Corpus compilation analysis and findings*. Amsterdam, Philadelphia: John Benjamins.

Stoffel, C. (1901). *Intensives and down-toners: A study in English adverbs*. Heidelberg: Winter.

Swales, J., & Burke, A. (2003). 'It's really fascinating work': Differences in evaluative adjectives across academic registers. In P. Leistyna & C. F. Meyer (Eds.), *Corpus analysis: Language structure and language use*. Amsterdam, New York, NY: Rodopi.

Tagliamonte, S. A. (2008). So different and pretty cool! Recycling intensifiers in Toronto. Canada. *English Language and Linguistics*, *12*(2), 361–394.

Tagliamonte, S. A., & Roberts, C. (2005). So weird; so cool; so innovative: The use of intensifiers in the television series *Friends*. *American Speech*, *80*(3), 280–300.

Tagliamonte, S. A., & Ito, R. (2002). Think really different: Continuity and specialization in the English dual form adverbs. *Journal of Sociolinguistics*, *6*(2), 236–266.

Waksler, R. (2012). *Super. uber. so* and *totally*: Over-the-top intensification to mark subjectivity in colloquial discourse. In N. Baumgarten, I. Du Bois, & J. House (Eds.), *Subjectivity in language and in discourse* (pp. 17–31). Bingley: Emerald.

Wee, L., & Tan, Y. Y. (2008). *That's so last year!* Constructions in a socio-cultural context. *Journal of Pragmatics*, *40*, 2100–2113.

Xiao, R., & Tao, H. (2007). A corpus-based sociolinguistic study of amplifiers in British English. *Sociolinguistic Studies*, *1*(2), 241–273.

Yaguchi, M., Iyeiri, Y., & Baba, Y. (2010). Speech style and gender distinctions in the use of *very* and *real/really*: An analysis of the corpus of spoken professional American English. *Journal of Pragmatics*, *42*, 585–597.

Zwicky, A. (2011). *GenX so*. Retrieved from http://arnoldzwicky.org/2011/11/14/gnx-so/

7 Canonical Tag Questions in Contemporary British English

Karin Axelsson

7.1 Introduction

This study deals with *canonical tag questions* (TQs), where an interrogative tag is appended to another clause as demonstrated in example (1), prototypically used to ask for confirmation of the proposition in the anchor. TQs have thus two parts: an *anchor* (single underlining) and a *tag* (double underlining).

(1) It's pretty English, isn't it? (BNC2014 SWF6; S0331)[1]

           anchor   tag
      tag question (TQ)

The form of the tag varies as it reflects the basic elements of the anchor: the anchor subject is repeated as shown in examples (2a) and (2c)–(2d) or just co-referred to if the anchor subject is not a personal pronoun as in (2b); the anchor finite auxiliary (the operator) is repeated as in (2b)–(2d) or, if the finite verb in the anchor is lexical, a form of *do* is used in the tag, as in (2a). If the anchor is positive, the tag is usually negative as in (2a)–(2b) (*reversed polarity*), but the tag may also be positive as in (2c) (*constant polarity*). If the anchor is negative, the tag is normally positive, as in (2d), i.e., another case of reversed polarity. Most TQs have a declarative anchor; such *declarative tag questions* (DecTQs) are the focus in the present study.

(2a) we all know that don't we?   (BNC2014 S7WY; S0325)
(2b) the vapour'll ignite won't it?   (BNC2014 SF2F; S0037)
(2c) oh you do that do you?   (BNC2014 SJ5D; S0144)
(2d) it doesn't make sense does it?   (BNC2014 SU82; S0041)

Invariant tags such as *eh, right* and *isn't that so* are not treated in the present study, but non-standard tags with a similar structure to standard canonical tags are included, e.g., *ain't it* and *innit*. During the last few decades, *innit* has become a standardised spelling in both dictionaries and corpora of the non-standard reduced pronunciation /ˈɪnɪt/. However, in the corpora used in the present study, the orthographic word *innit* is tokenised as consisting of three separate tokens (*in n it*) similar to *isn't it* (*is n't it*)—the *–s* form of the verb BE + negation + personal pronoun—which reflects the assumption that *innit* derives from a standard canonical tag (Andersen, 2001, p. 106). *Innit* has received a great deal of interest (e.g., Erman, 1998; Krug, 1998; Andersen, 2001; Stenström, Andersen, & Hasund, 2002; Cheshire, Kerswill, & Williams, 2005; Torgersen, Gabrielatos, Hoffmann, & Fox, 2011; Pichler, 2013, 2016; Palacios Martínez, 2015), in particular for its capacity to sometimes be employed invariantly, i.e., not only replacing *isn't it* but any standard tag, as in example (3), where *aren't you* is the expected standard tag, and for having a somewhat wider functional potential than standard canonical tags.

(3) so you're helping innit? (BNC2014 SBYQ; S0086)

The use of TQs in British English conversation has previously been studied based on data from the spoken part of *ICE–GB*[2] (e.g., Kim & Ann, 2008; Dehé & Braun, 2013; Gómez González, 2012, 2014; Barron, Pandarova, & Muderack, 2015; Kimps, 2016) and the spoken demographic part of the *British National Corpus* (the Spoken BNC1994DS), i.e., a subcorpus of everyday conversations (e.g., Tottie & Hoffmann, 2006; Axelsson, 2011; for more information on the BNC, see Section 7.2 as well as Burnard, 2000, 2007). However, these two corpora reflect the language of the early 1990s, i.e., more than twenty years ago.

From the sociolinguistic point of view, the most interesting factors in the use of DecTQs are probably age, gender and social class. Tottie and Hoffmann (2006) found that young speakers (younger than in their mid-twenties) use fewer canonical TQs than older speakers. Based on this result combined with Stenström et al. (2002)'s finding that invariant tags are used most by adolescents, they propose that there is "a shift in the type of tags used by different age groups" (2006, p. 306). Tottie and Hoffmann are uncertain whether this shift reflects real linguistic change or age-grading (change in linguistic behaviour as one gets older) and propose further research into the matter. The social variable which has been studied most in relation to TQs is gender. Such research was initiated by Lakoff (1973), who proposed that women use more TQs and that this would be the case as they want to sound more tentative and less assertive. However, TQ studies on gender have provided inconsistent results over the years. Calnan and Davidson (1998) found little difference and suggest that "[p]erhaps there are simply no differences between men and women in their use of tag questions and that the differences found in past research are simply the product of the situation studied" (1998, p. 31) and that "[conversational] role may be a more important factor" (1998, p. 33). The social class effect on the use of DecTQs has not so far received much attention (see Krug, 1998 for an exception).

In sum, previous research on TQs reflected the language of the early 1990s and has not paid enough attention to important sociolinguistic factors such as social class. This study addresses this gap by focusing on the use of canonical DecTQs in contemporary spoken British English using the *Spoken BNC2014* (Love, Dembry, Hardie, Brezina & McEnery, 2017), which comes with comprehensive sociolinguistic information. It contains about ten million tokens of transcribed informal conversation. In the present study, an early-access Sample of the Spoken BNC2014 is used (henceforth the Spoken BNC2014S).[3] This subcorpus contains about 4.8 million tokens and it is thus comparable in size and content to the five-million-token demographic part of the original BNC (henceforth the Spoken BNC1994DS).

The first aim of the present study is to investigate the frequencies and formal features (i.e., elements of the tags, polarity patterns etc.) of DecTQs in the Spoken BNC2014S and make comparisons with the frequencies and formal features of DecTQs in the Spoken BNC1994DS (Axelsson, 2011). The second aim is to compare the datasets as to sociolinguistics features: gender, age and social class. The third aim is to discuss any comparability issues between the two corpora which might affect a study on TQs, and possibly also other comparative studies.

7.2 Method

7.2.1 Data

The Spoken BNC2014S and Spoken BNC1994DS are of roughly equal size: 4,789,185 and 5,014,655 tokens, respectively. Both contain spoken informal conversations and provide sociolinguistic information about most of the speakers. The most important difference is the date of compilation, early 1990s and early 2010s respectively, which allows a diachronic study of DecTQ.

Some additional differences between the corpora need to be briefly noted: whereas the contributors (i.e., those making the recordings) for the Spoken BNC1994DS were selected in order to achieve a demographically balanced corpus, a PPSR (public participation in scientific research) method was used for the Spoken BNC2014. The sociolinguistic information about the speakers is more comprehensive in the Spoken BNC2014 than in the Spoken BNC1994DS, where the sociolinguistic features of many speakers are "unknown"; on the other hand, the Spoken BNC2014 (at least in its Sample version) is demographically less well-balanced. A further methodological challenge was connected to the fact that the sociolinguistic categories in the Spoken BNC2014S were not the same as in the Spoken BNC1994DS for several features, e.g., age spans (see Section 7.3.3.3).

A typical recording for the Spoken BNC2014S was made at home with a small group of family and/or close friends who were all aware of the recording taking place and the requirement of a good recording. In contrast, the contributors for the Spoken BNC1994DS were asked to record all their spoken conversations during two to seven days, usually only asking for permission after the recordings (Burnard, 2007); this means that there is a wide variety of spoken interaction in many different situations. This difference in recording procedures might affect the language use, probably in particular for interactional features such as TQs. Comparability considerations between the two BNC corpus materials, due to differences in compilation and transcription, are further discussed in Section 7.4.2.

7.2.2 Procedure

The Spoken BNC2014S data was retrieved via the online tool *CQPweb* (Hardie, 2012) and then analysed for formal features and sociolinguistic patterns, whereas the Spoken BNC1994DS dataset of 1,315 DecTQs with the analysis of their formal features was taken from Axelsson (2011). As the version of *BNCweb* used in Axelsson (2011) (a beta version of the online tool BNCweb in SGML-format for the BNC World Edition (Axelsson, 2011, p. 7)) is no longer accessible, the current version of the BNCweb tool in XML format (Hoffmann, Evert, Smith, Lee, & Berglund Prytz, 2008) was used for complementary searches and analyses of data in the Spoken BNC1994DS, in particular as to sociolinguistics (gender, age and social class), which was not treated in Axelsson (2011). The BNC1994 may also be accessed via CQPweb, but BNCweb was preferred as it offers additional features necessary for the retrieval of sociolinguistic information on the speakers of DecTQs in the Spoken BNC1994DS: the display of which speaker utters a turn and also links to metadata on each speaker. Moreover, the possibility in BNCweb to browse the corpus for a certain file and sentence number provided easy access to the DecTQs already stored in the Spoken BNC1994DS database.

In both corpus materials, the searches conducted for tags were lexical, i.e., intended to retrieve all possible lexical combinations of elements in tags: potential auxiliaries (*is, have, can* etc.) with or without the enclitic negation *n't* (a separate token) were combined with potential pronominal subjects (*it, you, we* etc., as well as *there*) into long search strings, which also included non-standard forms such as *ain't it* and *innit* (Axelsson, 2011, p. 39). Non-enclitic negation, as in example (4), is also possible in DecTQs and such cases might be identified when the immediate subsequent context of lexical matches are checked (Axelsson, 2011, p. 39). However, no such instances were found in the Spoken BNC2014S and only two instances of non-enclitic negation (0.2% of all DecTQs) occurred in the Spoken BNC1994DS (Axelsson, 2011, p. 98).

(4) And <u>they closed that er school</u> <u>did they not?</u> (BNC1994; KB8 7784)[4]

The searches for tags in the two BNC corpora produced a very large number of matches, which had to be randomly downsampled to receive manageable datasets (see Table 7.1). The first random thinning was done automatically with corpus tools; in the second pass, only the concordance lines of every second match were considered. In the dataset from the Spoken BNC1994DS, 1,315 instances were identified and analysed; the analysis was very time-consuming (Axelsson, 2011) and therefore a smaller sample was extracted from the Spoken BNC2014S, which, however, provided the same range of features. In the dataset from the Spoken BNC2014S, 497 DecTQs were identified and analysed.

At an early stage of the analysis of the 497 DecTQs of the Spoken BNC2014S, it became apparent that a few speakers were represented with very large proportions of the data; the speaker with most DecTQs in the Spoken BNC2014S (speaker 0012) produced almost 10% of the DecTQs, and just nine speakers used almost half of all DecTQs. As this could skew the results, a subcorpus, BNC2014SR, was created without the fourteen largest contributors (those with more than 75,000 words).[5] The size of the BNC2014SR is 2,887,503 tokens, distributed across 362+[6] speakers. In the BNC2014SR DecTQ dataset, there are 238 instances distributed across 119 speakers (no individual speaker produced more than eight DecTQs, i.e., 3.4% of the dataset). The fourteen most prolific speakers in the Spoken BNC2014S constitute a subcorpus henceforth called the BNC2014SP. Table 7.2 provides an overview of the number of tokens and speakers in the different subcorpora, as well as the number of DecTQs and DecTQ speakers in the DecTQ datasets from the Spoken BNC2014S.

Table 7.1 Matches in the Lexical Searches for DecTQs

Total Matches in BNC1994DS	Matches After an Automatic Random Thinning (to 12%)	Matches After a Manual Thinning (to 6%)	Relevant Matches After Thinnings = DecTQ
80,443	10,074	5,037	1,315
Total Matches in BNC2014S	Matches After an Automatic Random Thinning (to 6%)	Matches After a Manual Thinning (to 3%)	Relevant Matches After Thinnings = DecTQ
72,221	4,333	2,166	497

Table 7.2 Tokens, speakers and DecTQs in the Spoken BNC2014S subcorpora

Subcorpus	Tokens	Speakers	DecTQs in Dataset	DecTQ Speakers in Dataset
BNC2014S	4,789,185	376+	497	133
BNC2014SR	2,887,503	362+	238	119
BNC2014SP	1,901,682	14	259	14

For comparison, in the dataset from the Spoken BNC1994DS the identified speaker with most DecTQs (Wendy in file KE6) has 2.7% of the whole dataset. The risk of skewed results due to idiolects is thus comparatively small in the Spoken BNC1994DS dataset, so no reduction of that dataset was deemed necessary.

7.3 Results

7.3.1 Frequencies

Normalised frequencies in the present study apply the measure per million tokens (pmt) as used in CQPweb. For further discussion of frequency measures, see Section 7.4.1. The 238 DecTQs in the BNC2014SR equal a normalised frequency of 2,747 pmt. If the full dataset of 497 instances had been considered, the frequency would have been 3,459 DecTQs pmt. The speakers in BNC2014SP (i.e., the fourteen most prolific speakers) use 259 DecTQs, equalling 4,540 DecTQs pmt, which is significantly more than in the BNC2014SR (LL 31.18, Bayes 19.30);[7] this justifies the reduction of the dataset to the BNC2014SR. For an overview of raw and normalised frequencies of DecTQs in the Spoken BNC2014S, see Table 7.3.

The normalised frequency of DecTQs in the BNC2014SR (2,747 pmt) is far lower than that of the Spoken BNC1994DS, 4,371 pmt,[8] as shown Figure 7.1 (the black bars). This difference in normalised frequency is statistically significant (LL: 48.23) with a strong effect size (Bayes: 35.36). If the full dataset of 497 DecTQs in the Spoken BNC2014S (including the very prolific speakers) had been used, the difference would still have been statistically significant (LL: 17.45), whereas the effect size would have been clearly weaker but nevertheless positive (Bayes: 4.45). The frequencies of DecTQs in the Spoken BNC2014S and BNC2014SP are represented in Figure 7.1 by grey and white bars, respectively. Figure 7.1 also illustrates that the fourteen most prolific speakers in the Spoken BNC2014S (the BNC2014SP) use DecTQs at a similar frequency as the speakers in the Spoken BNC1994DS.

It might be the case that this difference in DecTQ frequency between the Spoken BNC1994DS and BNC2014SR reflects language change between

Table 7.3 Size of the Spoken BNC2014S Subcorpora and the Frequencies of DecTQs in These Subcorpora

Subcorpus	Tokens, Total	Tokens Thinned to 3%	N = DecTQs in Dataset	DecTQs pmt
BNC2014S	4,789,185	143,676	497	3,459
BNC2014SR	2,887,503	86,625	238	2,747
BNC2014SP	1,901,682	57,050	259	4,540

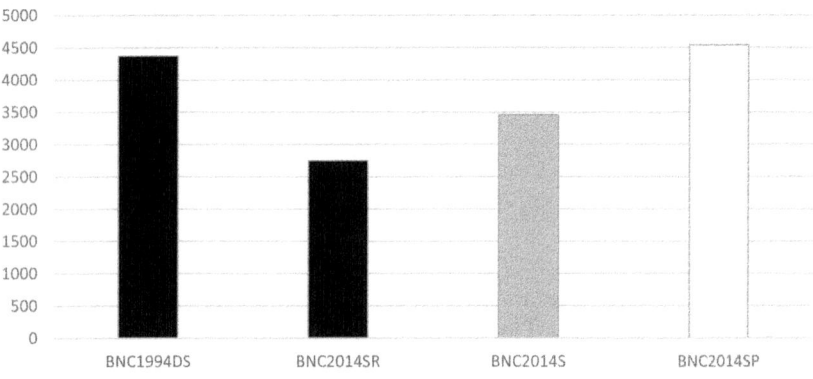

Figure 7.1 Frequencies of DecTQs pmt

the early 1990s and the early 2010s, i.e., that there has been an actual drop in the use of DecTQs. However, there are potentially confounding factors to consider, viz. that the two corpora may have different content due to being compiled (and transcribed) in different ways, and in particular, the fact that the Spoken BNC2014S is limited to fairly 'focused' conversations, whereas the Spoken BNC1994DS includes all kinds of interactions, including when the main activity is something else, such as taking care of children, watching TV or working. *'Focused' conversation* is here defined as the kind of conversation which family members and close friends are having when they know that they are being recorded and are motivated to concentrate on that particular conversation, rather than also doing something else at the same time. More 'focused' speakers probably lead to more coherent dialogues and perhaps also to somewhat less informal language (this will be further discussed in Section 7.4.2).

Interestingly enough, the frequency of DecTQs in face-to-face conversations in ICE–GB (also recorded in the early 1990s but restricted to informants having completed secondary schooling) is even somewhat lower than in the Spoken BNC2014SR: 2,165 per million words (pmw)[9] (Gómez-González pers. comm.).[10] Going back in time to the 1960s and 1970s, based on information in Nässlin (1984, pp. 90–91, 189, 192), the frequency of DecTQs in *A Corpus of English Conversation* (where almost all speakers were educated at university level) can be calculated at 2,235 pmw. This indicates that the Spoken BNC1994DS displays an extremely high use of DecTQs compared to other corpora, both previous and subsequent. It might be the case that the number of DecTQs would have been lower in a BNC from the 1990s if the same compilation principles had been adhered to as in the Spoken BNC2014. The comparison of formal features and sociolinguistics of the DecTQs in the two BNC corpora in the following sections may shed some light on the lower normalised frequency of DecTQs in the BNC2014SR than in the Spoken BNC1994DS.

7.3.2 Formal Features

The formal features treated in this section are elements of the tags, polarity patterns and subject ellipsis in the anchors. More detailed information on the formal features of DecTQs in the Spoken BNC1994DS can be found in Axelsson (2011, pp. 89–132).

The tag subject is mostly *it*[11] in both the BNC2014SR (45.4%) and Spoken BNC1994DS (41.4%); this small difference is not significant. Neither are there any significant differences between the two BNC corpus materials for the other personal pronouns or *there*. The descending order in the BNC2014SR is *it* (108 instances), *they* (38), *you* (37), *he* (16), *she* (12), *there* (10), *I* (9) and *we* (8).

The predominant tag operator is IS[12] in both datasets (40.3% in the BNC2014SR vs. 33.8% in the Spoken BNC1994DS) and the tag verb is BE (*am/are/is/was/were* etc.) in a majority of the cases (53.8% in the BNC2014SR vs. 52.5% in the Spoken BNC1994DS). Again, these differences are too small to be significant. The only significant difference (p<0.5) as to the operators/verbs is that the tag verb HAVE[13] (*have/has/had*) has a smaller proportion in the BNC2014SR (4.6%) than in the Spoken BNC1994DS (9.7%). The descending order of tag verbs in the BNC2014SR is BE (128 instances), DO (67), WILL/WOULD (18), other modal verbs (14) and HAVE (11).

The distributions of different word combinations in tags are similar in the two corpus materials except for *isn't it* and *innit*. The standard tag *isn't it* has a significantly higher proportion (p<0.001) of DecTQs in the BNC2014SR (24%) than in the Spoken BNC1994DS (13%), whereas the non-standard tag *innit* has a significantly lower proportion (p<0.001) in the BNC2014SR (2%) than in the Spoken BNC1994DS (9%). In the BNC1994DS, there are also other non-standard tags on the cline between *isn't it/ain't it* and *innit*: *in't it*, *int it* and *in it*. If these nonstandard forms as well as *innit* and *ain't it* are regarded as variants of *isn't it*, the proportions of *isn't it* are similar in the two corpus materials (26.5% in the BNC2014SR vs. 22.9%, in the Spoken BNC1994DS).

The very low frequency of *innit* in the Spoken BNC2014S is remarkable; only five instances gives a normalised frequency of 58 pmt compared to 332 pmt in the Spoken BNC1994DS (not including the alternatives *in 't it*, *int it* and *in it*). As there were so few *innit* in the 3%-dataset from the BNC2014SR, all instances of *innit* in the whole BNC2014SR subcorpus were retrieved: the normalised frequency is then somewhat higher (70 pmt) but still far from the frequency in the Spoken BNC1994DS. One hypothesis is that the more 'focused' conversations in the Spoken BNC2014S contribute to keep the use of *innit* down. For a more detailed study of *innit* in the Spoken BNC2014, see Axelsson (in prep.).

As to polarity patterns, only 12 out of the 238 DecTQs in the BNC2014SR (5.0%) display constant polarity, as in example (2c). This is significantly lower (p<0.5)[14] than in the Spoken BNC1994DS, where the percentage is 9.6% (123 out of 1,277 instances) (Axelsson, 2011, p. 119). The polarity patterns are illustrated in Figure 7.2.

However, Tottie and Hoffmann (2006, p. 290) report a somewhat lower proportion of constant-polarity TQs[15] in their investigation on the Spoken BNC1994DS: 8%. In ICE-GB, the proportion of constant-polarity DecTQs in private informal conversation is higher: 13.2% (Gómez-Gonzalez, pers. comm.). The proportion of constant-polairty DecTQs in A Corpus of English Conversation, recorded in the 1960s and 1970s, is even higher: around 15% (a calculation based on figures in Nässlin (1984, pp. 189–192)). Hoffmann (2006, p. 44), in his study of TQs in old drama, shows that the proportion of constant-polarity TQs was highest in the middle of the 18th century (about 40%) and that it slowly decreased to just below 20% in the early 20th century. He suggests that the proportion of constant-polarity TQs has decreased during the 20th century. The low proportion of constant-polarity DecTQs in the present study may indicate that this gradual decrease is continuing,

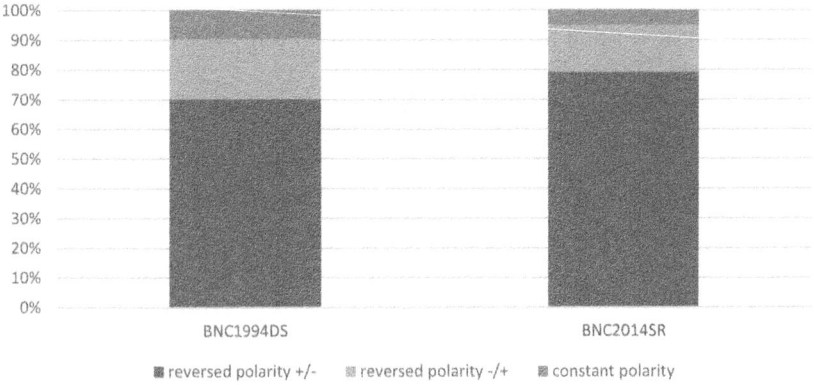

Figure 7.2 Proportions of Polarity Patterns in DecTQs

but it might alternatively be associated with the more 'focused' conversations in the Spoken BNC2014S, as constant-polarity DecTQs "exhibit a low degree of commitment towards the truth of the proposition by the speaker and a high responsibility towards the hearer" (Kimps, 2007, p. 289), and might therefore be used, among others things, to seek verification when somewhat less attentive speakers take part in somewhat less coherent spoken interactions as in the Spoken BNC1994DS. Figure 7.2 also shows that, among the reversed-polarity DecTQs, the proportion of the pattern negative anchor + positive tag is slightly more predominant in the BNC2014SR than in the Spoken BNC1994DS, but this difference is not statistically significant.

In the anchors of DecTQs, the subject may be ellipted, as in example (5a), where *they* is ellipted, and in example (5b), where both the subject *it* and the finite verb *is* are ellipted.

(5a) <u>don't get much do they?</u> (BNC2014 SQPN; S0376)
(5b) <u>extraordinary isn't it?</u> (BNC2014 S7KK; S0270)

Subject ellipsis in the anchors of DecTQs is clearly less frequent in the BNC2014SR than in the Spoken BNC1994DS. As subject ellipsis is more common for DecTQs with constant than reversed polarity in the Spoken BNC1994DS (Axelsson, 2011, p. 121), and as the proportion of constant-polarity DecTQs is low in the BNC2014SR, only the reversed-polarity DecTQs were compared for subject ellipsis. Figure 7.3. displays that subject ellipsis is found in only 8% of the reversed-polarity DecTQs in the BNC2014SR compared to 16.5% in the Spoken BNC1994DS; this difference is statistically significant ($p<0.01$). The lower use of subject ellipsis in the BNC2014SR is not likely to be due to language change; it is probably a matter of style difference between the two corpora. The more 'focused' conversations in the Spoken BNC2014S may have led to a tendency to be less informal. Kim and Ann (2008, p. 10) report only 7% ellipted anchor subjects in ICE-GB so, again, the Spoken BNC1994DS stands out in comparison to both earlier and subsequent corpora.

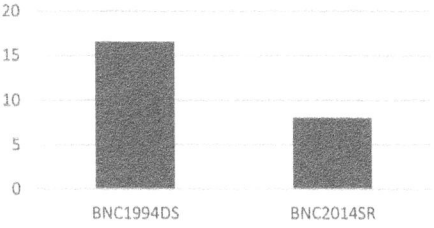

Figure 7.3 Percentage of Subject Ellipsis in the Anchors of Reversed-Polarity DecTQs

7.3.3 Sociolinguistic Factors

7.3.3.1 Sociolinguistic Information in the Corpus Materials

As Axelsson (2011) does not include the study of sociolinguistic factors behind the use of DecTQs, the present project involved additional work on the Spoken BNC1994DS database: gender, age and social grade of the speakers of the DecTQs were retrieved by re-accessing each of the 1,315 DecTQs in BNCweb. Unfortunately, the sociolinguistic information on the speakers in the Spoken BNC1994DS is far from complete. Moreover, the assignment of utterances to a particular speaker in the Spoken BNC1994DS is not entirely reliable. For 14 of the 1,315 DecTQs, the DecTQ speaker seems to have a dialogue with himself/herself as there is overlap indicated without a change of speaker in the DecTQ utterance and/or in the immediate context, as in example (6). In the nine cases (out of the fourteen) where audio files are now available, it is clear that two voices have been transcribed as pertaining to one speaker in passages with DecTQs.[16]

(6) *Keith:*   [. . .] how long it should take you to <-l-> **get there** <-l->
     Keith: <-l-> **to get** <-l-> there, yeah, <u>you can put the time of the day in as well</u> <u>can't ya?</u>

                                                    (BNC1994; KCY 2003–2004)

In contrast, the sociolinguistic information on the speakers in the Spoken BNC2014S is comprehensive and seems overall reliable. The sociolinguistic metadata on individual speakers is easily accessible via links in the concordance lines. The Spoken BNC2014 project team provided the distributions of relevant sociolinguistic metadata across the whole Spoken BNC2014S and Spoken BNC1994DS.

7.3.3.2 Gender

In the Spoken BNC1994DS, female speakers account for 60.7% of all tokens where gender is supplied[17] but for 64.7% of the DecTQs, so female speakers use more DecTQs than male speakers there (4,751 vs. 4,005 pmt; LL 7.94 but Bayes –4.54). The predominance of tokens for female speakers is lower in the BNC2014SR (54.0%),[18] and as they use 55.0% of the DecTQs in the BNC2014SR, there is no significant difference between the genders in the BNC2014SR (women: 2,805 pmt; men: 2,689 pmt; LL 0.11). One reason behind the similar frequency of DecTQs for men and women in the BNC2014SR might be that they have fairly equal roles in the kind of conversations included in the Spoken BNC2014S; the speakers are mostly adults with similar power (close family and friends).

7.3.3.3 Age

As shown in Figure 7.4, the investigation of the age of DecTQ users in the Spoken BNC1994DS in the present study confirms the "cut-off somewhere in the twenty-year bracket" which Tottie and Hoffmann (2006, p. 304) reported. The leap between the age categories 15–24 and 25–34 in the present study is statistically significant (LL 18.39, Bayes 7.05).

The age spans used in the Spoken BNC2014S are different from those in the Spoken BNC1994DS (this was remedied in the final version of the Spoken BNC2014; see Love, Dembry, Hardie, Brezina & McEnery, 2017, which complicates a comparison. Table 7.4 displays the raw numbers and frequencies for each age category in the BNC2014SR.

As the dataset from the BNC2014SR is not very large and there are as many as ten different age categories, some of them with few DecTQs (and also few tokens overall), at both ends of the age ladder, are included in larger categories in Figure 7.5: Age span 11–18 is merged with age span 19–29 into a category called 11–29, and the age spans 70–79, 80–89 and 90–99 are merged with age span 60–69 into a category called 60+.

At first glance, the bar charts in Figure 7.4 and 7.5 seem to display similar patterns: there is a clear rise from the second to the third bar. However, as the age spans differ, the cut-off in the BNC2014SR data is not somewhere around 25 years of age but around 40 years of age. However, maybe because the dataset is small, the rise between age categories 30–39 (2,484 pmt) and 40–49 (3,695 pmt) is not statistically significant (LL 2.26). If, on the other hand, the dataset is divided into just two age categories, 11–39 (2,439 pmt) and 40–99 (3,247 pmt), there is a statistically significant difference (LL 6.18), although the effect size is negative (Bayes –5.18). Clear conclusions on the impact of age on the use of DecTQs in the BNC2014SR require a larger dataset than what was retrieved for the present study. A tentative conclusion is, however, that there is indeed a cut-off around the age of 40 in the BNC2014SR instead of at around 25, which suggests language change going on rather than age-grading. As the use of *innit* is spread over all age categories in the BNC1994DS (see Figure 7.4), and there are very few *innit* in the BNC2014SR (see Figure 7.5), the use of *innit* does not seem to affect the age patterns for DecTQs in general.

The distribution of tokens used by different age categories is better balanced in the Spoken BNC1994DS than in the BNC2014SR, where age category 19–29 is predominant (41%), age category 11–18 poorly represented (4%) and age group 0–10 virtually absent (0.03%). The fact that children hardly participate at all in the conversations in the Spoken BNC2014S not only makes it impossible to say anything about their use of DecTQs but may also affect the overall use of DecTQs in the corpus, as parents and other adults would probably tend to talk somewhat differently to children than to other adults. An indication that the age of the

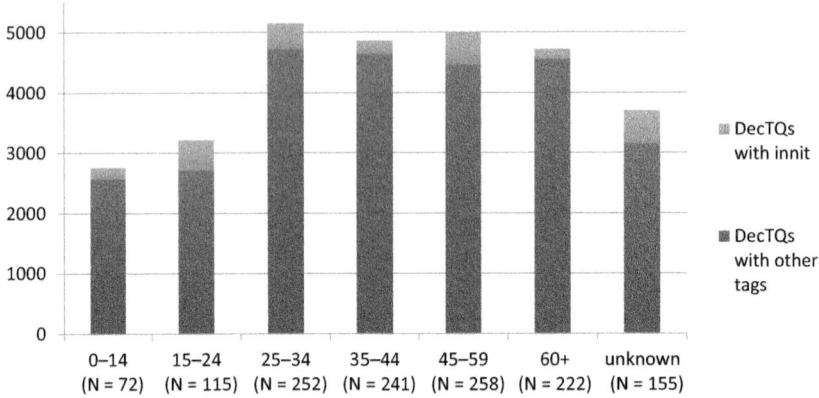

Figure 7.4 Frequency of DecTQs in the Spoken BNC1994DS pmt in Different Age Categories

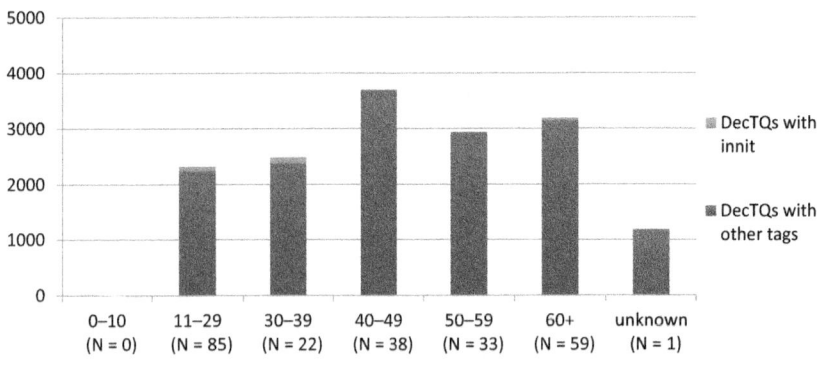

Figure 7.5 Frequency of DecTQs in the Spoken BNC2014SR pmt in Different Age Categories

addressee might matter is that TQs with imperative anchors (ImpTQs) in the second person are very rare in the Spoken BNC2014S: only eight instances in total, of which six are found in the BNC2014SR. This equals a frequency of about 1.5 instances pmt, which is extremely little compared to 32 pmt in the Spoken BNC1994DS (based on a search thinned to 30%; see Axelsson, 2011, p. 188). There are several examples of ImpTQs in the Spoken BNC1994DS data which are unlikely to be addressed to an adult, as in example (7), which is addressed to a 2-year-old girl.

(7) <u>Don't you wet the seat, will you?</u> (BNC1994; KBH 3071)

Table 7.4 Raw Number and Frequency of DecTQs in the BNC2014SR in Different Age Categories

	Separate Age Categories		Merged Age Categories			
	N	pmt	N	pmt	N	pmt
0–10	0	0	0	0	0	0
11–18	16	2,778	85	2,317	107	2,439
19–29	69	2,231				
30–39	22	2,484	22	2,484		
40–49	38	3,695	38	3,695	130	3,247
50–59	33	2,930	33	2,930		
60–69	44	3,131	59	3,189		
70–79	3	1,007				
80–89	10	7,396				
90–99	2	17,543				
Unknown	1	1,179	1	1,179	1	1,179
Total	238					

7.3.3.4 Social Class

The occupations of the speakers in the Spoken BNC2014S are coded according to the government-standard National Statistics Socio-Economic Classification (NS-SEC). There are no statistically significant differences as to the use of DecTQs between the different speaker occupation categories in the NS-SEC (see Table 7.5).

However, these codes are also mapped on to so-called social grades (the corresponding NS-SEC categories are given within brackets):

A   Higher managerial, administrative and professional (1.1 and 1.2)
B   Intermediate managerial, administrative and professional (2)
C1 Supervisory, clerical and junior managerial, administrative and professional (3 and 4)
C2 Skilled manual workers (5)
D   Semi-skilled and unskilled manual workers (6 and 7)
E   State pensioners, casual and lowest grade workers, unemployed with state benefits only (8 and those categorised as students/unclassifiable)

These social grades are also used in the Spoken BNC1994DS; however, some categories are conflated already in that corpus itself, resulting in only four categories: AB, C1, C2 and DE. Table 7.6 displays the distribution across social grades in both datasets. Categories for the BNC2014SR

Table 7.5 Speaker Occupations According to NS-SEC of DecTQ Speakers in the BNC2014SR (pmt)

	N	pmt
1.1 Large employers and higher managerial and administrative occupations	6	2,447
1.2 Higher professional occupations	31	2,435
2 Lower managerial, administrative and professional occupations	60	3,198
3 Intermediate occupations	41	3,254
4 Small employers and own account workers	9	3,140
5 Lower supervisory and technical occupations	4	1,433
6 Semi-routine occupations	9	3,835
7 Routine occupations	7	5,780
8 Never worked and long-term unemployed	34	3,173
Uncategorised/unknown	37	1,926
Total	238	

Table 7.6 Social Grades for DecTQ Speakers in the Spoken BNC1994DS and BNC2014SR

	BNC1994DS						BNC2014SR			
	N	pmt	N	pmt	N	pmt	N	pmt	N	pmt
A	213	4,166	451	4,231	213	4,166	37	2,437	97	2,791
B							60	3,066		
C1	238	4,291			504	4,755	50	3,234	54	2,958
C2	266	5,264	427	5,361			4	1,434		
D	161	5,529			161	5,529	16	4,496	86	2,629
E							70	2,401		
Unknown	437	3,812	437	3,812	437	3,812	1	1,297	1	1,297
Total	1,315						238			

are both presented per social grade and per merged social grades to facilitate the comparison between the two corpus materials and as the raw numbers in the BNC2014SR are small for several social grades.

Table 7.6 shows that, in the Spoken BNC1994DS, DecTQs are most frequent in social grades C2 and DE (5,361 pmt); together they are significantly more frequent than in grades AB and C1 together (4,231 pmt) (LL 12.23, but Bayes just 0.10). In the BNC2014SR, on the other hand, the frequency of DecTQs is very similar for social grades AB, C and DE. For each of these merged social grades, the use of DecTQs is lower in the BNC2014SR than in the corresponding merged grades in the Spoken BNC1994DS. These differences are all statistically significant (LL: AB 11.8, C 12.48 and DE 32.71) but only the last social grade category, DE, has a clear Bayes effect (21.68). This seems to indicate that the use of DecTQs has decreased most among the lower social grades from the early 1990s to the early 2010s. However, there are problems with both datasets: for the Spoken BNC1994DS, the social grades for as many as one-third of all DecTQs are unknown, and for the BNC2014SR, speakers of social grade C2 are heavily underrepresented with just 3.2% of the tokens, i.e., very low compared to the Spoken BNC1994DS, where C2 constitute 27.1% of the tokens assigned to a social grade of the speaker (social grade D is also very small in the BNC2014SR: 4.1%).

7.3.3.5 Individual Speakers and Speaker Communities

As shown in sections 7.3.3.2–7.3.3.4, there are no indications that the sociolinguistic factors of gender and social grade influence the use of DecTQs in the BNC2014SR, whereas age does to some extent. A more decisive factor than these three sociolinguistic factors may be the idiolect of the speaker. The fourteen prolific speakers in the BNC2014SP each contribute more than 75,000 tokens in the full corpus material and may therefore be well worth studying as individuals. The frequencies of DecTQs for these individuals range from 554 to 18,658 pmt (mean: 5,084; standard deviation: 5,187). This very large variation in individual frequencies makes it vital for the study of DecTQs that corpus material is spread over many individuals and that no individual is allowed to have a high share of the words/tokens.

The higher frequency of DecTQs for the fourteen speakers in the BNC2014SP (4,540 pmt) than in the BNC2014SR (2,747 pmt) may be analysed as being due to speaker S0012 and four other prolific speakers (S0013, S0008, S0024 and S0144) appearing in the same files as him. Among these five speakers, there is some variation for all the sociolinguistic features of gender, age and social grade. This group use 8,287 DecTQs pmt, whereas the group of nine other prolific speakers display a frequency similar to that of the reduced dataset: 2,677 pmt. This indicates that the use of DecTQs can be much higher than average in some speaker communities.

7.4 Discussion

7.4.1 Corpus Size and Frequency Measures

Deciding the size of a corpus is far from straightforward. Different software tools do not agree on the number of atomic units in the BNC (Brezina & Timperley, 2017), nor do they all use the same unit of measurement: both the BNC1994 and Spoken BNC2014 are divided into tokens (including punctuation tokens), but the tool BNCweb recalculates the number of tokens in the BNC1994 into words/w-units in order to disregard punctuation tokens, whereas the tool CQPweb applies tokens for all corpora, although the term *word* is sometimes used on the tool website.

In the present study, tokens are used as the unit of measurement in order to apply the same unit for both BNC corpus materials, and as corpus metadata for both materials was provided in tokens by the Spoken BNC2014 project team. However, the use of tokens is not unproblematic, as there are many more punctuation tokens in the BNC1994DS than in the Spoken BNC2014S: 684,858 vs. 82,104. The reason for this difference lies in the transcription guidelines for the Spoken BNC2014 being much more restrictive about punctuation; the transcribers were told not to use punctuation except for question marks (Love, Hawtin & Hardie, 2017, p. 37), whereas there are also many commas, full stops and other punctuation marks in the Spoken BNC1994DS. In tokens (i.e., including punctuation), the Spoken BNC2014S is 4.5% smaller (4,789,185) than the Spoken BNC1994DS (5,014,655 tokens). However, the number of tokens, excluding punctuation (≈'words'), is 4,707,081 in the Spoken BNC2014S and 4,329,797 in the Spoken BNC1994DS, i.e., the Spoken BNC2014S is instead larger than the Spoken BNC1994DS, no less than by 8.7% (see Figure 7.6).

If punctuation tokens were disregarded, the differences between the frequencies of DecTQs in the Spoken BNC1994DS (5,061 pmw) and BNC2014SR (2,795 pmt) would be larger than those presented in Section 7.3.1, and the figures for log-likelihood and effect size would be even higher (LL: 81.14; Bayes 81.08). It should also be noted that ICE-GB does not include any punctuation in spoken texts (Nelson, 2005, p. 32), so when previous studies on DecTQs based on ICE-GB are referred to in the present study, the unit of measurement is per million words.

Although relative frequency is, by convention, measured per million (or ten thousand etc.) tokens or words, it has been claimed that "relative frequency should be a measure of the number of times something occurs within the number of opportunities for it to occur" (Ball, 1994, p. 297); using frequency per token/words would then only be appropriate when measuring the occurrence of tokens/words, i.e., members of the

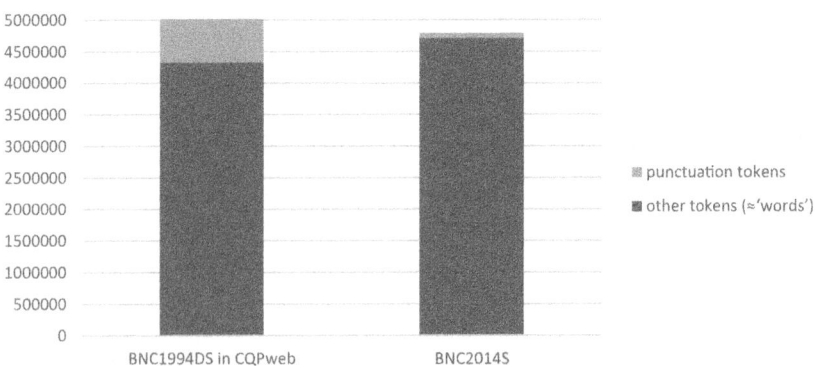

Figure 7.6 Corpus Size in Tokens With and Without Punctuation Tokens

same class. DecTQs apparently constitute another class than tokens as a DecTQ in itself consists of several tokens: at least three tokens (at least one token in the anchor and two or three tokens in the tag) and usually more tokens than that, with no clear upper limit. This also means that the number of opportunities are far lower than the number of tokens and that the number of opportunities does not necessarily stand in relation to the number of tokens in a corpus. Consequently, instead of using numbers of tokens/words in calculations of normalised frequencies, alternative ways of comparing the use of DecTQs between corpora might be to use the number of utterances, sentences, clauses or finite verbs. All these other measures have been considered for the present study, but have been rejected as they are difficult to apply and/or might give inaccurate results, as described below.

The number of utterances is similar in the two corpora (1% lower in the Spoken BNC2014S); however, it is unclear whether the same criteria for utterances have been used: the indication of overlap might, for example, affect the number of utterances, as a more detailed annotation of overlap may require a conversation to be divided into more turns. In the Spoken BNC1994DS, both the beginning and the end of overlaps are marked, whereas the Spoken BNC2014S indicates an overlap "[w]here the beginning of one speaker turn overlaps in time with the end of the previous turn" no matter where in the utterance the overlap actually starts (Love, Hawtin & Hardie, 2017, p. 39). Moreover, not all utterances are possible to add a tag to (e.g., *wh*-questions and short responses such as *Yes*), nor is there a maximum of one DecTQ per utterance, as shown in (8), where there are two DecTQs in the same utterance.

(8) but the timetable seems a bit variable doesn't it? there isn't really a set pattern to it I don't think is there? (BNC2014 S59R; S0251)

The number of sentences is available for the Spoken BNC1994DS but not for the Spoken BNC2014S, where punctuation marks are not generally used to delimit 'sentences'. The term used in the Spoken BNC1994DS is actually not sentence but *s-unit*, which means sentence-like unit. This indicates that it is often difficult to decide what a *sentence* is when spoken conversation is transcribed. The number of clauses is difficult to calculate in both corpora; however, it is possible to compare the frequencies of finite verbs, which is related to the number of finite clauses.

By combining all POS-tags for finite verbs,[19] the numbers of finite verbs in both corpus materials were queried: the number proved to be 7.4% higher in the Spoken BNC2014S (747,095) than in the Spoken BNC1994DS (695,923). This is very close to the 8.7% difference in corpus size by 'words' (excluding punctuation tokens), which indicates that the number of finite verbs is closely related to the number of 'words'. However, there are several complications. Firstly, some of the POS-tags for finite verbs also include imperatives and subjunctives, which are not found in anchors of DecTQs. Secondly, different POS-taggers have been used (CLAWS5 in the BNC1994 and CLAWS6 in the BNC2014) and the POS-tagging was improved with the Template Tagger in the BNC1994 (Burnard, 2000) but not in the BNC2014. Even so, VVB (the finite forms of lexical verbs) has been identified as the most error-prone POS-tag in the BNC1994 (Burnard, 2007). Thirdly, finite subclauses are seldom tagged, finite verbs occur in the tags themselves, and elliptical clauses without a finite verb may also be tagged, as in example (9).

(9) A bit drastic, <u>isn't it?</u> (BNC2014 S2PS; S0068)

In sum, practical corpus problems, as well as difficulties in defining the opportunities for DecTQs, made it impossible to apply other measures than per million tokens in the present study. The use of 'words' instead of tokens would probably have been more relevant, but the Spoken BNC2014S and its metadata (as well as the sociolinguistic metadata on the Spoken BNC1994DS) came in tokens, which made the use of words as the unit of measure too complicated to apply consistently.

7.4.2 Corpus Comparability

The somewhat surprising result that DecTQs occur clearly less frequently in the BNC2014SR than in the Spoken BNC1994DS may partly be explained by the fact that there are differences in compilation and transcription. As mentioned in Section 7.2.1, the Spoken BNC2014 project required better recordings and the consent of all speakers, which might have encouraged more 'focused' conversations. This is likely to have favoured more coherent conversations with less informal language, as indicated by, in relation to the Spoken BNC1994DS, the very low frequency of *innit*, the lower proportion of subject ellipsis in the anchors and the lower proportion of constant-polarity patterns (see Section 7.3.2 on formal features).

The transcription guidelines for the two BNC corpora differ in several ways. In addition to the different punctuation principles (see Section 7.4.1), there are, for example, differences as to the extent of paralinguistic annotation (e.g., voice quality, non-verbal sounds and pauses) and the markup of overlap (see also Section 7.4.1). There are also corpus comparability issues related to sociolinguistics: not all social categories from the Spoken BNC1994DS can be matched with the BNC2014SR.

7.4.3 Sociolinguistic Implications

When comparing two datasets from the sociolinguistic perspective we need to pay special attention to their comparability in the key social factors; some limitations are mentioned in Section 7.4.4. In addition, the process of analysis of different factors such as the contribution from individual speakers also need to be considered. The sociolinguistic results from the present study on the BNC2014SR should first be regarded on their own: What are the sociolinguistic factors behind the use of DecTQs in informal but 'focused' conversations among adult British English-speaking family members and close friends in the early 2010s? In the BNC2014SR, men and women use DecTQs to similar extents, maybe because their roles and power are similar: they are having relaxed and informal but still 'focused' conversations with family and friends. Neither are there indications that social grade matters for the use of DecTQs in the BNC2014SR. However, as to age in the BNC2014SR, speakers over 40 use more DecTQs than those under 40.

In the Spoken BNC1994DS, women used DecTQs somewhat more often than men, so the gender distribution is more equal in the BNC2014SR. As to age, the use of DecTQs in the Spoken BNC1994DS rose for speakers above around 25, about fifteen years earlier than the rise in the BNC2014SR. As the Spoken BNC2014S was recorded about twenty years after the Spoken BNC1994DS, this may indicate language change: that young speakers, who did not use that many DecTQs in their youth, have not increased their use of DecTQs when they have entered middle age. The use of DecTQs was higher in all social grades in the BNC1994DS than in the BNC2014SR, but the decrease in BNC2014SR is largest among the lower grades.

7.4.4 Future Work

One of the limitations of this study is incomplete social comparability of the two datasets used. The present study would also have benefited from a larger dataset of DecTQs from the Spoken BNC2014S. The goal was to have about half as many instances (around 650) as in the dataset from the Spoken BNC1994DS. However, as there turned out to be clearly fewer DecTQs than expected in the Spoken BNC2014S, and as the dataset had to be reduced to avoid skewed results due to some prolific speakers being too predominant in the Spoken BNC2014S, only 238 DecTQs were investigated. Still, several statistically significant results have been presented in this study. Nevertheless, a study based on a larger dataset from the final, more balanced, version of the Spoken BNC2014 is desirable. A larger sample would also allow multifactorial calculations of correlations between, for example, sociolinguistic factors. If the Spoken BNC2014 is marked-up prosodically and/or the audio files become available, the accuracy of some of the analysis might also be improved. Further studies on the number of opportunities for DecTQs in a corpus would also be welcome, not only for the phenomenon in general but also for the distribution of different tag elements. Of course, the development of the use of the tag *innit* deserves further attention in the future, as well as the use of invariant tags.

7.5 Conclusion

The frequency of DecTQs in the Spoken BNC2014SR is closer to that in other corpora such as ICE-GB than to the Spoken BNC1994DS, so it is the Spoken BNC1994DS which stands out as extreme in the use of DecTQs. The more 'focused' conversations in the Spoken BNC2014SR compared to the Spoken BNC1994DS might partly explain the overall lower frequency of DecTQs, as well as the larger proportions of some formal features which may be linked to somewhat more coherent and less informal language: the tag *innit*, subject ellipsis and constant polarity. As to sociolinguistics, DecTQs in the Spoken BNC2014SR are used to an equal extent by the two genders and different social grade groups. The age patterns indicate that DecTQs may be on the decrease, particularly among young adults. The two corpora compared in the present study proved to be more different than expected. If diachronic studies on spoken language are to be made based on corpora collected at different times, it is vital that the compilation and transcription principles are as similar as possible.

Acknowledgements

I am grateful to the Department of Languages and Literatures at the University of Gothenburg for funding my post-doc position, enabling me to conduct this research. I wish to thank the editors for their comments and support: Karin Aijmer, for being a long-time mentor and colleague at the University of Gothenburg, Robbie Love, for responding to all my questions on the Spoken BNC2014, and Vaclav Brezina, for very helpful advice and editing at the last stages. I am also grateful to the participants at the *ICAME38* conference, held in Prague 24–28 May 2017, and the *9th International Corpus Linguistics Conference*, held in Birmingham 24–28 July 2017, and the foundations sponsoring my attendance at these conferences: Herbert and Karin Jacobsson's Foundation and The Royal Society of Arts and Sciences in Gothenburg.

Notes

1 Examples are, unless otherwise indicated, taken from the Spoken BNC2014 Sample. The first code refers to the file and the second code to the individual speaker of the utterance.
2 For information on ICE-GB, see Nelson, Wallis, and Aarts (2002).
3 The Spoken BNC2014S is available as a subcorpus in the final version of Spoken BNC2014.

4 Examples from the original BNC are labelled 'BNC1994' and are then followed by a file code and a number referring to the position within that file.
5 The following speakers were excluded: S0008, S0012, S0013, S0018, S0024,
S0037, S0041, S0058, S0084, S0115, S0144, S0179, S0262 and S0439.
6 The plus means that apart from 362 identified speakers, there are a few utterances made by unknown speakers (only 0.5% of all tokens).
7 The statistical tests used here are log-likelihood (LL) for statistical significance and Bayes for effect size (http://ucrel.lancs.ac.uk/llwizard.html).
8 Cf. 5,210 DecTQs per million w-units in Axelsson (2011, p. 89). The concept
of w-unit is close to the concept of word and does not include punctuation
marks. For further discussion on corpus size and frequency measurements,
see Section 7.4.1.
9 For a discussion of per million tokens versus per million words, see Section
7.4.1.
10 The frequency of 2,300 TQs pmw reported in Gómez González (2012, p. 79)
also incudes non-declarative TQs.
11 This includes the cases when it is the last part of *innit* or *dunnit*; *dunnit* (a
reduced form of *doesn't it*) is found in the Spoken BNC1994DS but not in the
Spoken BNC2014S.
12 This includes cases when IS is the first part of *innit*, *in 't it*, *int it* or *in it*. The
first part of *ain't* is also analysed as IS if *ain't* is used in a tag when *isn't* is
expected.
13 This includes cases when the first part of *ain't* is analysed as a form of HAVE.
14 The statistical significance of proportions is calculated with the SIGIL Corpus
Frequency Wizard (http://sigil.collocations.de/wizard.htm).
15 Tottie and Hoffmann's TQs include a small number of TQs with other
anchors than declaratives, viz. imperatives and interrogatives (2006, p. 289).
16 The eight other cases are found in KD8 8334 (Martine), KC0 5891 (Enid),
KBX 1647 (Donald), KB6 218 (Angela), KCX 8785 (Kathleen), KBE 2313
(Betty) and KCP 4569 (Joy).
17 Information on gender is missing for 12.5% of the tokens in the Spoken
BNC1994DS, but only for 0.002% of the tokens in the Spoken BNC2014S.
18 In the whole Spoken BNC2014S, female speakers account for 60.0% of the
tokens but only for 51.5% of the DecTQs. This is an indication of how the
very prolific speakers may skew the results in the Spoken BNC2014S.
19 The search strings were (_VBB|_VBD|_VBZ|_VDB|_VDD|_VDZ|_VHB|_VHD|_
VHZ|_VM0|_VVB|_VVD| _VVZ) in the Spoken BNC1994DS and (_VB0|_
VBDR|_VBDZ|_VBM|_VBR|_VBZ|_VD0|_VDD|_VDZ|_VH0|_VHD| _VHZ|_
VM|_VMK|_VV0|_VVD|_VVZ) in the Spoken BNC2014S.

References

Andersen, G. (2001). *Pragmatic markers and sociolinguistic variation: A rele-
vance-theoretic approach to the language of adolescents*. Amsterdam: John
Benjamins.
Axelsson, K. (2011). *Tag questions in fiction dialogue*. Ph.D Gothenburg: Uni-
versity of Gothenburg.
Axelsson, K. (in prep). *Innit in the spoken BNC2014*.
Ball, C. N. (1994). Automated text analysis: Cautionary tales. *Literary and Lin-
guistic Computing*, 9(4), 295–302.
Barron, A., Pandarova, I., & Muderack, K. (2015). Tag questions across Irish
English and British English: A corpus analysis of form and function. *Multilin-
gua*, 34(4), 495–525.

Brezina, V., & Timperley, M. (2017). How large is the BNC? A proposal for standardised tokenization and word counting. Paper presented at *Corpus Linguistics International Conference 2017, Birmingham, 24–28 July 2017*. Retrieved from www.birmingham.ac.uk/Documents/college-artslaw/corpus/conference-archives/2017/general/paper303.pdf. Accessed 1 September 2017.

Burnard, L. (2000). *Reference guide for the British national corpus (World Edition)*. Retrieved from www.natcorp.ox.ac.uk/archive/worldURG/index.xml. Accessed 21 September 2017.

Burnard, L. (2007). *Reference guide for the British national corpus (XML Edition)*. Retrieved from www.natcorp.ox.ac.uk/docs/URG. Accessed 13 February 2017.

Calnan, A. C. T., & Davidson, M. J. (1998). The impact of gender and its interaction with role and status on the use of tag questions in meetings. *Women in Management Review, 13*(1), 19–36.

Cheshire, J., Kerswill, P., & Williams, A. (2005). Phonology, grammar, and discourse in dialect convergence. In P. Auer, F. Hinskens, & P. Kerswill (Eds.), *Dialect change: Convergence and divergence in European languages* (pp. 135–167). Cambridge: Cambridge University Press.

Dehé, N., & Braun, B. (2013). The prosody of question tags in English. *English Language and Linguistics, 17*(1), 129–156.

Erman, B. (1998). '*Just* wear the wig *innit!*' From identifying and proposition-oriented to intensifying and speaker-oriented: Grammaticalization in progress. In T. Haukioja (Ed.), *Papers from the 16th Scandinavian conference of linguistics* (pp. 87–100). Turku: Turun Yliopisto.

Gómez González, M.D.L.Á. (2012). The question of tag questions in English and Spanish. In I. Moskowich & B. Crespo (Eds.), *Encoding the past, decoding the future: Corpora in the 21st century* (pp. 59–97). Newcastle Upon Tyne: Cambridge Scholarly Press.

Gómez González, M.D.L.Á. (2014). Canonical tag questions in English, Spanish and Portuguese. *Languages in Contrast, 14*(1), 93–126.

Hardie, A. (2012). CQPweb—combining power, flexibility and usability in a corpus analysis tool. *International Journal of Corpus Linguistics, 17*(3), 380–409.

Hoffmann, S. (2006). Tag questions in Early and Late Modern English: Historical description and theoretical implications. *Anglistik, 17*(2), 35–55.

Hoffmann, S., Evert, S., Smith, N., Lee, D., & Berglund Prytz, Y. (2008). *Corpus linguistics with BNCweb—a practical guide*. Frankfurt am Main: Peter Lang.

Kim, J-B., & Ann, J-Y. (2008). English tag questions: Corpus findings and theoretical implications. *English Language and Linguistics (Korea), 25*, 103–126.

Kimps, D. (2007). Declarative constant polarity tag questions: A data-driven analysis of their form, meaning and attitudinal uses. *Journal of Pragmatics, 39*(2), 207–291.

Kimps, D. (2016). *English variable tag questions: A typology of their interpersonal meanings*. Ph.D. Leuven: KU Leuven.

Krug, M. (1998). British English is developing a new discourse marker, *innit?* A study in lexicalisation based on social, regional and stylistic variation. *Arbeiten aus Anglistik und Amerikanistik, 23*(2), 145–197.

Lakoff, R. (1973). Language and woman's place. *Language in Society, 2*, 45–80.

Love, R., Dembry, C., Hardie, A., Brezina, V., & McEnery, T. (2017). The spoken BNC2014: Designing and building a spoken corpus of everyday conversations. *International Journal of Corpus Linguistics, 22*(3), 311–318.

Love, R., Hawtin, A., & Hardie, A. (2017). *The British National Corpus 2014: User manual and reference guide (version 1.0)*. Lancaster: ESRC Centre for Corpus Approaches to Social Science. Retrieved from http://corpora.lancs. ac.uk/bnc2014/documentation.php. Accessed 21 November 2017.

Nässlin, S. (1984). *The English tag question: A study of sentences containing tags of the type isn't it?, is it?* Stockholm: Almqvist & Wiksell International.

Nelson, G. (2005). *The ICE tagging manual*. Retrieved from http://ice-corpora. net/ice/manuals.htm. Accessed 20 September 2017.

Nelson, G., Wallis, A., & Aarts, B. (2002). *Exploring natural language: Working with the British component of the international corpus of English*. Amsterdam: John Benjamins.

Palacios Martínez, I. M. (2015). Variation, development and pragmatic uses of *innit* in the language of British adults and teenagers. *English Language and Linguistics, 19*(3), 383–405.

Pichler, H. (2013). *The structure of discourse-pragmatic variation*. Amsterdam: John Benjamins.

Pichler, H. (2016). Uncovering discourse-pragmatic innovations: *innit* in Multicultural London English. In H. Pichler (Ed.), *Discourse-pragmatic variation and change in English: New methods and insights* (pp. 59–85). Cambridge: Cambridge University Press.

Stenström, A-B., Andersen, G., & Hasund, I. K. (2002). *Trends in teenage talk: Corpus compilation, analysis and findings*. Amsterdam: John Benjamins.

Torgersen, E. N., Gabrielatos, C., Hoffmann, S., & Fox, S. (2011). A corpus-based study of pragmatic markers in London English. *Corpus Linguistics and Linguistic Theory, 7*(1), 93–118.

Tottie, G., & Hoffmann, S. (2006). Tag questions in British and American English. *Journal of English Linguistics, 34*(4), 283–311.

8 *Yeah, Yeah Yeah* or *Yeah No That's Right*

A Multifactorial Analysis of the Selection of Backchannel Structures in British English

Deanna Wong and Haidee Kruger

8.1. Introduction

Conversation is composed of more than just words and grammatical structures. In spoken interaction, this syntactic infrastructure is surrounded by an envelope of features that enable communication. One such communicative feature is *backchannels*. Backchannels, or the speech of listeners, are an intrinsic part of spoken communication. They are used to express ongoing support for both the content of the talk, and for the speaker who has the main turn at talk. However, identifying the full range of these forms has been problematic as they are often difficult to identify, quantify and adequately describe.

Backchannels are often short, and take nonlexical or irregular forms which can be scattered throughout the talk. They also tend to overlap the speaker's talk, yet they do not interrupt it, and do not receive replies. The elusive nature of backchannels is intriguing: why do listeners talk when they are listening, particularly when the turn-holder provides no acknowledgement of, nor response to, their talk? In investigating these questions, one assumption has been that the forms taken by backchannels contribute to their conversational function. Early research, relying on the intricate analysis of small samples, identified links between specific backchannel forms and backchannel functions. However, it is difficult to establish if there is any fixed relationship between form and function, particularly as the most frequent backchannel forms appear to be multifunctional. While large-scale corpus analyses examining backchannels have provided some insight into this relationship, many have relied on the analysis of a pre-determined set of forms rather than examining the full range of potential forms, thus limiting their conclusions.

Rather than attempting to derive form/function relationships, the research reported here takes a different approach by abstracting away from individual backchannel forms and focusing on backchannel structures. The aim of the research is to establish the factors that condition the selection of specific backchannel structures in a large corpus of conversational data. By relying on more abstract identification criteria, in this case backchannel structure, we aim to avoid the challenges associated with the analysis of backchannels based on form/function paradigms. It is foreseen that the analysis of the factors that condition the choice of backchannel structures may lay the groundwork for future research on the potential functions of different backchannel structures. We use corpus annotation to identify backchannel structures, and then use the speaker metadata associated with each utterance as predictors of backchannel choice. These predictors include sociolinguistic factors (age, gender, socio-economic status), an interpersonal factor (relationship between speakers), and a linguistic factor (grammatical category of the single or anchor item of the backchannel).

In Section 8.2, the chapter first considers pertinent conceptual issues associated with the analysis of backchannel form, function and structure, as well as methodological concerns in the analysis of backchannels. Based on this overview of conceptual and methodological issues in the analysis of backchannels, the research gap that this study addresses is identified, and the research questions presented. Section 8.3 describes the methodological approach used to identify and analyse backchannels, while Section 8.4 presents the findings of the study. Section 8.5 concludes with a summary of findings, a reflection on the limitations of the method, and suggestions for future research.

8.2 Conceptual and Methodological Challenges in the study of Backchannels

Backchannels are intrinsically linked to a level of successful interaction that extends beyond the content of the talk into an interpersonal dimension. For example, McCarthy (2003, p. 59) notes that backchannels function to manage the affective aspects of the ongoing talk, and are an important component of "the nontransactional stratum of talk". Pullin (2015) sees backchannel use as a marker of group cohesion, while Ameka (1992) regards backchannels as phatic interjections that are directed 'at' conversationalists rather than 'to' them. As such, backchannels form part of a category of "interactive competencies" (Barron & Black, 2015, p. 112) that can help to shape the talk, primarily by providing support to the speaker, or to the content of the speaker's talk. However, as pointed out in the introduction to this chapter, there are several conceptual and methodological difficulties in the study of backchannels. This section discusses some of these challenges in turn.

8.2.2 Backchannel Form, Function and Structure

The concept of supportive listener-speech has been discussed since the mid-20th century (see Dittman & Llewwllyn, 1968; Fries, 1952). However, the term *backchannel* was not fused until 1970 when Yngve (1970) made a distinction between the speech produced by the person holding the turn at talk in the 'main' channel, and the listener, who occupies the 'back' channel of the communication. Yngve (1970) proposed that speech produced by listeners is therefore best described as 'backchannels'. A variety of forms are associated with the descriptor backchannel, ranging from the nonlexical, e.g., *mm, mhm, uhuh*, to single lexical forms such as *true* and *right*, and variants of *yes* and *no*, e.g., *yeah, nah*. Researchers have also identified backchannels composed of complex constructions with a sophisticated level of structure in the form of a "microsyntax" that takes the form of *that + is + descriptor* such as *that's so true* (Jurafsky, Shriberg, Fox, & Curl, 1998, p. 6).

Functionally, backchannels are often presented as either belonging to specific functional categories or forming part of a functional continuum, with researchers exemplifying these functions by linking them to specific forms. For example, when linking backchannel forms to specific functional categories, backchannels have been described as acting as "continuers" (Schegloff, 1982, p. 81), which encourage the speaker to keep talking, through to "acknowledgement tokens" (Jefferson, 1984) which signal receipt of the speaker's message. Tottie (1991, p. 256) presents similar functional categories, but labels the forms functionally described by Schegloff (1982) as *continuers* as "regulative", and those that function as *acknowledgements* as "supportive" features within the interaction. Descriptions that model backchannel function along a continuum include Stenström's (1994, p. 82) Feedback Gradient which identifies a cline of backchannel forms that shift in their function from signalling indifference (e.g., *m*) to involvement (e.g., *hell*). A more complex functional cline, labelled the Verbal Feedback Continuum, is suggested by Holmes and Stubbe (1997, p. 10), who match signals of high or low involvement and affect with the complexity of backchannel forms.

However, there is an overlap in the literature that tends to blur classifications quantifying the form and function of backchannels. Functional descriptions of backchannels that seek to differentiate form by function do not always remain consistent across datasets. For example, the nonlexical form *mm* has had various functions attributed to it indicating different levels of interaction with the speaker's talk. These indicators of interactive magnitude shift from indifference (Stenström, 1994) to neutrality (Holmes & Stubbe, 1997) to engagement (Gardner, 2001). In addition, *yeah* has attracted contradictory functional labels, with some describing it as signalling "imminent speakership" (Jefferson, 1984, p. 202) or "speakership incipiency" (Drummond & Hopper, 1993, p. 158), whilst others describe it as an indicator of message receipt, an "acknowledgement token" (Gardner, 2001) and a lack of desire to take the turn at talk, "horizontal transitions" (Bangerter & Clark, 2003, p. 198). These apparently contradictory relationships between backchannel form and function suggest that some forms are multifunctional. As a result, the reported links between the shape of individual backchannels and their function are best explained within the specific contexts that inform such conclusions, and are less effective once these relationships are extrapolated to larger and more diverse datasets.

An alternative approach to the analysis of backchannels is to consider their structure. More abstract than the approaches described earlier, this method identifies patterns in backchannel structure based on their location in the talk. In other words, rather than relying on backchannel form as an identifying criterion, backchannels are identified first by their overlapping, non-interruptive and unacknowledged status, and then by their 'shape'. The resulting model sees backchannels categorised as either *single backchannels*, or as *backchannel clusters* (Wong & Peters, 2007, pp. 493–494). The backchannel cluster category is further differentiated with *compound backchannel* clusters, and *reduplicate backchannel clusters*. Singles are comprised of a single whole or partial form such as *yeah* in Extract 1. Reduplicate backchannel clusters consist of more than one repetition of identical forms, which in Extract 1 takes the form of *yeah yeah*. The final structural category encompasses all other backchannel cluster forms, those composed of more than one unit of a range of forms, such as *yeah no I'm not at all yeah* in Extract 1.

While the structural model for backchannel identification proposed by Wong and Peters (2007) does allow for a classification system of backchannels that avoids presumption of form or function, it is not without its problems. The model is not as fine-grained as those described, and does not offer a one-to-one link between individual forms and their function. It has also only been tested on a relatively small sample of orthographically transcribed spoken telephone conversations drawn from the distanced conversation section of the Australian subcorpus of the International Corpus of English (ICE) (see Greenbaum, 1996 for more information about ICE). It has also not been tested on face-to-face interaction. Analysis by structure may also be problematic as there is no research to indicate why one type of backchannel structure may be selected rather than another one. However, the model does offer a broader descriptive tool for large-scale exploratory research seeking to differentiate backchannels within interaction.

S0303: and it's very rational and it's very I'm just not really like that
S0262: >> yeah yeah [2]
S0303: I'd love to be like that
S0262: >>—UNCLEARWORD yeah [3]
S0303: >> but I'm not I just
S0262: >> yeah no I'm not at all yeah [3]

S0303: >> and—ANON-name-f's like she's always giving me all this
S0262: >> yeah [1]
S0303: >> advice about like what to do about like selling the flat and
S0262: >> yeah yeah [2]
S0303: like about the

(BNC2014 S6HP)

Extract 1 Single (1), Reduplicate Cluster (2) and Compound Cluster (3)
Backchannels (Indicated in Bold Text) in Dyad S6HP from the Spoken British National Corpus 2014 Sample (Spoken BNC2014S) [1]

8.2.3 Methods for the Analysis of Backchannels in Conversation

The availability of large-scale spoken corpora such as the Spoken BNC2014
(Love, Dembry, Hardie, Brezina & McEnery, 2017) provides an opportunity to examine the use of backchannels in conversation quantitatively,
across a large set of speakers. This method offers distinct advantages in
comparison to earlier research broadly grouped under the label *conversational analysis* (CA). CA is a data-driven approach that focuses on the
analysis of "fine-grained transcripts" (Gardner, 2001, p. 252) of spoken
interaction. It takes a qualitative approach to interaction, and is driven
by the premise that it is "possible that detailed study of small phenomena
may give an enormous understanding of the way humans do things and
the kinds of objects they use to construct and order their affairs" (Sacks,
1984, p. 24). Research from, for example, Jefferson (1984) and Schegloff
(1982), which made use of the CA approach, set the scene for interest in
backchannels in conversation. However, their investigations were based
on small numbers of conversations, usually conducted by speakers of
North American English. Further, due to the meticulous nature of the
CA method, which in these early studies involved manual transcription,
annotation and analysis, the size and scale of these investigations was
necessarily limited.

Linguistic corpora provide access to large samples of spoken language,
most often orthographically transcribed. Corpora have been used to
investigate backchannels, or backchannel-like features, in several varieties of English, including Australian English using the Australian component of ICE (Wong & Peters, 2007; Peters & Wong, 2015), and in New
Zealand English (Holmes & Stubbe, 1997) using the Wellington Corpus
of Spoken English (Holmes, Vine, & Johnson, 1998). Perhaps the most
studied variety of English using corpus techniques is British English. For
example, Stenström (1994) examined the London Lund Corpus (LLC)

(Svartvik, 1990) and found that in British English interaction, simple nonlexical constructions e.g., *m, ah, oh, mhm, yes*, and lexical forms e.g., *good heavens, I see, of course*, and *oh dear* are used by listeners when producing a backchannel. Kjellmer (2009) focused his analysis on the most frequent forms in his sample from the CobuildDirect Corpus, which are largely nonlexical forms or those that function as interjections or signal of agreement.

In this research, British English is also often considered in contrast to another variety of English. For example, Tottie (1991) found that backchannels are produced less often in British English than in American English. Although listeners in both groups tend to use short backchannels, British listeners prefer *yes* while American listeners prefer *yeah* as their most frequent backchannel response. A comparison between British and Irish English found that British single-word forms of feedback have more in common with American English than they do with Irish English, with responses such as *yes* having no equivalent form in the Irish data (O'Keeffe & Adolphs, 2008). In another comparison between British and American English, McCarthy (2003) found that British and American English listeners draw on a similar repertoire of forms when producing backchannels.

The samples upon which these analyses are based vary in size. The largest sample size is reported by Kjellmer (2009, p. 85) who analysed the 9,272,579 word CobuildDirect Corpus. McCarthy (2003) and O'Keeffe and Adolphs (2008) analysed samples drawn from the 5,000,000 word Cambridge and Nottingham Corpus of Discourse in English (CAN-CODE) Corpus (McCarthy & Carter, 2001). At the other end of the spectrum, Stenström (1994) analysed the 500,000 word London Lund Corpus (LLC) (Svartvik, 1990). The smallest sample considered in this set of research is that reported by Tottie (1991), who used samples from both the LLC (500,000 words) and the Santa Barbara Corpus of Spoken American English (249,000 words) (Du Bois et al., 2000–2005). However, her investigation examined one nineteen-minute conversation in American English, and two short conversations in British English. The range in corpus and sample sizes obviously allows for both very broad and quite narrow analyses.

All these corpora are based on orthographically transcribed spoken language. One of the challenges for the creators of these spoken corpora is to adequately capture the features of interaction that do not comply with the idealised "one party talks at a time" concept of turn-taking (Sacks, Schegloff, & Jefferson, 1974, p. 700). Backchannels are one such feature whose placement—as partial or total overlaps—challenges this concept. Some corpus designers incorporate markup systems to help capture overlapping speech. For example, the spoken language tagset for the International Corpus of English (ICE) made use of "overlapping string" tags which indicated the beginning and end of an overlap, and "overlapping string sets" which indicated the beginning and end of a series of overlapping strings (Wong, Peters, & Cassidy, 2011, p. 124). The design of the spoken component of the original British National Corpus (the Spoken BNC1994) also incorporated an annotation scheme for overlapping speech designed to indicate the location and source of interruptions (Crowdy, 1994). Its successor, the Spoken BNC2014, also marks overlaps using a simplified scheme that is incorporated into the underlying XML (Love, Dembry, Hardie, Brezina & McEnery, 2017).

8.3 Research Aims and Questions

Against the background of the conceptual and methodological challenges for the analysis of backchannels, the central aim of this investigation is to advance the description of backchannels in casual, face-to-face British English conversation by focusing on aspects of backchannel use that have not been widely explored using quantitative corpus-based methods, and by applying statistical methods drawn from variationist linguistics. In particular, we narrow the focus to backchannel structures, and investigate the relationship between the selection of these structures, and a number of speaker-related and grammatical variables. To our knowledge, the notion that the choice of backchannel structures (like the choice of many other linguistic structures) may be conditioned by particular sociolinguistic and grammatical variables has not been previously investigated. The aims of this study are therefore to:

1. quantify the overall frequency of different backchannel structures in a large corpus of authentic British conversational English; and
2. develop a better understanding of the factors that affect the selection of particular backchannel structures, including sociolinguistic, interpersonal, and grammatical factors, using monofactorial and multifactorial methods.

8.4 Method

8.4.1 *Operational Definitions*

The aim of this research was to examine listener-produced backchannels used in conversations conducted by British English[2] speakers. Thus, a *Listener* was operationally defined as the participant in the talk who did not have the main turn at talk, and was ostensibly refraining from taking the turn. In contrast, the *Speaker* was operationally defined as the participant who held the main turn at the talk. In terms of Listener behaviour, a *Backchannel* was operationally defined as Listener talk that overlapped a Speaker's turn, but did not interrupt it, did not receive a response, and did not result in a change of turn-holders. Talk that overlapped the Speaker's turn and resulted in a change of turn-holder, or received a response, was operationally defined as an *Interruption*. Any talk that was unclear or ambiguous was defined as *Other*.

8.4.2 Data Source

The data for the analysis were extracted from the 4,789,185-word Spoken BNC2014 Sample (see Chapter 1). As well as providing orthographic transcriptions of spoken interactions, the corpus was annotated using Version 6 of the UCREL Constituent Likelihood Automatic Word-tagging System (CLAWS 6) tagset (http://ucrel.lancs.ac.uk/claws/).

8.4.3 Data Extraction

In order to avoid assumptions about potential forms in the British back-channeling repertoire, the method used in this investigation followed Wong and Peters' (2007) approach, which relies on corpus markup to identify possible backchannel placement. Potential backchannels were identified in the data using the underlying XML corpus markup that indicated overlapping sections of the text. Potential targets were selected via a restricted search that made use of the underlying XML markup, primarily the <u_trans> tagset which marked utterance transitions. Potential targets were not identified using the CLAWS 6 part-of-speech (POS) tagset, as relying on markup identifying a pre-existing grammatical category (for example, the UH tag which marked the category *Interjections*) may not have been successful in capturing all potential backchannel forms.[3]

Extraction of the target data made use of restricted searches, in the first instance to ensure that the potential effects of confounding variables (like the number of participants in the conversation, and the linguistic or cultural background of the participants) could be controlled for in the sampling. Only interactions involving two people were included in the data set, and those individuals had to be identified as from England. All other speakers (including Scottish, Welsh and Irish) were excluded. The subcorpus created in this way is termed the Dyad subcorpus.

The restricted search also relied only on those overlaps marked with a high attribution confidence that ensured that only utterances produced by an identifiable speaker were included in the sample. Finally, to capture as many potential backchannels as possible, the search made use of wildcards permitting strings of up to nineteen words to be included in the search. This approach had the benefit of capturing as many instances of overlapping speech as possible without needing to rely on any specific letter combination, grammatical tag or word form in the data.

The CQPweb search results presented several challenges for the analysis of backchannels. While the sections of talk overlapping talk are marked, the talk that was overlapped, and the extent of those overlaps, did not appear to correlate with the perceived length of the text marked as over-lapping—nor was the transcription scheme designed to capture this information (Love, Hawtin & Hardie, 2017). The Spoken BNC2014's simple system of marking overlapping talk protocolled that only the fact that a given turn overlapped with the previous turn, in any way, was marked. For example, the duration of the two-syllable backchannel *mm mm* produced by Speaker 0426 in Extract 6 (below) was not likely to have been equivalent in length to the string of more than 20 words it was marked as overlapping. In addition, when talk was marked as overlapping, no other text was marked to show what part of the talk was being overlapped. Extract 2 illustrates this occurrence, with Speaker 0002's utterance *yes yes* marked as overlapping, but none of Speaker 0281's preceding talk marked as having been overlapped.

S0281: interesting the evening is getting interestinger and inter-estinger
S0002: >> yes yes
S0281: do you know why we say m- more interesting rather than interestinger?

(BNC2014 S9EP)

Extract 2 An Example of the Lack of Corresponding Overlaps in the Transcribed Talk from BNC2014 S9EP

Because of this, the decision was made to rely on the transcriber's judgement. Therefore, the text marked as overlapped was considered within the talk it occurred, and was treated according to the operational definitions described in Section 3.1. Thus, if text was marked as overlapping, if it did not interrupt the turn-holder's talk, and if it did not receive a response, the text was categorised as a backchannel.

8.4.4 Data Classification

The data were first categorised as *Backchannel, Interruption* or *Other* according to the operational definitions in Section 8.4.1. Once this preliminary categorisation had been completed, a structural classification of the backchannels was done. The structure of the backchannel is the dependent variable of interest in this study. This classification is discussed in more detail in Section 8.4.5. After this, each observation was further annotated for a range of sociolinguistic, interactional and grammatical variables, used as independent variables in analysing which factors most reliably predict the selection of particular backchannel structures. These variables and their annotation are discussed in more detail in Section 8.4.6

8.4.5 Structural Classification of Backchannels

Data categorised as backchannels were broken down into three structural categories—**single** backchannels, **reduplicate** backchannel clusters, and **compound** backchannel clusters (after Wong & Peters, 2007). For ease of discussion, the three structures will be described as S-structures (single backchannels), R-structures (reduplicate backchannel clusters), and C-structures (compound backchannel clusters) in the ensuing discussion. All three structural categories occurred as overlapping, non-interruptive lexical words or nonlexical forms that did not interrupt the speaker's turn, and did not receive a response. Each of the categories are described below, illustrated by extracts drawn from the Dyad subcorpus.

S-structures were identified as single (whole or partial) lexical words or nonlexical forms, such as *exactly* and *yeah* in Extract 3.

S0450: oh even if you live with someone it doesn't mean you're always gonna be free when they want

S0439: >> **exactly**

S0450: >> to do something

S0439: and it's kind of like she just expects me to be free and it's like I'm not become so used to you just being in your bedroom that I've gone out and made plans you know like

S0450: >> **yeah**

S0439: I go out and I see people and I go to the cinema or I go for dinner and you're not a part of that because

(BNC2014 SZQX)

Extract 3 The Single Backchannels *Exactly* and *Yeah* in Sample BNC2014 SZQX

C-structures were identified as any string of two or more (whole or partial) lexical words or nonlexical forms. In Extract 4, the cluster *that's ridiculous* contains a string of lexical forms that provide a commentary on the topic of the speaker's talk. The cluster *oh yes yeah* in Extract 5 expresses agreement through a combination of the interjection *oh*, the affirmative *yes* and its informal variant *yeah*.

S0378: what am I supposed to do? I have no money to to eat to get the bus to my job interview

S0167: >> that's ridiculous
S0378: so then they gave me like I think it was a month's travel card

(BNC2014 S9MK)

Extract 4 The Compound Backchannel Cluster (C-structure) *That's Ridiculous* in BNC2014 S9MK

S0281: there's always something isn't there? before Christmas it was a stomach virus and now skin thing
S0002: sorry?
S0281: before Christmas there was a stomach problem
S0002: >> oh yes yeah
S0281: and now a skin thing
S0002: good god is it? well the other thing is er change of er washing powder that can sometimes do that

(BNC2014 S9EP)

Extract 5 The Compound Backchannel Cluster, or C-structure *Oh Yes Yeah* in BNC2014 S9EP

R-structures were identified as strings of one or more (whole or partial) lexical words or nonlexical forms that consist of repeated forms. Reduplicated words or forms could be repeated two or more times in the backchannel. Extract 5 shows a short exchange where Speaker 0426 produces three reduplicates: the repeated nonlexical forms in *mm mm*, and the lexical *right right* and *sure sure*.

S0427: >> I think that's true and the other thing is that although the police are also er er er a sort of a ranked organisation
S0426: >> mm mm
S0427: and they've set great store by it erm what's different is that a PC always exercises discretion
S0426: right
S0427: you can't
S0426: >> right right
S0427: >> order a PC to do something

> S0426: >> sure sure
> S0427: >> wrong so to speak there's always
> S0426: >> well sure
> S0427: >> the element of discretion
>
> (BNC2014 SVN6)
>
> Extract 6 Reduplicate Backchannel Structures, or R-structures, in Dyad BNC2014 SVN6

A **backchannel anchor** was identified as the initial lexical word or non-lexical form in a backchannel cluster or reduplicate. For example, in Extract 5, the reduplicate backchannels *mm mm, right right*, and *sure sure* are anchored by *mm, right*, and *sure*. Also in Extract 6, the compound backchannel cluster *well sure* is anchored by the word *well*. In keeping with the labelling scheme described earlier, anchors in compound backchannel clusters are identified as **C-anchors**, while anchors in reduplicate structures are identified as **R-anchors**.

8.4.6 Annotation of Grammatical, Interpersonal and Sociolinguistic Variables

Drawing on the methodology of (sociolinguistic) variationist studies (see, for example, Tagliamonte, 2012), a range of grammatical, interpersonal and sociolinguistic variables were identified that might potentially condition the choice between the three backchannel structures identified in Section 3.4.1. In this section, we briefly discuss the annotation of these features in the data set, using the metadata available for the Spoken BNC2014 Sample corpus.

In the first instance, the **grammatical structure** of S-structures, C-anchors and R-anchors (in other words, the first or only item in the backchannel) was classified, using the CLAWS 6 POS annotation. While the CLAWS 6 set is composed of 148 tags, only 103 appeared in the data. However, even this reduced set of 103 tags contained too many variables for a coherent analysis, and the decision was made to collapse these into sixteen categories under the variable heading SATAG. Most of the SATAG categories are superordinates of the existing categories. For example, the twenty-two tags marking a range of nominal forms were grouped in the category *Noun*. However, some tags were not collapsed. These were categories that did not easily fit into a combined one, and included *Existential There, Infinitive Marker, Interjection, Negative* and *Unclassified*. The collapsed set of sixteen SATAG Categories is shown in Table 8.1.

Table 8.1 CLAWS 6 Tags Included in Each SATAG Category

Tags	SATAG: Full Form	SATAG
JJ, JJR, JJT, JK	Adjective	A
RA, REX, RG, RGQ, RGQV, RGR, RGT, RL, RP, RPK, RR, RRQ, RRQV, RRR, RRT, RT	Adverb	B
ZZ1, ZZ2	Alphabetic	C
APPGE, AT, AT1	Article	D
CC, CCB, CS, CSA, CSN, CST, CSW	Conjunction	E
DA, DA1, DA2, DAR, DAT, DB, DB2, DD, DD1, DD2, DDQ, DDQGE, DDQV	Determiner	F
EX	Existential There	G
UH	Interjection	H
XX	Negative	I
ND1, NN, NN1, NN2, NNA, NNB, NNL1, NNL2, NNO, NNO2, NNT1, NNT2, NNU, NNU1, NNU2, NP, NP1, NP2, NPD1, NPD2, NPM1, NPM2	Noun	J
MC, MC1, MC2, MCGE, MCMC, MD, MF	Number	K
IF, II, IO, IW	Preposition	L
PN, PN1, PNQO, PNQS, PNQV, PNX1, PPGE, PPH1, PPHO1, PPHO2, PPHS1, PPHS2, PPIO1, PPIO2, PPIS1, PPIS2, PPX1, PPX2, PPY	Pronoun	M
FU	Unclassified	N
VB0, VBDR, VBDZ, VBG, VBI, VBM, VBN, VBR, VBZ, VD0, VDD, VDG, VDI, VDN, VDZ, VH0, VHD, VHG, VHI, VHN, VHZ, VM, VMK, VV0, VVD, VVG, VVGK, VVI, VVN, VVNK, VVZ	Verb	O
TO	Infinitive marker	P

Sociolinguistic variables included in the analysis include **gender, age** and **socio-economic status**. The **relationship between the participants** in the dyad, an interpersonal or discourse feature that may also be seen as related to sociolinguistic variables, was also annotated. All these annotations are based on metadata available for the Spoken BNC2014S.

Gender was coded directly, using the available metadata. The sample included 72 female speakers and 51 male speakers. The **age** of speakers was encoded in the Spoken BNC2014S as either a specific number or as fitting into an age band of ten years. For the analysis, these age bands were further collapsed into three groups spanning 30 years each: 0–29 years (49 speakers), 30–59 (48 speakers), and 60–89 years (26 speakers). These categories made up the levels for the variable AGE (see Table 8.2).

The **socio-economic status** of BNC2014 participants was recorded using the National Statistics Socio-economic Classification (NS-SEC) scale, devised and used by the Office for National Statistics in the United Kingdom (ONS). This set, which consists of eight categories, was

Table 8.2 The Spoken BNC2014S Age Categorisation Versus the Collapsed AGE Categories

Spoken BNC2014S Age Bands	*AGE*
11_18	0–29
19_29	
30_39	30–59
40_49	
50_59	
60_69	60–89
70_79	
80_89	

Table 8.3 The BNC2014S NS-SEC Age Categorisation Versus the Collapsed NS-SEC Categories (After ONS, 2012)

Spoken BNC2014S NS-SEC	*Description*	*NS-SEC-Modified*
1_1	Large employers and higher managerial and administrative occupations	1: Managerial and professional occupations
1_2	Higher professional occupations	
2	Lower managerial, administrative and professional occupations	
3	Intermediate occupations	2: Intermediate occupations
4	Small employers and own account workers	
5	Lower supervisory and technical occupations	
6	Semi-routine occupations	3: Routine and manual occupations and
7	Routine occupations	
8	Never worked and long-term unemployed	Never worked and long-term unemployed
Uncategorised	Includes full-time students, occupations not stated or inadequately described, and not classifiable for other reasons	UNCAT

reduced to three categories following guidelines published by the ONS (ONS, 2012), and included in the analysis as the variable NS-SEC (see Table 8.3). The new categories were comprised of 55 speakers in Category 1, 26 speakers in Category 2, 19 speakers in Category 3, and 23 Uncategorised speakers.

As far as the **relationship** between interlocutors is concerned, the initial BNC2014 categories (Acquaintances, with a subset labelled Acquaintances; Close family; Partners, Very close friends; Colleagues; Friends;

Table 8.4 The Spoken BNC2014S Categories for Relationship Between Speakers Versus the Collapsed RSHIP Categories

Spoken BNC2014S classes for relationship between speakers	RSHIP
Close family	Close
Partners	
Very close friends	
Acquaintances	Wider
Colleagues	
Friends	
Wider family circle	
Strangers	

Wider family circle; Strangers) were collapsed into two categories, Wider and Closer, for the variable RSHP (see Table 8.4).

8.4.7 Statistical Analysis

The statistical analysis was done based on a total of 13,577 cases of utterances with backchannels, produced by 123 different speakers. Each case was annotated for the structure of the backchannel, as well as the grammatical, interpersonal and sociolinguistic variables outlined earlier.

The analysis proceeds in two main steps. The first step has two components. First, an overall analysis of the normalised frequency of backchannels overall and per group is presented. Second, an exploratory analysis of the relationship between each of the five individual independent variables (AGE, GENDER, SATAG, SSEC, RSHIP) and the relative frequency of selection of the three structural categories of backchannels (Single = S, Clusters = C and Reduplicates = R) is carried out. This exploratory mono-factorial analysis makes use of contingency tables (crosstabulations), visualised as spine plots produced using the software R (R. Core Team, 2015). The statistical analyses are supplemented with detailed qualitative analyses of individual forms.

The monofactorial analysis, however, cannot account for the potential relationships and interactions between the individual independent variables. For this reason, the second step of the analysis carries out a multi-factorial analysis of the effects of the five independent variables. For this purpose, we use conditional inference tree modelling, as implemented in the ctree function in the R-package 'partykit' (Hothorn, Hornik, & Zeileis, 2006; Hothorn & Zeileis, 2015). Conditional inference trees

> estimate a regression relationship by binary recursive partition-
> ing in a conditional inference framework. Roughly, the algorithm
> works as follows: 1) Test the global null hypothesis of independ-
> ence between any of the input variables and the response (which may

be multivariate as well). Stop if this hypothesis cannot be rejected. Otherwise select the input variable with strongest association to the response. This association is measured by a p-value corresponding to a test for the partial null hypothesis of a single input variable and the response. 2) Implement a binary split on the selected input variable. 3) Recursively repeat steps 1) and 2).

(Hothorn & Zeileis, 2016, pp. 7–8)

Tagliamonte and Baayen (2012, p. 135) argue that conditional inference trees are a useful tool for variationist analyses, since they straightforwardly visualise how multiple predictors (or independent variables) operate together. They are particularly useful in cases where there are many higher-order interactions, and large numbers of predictors (Levshina, 2015, p. 292), as is the case for this analysis. We therefore use conditional inference tree modelling to assess the interaction of the predictors in affecting the choice of backchannel structure.

8.5 Results and Discussion

The following section considers the distribution of backchannel structures across the sample. Sections 8.5.1 to 8.5.3 consider the distribution of the structures and the most common forms associated with each structure, and also reflects in more detail on the usage patterns for the most common forms. In Section 8.5.4, we present the monofactorial analysis, which considers each of the five independent variables (gender, age, socio-economic status, relationship, and grammatical structure) in relation to the independent variable, backchannel structure. The section concludes with the multifactorial analysis in Section 8.5.5, which investigates how the five variables interact in conditioning the selection of the backchannel structure.

8.5.1 Backchannel Structures and Associated Forms in the Dyad Subcorpus

All three structural types of backchannel occur in the Dyad subcorpus. However, backchannels spoken by British English speakers are far more likely to be part of a C-structure (9,606 cases or 70.8% of cases) than any other type of backchannel structure. The next most frequent form were S-structures (3,505 cases, or 25.1% of cases), and the least most frequent form were R-structures (466 cases, or 3.4% of cases).

Within each of the structures, a range of forms were used by listeners. However, as Figure 8.1 shows, a small set of forms are repeatedly chosen by speakers to be used as a single backchannel, or to begin a cluster. Figure 8.1 demonstrates that in terms of forms, the S- and R-categories are generally similar in preferences. *Yeah* dominates the S- and R- categories,

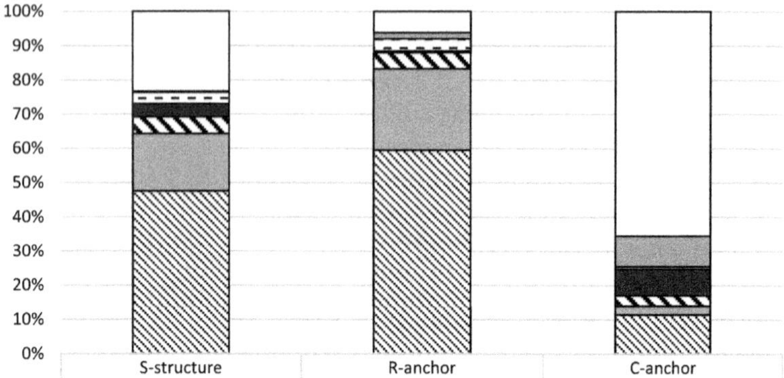

Figure 8.1 Comparison of the Distributions of the Most Frequent S-structure, R-anchor, and C-anchor Forms as Proportions of Structural Group, With Raw Frequencies

	S-structure	R-anchor	C-anchor
Other	818	29	6300
I	8	8	870
yes	120	17	71
oh	137	2	729
no	171	22	303
Variants of mm	584	111	241
yeah	1667	277	1092

accounting for nearly 60% of all R-anchors produced, and under half of S-structures (47.6%). The "Other" category is more strongly represented for S-structures than for R-anchors, to the extent that it is proportionally the second most frequent form (23.3%) for S-structures. Variants of *mm* were proportionally the second most frequent form for R-anchors (23.8%), and the third for S-structures (16.7%). *No, oh, yes* and *I* occur at similarly low frequencies as S-structures and R-anchors. These findings suggest that the R-structure is a kind of specialised and formally restricted elaboration of S-structures predominantly with *yeah* and variants of *mm*, which together make up more than 80% of anchors in R-structures.

The forms typically used as C-anchors show very different distributional patterns. *Yeah* is proportionally much less frequent as C-anchor (accounting for just 11.4% of cases), as are variants of *mm* (2.5%). The most dominant forms used as C-anchors are, in fact, the category "Other" (65.6% of cases), with *I* and *oh* proportionally much more frequent than in S- and R-structures, at (9.1% and 7.6%, respectively). This difference in distribution is an indicator of the more noticeable presence of lexical structures in C-structures. While the high frequencies of *I* as a C-anchor may be a marker of listeners signalling increased engagement with the speaker or the topic, the sizable proportion of Other (65.6%) indicates the broad variation that occurs within that structure.

The following sections consider two specific aspects of backchannel structure and forms in the corpus that emerge from the above. We first consider the use of the most frequent backchannel form, *yeah*, and the influence of individual variation. Subsequent to this we analyse the use of *no* as a supporting backchannel. *No* accounts for between 3% and 5% of backchannels or backchannel anchors. Its presence as backchannel is somewhat counterintuitive, warranting further investigation.

8.5.2 *Yeah and Individual Variation*

The British English listeners in the Dyad subcorpus clearly prefer *yeah* as a single backchannel, or as part of a reduplicate cluster (see Figure 8.1). However, it should be noted that the production of backchannels as singles or as reduplicates anchored by *yeah* is not evenly distributed across speakers. In particular, one speaker, Speaker 0262, dominated both distributions, producing 207 single *yeah*s (compared to a mean of 19 for all other speakers), and 67 *yeah*-anchored reduplicates (compared to a mean of 6 for all other speakers).

Speaker 0262 was one of the most productive speakers in terms of her backchannel production. She produced the most backchannels overall (1,247), the most single backchannels (377); the most reduplicates (98); and the second-largest number of clusters (772). In terms of the proportion of backchannels she contributed to the sample, overall, she contributed 9% of all backchannels. Note, however, that although she was highly productive in terms of her backchannel output, Speaker 0262 was not the most productive speaker overall, and ranked as the eighth most productive speaker in terms of the number of utterances she produced (12,870) and seventh in terms of the number of words she produced (120,256). This suggests that rather than a prolific speaker, she was an enthusiastic listener, who actively engaged with the other speaker's talk.

What is notable about Speaker 0262 is her use of the form *yeah*. Just under a third (380) of her 1,247 backchannels were, or began with, *yeah*. More than half of those *yeah*s appeared as single backchannels (207), with the remainder located as R-anchors (67) or C-anchors (106). Most interesting are her reduplicate backchannels, where more than two-thirds of her total R-structure output were composed of reduplications of the word *yeah*. *Yeah yeah* was the most common reduplication of *yeah* from Speaker 0262 (54), and her contribution accounted for just under a quarter of all the *yeah yeah*s produced in the corpus. Her use of *yeah yeah yeah* (11) and *yeah yeah yeah yeah* (1) each accounted for around a fifth of all of those forms in the corpus. However, Speaker 0262 was the only speaker to produce a backchannel with six repetitions of *yeah*.

Clearly, Speaker 0262 favoured *yeah* when producing single and reduplicate backchannels. One possibility is that she was influenced by another listener, and imitated that speaker's listening behaviours. However, she was recorded speaking with nine different people, and only two of those individuals appear in the top twenty most frequent backchannel producers (Speaker 0303 ranked eleventh, and Speaker 0353 ranked seventeenth). The influence of situational context can also be countered by the fact that she was recorded in twelve different locations, suggesting that Speaker 0262's backchannel production is purely idiosyncratic and influenced neither by conversationalists nor context.

These findings on individual variability raise some challenges for the present research, as it clearly suggests that backchannel use may form part of highly idiosyncratic listening behaviours that should be accounted for as individual variation in a statistical model. This matter is discussed in further detail in Section 5.

8.5.3 Backchannel Forms and Complex Meaning: The Use of No as a Backchannel

Listeners' use of *no* could be interpreted as counter-intuitive, particularly given the denotation that accompanies the form. However, it occurs at non-negligible frequencies across all three structures (see Figure 8.1). One explanation is that the relationship between the form and apparent meaning of backchannels is a complex one, and it is likely to be determined by context as much as the forms used. Exchanges such the one presented in Extract 7 illustrate the complexity of the support directed from the backchannel of the conversation. In this interaction, Speaker 0238 is agreeing with the Speaker 0239's claim about a lack of decomposition, with the first unit of her backchannel *no yeah yeah* marking agreement with Speaker 0239's negative *don't*. Interestingly, the *yeah yeah* that follows *no* could be a response to both Speaker 0239's statement and to the "monitoring device" (Biber, Johansson, Leech, Conrad, & Finegan, 1999, p. 1092) *you know* inserted following the first use of *decompose* as well as general agreement with the gist of Speaker 0239's ongoing talk.

S0239: yeah but they started them with these bags
S0238: oh
S0239: and they they decompose you know they don't decompose here they
S0238: >> no yeah yeah
S0239: >> decompose later and that's really good and we put that out and there's another bin outside you can put it into

(BNC2014 SMEB)

Extract 7 Directed Support Using *No Yeah Yeah* in Dyad BNC2014 SMEB

A more complex example of directed support appears in dyad BNC2014 SY5E in Extract 8. In the exchange, a discussion about the reliability of food storage practices, Speaker 0198's talk is supported by two backchannels produced by Speaker 0229. The backchannels appear as *yeah no* and *no*. While the forms incorporated into these backchannels are limited to a combination of *yeah* and *no*, the functional complexity achieved through these forms belies their apparent simplicity. As with the example in Extract 7, the apparently contradictory content of Speaker 0229's first backchannel *yeah no*, functions to indicate both broad and targeted agreement for Speaker 0198's claim about the age of stored watermelons. Broad agreement for Speaker 0198's statement is evident in the use of *yeah* which is likely to express support for both the ongoing talk and possibly Speaker 0198's right to continue in the turn. The second word, *no*, provides more specific semantic agreement about the content of Speaker 0198's talk through reinforcing the twice-repeated negative structure *you don't* with a similarly negative structure. Speaker 0198 then provides a second backchannel which again expresses agreement with Speaker 0229's nutritional claim with another *no*, once again expressing support with a backchannel that mirrors the semantic content of the talk, rather than taking a more axiomatic marker of agreement such as *yeah*. The complexity of meaning inherent in the small slice of interaction in Extract 8 points to the challenges presented to researchers who rely entirely on the forms of backchannels to inform their analysis.

S0198: you don't that's the problem with fr- everything fruit vegeta-
bles you don't know how old that watermelon is
S0229: >> yeah no
S0198: don't know how good those you don't know if there's actu-
ally any vitamins left in it any more
S0229: >> no
S0198: cos it's travelled so far

(BNC2014 SY5E)

Extract 8 Directed Support Using *Yeah No* and *No* in Dyad BNC2014 SY5E

The following section considers each of the structures discussed here—S-structures, R-structures, and C-structures—and their relationship to the five independent variables identified in Section 8.4.6.: gender, age, socio-economic status, relationship between speakers, and grammatical category. The analysis presented in this section is an exploratory precursor to the multifactorial analysis presented in Section 8.5.5.

8.5.4 Monofactorial Analysis of the Effect of Individual Independent Variables on the Selection of Backchannel Structure

The sociolinguistic factors considered in this analysis were gender, age and socio-economic status. The proportional frequency of C-structures, S-structures and R-structures by these groupings is shown in Figure 8.2.

As far as gender is concerned, females produced proportionally more backchannels than males (64.6% vs. 35.4%). This is unsurprising, given the difference in representation of the genders in the sample. When the frequency of backchannels is considered as a normalised frequency per 1,000 words per speaker (see Figure 8.3), there is very little difference between males and females. Female speakers use backchannels at a mean frequency of 4.75 per 1,000 words (SD = 4.72), whereas male speakers use backchannels more frequently, at a mean of 6.46 times per 1,000 words (SD = 8.52). Using a two-sample t-test, however, the difference between the two groups is not significant (t = –1.30, p = 0.20).[4] Female and male speakers also produced comparably similar proportions of C-structures (70.6% vs. 71.04%), S-structures (26.0% vs. 25.44%) and R-structures (3.4% vs. 3.52%) to male speakers, as evident in Figure 8.2.

Within the age comparison, which compared three age bands of thirty years each, the 30–59 age group produced the largest proportion of

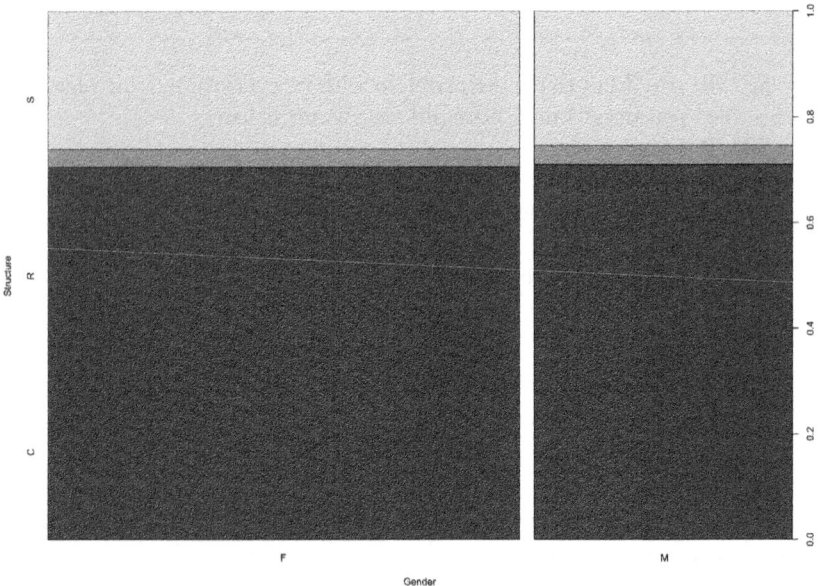

Figure 8.2 Spine Plots Comparing the Distribution of Backchannel Structures Across the Three Sociolinguistic Variables Gender, Age and Socio-Economic Status

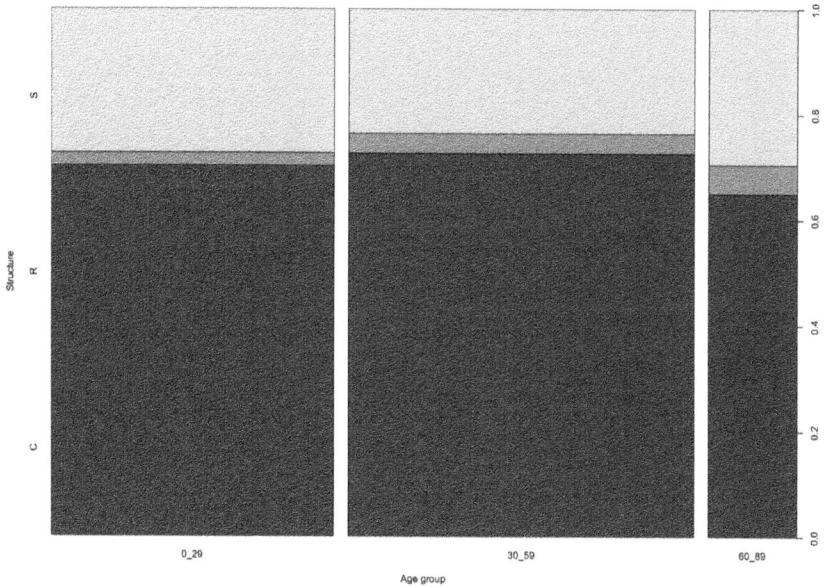

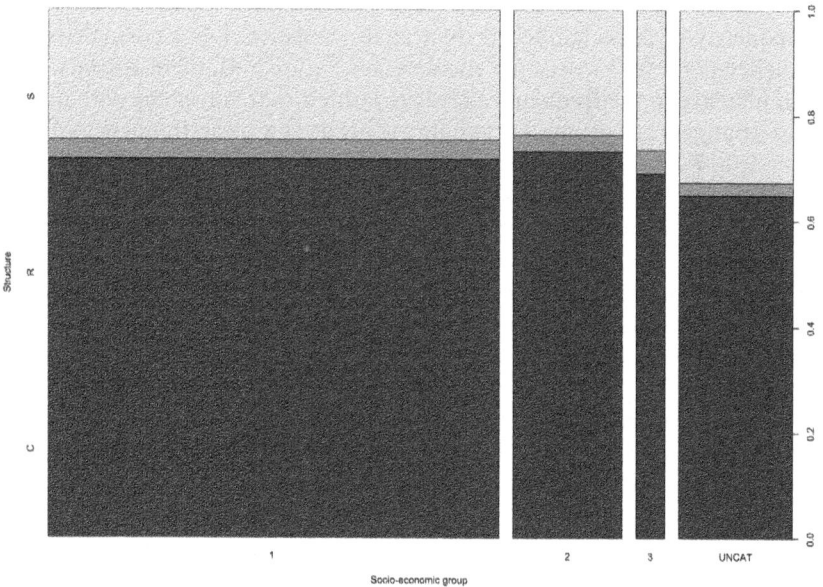

Figure 8.2 Continued

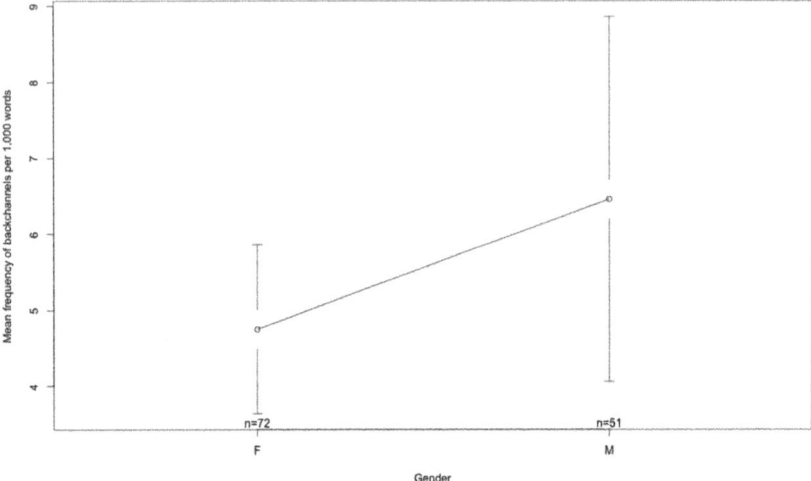

Figure 8.3 Comparison of Female Versus Male Backchannel Frequency Normalised Per 1,000 Words Per Speaker

backchannels (48.1%), whilst the oldest age group, 60–89 years old, produced the smallest proportion of backchannels (12.3%). When the frequency of backchannels is once again considered as a normalised frequency per 1,000 words per speaker (see Figure 8.4), there appears to be an increase in the frequency of backchannels that correlates with age. In the youngest age group, backchannels occur at a mean frequency of 4.72 per 1,000 words (SD = 5.82), whereas in the age group 30–59 years, this increases to 5.58 per 1,000 words (SD = 5.72). Speakers older than 60 used backchannels on average 6.62 times per 1,000 words (SD = 9.12) (see Figure 8.4). Using one-way ANOVA, however, the difference between the three groups is not significant (F = 0.72, p = 0.50).

There appears to be some relationship between age and preference for particular structures, although the pattern in Figure 8.2 is difficult to interpret.

Socio-economic status was compared using the four classification groups outlined in Table 8.3, and the resulting spine plot (Figure 8.2) shows that speakers from Category 1 (managerial and professional occupations) produced by far the most backchannels in the sample (64.2%). When the frequency of backchannels is considered as a normalised frequency per 1,000 words per speaker, speakers in Category 1 still produce on average the most backchannels, with the highest degree of variability (6.40 per 1,000 words; SD = 8.33). Speakers in the other three categories have mean values that are very similar, at 4.80 (SD = 5.00), 4.29 (SD = 4.49) and 4.93 (SD = 4.68) respectively for the Category 2,

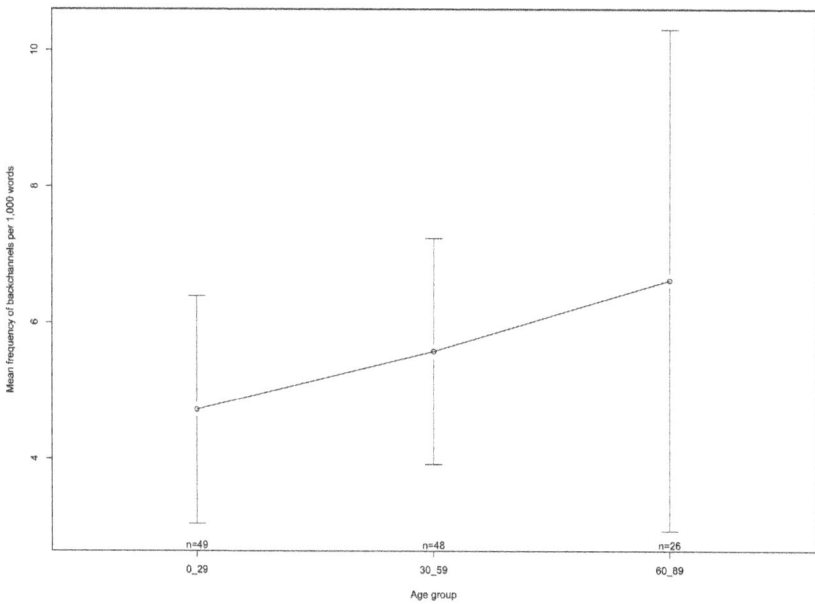

Figure 8.4 Comparison of Backchannel Frequency Based on Age of Speakers (Normalised Per 1,000 Words)

Category 3, and Uncategorised groups (see Figure 8.5). Using one-way ANOVA, however, differences between the groups are not significant (F = 0.70, p = 0.60).

The distribution of structures within this category was also the most like the overall distribution of backchannels, with 71.7% C-structures, 3.7% R-structures and 24.6% S-structures (see Figure 8.2). The proportional distribution across Groups 1 and 2 is relatively similar, with only the Uncategorised group (largely composed of full-time students and unclassifiable individuals) demonstrating an ostensibly different distribution, with proportionally more S-structures (32.6%) and fewer C-structures (65.0%). The distribution for Group 3 (combining speakers in routine and manual occupations with those who are unemployed) falls somewhat between that for Group 1 and 2, and the Uncategorised group, but this group accounts for a small number of utterances.

The interpersonal variable of relationship between speakers is composed of two categories, Close and Wider, with more utterances produced in Close relationships (66.8% vs. 33.2%; see Figure 8.6). Because the individual speakers in the sample communicated in both Close and Wider relationships, it is not possible to calculate a normalised frequency of backchannels by relationship, per speaker.)

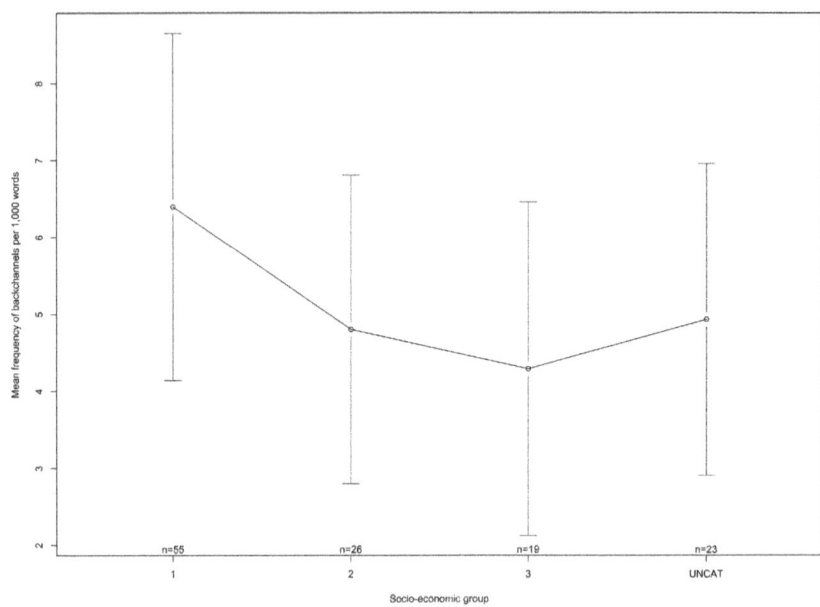

Figure 8.5 Comparison of Normalised Backchannel Frequency Based on Socio-Economic Status

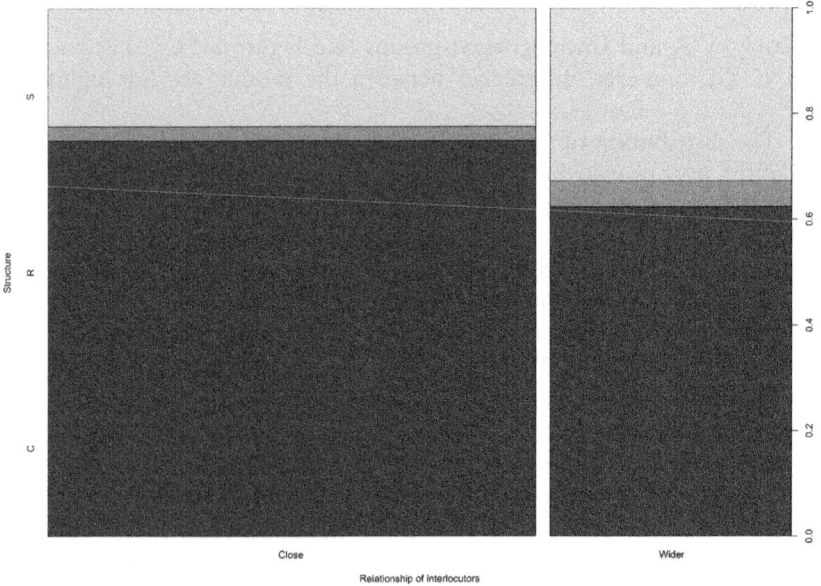

Figure 8.6 Spine Plot Comparing the Relationship Between Speakers and Backchannel Structure

As shown in Figure 8.6, for speakers interacting in a close relationship, which includes close family, partners and very close friends, the C-structure dominates proportionally (74.9%, which is at a proportion similar to that in the overall sample, vs. 62.4% for wider relationships). In comparison, speakers interacting with their wider circle of family or friends, or acquaintances, colleagues and strangers, make proportionally considerably more use of S-structures (32.7% for wider vs. 22.4% for close relationships) and R-structures (4.9% for wider vs. 2.7 for close relationships).

The analysis of the relationship between the grammatical category of the first or only element of a backchannel and the three structures was the most complex, with sixteen categories to compare. As shown in Figure 8.8, the largest grammatical category is Interjections (H; 42.3% of all structures), which shows a substantial and striking deviation from the overall preference for C-structures that characterises the sample as a whole, with almost equal proportions of C-structures (44.5%) and S-structures (48.1%), and a notably larger proportion of R-structures (7.4%). Interjections thus appear to be the most versatile of grammatical categories as far as backchannels are concerned, allowing for the greatest

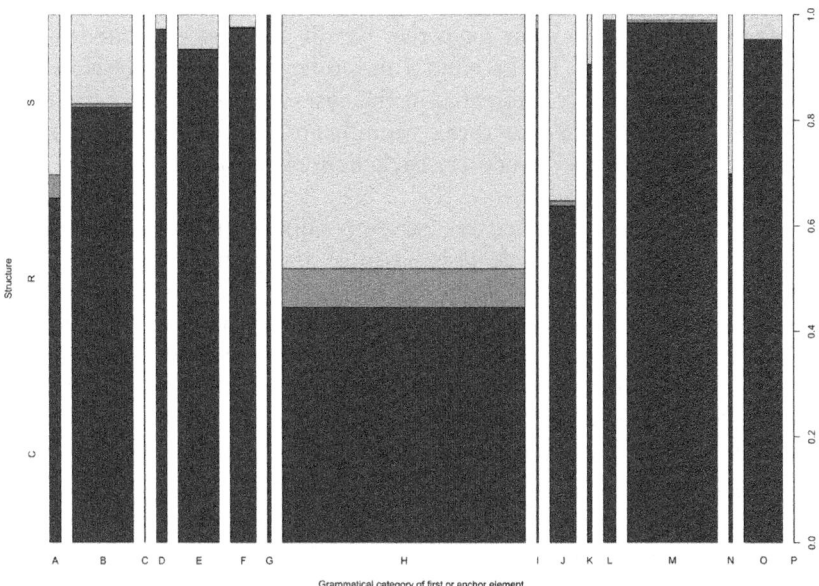

Figure 8.7 Spine Plot Comparing the Grammatical Category of S-structures and Anchors With Backchannel Structure (Key: A= Adjective; B= Adverb; C= Alphabetic; D= Article; E= Conjunction; F= Determiner; G= Existential There; H= Interjection; I= Negative; J= Noun; K= Number; L= Preposition; M= Pronoun; N= Unclassified; O= Verb, P=Infinitive marker)

range of structures. Three other categories also have a proportionally higher frequency of S-structures, namely Adjective (A; 30.4%), Noun (J; 35.3%) and Unclassified (N; 30.2%) (although the Adjective and Unclassified categories have very low numbers of cases), with the S-structure also more frequent for Adverbs (B; 16.9%) than is the case in the overall sample.

Two categories are completely composed of C-structures, with no S-structures or R-structures (Existential *there* (G) and Infinitive marker (P)). Several other categories do not appear as R-structures, including Negative (I), Noun (J), Number (K), Preposition (L), Unclassified (N), Verb (O), and Infinitive Marker (P).

The discussion in this section suggests that some sociolinguistic, interpersonal and grammatical variables play a role in conditioning the choice of backchannel structure. However, this analysis can be exploratory only, as it does not take account of the potential interactions between these variables. The following section turns its attention to the results of the multifactorial analysis in the form of the conditional inference tree.

8.5.5 Multifactorial Analysis

Overall, compound backchannel clusters are by far the most frequent, default option, as evident from the overall analyses presented in Sections 8.5.1 to 8.5.4. In the conditional inference tree analysis, we are therefore particularly interested in the cases where the distribution of choices for single (S-structure), reduplicate cluster (R-structure), or compound cluster (C-structure) backchannels deviates from this overall distribution.

The conditional inference tree (see Appendix 1) shows that the highest level split in the data (node 1) is based on the grammatical category of the initial or only element of the backchannel (SATAG, which for single backchannels is the only element, and for clusters and reduplicates is the anchor element)[5] suggesting that the choice between the three structural variants is significantly different when the backchannel (anchor) is either an adjective, an interjection, a noun or unclassified (A, H, J, N; the left branch of node 1) compared to other grammatical categories (B, C, D, E, F, G, I, K, L, M, O, P; the right branch of node 1). For adjectives, interjections, nouns and unclassified backchannels/backchannel anchors, there is a great deal more variability in the choice among the three structures (as evident in the terminal nodes on the left side of the tree), whereas for all other grammatical categories, the C-structure very strongly dominates (as evident in the terminal nodes on the right side of the tree). The following discussion follows these main splits in the tree, and considers the interaction between SATAG and the variables RSHIP, AGE and NSSEC3. Note that GENDER was not identified as being a significant conditioning variable in the multifactorial analysis.

8.5.6 *Right Branch of Node 1: C-structures and Grammatical Categories*

As pointed out, the right branch of node 1 overall reflects the distribution of the overall sample, and the subsequent splits are the most predictable given the dominance of compound clusters in the overall frequencies and distributions discussed previously. In this branch, SATAG is the strongest predictor, with RSHIP and AGE playing some conditioning role in structural choices. NSSEC3 does not play a role in conditioning the choice between the three structures.

The subsequent split on this side of the tree (on node 25) is also for SATAG, isolating adverbs and alphabetics in the left branch. The relationship between speakers is a key conditioning factor when the grammatical category of a backchannel (anchor) takes the form of an Adverb, e.g., *well* (400); *so* (203); *okay* (87); or *just* (70)[6] or an Alphabetic, e.g., *i-* (7) (node 26). When the conversationalists are in a close relationship (terminal node 27), the C-structure dominates (over 80%). However, when they are in a more distant relationship (the right branch of node 26), speakers' choice of C-structure is further conditioned by age. Here, speakers tend to produce somewhat more C-structures when aged 30–59 (over 80%; terminal node 30) then they do when they are younger or older (below 75%; terminal node 29).

Returning to node 25, when the backchannel (anchor) is an article (D), conjunction (E), determiner (F), existential *there* (G), negative (I), number (K), preposition (L), pronoun (M), verb (O), or infinitive marker (P), the subsequent split is again based on the grammatical category of the backchannel (anchor) (node 31). This split separates out the categories conjunction, with the most frequent forms *and* (351), *but* (252), *cos* (104), *or* (65); Number, e.g., *one* (10), *three* (nine), *ten* (seven); and Verb, e.g., *is* (88), *do* (81), *like* (43), *did* (37), to the left. This set is then conditioned by the age of the speaker, where those belonging to the 30–59 age group are more likely to choose a C-structure (above 95%; terminal node 34) than those from other age groups (terminal node 33). The right branching from node 31, where the grammatical categories article, e.g., *the* (121), *a* (52), *no* (23), *my* (17); Determiner, e.g., *that* (325), *what* (164), *which* (32), *this* (28); Existential *there* (50); Negative, e.g., *not* (37); Preposition, e.g., *like* (61), *in* (56), *for* (27), *with* (27); Pronoun, e.g., *I* (842), *it* (487), *you* (289), *they* (153); and Infinitive marker *to* (42) account for terminal node 35, results in a distribution with the strongest dominance of C-structures (over 98%), the fewest S-structures and no R-structures. This terminal node also contains the largest number of observations (N = 3,408).

8.5.7 *Left Branch of Node 1: Adjectives, Interjections, Nouns, and Unclassified Categories*

The outcomes for the branches of the left-hand side of the tree (from node 2) are less predictable: across all the terminal nodes there is evidence of variability in the distribution, and seven out of the twelve terminal nodes show a higher frequency of S-structures rather than C-structures, which is different to the overall distribution of the sample.

- Grammatical categories of backchannel (anchors): adjective, noun and unclassified

The left branch of node 1 isolates the grammatical categories adjective (A), interjection (H), noun (J), and unclassified (N). The first node in this branch (node 2) splits this set so that adjectives, nouns and unclassified cases (the left branch of node 2) are separated from interjections (the right branch of node 2). For adjectives, nouns and unclassified cases, the choice between structures is subsequently conditioned by the relationship between the speakers (node 3). When speakers are in a close relationship, they are more likely to favour C-structures (around 75%; terminal node 4), about three times as much as they do S-structures (around 25%), with almost no R-structures. However, when the relationship between speakers is less close, the subsequent split is determined by the age of the speakers (node 5). When speakers fall into the 30–59 age group, they favour C-structures less strongly (around 60%) with S-structures represented more strongly (around 38%) (terminal node 9). Younger and older speakers make an additional determination based on grammatical category of the backchannel (anchor) (node 6). When the grammatical category of the backchannel (anchor) takes the form of an adjective, they are more likely to produce an S-structure (about 50%) than a C-structure (about 30%), and show one of the strongest tendencies to select an R-structure (more than 15%; terminal node 7). When speakers use nouns or unclassified forms, they are still more likely to prefer S-structures (terminal node 8). However, the difference between S-structures and C-structures in terminal node 8 is much smaller in comparison to that in terminal node 7, and includes fewer R-structures.

- Grammatical categories of backchannel (anchors): interjections

When a backchannel (anchor) appears in the form of an interjection, which includes *yeah*, variants of *mm*, *oh* and *no*, at node 2, speakers again vary their structural choices based on the relationship between speakers (node 10). For those in a close relationship, the choice is further conditioned by socio-economic status (node 11). Here, speakers in Groups 1, 2, and 3 are more likely to favour C-structures (terminal node 12). Those speakers belonging to the Uncategorised socio-economic group, which is largely composed of students and other undefined individuals, are split based on age (node 13), where all speakers, apart from those in the 60–89 age group, favour S-structures over C-structures (terminal node 14). In contrast, the oldest age group (60–89) are more likely to favour C-structures (about 45%; terminal node 15). However, this category also produced the most R-structures (over 20%), which, combined with S-structures (nearly 35%), suggests a preference for simple and repetitive backchannel structures in this group.

In the right branch of node 10, when the relationship between speakers is less close, the distribution is conditioned by socio-economic status (node 16). Speakers belonging to Group 1, 3 and Uncategorised are further split based on age (node 17). Here, younger speakers (0–29 years) are more likely to choose S-structures than C-structures (terminal node 18). However, all other ages are further split at node 19 based on the socio-economic status of the speakers (node 19). Here, those working in managerial and professional occupations (Group 1) also favour S-structures (terminal node 20), although they do not show as strong a preference for these structures as those in Group 3 and Uncategorised (terminal node 21).

Returning to node 16, for speakers working in Intermediate occupations (Group 2) the choice is further conditioned by age (node 22), with older speakers (60–89 years) preferring S-structures (terminal node 24), and all other age groups preferring C-structures (terminal node 23).

In summary, it appears that where S-structures are more frequent than C-structures, they occur in contexts where the backchannel takes the form of an adjective, noun, interjection or unclassified form. For adjectives and nouns (and unclassified forms), the type of relationship and age are important conditioning factors. Speakers aged either 0–29 or 60–89 years, communicating within their wider network, tend to prefer S-structures rather than C-structures. Within this group, R-structures are preferred in the form of adjectives e.g., *sure, good, okay* and *sorry*.

For interjections, socio-economic status, as well as age and relationship, are important conditioning factors. In close relationships, speakers who are full-time students (or otherwise uncategorised in socio-economic status) and under the age of 60 prefer S-structures in the form of interjections more strongly—although those in the other three socio-economic groups also demonstrate a relatively higher frequency of S-structures when using interjections in close relationships. R-structures occur at a particularly high frequency when speakers over 60 in the unclassified socio-economic group use interjections as backchannels. For wider relationships, those from all socio-economic categories bar those in intermediate occupations, and from all age groups within those categories prefer S-structures, though at various levels of preference.

8.6 Summary and Conclusion

8.6.1 Findings

Analysis of the Dyad subcorpus of the Spoken BNC2014S provides insights into the listening behaviours of British English conversationalists. Two stated aims guided the investigation. The first focused on backchannel structure and sought to quantify the overall frequency of different backchannel structures in authentic British conversational English. We found that British English conversationalists are most likely to use compound backchannel clusters (C-structures) such as *oh yeah, oh right* and *I know*, followed by single backchannels (S-structures) such as *yeah, mm* and *no*, and least likely to use reduplicate backchannel clusters (R-structures) such as *yeah yeah, mm mm* and *yeah yeah yeah*. By considering the initial unit of backchannel clusters, the backchannel anchor, or the only unit of a single backchannel, we found a marked preference for *yeah* as an S-structure, and as the first unit of R-structures. In contrast, for C-structures there is much more variability in the form of the first unit, with forms such the pronoun *I*, and interjections such as *oh* and *no* amongst the most frequent.

The second aim of this research was to identify the factors that affect the selection of specific backchannel structures. Thus, for this investigation, we considered five independent variables: three sociolinguistic, one interpersonal and one grammatical variable. The analysis of these variables was conducted first as a monofactorial analysis that considered each variable individually in relation to the dependent variable of backchannel structure. The second was to consider all five independent variables simultaneously in a multifactorial analysis of backchannel structure.

The findings of the study show no significant differences in the frequency of backchannels, as such, for female and male speakers, speakers of different age groups and socio-economic backgrounds, and in closer or wider relationships. In the monofactorial analyses, we found that backchannel clusters are the most frequent structure across the three sociolinguistic variables of gender, age and socio-economic status, and the interpersonal variable, relationship between speakers. This remained stable regardless of the fact that the sample has more female than male speakers, more younger than older speakers, more speakers employed in managerial or professional occupations than any other socio-economic group, and more people in close relationships rather than distant ones. However, some variation is evident in the use of S-structures, with older people, those in full-time study and undefined occupations, and those in wider relationships more likely to favour S-structures than others in their categories.

The monofactorial analysis shows that the largest variation in backchannel structure is accounted for by the grammatical category of the only (for single backchannels) or the initial (for clusters) unit of a backchannel. British conversationalists prefer interjections—a broad category composed of non-lexical and lexical items such as *yeah, mm, oh* and *no* whose function seems more important than their form—at the beginning of single and cluster backchannels. However, interjections are not spread evenly across structures, and are more heavily used as an S-structure and R-anchor, than as a C-anchor. C-anchors instead show a much broader

variation, with the most frequent grammatical categories including pronouns such as *I* and *you*, and adverbs such as *really, right* and *okay*.

The monofactorial analysis also provides an insight into the interpersonal aspects of listening behaviours. For example, when considering the
relationship between speakers, there is a difference in the structure of
a backchannel based on how close the relationship is. This means that
those in more distant relationships are more likely to use single or reduplicate backchannels. The most frequent of these forms, *yeah* and *yeah
yeah*, are axiomatic: they are the most cited in the literature, and consequently the most predictable. However, speakers in a close relationship
are more likely to use a compound cluster as a backchannel. These show
broad variation in form, and are therefore much less predictable, and
presumably more context-dependent. This suggests that the less familiar
a speaker is with a conversationalist, the more likely they are to rely on
short, less lexical, and more predictable backchannel forms when providing feedback from the back channel of conversation. It is possible that
this is an indicator of a listener-specific politeness strategy, and requires
further investigation, particularly as this has implications for fields as
varied as English as a Second Language teaching and the development of
dialogue systems.

The multifactorial analysis reinforces the importance of the grammatical category and its effect on the selection of S-structures, C-anchors
and R-anchors. This is further conditioned by the age of speakers, their
relationships, and their socio-economic status. However, gender does not
play a role in determining a speaker's choice of backchannel structure.
The multifactorial analysis further confirms that deviations from the
preference for C-structures are linked to the use of interjections, and to a
lesser extent, adjectives, nouns, and unclassified forms.

8.6.2 Limitations of the Current Research

The size of the Dyad subcorpus provides a rare large-scale insight into
British English dyadic conversation. In addition, features such as the
annotation of speaker turns, overlapping speech, extensive metadata,
and grammatical annotation were invaluable in the analysis reported
here. However, there are several limitations to this study. First, the sample itself is problematic, primarily because it has many more female than
male speakers, more younger speakers, more people in close relationships
and a clear majority employed in managerial and professional roles. On
a national level, more data from Scotland, Wales and Northern Ireland
would have allowed a comparison of truly British listening behaviours.
Second, the orthographic transcriptions, while comprehensive, do not
provide enough information about the exchanges. There is very little
information about paralinguistic features such as tone, silence or speech
rate, beyond a question mark tag flagging a high rising terminal tone.

Of more concern is the absence of any information about the nonverbal dimension of each exchange, including gaze direction, gesture, posture and even touch. Variations in any of these factors adds a dimension to the meaning of an exchange that is not always evident in the words being used. A ready solution for future projects could be to sample more broadly in the first instance, and to include additional levels of markup tracking both paralinguistic and nonverbal cues in the interaction in the second. However, given the size, challenges inherent in collecting spoken data, and the probable cost of developing a corpus the size of the Spoken BNC2014, these limitations are ones most likely to be a niche concern and not ones that should be taken as failings of the corpus itself.

In terms of the analysis, an additional limitation is the potential effect individual variation may have had on the results. However, given the number of participants, the sample size, and the consistent dominance of grammatical forms such as interjections across structures and speakers, this is not likely to be a major issue. Nevertheless, future research will use alternative methods such as linear mixed-effect modelling to account for the influence of individual variation.

8.6.3 Future Research

The research presented in this chapter provides an overview of the backchannel structures used by British English listeners in dyadic conversations. As such, future research should be focused more narrowly on the features of specific backchannel structures and their use. For example, a closer examination of 'micro-syntax' (Jurafsky et al., 1998) in compound backchannel clusters may provide an insight into whether the formulaic use of backchannel forms such as *yeah* as a single and reduplicate is mirrored in a predictable structure to compound clusters. This would in turn establish if there is a typical 'type' of compound cluster, which would be particularly important given the apparent variation evident at the level of C-anchors.

Further, more work needs to be done comparing backchanneling behaviours in regional varieties of English to establish whether there is a universal listening behaviour, or if listening behaviours are unique to specific sociolinguistic or cultural groups. This in turn leads to a need to establish if those behaviours vary not only based on the sociolinguistic dimensions, but also on the communication method. While early research (Dittman & Llewwllyn, 1968) has hinted that distanced conversation (by telephone or other voice-only means) may produce listening behaviours that differ from those that occur in face-to-face contexts, there has been no recent research considering this potential difference. This difference could be an important one, both from a methodological standpoint (comparing apples with oranges), but also from a practical standpoint given the ongoing development of speech-based interaction agents that need to mimic natural interactive processes in order to ensure engagement with their human users.

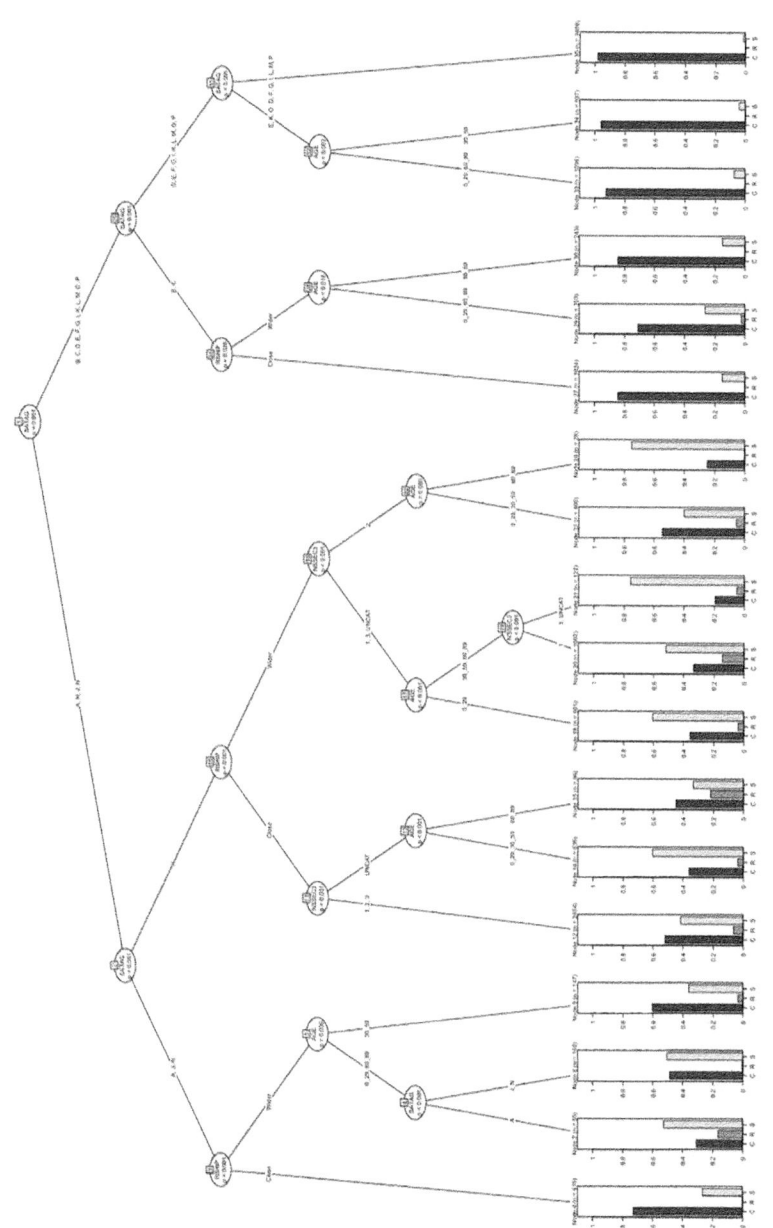

Appendix 1 Conditional Inference Tree

Notes

1 The transcriptions included as extracts have been modified to remove the spaces which were inserted before sentence final punctuation marks, and within contracted or truncated words such as you 're and gon na for annotation purposes. Overlapping speech is marked with double chevrons >> following the speaker's identification number. Backchannels are indicated in bold text. Names that were not anonymised in the extracted data were anonymised by the lead author, and replaced with 'NAME'. The source corpus file is indicated in round brackets at the end of the transcript.
2 For the purposes of this investigation, the term 'British English' is taken to mean 'English spoken in England'. This is due to the overwhelming dominance of data extracted from England in the Dyad subcorpus (see Section 3.3), where the sample sizes for the English, Welsh, Scottish and Northern Irish data sets were markedly unequal. The English data set (2,435,960 words) accounted for 98.3% of the Dyad subcorpus. In contrast, the Welsh (35,612 words) and the Northern Irish (6,178 words) sets accounted for just 1.4% and 0.2% of the Dyad subcorpus respectively. Finally, there was no Scottish data in the Dyad subcorpus. Therefore, the investigation will focus solely on the England dataset.
3 There were a few instances in the transcripts where nonlexical forms were orthographically transcribed with slight variations, which did not appear to represent a significant phonetic equivalent in the spoken form. For example, the forms *mm, hmm, hm*, and *mmm* were combined as variants of *mm*. Similarly, *uhu, uh, huh*, and *uh-huh* were combined as variants of *uhuh*. However, it is important to note that nonlexical forms such as *aha* were not combined with variants of *uhuh* as the vowels were considered too different.
4 While the data did not meet the assumption of normal distribution, the parametric t-test and one-way ANOVA are relatively robust to deviations from normality where sample sizes are large, as is the case here. We therefore use parametric tests to test for significance; however, non-parametric tests likewise indicated no significant difference between groups.
5 In the remainder of the discussion, we refer in shorthand to the "grammatical category of the backchannel (anchor)", to reflect that for single backchannels this is the grammatical category of the sole element in the backchannel, and for clusters and reduplicates this is the grammatical category of the first element in the backchannel, the anchor.
6 Each of the examples provided are based on the top four most frequent forms with a count greater than one in the category.

References

Ameka, F. (1992). Interjections: The universal yet neglected part of speech. *Journal of Pragmatics*, *18*, 101–118.

Barron, A., & Black, E. (2015). Constructing small talk in learner-native speaker voice-based telecollaboration: A focus on topic management and backchanneling. *System*, *48*, 112–128. Retrieved from http://dx.doi.org/10.1016/j.system.2014.09.009

Biber, D., Johansson, S., Leech, G., Conrad, S., & Finegan, E. (1999). *Longman grammar of spoken and written English*. Harlow, England: Pearson Education Limited.

Crowdy, S. (1994). Spoken corpus transcription. *Literary and Linguistic Computing*, *9*(1), 25–28. Retrieved from http://doi.org/10.1093/llc/9.1.25

Dittman, A. T., & Llewwllyn, L. G. (1968). Relationship between vocalizations and head nods as listener responses. *Journal of Personality and Social Psychology*, 9(1), 79–84.

Drummond, K., & Hopper, R. (1993). Back channels revisited: Acknowledgment tokens and speakership incipiency. *Research on Language & Social Interaction*, 26(2), 157–177.

Du Bois, J., Chafe, W. L., Meyer, C., Thompson, S. A., Englebretson, R., & Martey, N. (2000–2005). *Santa Barbara corpus of spoken American English, Parts 1–4*. Philadelphia: Linguistic Data Consortium.

Fries, C. C. (1952). *The structure of English: An introduction to the construction of English sentences*. New York, NY: Harcourt Brace.

Gardner, R. (2001). *When listeners talk: Response tokens and listener stance*. Amsterdam: John Benjamins.

Greenbaum, S. (1996). *Comparing English worldwide: The international corpus of English*. Oxford: Oxford University Press.

Holmes, J., & Stubbe, M. (1997). Good listeners: Gender differences in New Zealand conversation. *Women and Language*, 20(2), 7–14.

Holmes, J., Vine, B., & Johnson, G. (1998). *The Wellington corpus of spoken New Zealand English: A users' guide*. Wellington: School of Linguistics and Applied Language Studies, Victoria University of Wellington. Retrieved September 5, 2010, from http://archive.lib.msu.edu/LDC/rawcds/cd421/MANU ALS/WSC/INDEX.HTM; for updated information, see www.victoria.ac.nz/lals/resources/corpora-default/corpora-wsc

Hothorn, T., Hornik, K., & Zeileis, A. (2006). Unbiased recursive partitioning: A conditional inference framework. *Journal of Computational and Graphical Statistics*, 15(3), 651–674.

Hothorn, T., & Zeileis, A. (2015). partykit: A modular toolkit for recursive partytioning in R. *Journal of Machine Learning Research*, 16, 3905–3909. Retrieved from http://jmlr.org/papers/v16/hothorn15a.html

Hothorn, T., & Zeileis, A. (2016). *Package 'partykit': CRAN*. Retrieved from https://cran.r-project.org/web/packages/partykit/partykit.pdf. Accessed 8 August 2016.

Jefferson, G. (1984). Notes on a systematic deployment of the acknowledgement tokens "yeah" and "mm hm". *Papers in Linguistics*, 17, 197–216.

Jurafsky, D., Shriberg, E. E., Fox, B., & Curl, T. (1998). Lexical, prosodic, and syntactic cues for dialog acts. *Proceedings of ACL/COLING-98 Workshop on Discourse Relations and Discourse Markers*, 114–120.

Kjellmer, G. (2009). Where do we backchannel? On the use of mm, mhm, uh huh and such like. *International Journal of Corpus Linguistics*, 14(1), 81–112. Retrieved from http://doi.org/10.1075/ijcl.14.1.05kje

Levshina, N. (2015). *How to do linguistics with R: Data exploration and statistical analysis*. Amsterdam: John Benjamins.

Love, R., Dembry, C., Hardie, A., Brezina, V., & McEnery, T. (2017). The spoken BNC2014: Designing and building a spoken corpus of everyday conversations. *International Journal of Corpus Linguistics*, 22(3), 319–344.

Love, R., Hawtin, A., & Hardie, A. (2017). *The British national corpus 2014 user manual and reference guide (version 1.0)*. Lancaster: ESRC Centre for Corpus Approaches to Social Science. Retrieved from http://corpora.lancs.ac.uk/bnc2014

McCarthy, M. (2003). Talking back: "Small" interactional response tokens in everyday conversation. *Research on Language and Social Interaction*, 36(1), 33–63. Retrieved from http://doi.org/10.1207/S15327973RLSI3601_3

McCarthy, M., & Carter, R. (2001). Size isn't everything: Spoken English, corpus, and the classroom. *TESOL Quarterly, 35*, 337–340. doi:10.2307/3587654

Office for National Statistics (ONS). (2012). *The National Statistics Socio-Economic Classification (NS-SEC rebased on the SOC2010)*. Retrieved from http://webarchive.nationalarchives.gov.uk/20120315042155/www.ons.gov.uk/ons/guide-method/classifications/current-standard-classifications/soc2010/soc2010-volume-3-ns-sec—rebased-on-soc2010—user-manual/index.html

O'Keeffe, A., & Adolphs, S. (2008). Response tokens in British and Irish discourse: Corpus, context and variational pragmatics. In K. P. Schneider & A. Barron (Eds.), *Variational pragmatics* (pp. 69–98). Amsterdam, Philadelphia: John Benjamins.

Peters, P., & Wong, D. (2015). Turn management and backchannels. In K. Aijmer & C. Rühlemann (Eds.), *Corpus pragmatics: A handbook* (pp. 408–429). Cambridge: Cambridge University Press.

Pullin, P. (2015). The application of English as a Lingua Franca (ELF) research findings to the teaching of pragmatic competence. In K. Beeching & H. Woodfield (Eds.), *Researching sociopragmatic variability: Perspectives from variational, interlanguage and contrastive pragmatics* (pp. 276–296). Hampshire: Palgrave Macmillan Ltd.

R. Core Team. (2015). *R: A language and environment for statistical computing*. Vienna, Austria: R. Foundation for Statistical Computing. Retrieved from www.R-project.org/

Sacks, H. (1984). Notes on methodology. In J. M. Atkinson & J. Heritage (Eds.), *Structures of social action: Studies in conversational analysis* (pp. 21–27). Cambridge: Cambridge University Press.

Sacks, H., Schegloff, E. A., & Jefferson, G. (1974). A simplest systematics for the organization of turntaking for conversation. *Language, 50*(4), 696–735.

Schegloff, E. A. (1982). Discourse as an interactional achievement: Some uses of 'uh huh and other things that come between sentences. In D. Tannen (Ed.), *Analyzing discourse: Text and talk* (pp. 71–93). Washington, DC: Georgetown University Press.

Stenström, A-B. (1994). *An introduction to spoken interaction*. London: Longman.

Svartvik, J. (Ed.). (1990). *The London corpus of spoken English: Description and research*. Lund: Lund University Press.

Tagliamonte, S. A. (2012). *Variationist sociolinguistics: Change, observation, interpretation*. Oxford: Wiley-Blackwell.

Tagliamonte, S. A., & Baayen, R. H. (2012). Models, forests, and trees of York English: *Was/were* variation as a case study for statistical practice. *Language Variation and Change, 24*(2), 135–178.

Tottie, G. (1991). Conversational style in British and American English: The case of backchannels. In K. Aijmer & B. Altenberg (Eds.), *English corpus linguistics* (pp. 254–271). London: Longman.

Wong, D., Cassidy, S., & Peters, P. (2011). Updating the ICE annotation system: Tagging, parsing and validation. *Corpora, 6*(2), 115–144.

Wong, D., & Peters, P. (2007). A study of backchannels in regional varieties of English, using corpus mark-up as the means of identification. *International Journal of Corpus Linguistics, 12*(4), 479–509.

Yngve, V. (1970). On getting a word in edgewise. In *Papers from the sixth regional meeting Chicago linguistics society* (pp. 567–577). Chicago: Chicago Linguistics Society.

Part III
Morphosyntax

9 Variation in the Productivity of Adjective Comparison in Present-Day English

Tanja Säily, Victorina González-Díaz and Jukka Suomela

9.1 Introduction

English adjective comparison has received a great deal of attention in corpus-based research, particularly in the functional competition between inflectional (*-er*) and periphrastic (*more*) strategies (e.g., Mondorf, 2003; González-Díaz, 2008; Matsui, 2010). There is, however, a key area of competition that remains relatively unexplored, namely, the productivity of either comparative strategy. The received wisdom is that inflectional affixes are fully productive, which would suggest lack of variation within the productivity of *-er*. However, recent research using novel methodologies (Säily, 2014) crucially shows *sociolinguistic* variation in the productivity of extremely productive derivational suffixes. Whether the same variation applies to the productivity of inflectional processes therefore remains an open question.

Our study explores intra- and extra-linguistic variation in the productivity of comparative strategies. Intra-linguistic factors include syntactic position, the presence of premodifiers, complements and a second term of comparison, and the length of the adjective. The extra-linguistic determinants focus on gender, age, socio-economic status, conversational setting and roles of the interlocutors. Rather than limiting ourselves to the relatively small number of adjective types in which both inflectional and periphrastic comparison can occur, we take a holistic approach and consider the entire range of types within each strategy using the methodology and software recently developed by Säily and Suomela (2009) and Suomela (2016) for the study of derivational productivity (*types2*). The Spoken BNC2014 (Love, Dembry, Hardie, Brezina, & McEnery, 2017) is instrumental to the project, as it is the only up-to-date corpus of Present-Day English (PDE) providing access to both intra- and extra-linguistic information across a representative sample of British society. To provide our study with a diachronic dimension, we will compare the corpus with the spoken component of the original British National Corpus (BNC1994).

Our research constitutes a timely contribution to current knowledge of adjective comparison and morphological theory-building. It not only provides greater descriptive adequacy as regards the factors shaping the growth and development of the English comparative system, but also deals with much-debated issues concerning analytic vs. synthetic trends in the history of English. Past empirical work on analyticity and syntheticity has often excluded the study of derivational morphology (e.g., Szmrecsanyi, 2012), partly because of the strict compartmentalisation of inflectional and derivational morphology. The idea that there is a derivation-to-inflection cline rather than a sharp divide between the two has of course been expressed in previous literature (e.g., Brinton & Traugott, 2005; Bauer, 2004). However, more empirical evidence is still needed to support this hypothesis. If our results were to show variation and change in the productivity of inflectional comparison (as an example of inflectional morphology) similar to that previously observed in derivational morphology (e.g., Säily, 2014), then this would provide further support for the 'cline' view. Furthermore, the existence of a cline would mean that *both* derivation and inflection contribute to syntheticity, which is also the view expressed by Danchev (1992).

The chapter is organised as follows. Section 9.2 summarises previous research on adjective comparison and morphological productivity. Section 9.3 describes the material and methods used. Sections 9.4 and 9.5 focus on the data analysis and discussion of the findings, whereas Section 9.6 considers the theoretical implications of the study.

9.2 Background

9.2.1 English Adjective Comparison

Adjective comparison has been a long-standing topic of interest in English linguistics from the early 20th century onwards. Lexicographical works of the early to mid-20th century (e.g., Poutsma, 1914; Curme, 1931; Jespersen, 1949) provide a description of the two structures available in PDE (inflectional comparison—e.g., *friendlier*—and periphrastic comparison, e.g., *more friendly*) and of the main factors governing the choice of one (inflectional) or the other (periphrastic) strategy (see also Quirk, Greenbaum, Leech, & Svartvik, 1985 or Huddleston & Pullum, 2002). These factors are normally of a phonological and morphosyntactic nature, i.e., the number of syllables of the adjective (adjectives of more than three syllables normally take periphrastic comparison and monosyllabic ones prefer the inflectional form) and/or its ending and stress pattern (e.g., *-ive*, *-ous* or *-ful* adjectives normally take periphrastic comparison). Another frequently-discussed issue in early lexicographical works is the origin of the periphrastic construction (e.g., Mossé, 1952; Strang, 1970; but see also Knüpfer, 1921).

Scholarly interest in adjective comparison grew in the second half of the 20th century, especially in works couched within the generative tradition.

These studies often focused on the development of theoretical models that could account for the semantics and syntax of comparatives in an efficient manner (see Cresswell, 1976; Rusiecki, 1985 or, more recently van Rooij, 2010, 2011), as well as on the constraints leading to the derivation of comparatives (e.g., Huddleston, 1967; Bresnan, 1977). Controversies about the nature of over-generalisations also sparked an interest in the acquisition and use of comparatives (see Gathercole, 1979, 1985; Gitterman & Johnston, 1983 or, more recently, Graziano-King, 1999; Graziano-King & Cairns, 2005; Hohaus, Tiemann, & Beck, 2014).

The growth of computer-based English linguistics in the late 1980s elicited new synchronic and diachronic interest in the comparative system. On the synchronic front, recent corpus-based scholarship has primarily focused on the factors governing the functional distribution of inflectional and periphrastic strategies in PDE. Thus, alongside length and ending, a number of other prosodic, syntactic, semantic and cognitive-pragmatic determinants of variation have been put forward, e.g., syntactic position and presence of premodifiers, complements and a second term of comparison (syntax); concrete vs. abstract meanings (semantics); and frequency of adjectival use, complexity of the context and previous mention in discourse (cognitive-pragmatic) (see, among others, Leech & Culpeper, 1997; Lindquist, 2000; Mondorf, 2003, 2007, 2009; Szmrecsanyi, 2005; González-Díaz, 2008; Hilpert, 2008, 2010). Although some discrepancies can be found as regards how influential each of these factors is, these works present a unified picture as far as they show that "the true extent of variability in this area appears to have been underestimated in the past" (Mondorf, 2009, p. xiii).

Diachronic studies of adjective comparison are relatively less numerous. Some concomitances can nevertheless be found across works: namely, an interest in ascertaining possible usage trends in comparative strategies across time (Kytö, 1996 and Kytö & Romaine, 1997, 2006 observe a tendency for the inflectional strategy to prevail over the periphrastic one over time), and a willingness to further explore previous claims on the origin of the periphrastic construction. In addition, accounts of genre-based distribution of comparatives as well as socio-stylistic analyses of non-standard comparative strategies (double comparison, e.g., *more friendlier*) are also found (see Kytö, 1996; González-Díaz, 2004, 2006, 2008; Mondorf, 2009).

The brief outline above attests to the wealth of research already produced on the English comparative system. There are, however, particular aspects where the application of recent developments, be they corpora or methodologies, may lead to new insights about comparison. Corpus-wise, the Spoken BNC2014 constitutes a valuable resource to confirm and/or reject previously observed shifts and trends in the recent history of the British English comparative. On the methodological front, previous corpus-based research on the competition between inflectional and periphrastic forms has traditionally focused on a small number of adjective types (normally disyllabic adjectives) which can take both comparative strategies. New software such as the *types2* program used in this chapter allows for reliable comparisons of adjective types regardless of their default comparative preferences. This in turn opens up new avenues of investigation—in our case, it allows us to study variation within the productivity of either comparative strategy across internal and external factors of change. Note, in this connection, that although the received wisdom is that inflection is fully productive—and consequently we would expect to find no variation within the productivity of synthetic *-er* comparatives—the existence of sociolinguistic variation in the productivity of extremely productive derivational suffixes has been observed (see Säily, 2014). Whether the same variation applies to the productivity of inflectional processes remains an open question, which we will pursue in the following sections.

9.2.2 Morphological Productivity

The concept of morphological productivity is difficult to define. Bolinger (1948, p. 18) refers to a "degree of animation" as an essential property of morphemes that amounts to a "statistically determinable readiness with which an element enters into new combinations". Baayen (e.g., 2009, 1992, 1993) specifies three aspects of productivity: realised, expanding and potential productivity, measured in different ways. The measures are based on the frequencies of tokens (all words containing the affix or morphological category in question), types (different words containing the affix) and hapax legomena (words occurring only once) in a corpus. **Realised productivity** is measured in type frequency: the number of different words formed using the affix estimates how the productivity has been realised up to the point or period in time represented by the corpus. **Potential productivity** is measured as the proportion of hapax legomena containing the affix out of all tokens containing the affix: this assesses the growth rate of the category. Put simply, the reasoning behind this is that hapax frequency approximates the number of new types, as it is among hapax legomena that most new types are found (Baayen, 1993, p. 189). Finally, **expanding productivity** is measured as the proportion of hapax legomena containing the affix out of all hapax legomena in the corpus: this estimates the rate at which the category is expanding relative to the overall lexicon. When comparing the productivity of affixes, they may be ranked in a different order depending on the measure used, as the measures represent different facets of productivity. Where possible, therefore, all three measures should be taken into account when estimating productivity; however, it has been shown that measures based on hapax legomena yield unreliable results in smaller corpora, including the demographically sampled spoken subcorpus of BNC1994 (Baayen, 1993; Säily & Suomela, 2009; Säily, 2011; see further Section 9.3.2 below).

Studies of morphological productivity have tended to focus on derivation (e.g., Plag, 1999). Inflection is traditionally regarded as more productive than derivation (Stump, 1998, p. 16) and has even been claimed to be fully productive (Haspelmath, 2002, p. 75; Plag, 2003, p. 16). Previous sources, however, make further distinctions between contextual (syntax-dependent) and inherent inflection (which is not required by syntax; cf., e.g., Booij, 1996, pp. 2–3). Examples of inherent inflection include number-marking in nouns, or comparative and superlative degree for adjectives. Booij (1996) argues that inherent inflection is more similar to derivation and may be subject to similar lexicalisation tendencies and constraints on productivity. To give an example, some nouns in English cannot be pluralised because their semantics does not allow for the addition of an affix meaning 'more than one instance of'. Along the same lines, Gaeta (2007) studies a range of derivational and inherently inflectional affixes in Italian and shows not only that the potential productivity of the affixes forms a cline from derivation to inflection, but also that inflectional productivity varies across both affixes and entire inflectional categories. The study also suggests that some of this variation may be due to competing periphrastic forms.

Productivity, then, is not just a property of morphology. As recent work within Construction Grammar shows, productivity can be applied to different types of form–content pairings ('constructions') at different levels of granularity (see Perek, 2016; Zeldes, 2009, 2013; Hilpert, 2013). Furthermore, as noted above, productivity may be either constrained or influenced by various factors. Plag (2006, pp. 550–551) lists a number of structural factors, which are mostly process-specific and include phonological, morphological, syntactic and semantic constraints. External factors have chiefly been studied with respect to derivational productivity and focus on pragmatic, stylistic and sociolinguistic considerations (the latter including gender, age, region, education, socio-economic status, and register in terms of participant relations; see Štekauer et al., 2005; Keune, van Hout, & Baayen, 2006; Schröder, 2008; Palmer, 2009; Gardner, 2013; Säily, 2014). Even though social factors were already regarded as important by Romaine (1983), they have only recently started to be studied in more detail. Moreover, the extent to which these factors are applicable to non-derivational kinds of productivity is yet to be determined.

Our goal is therefore to extend previous work that has challenged the strict separation of derivation and inflection. While Gaeta (2007) found a cline between the productivity of inflectional and derivational affixes, we wish to see if there is variation and change within the productivity of individual inflectional affixes (in our case, in the use of the *-er* comparative strategy) and if so, whether it is similar to that discovered in derivational affixes (e.g., Säily, 2014). In this respect, we are particularly interested in whether the productivity of inflectional comparison may be constrained by external factors of change. We will also study productivity beyond morphology by including in our analysis the periphrastic comparative construction [*more* +ADJ]. Although our work cannot be couched within any specific theoretical framework, it will pay attention to both internal and external factors as both are considered crucial to understanding language variation and change (cf. the embedding problem presented by Weinreich, Labov, & Herzog, 1968).

9.3 Materials and Methods

9.3.1 Materials

Our data comes from two main sources, the spoken subcorpus of the original British National Corpus (the Spoken BNC1994) and the Spoken BNC2014S—the early-access Sample of the newly compiled Spoken British National Corpus 2014 (see Chapter 1). The reason behind this dual-corpus choice was not only to increase the robustness of our claims (as noted in the previous section, we adopt a holistic approach to type analysis), but also to allow for a short-term diachronic dimension in our study.

We considered all of the BNC2014 data made available to us (see Section 9.3.2). From the Spoken BNC1994, however, we took a random sample of 500 speakers from the 'demographically sampled' part of the collection (the Spoken BNC1994DS, recorded c. 1991–1993), which is the part of the BNC1994 subcorpus that matches best the new BNC2014 (meta)data and therefore allows for greatest reliability of short-term diachronic comparisons. Overall, our dataset comprises c. six million words: 1.33 million words from the Spoken BNC1994DS, and 4.76 million words from the Spoken BNC2014S.

9.3.2 Methods

The data was retrieved via CQPweb (Hardie, 2012) using a combination of lemma and POS tag searches and then post-processed with Python scripts; we used the search term *er_AJC or *er_JJR for inflectional comparatives (e.g., *friendlier, colder*) and more *_AJ0 or more *_JJ for the periphrastic ones (e.g., *more friendly, more interesting*).[1] The initial dataset was later manually checked and pruned down to relevant types and tokens. Discarded examples comprised:

- Incorrectly tagged lexemes. For instance, the nouns *lighter* or *cooler* (e.g., *do you have a **lighter**?*) or verbs such as *lower* (e.g., ***lower** the tax rate*).

- Instances where the relevant comparative forms are part of a set phrase or expression (e.g., *the **bigger** the **better**; it makes it all the **more serious***). In these cases, the productivity of the individual lexical element may be compromised by its function within a bigger unit.
- Cases where the comparative is part of a nominal, adjectival or verbal lexeme (e.g., ***higher** education, the **greater** good*).
- Examples featuring comparative forms in adverbial functions (e.g., *I cycle so much **faster**/you could have delivered **funnier** that kind of thing*), as well as cases where *more* performs determinative functions (e.g., *we need **more** modern literature in the department/I have **more** grey hair than she does*).
- Double comparative tokens (e.g., *He is **more poorer** than X*). The frequency of these structures was, across BNC compilations, too low to draw any meaningful results from the analyses.
- Cases where the speaker hesitates and repeats the comparative (e.g., *it is easier it is **easier** to see*). The first comparative token of the repetition was systematically discarded from the tally (see underlined *easier* above), the second (repeated) form was included.

In line with previous literature, the relevant tokens were classified according to a set of intra- and extra-linguistic factors. Intra-linguistically, the data was coded for the following well-established morphosyntactic considerations:

- Number of syllables of the positive adjective
- Syntactic position (attributive/predicative/postpositive comparatives)
- Presence/absence of a second term of comparison (a *than* phrase)
- Presence of adverbial premodifiers (e.g., ***much/a bit/a lot** more friendly*)
- Presence of complements (e.g., *he was more aware [of X]/I am a lot more careful [**with X**]*)

The external variables considered included the **gender, age** and **social class** of the speaker. Speakers whose gender and/or age group was unknown were discarded from the tally. Note also that some slight mismatches were observed in the age and social class categories used across BNC compilations. To elaborate, the BNC1994 works with the age groups [0–14], [15–24], [25–34], [35–44], [45–59] and [60+], whereas the Sample version of the BNC2014 uses the categories [0–10], [11–18], [19–29], [30–39], [40–49], . . . , [90–99]. To make the categories more comparable, we collapsed them into three groups for both corpora: [0–24], [25–44] and [45–99] for the BNC1994, and [0–29], [30–49] and [50–99] for the BNC2014. Similarly, the social class distinctions were somewhat different in the two corpora, but we were provided with an automatic mapping from the BNC2014 categories to the BNC1994 categories, which are based on Social Grade, determined by occupation (National Readership Survey, 2015). For ease of analysis, we collapsed the categories into two groups: middle class (A+B+C1) and working class (C2+D+E). In the BNC2014, we also had access to the external factor of **education**: secondary school, college/sixth form and university. Regional variation was not examined as our initial explorations did not yield (socio)linguistically interesting results.

We also considered the influence of **register**, in order to check whether our sociolinguistic results remained the same when focusing on speech in a similar setting. In particular, we were interested in everyday discussions among family and close friends at home, as this is the setting that represents the widest range of social groups (as opposed to, e.g., 'work', which only represents those who work and is male-skewed at least in the BNC1994). Again, the differences in the corpus metadata made such comparisons somewhat challenging: in the BNC1994DS we had access to the locale of the conversation, while in the BNC2014S locale was not directly available but there was information on the relationship between the speakers. Hence for register-specific comparisons, in the BNC1994 we focused on conversations that took place at home (e.g., 'home', 'kitchen', 'bedroom') and in the BNC2014 we focused on conversations among close family, partners, and very close friends.

In our quantitative analysis of productivity, we focused on realised productivity, as measured by **type frequency** (for a justification of this, see Säily, 2014, pp. 238–239).[2] For example, to assess whether there was change in the productivity of inflectional adjective comparison over time, we initially counted the number of different adjectives used in such comparisons in both the Spoken BNC1994DS and Spoken BNC2014S, and compared these numbers with each other. Similarly, to study sociolinguistic variation in productivity, we first considered similar comparisons across subcorpora that represented different social categories. Here we faced three methodological challenges:

- How to compare type frequencies among **corpora of different sizes**? If we observe one hundred types in a corpus with one million words, how many types would we expect to see in a corpus with two million words?
- How large a difference in type frequencies is **statistically significant**? Could the findings be explained by mere random chance?
- How to deal with **outliers**? How do we know if our findings are representative of the entire social category, and not, e.g., of the influence of a speaker's idiolectal preferences?

To address these challenges, we first divided the corpus into relatively large **samples** so that, e.g., individual idiosyncrasies or one-off events only influenced a small number of samples. In our case, we made the choice that one sample corresponded to all utterances of **one speaker in one setting** (in total 2,800 samples in the Spoken BNC1994DS and 1,493 samples in the Spoken BNC2014S). This allowed us to unambiguously associate both speaker-specific metadata (e.g., age and social class) and register-specific metadata (e.g., locale) with each sample. Then we constructed a large number of **random re-orderings** (permutations) of the samples, in order to learn the typical relationship between type frequency and token frequency in the corpus under study. This information can be represented as a **type accumulation curves** (see Figure 9.1).

Figure 9.1 presents the type accumulation curve for inflectional adjective comparison in the entire dataset that consists of both BNC1994 and BNC2014 samples. The x axis shows the token frequency, while the y axis records the type frequency. The darker shading indicates more typical values; for example, a random collection of samples with 1,000 tokens is expected to contain c. eighty to ninety-five types, whereas a collection with 2,000 tokens is expected to contain c. 105–120 types.

The method allows us to pick a subcorpus of interest—e.g., the subcorpus that consists of the BNC1994 samples only, or the subcorpus of female speakers—and compare the number of types and tokens in it with

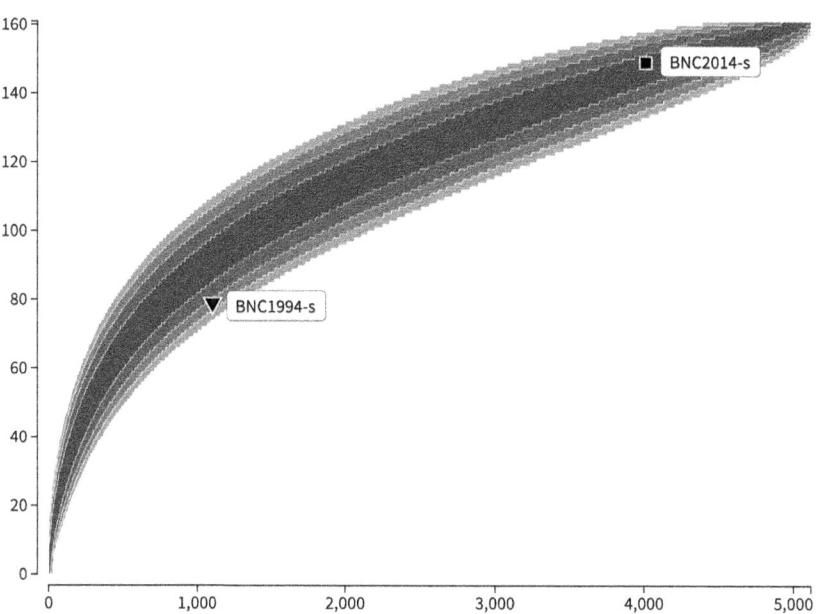

Figure 9.1 Type accumulation curve: type frequency (y axis) vs. token frequency (x axis). Inflectional adjective comparison in the entire corpus (BNC1994-s + BNC2014-s). Dark shading indicates the range of the most common values.

the overall type accumulation curve. We can also zoom in on internal factors: to give an example, we can calculate type and token frequencies for only those adjective comparisons with adverbial premodifiers and see if similar variation between subcorpora is present in this dataset (see Section 9.4 below). Note, however, that in order to compare internal factors with each other, a slightly different (and cruder) approach was taken: we split the corpus into samples that consisted of just one occurrence of adjective comparison. Here, more care was needed in the interpretation of the results, as a single speaker was potentially represented by a large number of samples.[3]

Overall, the three above-mentioned challenges were met in that:

- We do not need to compare, e.g., the BNC1994 and BNC2014 with each other; we can compare, e.g., the BNC1994 with random collections of samples from the BNC1994 and BNC2014 that happen to have the same token frequency as the BNC1994.
- We can directly assess the statistical significance of the findings (see Section 9.4.1 for a concrete example). In essence, we are testing hypotheses using the statistical technique of permutation testing.
- The findings are robust to outliers: a small number of highly atypical samples cannot have much influence on the findings.

Some computer programs were naturally needed to conduct this kind of study. We imported our data to the *types2* **software** (Suomela, 2016), which takes care of the numerical calculations related to the permutation testing, and produces interactive visualisations that can be used to explore type and token frequencies in different subcorpora. The tool also takes care of the issue of **false discovery rate** (FDR) control in studies in which we test a large number of hypotheses. For more details on the methodological background and on the software that we use, see Säily and Suomela (2009, 2017).

9.4 Analysis

9.4.1 Overview

Let us first examine the overall type and token frequencies of inflectional and periphrastic comparison in our two corpora. In the Spoken BNC1994DS, we find seventy-eight types and 1,106 tokens for inflectional comparison, and seventy-nine types and 114 tokens for periphrastic comparison.[4] As periphrastic comparison achieves a similar number of types to inflectional comparison in a much lower number of tokens, it is clearly the more productive of the two strategies. However, the difference between the strategies is much less obvious when we focus on disyllabic adjective types (where the two strategies alternate), and we are unable to determine which of the two strategies is more productive in this case.[5] In the Spoken BNC2014S, we find 149 types and 4,010 tokens for inflectional comparison, and 525 types and 1,249 tokens for periphrastic comparison, making the latter again clearly more productive. This time similar results are also obtained for disyllabic types.

Figure 9.1 shows the type accumulation curve for **inflectional comparison** in the BNC1994 and BNC2014 data combined, plotting each corpus on the curve. The BNC1994 has few types compared to randomly sampled subcorpora of the same size: it contains 1,106 tokens and seventy-eight types, and only c. 0.32% of the random collections of samples of this size have such a low number of types. The significantly low productivity of inflectional adjective comparison in the BNC1994 ($p < 0.0032$) implies an **increase in the productivity** of inflectional comparison over time, which will be studied further in Section 9.4.2 below.

As regards **periphrastic comparison**, a noticeable **increase in token frequency** is observed, from 85.5 instances per million words in the BNC1994 to 262.6 in the BNC2014. Moreover, this change does not seem to be due to a small number of outliers, but it is representative of the whole corpus (see Figure 9.2). However, the results do not record any significant change in the productivity, or type frequency, of periphrastic comparison.

Another question of interest concerns the influence of intra- and extra-linguistic factors on the productivity of either comparative strategy. The data analysis reveals **no sociolinguistic variation in the productivity of**

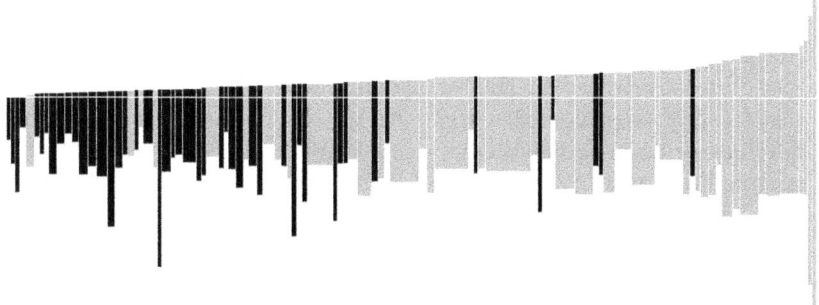

Figure 9.2 Speakers with at least 20,000 words in the corpus; black bars represent speakers in the Spoken BNC1994DS (this also includes speakers outside our random sample of 500) and grey bars represent speakers in the Spoken BNC2014S. The top part indicates the relative frequency of *more* followed by a general adjective not inflected for degree (typically periphrastic adjective comparison), while the bottom part indicates the relative frequency of other occurrences of *more*. The speakers are ordered by the frequency of *more* + adjective; clearly most speakers from the BNC1994 have a low frequency, while most speakers from the BNC2014 have a high frequency.

periphrastic comparison in either corpus, even when the corpora are considered jointly as in Figure 9.1. Although the Spoken BNC2014S shows a non-significant tendency for older speakers and those with a college education to use periphrastic comparison less productively, the trend disappears when we restrict the dataset by register (see Section 9.3.2). Inflectional comparatives feature a somewhat different distribution, as social class and gender considerations do appear to have an impact on their productivity across corpora (see Section 9.4.2.2).

Moving on to a consideration of intra-linguistic factors, **periphrastic comparison** in the BNC2014 appears to be significantly *un*productive when accompanied by an **infinitival or prepositional complement** (see Figure 9.3), and highly productive when no complement/modifier is present. Similar tendencies in terms of infinitival and no complementation are found in the BNC1994; while there is no evidence for the influence of prepositional complementation/postmodification, this may be due to data restrictions, as we took a sample of 500 speakers from the corpus rather than the whole corpus dataset. In other words, the internal factors influencing the productivity of periphrastic comparison seem to have remained qualitatively similar over time.

Along the same lines, **inflectional comparison** is used unproductively with **infinitival complements/modifiers** in both corpora, as can be seen in Table 9.1 (the other complementation patterns do not reach significance with the inflectional strategy). In other words, the number of different adjectives that are used with an infinitival complement/postmodifier is very low across the board. In the BNC2014, for example, only 14 different adjectives are used in inflectional comparison with infinitival complementation: *easier* (the most common type, e.g., *easier to see*), *better*, *cheaper, harder, quicker, nicer, longer, clearer, safer, faster, higher, simpler, slower* and *warmer*. The list is similar in the BNC1994, to the extent that the five most common types are the same, although in a slightly different order. The default option is clearly to have no complement/postmodifier at all, and all other complementation options are quite infrequent.

In addition, there are two internal factors that seem to influence inflectional but not periphrastic comparison. Inflectional comparison is used highly productively (1) in a **predicative position** and (2) with a **premodifying adverb**. Both seem to be new developments in the BNC2014 (see Table 9.2); however, there is also some indication in the BNC1994 of the connection between the predicative position and productivity, as the productivity of inflectional comparison is low in the other syntactic positions. When we consider the corpora jointly, we find further factors according to which the productivity of inflectional comparison has changed, such as the lack of a term of comparison; these will be discussed in the next section.

Overall, the data analysis indicates that, while shifts in usage are attested in periphrastic comparatives, it is the inflectional strategy that

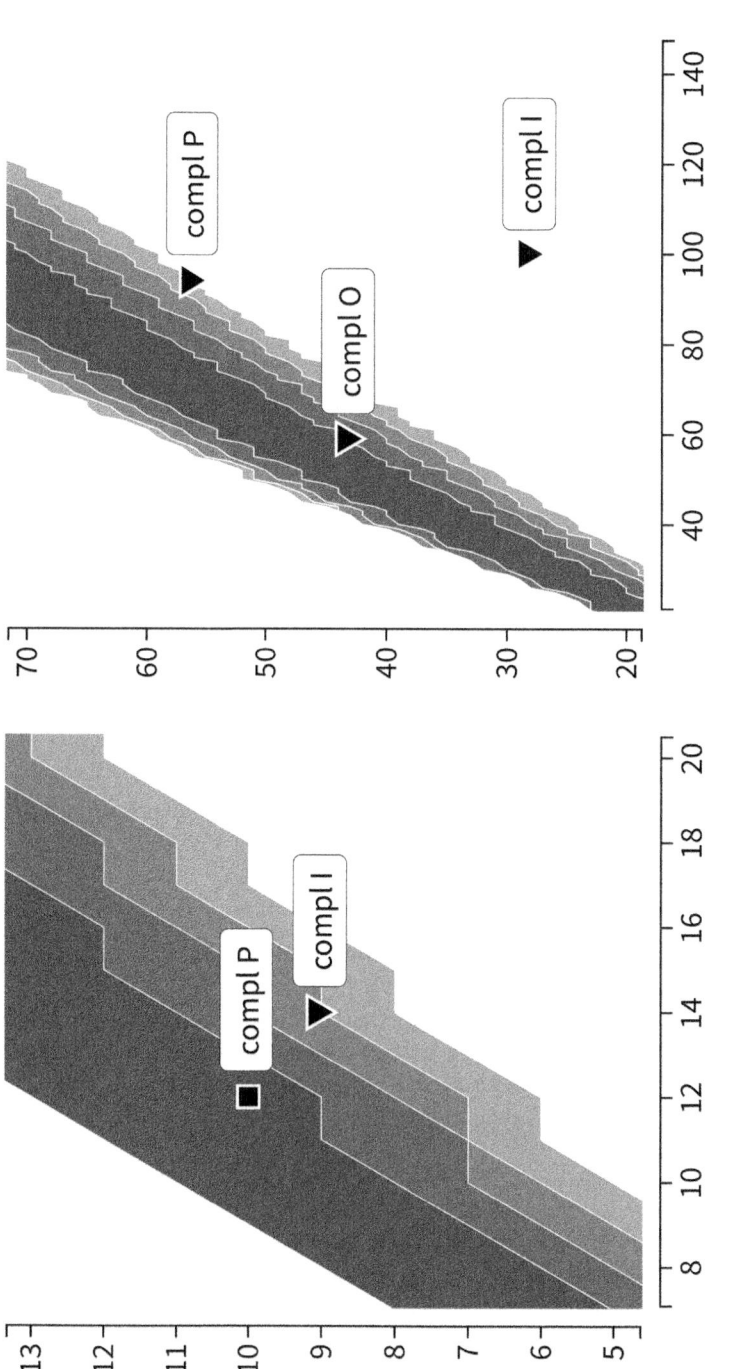

Figure 9.3 Productivity of periphrastic comparison across different complementation patterns in the Spoken BNC1994DS (left) and the Spoken BNC2014S (right), types (*y* axis) vs. tokens (*x* axis). I = infinitival, P = prepositional, O = other.

Table 9.1 Adjective comparison with infinitival complements/modifiers. In each case the number of types is low compared with the expected number of types in a random collection of tokens taken from the same corpus (significance indicated by *p*-values).

Internal Factor	Strategy	Corpus	Types	Tokens	p-Value
infinitival complement/ modifier	inflectional	BNC1994	10	65	< 0.00001
		BNC2014	14	259	< 0.00001
	periphrastic	BNC1994	9	14	0.008
		BNC2014	28	100	< 0.00001

Table 9.2 Internal factors that are associated with high productivity of inflectional comparison in the Spoken BNC2014S.

Internal Factor	Strategy	Corpus	Types	Tokens	p-Value
predicative position	inflectional	BNC1994	77	898	(0.4)
		BNC2014	137	2,685	0.02
premodifying adverb	inflectional	BNC1994	43	221	(0.6)
		BNC2014	96	725	0.0005

has undergone significant changes in productivity, both intra- and extra-linguistically, from the 1990s onwards. The changes and the motivations behind them will be further discussed in Section 9.4.2.

9.4.2 Change in the Productivity of Inflectional Comparison: Close-Up Analysis

9.4.2.1 Internal Factors

Exploratory analysis using *types2* shows that inflectional comparison is used less productively in the Spoken BNC1994DS than in the Spoken BNC2014S with respect to several structural factors: with a premodifying adverb, in the postpositive and predicative positions, with disyllabic adjectives, and when no term of comparison is present (see Table 9.3). This implies that the productivity of inflectional comparison has increased over time, especially within these categories.

How can we interpret these results? As the vast majority of all instances of inflectional comparison are used in the predicative position and/or without a term of comparison, these two categories naturally behave like the corpus as a whole. Nevertheless, the increase in the productivity of inflectional comparison in **predicative positions** is potentially interesting for, historically, the preference for inflectional forms is less marked in these predicative (as well as postpositive) environments, particularly from the 18th century onwards (see González-Díaz, 2008, p. 82).

Table 9.3 Exploring changes in productivity between the Spoken BNC1994DS and Spoken BNC2014S: top results.

Strategy	Corpus	Internal Factor	Type Richness	p-Value
inflectional	BNC1994 + BNC2014	(overall)	low in BNC1994	0.003
		premodifying adverb	low in BNC1994	0.004
		postpositive position	low in BNC1994	0.004
		disyllabic adjective base	low in BNC1994	0.005
		predicative position	low in BNC1994	0.005
		without term of comparison	low in BNC1994	0.008

More generally, the results seem to suggest a recent ongoing expansion of the functional realm of inflectional forms in Present-Day (British) English. This functional expansion is not syntax-specific only: one of the traditional semantic-pragmatic differences between inflectional and periphrastic comparison is that periphrastic comparison allows for a greater emphasis on the actual comparative/degree meaning by having a separate lexical element (*more*) (Curme, 1931, p. 504; Mondorf, 2003; Mondorf, 2009, p. 90ff), whereas the inflectional strategy not only lacks this possibility but also places the comparative element at the end of the word, which in a stress-timed language such as English is less than ideal. It is therefore possible that the **co-occurrence of inflectional comparatives with a degree adverb** (see Table 9.3, e.g., *a bit happier, much colder*) may have become a functional measure to compensate for the semantic difference between the two strategies. It should also be noted here that degree adverbs not only convey emphasis but are often used as indicators of social meanings, particularly as in-group markers (see Macaulay, 2002 among others). Social factors relevant to this change as well as to the overall increase in the productivity of inflectional comparison will be investigated in the next section.

9.4.2.2 *External Factors*

After computing the type accumulation curve for the BNC1994 and BNC2014 data combined (Figure 9.1), we can also plot subcorpora based on social groups onto the curve (Figure 9.4). Gender-based subcorpora show no significant differences, but when looking at social class, we find that working-class speakers ("C2+DE") use inflectional comparison significantly unproductively in the BNC1994, whereas, in the BNC2014, neither working-class nor middle-class speakers differ significantly from the corpus as a whole. Thus, working-class speakers seem to have caught up with middle-class speakers within the twenty-odd years that have elapsed between the two corpora (provided that we trust the categorisation of social classes in both corpora; cf. Section 9.3.2, Section 9.5).

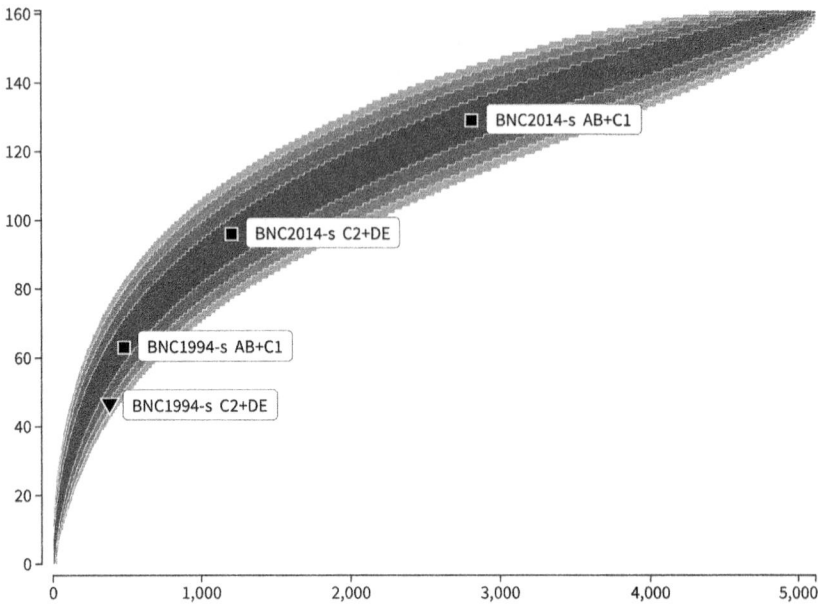

Figure 9.4 Working-class speakers ("C2+DE") use inflectional comparison unproductively in the Spoken BNC1994DS (cf. Figure 9.1). Type frequency (*y* axis) vs. token frequency (*x* axis).

A closer examination of the Spoken BNC1994DS reveals that it is particularly working-class *women* who use inflectional comparison unproductively (similar results are obtained when we restrict the dataset by register to home settings only). Although without reaching statistical significance, Figure 9.5 shows that there is approximately the same number of inflectional comparative tokens from both working-class men ("C2+DE Male") and working-class women ("C2+DE Female"), but the women use fewer adjective types, which implies lower productivity and a higher token frequency per type. Consider, in this connection, example (1) below. As previously noted (see fn. 4), *better* is, overall, one of the most frequently used inflectional forms in our data, and it is high-frequency types like this that are repeated more often by the women.

(1) Don't need that on. That's **better** innit?
                        (BNC1994, KCU 6538–6539, PS0GF: female,
                        working-class, age 24)[6]

Säily (2011, p. 130) finds a similar class-based gender difference in the productivity of the nominal suffix *-ness*. It is as if, in our sample of the BNC1994, lexical diversity is more of a concern for working-class men, whereas women of the same socio-economic status tend to be more

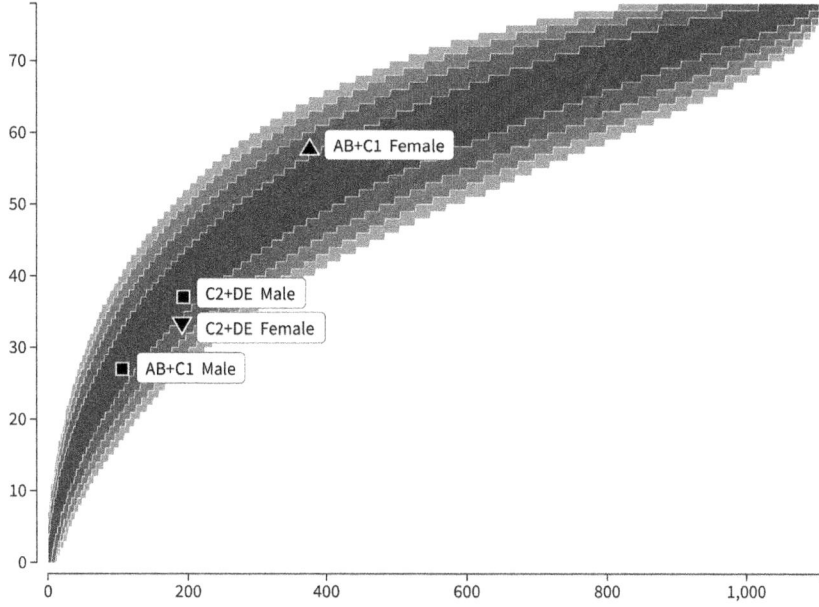

Figure 9.5 In the Spoken BNC1994DS, especially working-class women ("C2+DE Female") use inflectional comparison unproductively. Type frequency (*y* axis) vs. token frequency (*x* axis).

interested in keeping the conversation going by repeating the same few types. Of course, the difference in this case is small; an analysis of the entire demographically sampled spoken section of the BNC1994 would be needed to be able to gain more reliable results.

As noted in the previous section, the increased productivity of inflectional comparatives when premodified by a degree adverb could also be a question of style. Here we find a different pattern: in both the BNC1994 and BNC2014, male speakers have a (non-significant) tendency to use inflectional comparison productively with a premodifying adverb (see Figure 9.6), while social class has no effect. The gender difference seems to have grown more pronounced in the BNC2014, where male speakers use roughly the same number of types as female speakers despite the fact that there is much more data from the latter. While these results become weaker when the dataset is restricted by register, the tendency remains clear, especially in the BNC2014. Furthermore, there seems to be a combined effect of gender and age in the BNC2014 such that the most unproductive speakers are women representing the youngest age group, 0–29. Thus, in this case the change is not about a certain social group catching up with the rest but rather about an increasing difference between two social groups that also becomes more fine-grained over time. In (2), for instance, a male speaker uses *posher*, a hapax legomenon in the corpus. This is representative of the above-mentioned trend, where males

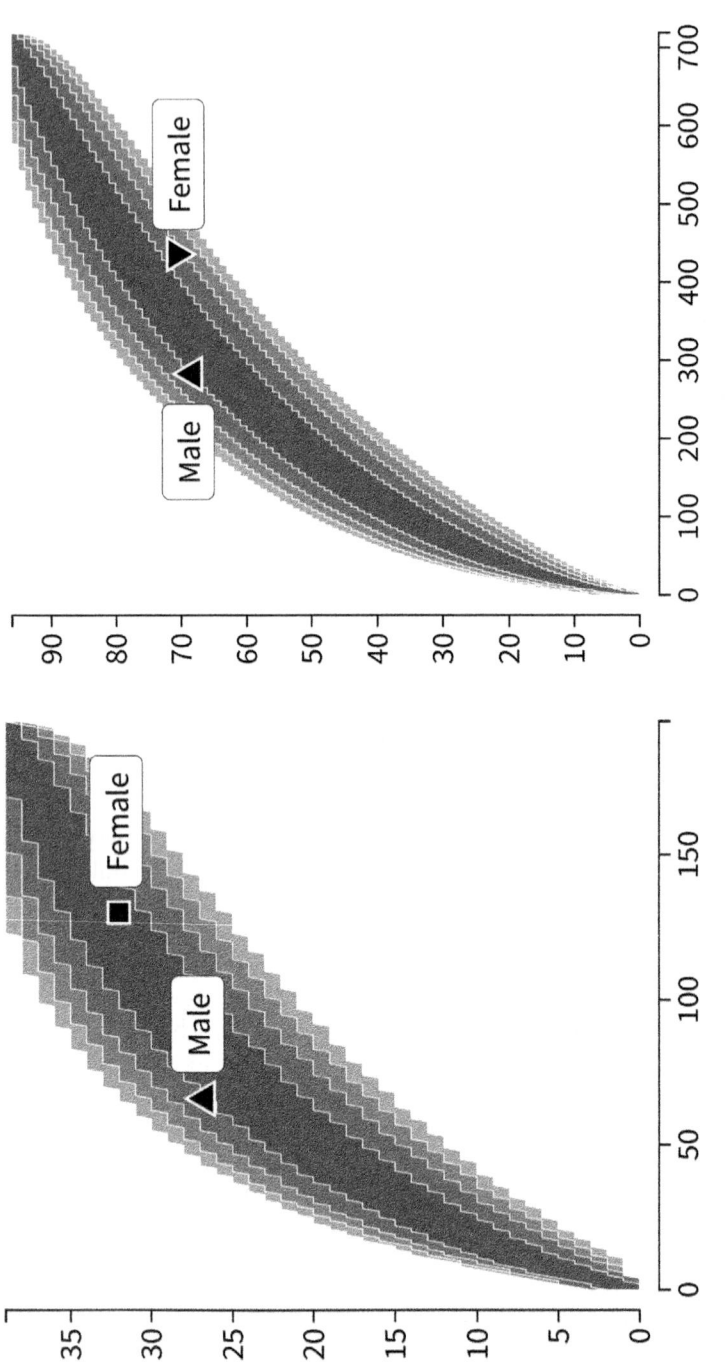

Figure 9.6 Gender variation in inflectional comparison with a premodifying adverb (Spoken BNC1994DS left, Spoken BNC2014S right). Type frequency (*y* axis) vs. token frequency (*x* axis).

consistently combine the *-er* inflectional strategy with a wider range of adjectival bases than their female counterparts.

(2) and older scouser and he moved away to the Wirral so he's probably
     a bit a bit **posher**
                    (BNC2014, SVFH, S0250: male, middle-class, age 26)

9.5 Discussion

The sections above record a noticeable difference in the behaviour of inflectional and periphrastic adjectival comparatives. Some internal factors (presence/absence of complements) seem to have some impact on the productivity of the periphrastic strategy in PDE; nevertheless, the overall picture is that of stability in its productivity over time and across social categories. By contrast, the productivity of inflectional comparison appears to have significantly increased in the recent history of British English and—more importantly for the overarching theme of the present volume—some of this change is clearly due to social factors.

Our results suggest that the change in the productivity of inflectional comparison seems to have been partly the result of working-class women increasing their usage of the strategy, which now closely matches that of the other social groups. This could perhaps be explained by recent changes in the social position of UK working-class women. In our corpora, the proportion of housewives/women not in the workforce has dropped from 13% to 0.5% between the 1990s and 2010s. This drop in the corpus figures partially matches recent statistics on female employment in Britain, which shows a consistent increase in the figures of working women (from 61.8% to 68.8%) in the period 1993–2015.[7] It would therefore not be unreasonable to assume that their incorporation into the UK workforce has had an indirect impact on working women's linguistic identity, causing a levelling of some aspects of their speech style with respect to other social groups. This interpretation, which focuses on both macro-level social categories and style as a means of identity construction, thus surfs on both the first and third waves of sociolinguistics (Eckert, 2012).

It is possible that some of the sociolinguistic variation and change we observed, particularly when it did not reach statistical significance, could be due to chance (cf. Rissanen's, 1989, p. 18 "mystery of vanishing reliability", which refers to dividing the data into ever more detailed categories that end up being too small and thus unrepresentative). However, even when a change is statistically significant, the question remains whether it is really social, or an artefact of the corpus. While our BNC1994 sample is based on the demographically sampled section of the British National Corpus (Burnard, 2007, sec. 1.5.1), the new Spoken BNC2014 has not been sampled demographically. Thus, although specific dialectal areas have been targeted, the sampling procedure has been somewhat "opportunistic" (McEnery & Hardie, 2012, p. 11) in that contributions by the general public were invited through an open call via traditional and social media rather than systematically contacting representatives of specific social groups (Love, Dembry, Hardie, Brezina, & McEnery, 2017). Hence, more research is needed to verify our results and to assess the representativeness of the entire Spoken BNC2014, of which we had at our disposal the early-access Sample (Spoken BNC2014S).

Note, also, that gender variation seems to remain alive and well in other environments, as evidenced by the result that male speakers tend to use inflectional comparison with premodifying adverbs more productively than female speakers in both the BNC1994 and BNC2014 data. Previous research has consistently shown that, in the case of other constructions where the conveyance of degree is at stake (e.g., adverbial intensifiers in adjective modifying functions, as in *very good*, *really important* or *pure fast*), it has been women and young people who have tended to lead the usage and renewal of lexical elements (e.g., Macaulay, 2006; Tagliamonte, 2008; Tagliamonte & Denis, 2014). However, our point of view is different in that we are not focusing on lexical change in individual adverbs, but on variation and change in a morphosyntactic system and, more specifically, in the variety of comparative adjective types used with any premodifying adverb (most often *much*, *a bit*, *a lot*). It may be worth noting here that some studies of derivational productivity (e.g., Keune, van Hout, & Baayen, 2006) have found the most productive speakers to be highly educated older men, so our results align well with theirs.

Finally, the internal factors we have analysed as potentially influencing productivity have previously been used to study the choice between the inflectional and periphrastic strategies. It is noteworthy that the factors seem to behave differently in the holistic study of productivity, on the one hand, and in the variationist study of strategy choice, on the other. While we have found that the productivity of inflectional comparison is high in the predicative position and in the presence of a premodifying adverb, previous research has found that where both inflectional and periphrastic strategies are possible, it is the periphrastic form that is chosen more frequently (in terms of token frequency) in these contexts (González-Díaz, 2008, p. 110ff). However, strategy choice has not yet been studied in the new Spoken BNC2014, so it is possible that preferences may have shifted towards the inflectional form after the early 1990s (cf. the discussion of functional expansion in 9.4.2.1 above). We therefore leave further investigation of this topic to future research.

9.6 Conclusion

The previous section has focused on the system-specific findings of the study. In this section, we briefly point to some of its wider implications.

Our findings have crucially shown that social factors—especially gender and social class—play a role in the productivity of inflectional morphology, opening new areas of inquiry to sociolinguistic research. Put differently, processes of variation and change seem to operate in similar ways across inflectional and derivational productivity. These findings contribute to morphological theory-building by providing concrete evidence of the existence of a cline between derivation and inflection, complementing previous research by, e.g., Gaeta (2007) and Bauer (2004). How that cline is operationalised, i.e., whether any trends could emerge in terms of, e.g., the incidence of factors within and across inflectional/derivational categories, needs to be ascertained by further research.

Furthermore, the study also engages with long-standing diachronic debates about synthetic vs. analytic shifts in English (see Kytö & Romaine, 1997; Szmrecsanyi, 2012, among others). In line with Schwegler (1994), we subscribe to the idea that analyticity and syntheticity are relative terms that can only be applied to particular systems and/or constructions within languages (as opposed to languages per se). Our research further warns about the relativity of such notions, as it records variable results depending on whether one (token) or another (type) principle is taken as starting point: the increase found in the (type) productivity of inflectional comparison would seem to point towards the increasing syntheticity of the comparative system in PDE. By contrast, the rise in token frequency of periphrastic comparison appears to contribute to increasing analyticity. Most importantly to our project, our findings support the hypothesis of a cline between derivation and inflection, which implies that derivation should be viewed as contributing to syntheticity alongside inflection. The rich array of productive derivational affixes in English could then further challenge the idea of increasing analyticity.

Acknowledgements

The authors wish to thank the anonymous reviewers for their helpful feedback. Thanks are also due to CSC—IT Center for Science, Finland, for computational resources. This work was supported in part by the Academy of Finland grant 276349 to the project 'Reassessing language change: the challenge of real time'.

Notes

1 Note that the POS tagset varies slightly across compilations: for example, AJ0 is the POS tag for a general adjective not inflected for degree in BNC1994 (see the CLAWS 5 POS tagset); the corresponding tag in BNC2014 is JJ (see the CLAWS 6 POS tagset). For more information on the different CLAWS tagsets, please see http://ucrel.lancs.ac.uk/claws/.

2 In brief, it could be argued that by only using type frequency and leaving out hapax-based measures, we end up measuring lexical diversity rather

than productivity in the sense of 'readiness to enter into new combinations'. However, measuring change in type frequency between two time periods does provide us with access to formations that are 'new' in the more recent time period in the corpus. While many of the 'corpus-new' formations may not be new to the language of the community as a whole, they may be productive uses in that they are not stored—or are only weakly activated, cf. Baayen (1993)—in the speaker's mental lexicon, so that the speaker produces the formation from its more strongly activated components in the speech situation (e.g., *posh + -er → posher*). This is more likely to happen if the formation is much less frequent than its base (e.g., *posh*: 396 instances in the entire BNC1994, *posher*: seventeen instances; cf. Hay & Baayen, 2002). Hence, many types that are not 'corpus-new' can also be formed productively. We would therefore argue that even though it is clearly imperfect, type frequency can still be a useful measure of productivity.

3 In particular, the *p*-values reported in Tables 9.1 and 9.2 were derived with token-level samples.

4 We have included the highly frequent inflectional type *better*, which has no base, in our analyses. If *better* is removed, the results become similar but weaker.

5 Not all disyllabic bases can take both kinds of comparison (e.g., disyllabic adjectives ending in *-ful* or *-ous* do not normally take inflectional comparison; e.g., ?*cautiouser*, ?*carefuller*). In order to make our results fully comparable, we could have further restricted the bases under analysis. In this chapter, however, we are more interested in variation and change *within* the productivity of either strategy as a whole and, therefore, such considerations were discarded.

6 References to the corpora are given in the following format: corpus, text, speaker: speaker attributes.

7 See www.ons.gov.uk/employmentandlabourmarket/peopleinwork/employ mentandemployeetypes/timeseries/lf25/lms (last accessed 10/02/2017). The word 'partially' needs indeed to be stressed here, as the UK Office for National Statistics does not, to the best of our knowledge, provide specific indication of the socio-economic status (working- or middle-class) of the female workforce recorded in their statistics.

References

Baayen, R. H. (1992). Quantitative aspects of morphological productivity. In G. Booij & J. v. Marle (Eds.), *Yearbook of morphology 1991* (pp. 109–149). Dordrecht: Kluwer.

Baayen, R. H. (1993). On frequency, transparency and productivity. In G. Booij & J. v. Marle (Eds.), *Yearbook of morphology 1992* (pp. 181–208). Dordrecht: Kluwer.

Baayen, R. H. (2009). Corpus linguistics in morphology: Morphological productivity. In A. Lüdeling & M. Kytö (Eds.), *Corpus linguistics: An international handbook* (pp. 899–919). Berlin: Mouton de Gruyter.

Bauer, L. (2004). The function of word-formation and the inflection-derivation distinction. In H. Aertsen, M. Hannay, & R. Lyall (Eds.), *Words in their places: A festschrift for J. Lachlan Mackenzie* (pp. 283–292). Amsterdam: Vrije Universiteit.

BNC1994 = *The British National Corpus*, version 3 (BNC XML edition). (2007). Distributed by Oxford University Computing Services on behalf of the BNC Consortium. Retrieved from www.natcorp.ox.ac.uk/

Bolinger, D. L. (1948). On defining the morpheme. *Word, 4*, 18–23.

Booij, G. (1996). Inherent versus contextual inflection and the split morphology hypothesis. In G. Booij & J. v. Marle (Eds.), *Yearbook of morphology 1995* (pp. 1–16). Dordrecht: Kluwer.

Bresnan, J. (1977). Variables in the theory of transformations. In P. W. Culicover, T. Wasow, & A. Akmajian (Eds.), *Formal syntax* (pp. 115–122). New York, NY: Academic Press.

Brinton, L. J., & Traugott, E. C. (2005). *Lexicalization and language change.* Cambridge: Cambridge University Press.

Burnard, L. (Ed.). (2007). *Reference guide for the British National Corpus (XML edition).* Published for the British National Corpus Consortium by the Research Technologies Service at Oxford University Computing Services. Retrieved from www.natcorp.ox.ac.uk/docs/URG/

Cresswell, M. J. (1976). The semantics of degree. In B. H. Partee (Ed.), *Montague grammar* (pp. 261–292). London, New York, NY: Academic Press.

Curme, G. O. (1931). *A grammar of the English language: Volume II: Syntax.* Boston, MA: D. C. Heath & Company.

Danchev, A. (1992). The evidence for analytic and synthetic developments in English. In M. Rissanen, O. Ihalainen, T. Nevalainen, & I. Taavitsainen (Eds.), *History of Englishes: New methods and interpretations in historical linguistics* (pp. 25–41). Berlin: Mouton de Gruyter.

Eckert, P. (2012). Three waves of variation study: The emergence of meaning in the study of sociolinguistic variation. *Annual Review of Anthropology, 41*, 87–100.

Gaeta, L. (2007). On the double nature of productivity in inflectional morphology. *Morphology, 17*(2), 181–205.

Gardner, A. (2013). *Derivation in Middle English: Regional and text type variation.* Ph.D dissertation. Zurich: University of Zurich.

Gathercole, V. (1979). *Birdies like birdseed the better than buns: A study of relational comparatives and their acquisition.* Ph.D dissertation. Lawrence, KS: University of Kansas.

Gathercole, V. (1985). More and more about more. *Journal of Experimental Child Psychology, 40*(1), 73–104.

Gitterman, D., & Johnston, J. R. (1983). Talking about comparisons: A study of young children's comparative adjective usage. *Journal of Child Language, 10*, 605–621.

González-Díaz, V. (2004). Adjectival double periphrastic comparison in EModE: A socio-stylistic analysis. *Folia Linguistica Historica, 25*, 177–210.

González-Díaz, V. (2006). The origin of English periphrastic comparison. *English Studies, 84*, 707–734.

González-Díaz, V. (2008). *English adjective comparison: A historical perspective.* Amsterdam: John Benjamins.

Graziano-King, J. (1999). *Acquisition of comparative forms in English.* Ph.D dissertation. New York, NY: The Graduate School of the City University of New York.

Graziano-King, J., & Cairns, H. S. (2005). Acquisition of English comparative adjectives. *Journal of Child Language, 32*, 345–373.

Hardie, A. (2012). CQPweb—combining power, flexibility and usability in a corpus analysis tool. *International Journal of Corpus Linguistics, 17*(3), 380–409.

Haspelmath, M. (2002). *Understanding morphology*. London: Arnold.

Hay, J., & Baayen, R. H. (2002). Parsing and productivity. In G. Booij & J. v. Marle (Eds.), *Yearbook of morphology 2001* (pp. 203–235). Dordrecht: Kluwer.

Hilpert, M. (2008). The English comparative—language structure and language use. *English Language and Linguistics, 12*(3), 395–417.

Hilpert, M. (2010). Comparing the comparative: A corpus-based study of comparative constructions in English and Swedish. In H. Boas (Ed.), *Contrastive studies in construction grammar* (pp. 22–41). Amsterdam: John Benjamins.

Hilpert, M. (2013). *Constructional change in English: Developments in allomorphy, word formation, and syntax*. Cambridge: Cambridge University Press.

Hohaus, V., Tiemann, S., & Beck, S. (2014). Acquisition of comparative constructions. *Language Acquisition, 21*(3), 215–249.

Huddleston, R. (1967). More on the English comparative. *Journal of Linguistics, 3*, 91–102.

Huddleston, R., & Pullum, G. K. (2002). *The Cambridge grammar of the English language*. Cambridge: Cambridge University Press.

Jespersen, O. (1949). *A modern English grammar on historical principles. Part VII: Syntax*. Copenhagen: Ejnar Munksgaard.

Keune, K., Hout, R. v., & Baayen, R. H. (2006). Socio-geographic variation in morphological productivity in spoken Dutch: A comparison of statistical techniques. In J-M. Viprey and Lexicometrica (Eds.), *Actes de JADT 2006 : 8es Journées internationales d'Analyse statistique des Données Textuelles* (pp. 571–581). Besançon: Université de Franche-Comté.

Knüpfer, H. (1921). Die Anfange der periphrastischen Komparation im Englischen. *Englische Studien, 55*, 321–389.

Kytö, M. (1996). 'The best and most excellentest way': The rivalling forms of adjective comparison in Late Middle and Early Modern English. In J. Svartvik (Ed.), *Words: Proceedings of an international symposium, Lund, 25–26 August 1995* (pp. 124–144). Stockholm: Kungl. Vitterhets Historie och Antikvitets Akademien.

Kytö, M., & Romaine, S. (1997). Competing forms of adjective comparison in Modern English: What could be more quicker and easier and more effective? In T. Nevalainen & L. Kahlas-Tarkka (Eds.), *To explain the present: Studies in the changing English language in honour of Matti Rissanen* (pp. 329–352). Helsinki: Société Néophilologique.

Kytö, M., & Romaine, S. (2006). Adjective comparison in nineteenth-century English. In M. Kytö, M. Rydén, & E. Smitterberg (Eds.), *Nineteenth-century English: Stability and change* (pp. 194–214). Cambridge: Cambridge University Press.

Leech, G., & Culpeper, J. (1997). The comparison of adjectives in recent British English. In T. Nevalainen & L. Kahlas-Tarkka (Eds.), *To explain the present: Studies in the changing English language in honour of Matti Rissanen* (pp. 353–373). Helsinki: Société Néophilologique.

Lindquist, H. (2000). Livelier or more lively? Syntactic and contextual factors influencing the comparison of disyllabic adjectives. In J. M. Kirk (Ed.), *Corpora galore: Analyses and techniques in describing English* (pp. 125–132). Amsterdam: Rodopi.

Love, R., Dembry, C., Hardie, A., Brezina, V., & McEnery, T. (2017). The Spoken BNC2014: Designing and building a spoken corpus of everyday conversations. *International Journal of Corpus Linguistics*, 22(3), 319–344.

Macaulay, R. (2002). Extremely interesting, very interesting, or only quite interesting? Adverbs and social class. *Journal of Sociolinguistics*, 6(3), 398–417.

Macaulay, R. (2006). Pure grammaticalization: The development of a teenage intensifier. *Language Variation and Change*, 18(3), 267–283.

Matsui, C. (2010). *-er* type or *more* type adjectives of comparison in English. *Studia Neophilologica*, 82(2), 188–202.

McEnery, T., & Hardie, A. (2012). *Corpus linguistics: Method, theory and practice*. Cambridge: Cambridge University Press.

Mondorf, B. (2003). Support for *more*-support. In G. Rohdenburg & B. Mondorf (Eds.), *Determinants of grammatical variation in English* (pp. 251–304). Berlin, New York, NY: Mouton de Gruyter.

Mondorf, B. (2007). Recalcitrant problems of comparative alternation and new insights emerging from internet data. In M. Hundt, N. Nesselhauf, & C. Biewer (Eds.), *Corpus linguistics and the web* (pp. 211–232). Amsterdam: Rodopi.

Mondorf, B. (2009). *More support for more-support: The role of processing constraints on the choice between synthetic and analytic comparative forms.* Amsterdam: John Benjamins.

Mossé, F. (1952). *A handbook of Middle English*. Baltimore, London: The John Hopkins University Press.

National Readership Survey. (2015). *Social grade*. Retrieved from www.nrs.co.uk/nrs-print/lifestyle-and-classification-data/social-grade/

Palmer, C. C. (2009). *Borrowings, derivational morphology, and perceived productivity in English, 1300–1600*. Ph.D dissertation. Ann Arbor, MI: University of Michigan.

Perek, F. (2016). Using distributional semantics to study syntactic productivity in diachrony: A case study. *Linguistics*, 54(1), 149–188.

Plag, I. (1999). *Morphological productivity: Structural constraints in English derivation*. Berlin: Mouton de Gruyter.

Plag, I. (2003). *Word-formation in English*. Cambridge: Cambridge University Press.

Plag, I. (2006). Productivity. In B. Aarts & A. McMahon (Eds.), *The handbook of English linguistics* (pp. 537–556). Oxford: Wiley-Blackwell.

Poutsma, H. (1914). *A grammar of Late Modern English*. Groningen: Noordhoff.

Quirk, R., Greenbaum, S., Leech, G., & Svartvik, J. (1985). *A comprehensive grammar of the English language*. London: Longman.

Rissanen, M. (1989). Three problems connected with the use of diachronic corpora. *ICAME Journal*, 13, 16–19.

Romaine, S. (1983). On the productivity of word formation rules and limits of variability in the lexicon. *Australian Journal of Linguistics*, 3(2), 177–200.

Rusiecki, J. (1985). *Adjectives and comparison in English: A semantic study*. London, New York, NY: Longman.

Säily, T. (2011). Variation in morphological productivity in the BNC: Sociolinguistic and methodological considerations. *Corpus Linguistics and Linguistic Theory*, 7(1), 119–141.

Säily, T. (2014). *Sociolinguistic variation in English derivational productivity: Studies and methods in diachronic corpus linguistics.* Helsinki: Société Néophilologique.

Säily, T., & Suomela, J. (2009). Comparing type counts: The case of women, men and *-ity* in early English letters. In A. Renouf & A. Kehoe (Eds.), *Corpus linguistics: Refinements and reassessments* (pp. 87–109). Amsterdam: Rodopi.

Säily, T., & Suomela, J. (2017). *types2*: Exploring word-frequency differences in corpora. In T. Hiltunen, J. McVeigh, & T. Säily (Eds.), *Big and rich data in English corpus linguistics: Methods and explorations.* Helsinki: VARIENG. Retrieved from http://www.helsinki.fi/varieng/series/volumes/19/saily_suomela/

Schröder, A. (2008). *On the productivity of verbal prefixation in English.* Habilitationsschrift, Martin-Luther-Universität Halle-Wittenberg.

Schwegler, A. (1994). Analysis and synthesis. In R. E. Asher & J. M. Y. Simpson (Eds.), *The encyclopedia of language and linguistics* (Vol. I, pp. 111–114). Oxford: Pergamon Press.

Štekauer, P., Chapman, D., Tomaščíková, S., & Franko, Š. (2005). Word-formation as creativity within productivity constraints: Sociolinguistic evidence. *Onomasiology Online, 6,* 1–55.

Strang, B. (1970). *A history of English.* London: Methuen.

Stump, G. T. (1998). Inflection. In A. Spencer & A. M. Zwicky (Eds.), *The handbook of morphology* (pp. 13–43). Oxford: Wiley-Blackwell.

Suomela, J. (2016). *types2: Type and hapax accumulation curves.* Computer program. Retrieved from http://users.ics.aalto.fi/suomela/types2/

Szmrecsanyi, B. (2005). Language users as creatures of habit: A corpus-based analysis of persistence in spoken English. *Corpus Linguistics and Linguistic Theory, 1*(1), 113–150.

Szmrecsanyi, B. (2012). Analyticity and syntheticity in the history of English. In T. Nevalainen & E. C. Traugott (Eds.), *The Oxford handbook of the history of English* (pp. 654–665). Oxford: Oxford University Press.

Tagliamonte, S. A. (2008). So different and pretty cool! Recycling intensifiers in Toronto, Canada. *English Language and Linguistics, 12,* 361–394.

Tagliamonte, S. A., & Denis, D. (2014). Expanding the transmission/diffusion dichotomy: Evidence from Canada. *Language, 90*(1), 90–136.

van Rooij, R. (2010). Explicit versus implicit comparatives. In P. Égré & N. Klinedinst (Eds.), *Vagueness and language use* (pp. 51–72). Houndsmills: Palgrave Macmillan.

van Rooij, R. (2011). Measurement and interadjective comparisons. *Journal of Semantics, 28,* 335–358.

Weinreich, U., Labov, W., & Herzog, M. I. (1968). Empirical foundations for a theory of language change. In W. P. Lehmann & Y. Malkiel (Eds.), *Directions for historical linguistics: A symposium* (pp. 95–188). Austin: University of Texas Press.

Zeldes, A. (2009). Quantifying constructional productivity with unseen slot members. In A. Feldman & B. Lönneker-Rodman (Eds.), *CALC '09: Proceedings of the NAACL HLT workshop on Computational Approaches to Linguistic Creativity* (pp. 47–54). Stroudsburg, PA: Association for Computational Linguistics.

Zeldes, A. (2013). Productive argument selection: Is lexical semantics enough? *Corpus Linguistics and Linguistic Theory, 9*(2), 263–291.

10 The Dative Alternation Revisited

Fresh Insights From Contemporary British Spoken Data

Gard B. Jenset, Barbara McGillivray and Michael Rundell

10.1 Motivation

A well-known feature of English grammar is the dative alternation, whereby a verb may be used in a V-NP-NP construction (*Give me the money*) or with a prepositional phrase in the pattern V-NP-PP, typically with the preposition *to* (*Give the money to me*). In this study, we use data from the early access Sample of the Spoken British National Corpus 2014 (the Spoken BNC2014S) to investigate the behaviour of six high-frequency verbs whose argument structure preferences include the dative alternation. Given that speakers have both patterns available to them, our goal is to discover whether the choice of pattern is motivated rather than arbitrary—and if so, which factors influence that choice.

Although the dative alternation is a well-researched topic, most published work draws either on introspection or on data from written sources. Using contemporary unscripted spoken text from face-to-face conversations takes us into new territory, especially as the linguistic data in the Spoken BNC2014S are complemented by rich sociolinguistic information on participating speakers. By "sociolinguistic information" we mean the social phenomena that co-occur with linguistic variables (Bayley, 2002, p. 118). The corpus represents a powerful new research resource, and in this chapter we show how it yields new insights into the use of the dative alternation.

10.2 Previous Research

The dative alternation is one of several English constructions that offer the speaker a choice in how to order the information in an utterance. Although such variation can be investigated from several perspectives (Arnold, Losongco, Wasow, & Ginstrom, 2000, p. 28), our starting point is the identification of factors that correctly predict the choice of construction. In the case of the dative alternation, it is well established that the structural complexity, or heaviness, of constituents plays a role (Arnold et al., 2000). This is in accordance with Behagel's Law, according to which short constituents occur before long ones (Köhler, 1999; Arnold et al., 2000, p. 29). Additionally, Arnold et al. demonstrated that information status, or 'givenness', plays a role, and that givenness and heaviness are partially independent constraints modulated by the strength of their effects. In their ground-breaking quantitative study of the English dative alternation, Bresnan, Cueni, Nikitina, and Baayen (2007) showed that intuitions are insufficient for investigating the intricacies of the dative alternation, and that the range of possible variation is greater than had previously been assumed. Using multivariate statistical techniques (generalised linear regression modelling), they confirmed that discourse factors have an independent role to play, and that these effects are significant even when conditioned on specific verbs and verb senses. Jenset and Johansson (2013) used a large set of data from the Web to study the effects of the semantics of the theme, e.g., the thing being given in sentences of the type "gave the X to her". They found semantic effects which suggest that the choice of construction is moderated by the semantics of the theme. However, to retrieve the data from unannotated text, Jenset and Johansson extracted only data with pronominal recipients, which might have affected the results.

In contrast with the discourse and grammatical factors influencing the dative alternation, the effects of sociolinguistic variables at the level of the individual is less clear. So far, sociolinguistic studies have mainly identified differences between major varieties of English, such as Australian English (Bresnan & Ford, 2010), New Zealand English (Bresnan & Hay, 2008) and African-American English (Kendall, Bresnan, & Van Herk, 2011). The results from these studies all point to a largely shared English grammar with respect to the dative alternation, but with minor probabilistic variations, such as the New Zealand tendency to produce more inanimate recipients in the V-NP-NP construction (Bresnan & Hay, 2008). However, this still leaves open the status of individual sociolinguistic variables such as age or education. In their study of the dative alternation in African-American English, Kendall et al. (2011) found that, with a binary logistic regression model, gender and age were not statistically significant predictors of the dative alternation. This result might be due to the use of written data, but other studies based on spoken data, such as Bresnan and Hay (2008) and Bresnan and Ford (2010), reach the same conclusion. However, these studies rely in part on the Switchboard corpus (Godfrey, Holliman, & McDaniel, 1992), which consists of recordings of telephone conversations between strangers. It is possible that a corpus of unscripted, face-to-face dialogue between speakers who know one another might lead to different results.

10.3 Research Goals

The objective of this study is to identify those factors that might influence speakers to prefer one dative pattern over the other in the Spoken BNC2014S data. The range of potentially significant features is broad, so there are numerous candidates to choose from. In the Spoken BNC2014S dataset, the raw language data are semantically tagged (based on UCREL's semantic analysis system, USAS, whose tags are available at http://ucrel. lancs.ac.uk/usas/), and further supplemented by rich sociolinguistic metadata, which provide a snapshot of speakers' age, gender, level of education, occupation, dialect and socio-economic status. The annotation also tells us about the closeness of the relationships between the participants in any interaction. Any or all of these factors could have a bearing on the choice of construction, as could contextual features such as the type of direct and indirect objects (which brings in questions of the verb's selectional preferences) and their length. Our goal, therefore, is to determine the effects, if any, of these variables on speakers' choices.

High-frequency verbs like the ones examined in this study are typically complex in terms of their semantics, syntax and phraseology. So the initial stage of data extraction, aimed at identifying relevant instances of the dative constructions, generated considerable noise. A manual process of cleaning and annotation followed, and the resulting set of around 2,000 concordance lines formed the basis for the investigation. However, with such a large number and wide range of potentially significant variables, the task of discovering whether the choice of construction is motivated (and if so, which factors play a part in motivating it) is one of considerable complexity. An important feature of this study is our use of state-of-the-art multivariate statistical techniques to account for the interplay of the potentially significant variables. Moreover, in seeking to model speakers' choices as a function of several variables, our research exploits many of the unique features of this rich dataset.

Our general goal is to discover why speakers select one dative pattern over another, and at a more specific level this involves determining whether speakers' choices are affected by linguistic or semantic aspects of the co-text, and/or by sociolinguistic factors such as age, gender and social status. Finally, we aim to learn whether the evidence in the Spoken BNC2014S data can help to confirm the results of previous studies.

10.4 Description of Corpus Data and Metadata

The source data for this study are the early access Sample of the Spoken BNC2014. More information can be found in Chapter 1. Suffice it to say that, as in the BNC of the early 1990s, the Spoken BNC2014S sampling frame includes a range of sociolinguistic categories, such as age, gender and socio-economic status. Speakers represent various combinations of these, and in the Spoken BNC2014S this information is available as a rich set of metadata which complements the transcribed recordings.

It is important to note, however, that for many of the key sociolinguistic indicators, speakers are not optimally distributed across the sampling frame. Looking at participants' ages, for example, over 40% of speakers in the data we studied are in the age range 19–29. Representation in the "middle" age ranges (30–49) shows a sharp decline, and rises again for the cohort of people aged 50 and over. The sample is similarly skewed in the case of social status. Speakers from social grades A and B (roughly speaking, higher-status middle-class individuals) are hugely over-represented, with close to half of all sentences in our sample coming from members of these groups, while groups A and B make up only 27% of the UK population at large. Social grades C1, C2 and D are thinly populated in the Spoken BNC2014S data, but grade E (non-working people, pensioners, etc.) is again over-represented, comprising almost one-third of speakers in the data we studied, against 8% in the national figures. The distribution of dialects is skewed towards southern English varieties; for example, the number of data points corresponding to speakers whose dialect is labelled as "south" is 970 (50% of the total in the dataset), and 387 (20%) are unspecified. It is useful to be aware of these imbalances, and a degree of caution is required when extrapolating any findings to the wider population.

10.5 Scope of the Research

To investigate the dative alternation, we needed to find verbs for which both patterns were equally acceptable, even if not equally frequent. We looked at a number of mid-frequency verbs, including *award, hand, grant* and *mail*, all of which include the two dative patterns among their syntactic preferences. These yielded too few usable data points, and it became clear that, if we were to collect adequate material for the study, in a corpus of fairly modest size, we would need to focus on high-frequency words.

The six verbs on which this study is based are: *give, lend, offer, sell, send* and *show*, and basic frequency data are shown in Table 10.1:

In this study, we look only at dative uses from the "core" meaning of each verb. The verbs are all polysemous, and dative uses can be found in other senses—and in some cases, the dative alternation is as normal as it is in the core meaning. For example:

> *you know somebody loves you they **show** you love* (V-NP-NP)
>   (BNC2014 SMCW)
> *but you need to be able to **show** a respect to your elders* (V-NP-PP)
>   (BNC2014 SGSY)

Table 10.1 The Six Verbs With Their Raw Frequency in the Corpus and the Number of Dative Instances in the Data

Verb	Frequency in the Spoken BNC2014S	Datives
give	3980	1000*
lend	65	38
offer	238	72
show	1066	276
sell	1063	103
send	1527	570

* Note that *give* is a special case: its frequency in the corpus (it occurs far more often than any of our other verbs) raised the possibility that the data for this one verb might skew our results. To minimise this risk we took a sample, and selected only the first 1,000 dative instances from the concordances for *give*.

> they are **selling** you the idea that you can publish (V-NP-NP) (BNC2014 SL46)
>
> didn't try to **sell** their faith to you (V-NP-PP) (BNC2014 SKDX)

But we assumed that a focus on core usage would minimise interference from other factors and yield a cleaner set of data to work with. This raises the question of what a core meaning is, and how a given occurrence of a verb can be reliably assigned to a particular sense. Identifying syntactic patterns (V-NP-NP, V-NP-PP) is straightforward, but disambiguating the meanings of a polysemous word is notoriously difficult—not least because the category "word sense" is inherently unstable (e.g., Hanks, 2013, pp. 65–83). Nonetheless, the interplay of patterns and co-text (notably selectional preferences) provides a robust working basis for word sense disambiguation. In the unsorted data for one of the verbs, for example, we find this dative (V-NP-PP) pattern:

> erm who actually is a lecturer and **lends credibility** to the whole thing (BNC2014 SZAP)

The V-NP-NP pattern would be equally expected here (*this **lends** it some **credibility***). This does not seem like a core instance of *lend*, and that intuition is supported by the nature of the direct and indirect objects—the "implicatures" as they are termed in Hanks's *Pattern Dictionary of English Verbs* (PDEV; http://pdev.org.uk). In PDEV's analysis of *lend*, the first two constructions listed are identical, and what distinguishes them are the things being lent (in the first case, physical objects or assets; in the second, things such as "weight, credibility, credence, support"). The core sense of *sell* can be similarly identified on the basis of what is being sold: in the FrameNet database, for example, the basic meaning of *sell* belongs to a Frame called "Commerce_sell" (https://framenet.icsi.berkeley.edu/fndrupal/framenet_data), which describes "commercial transactions involving a buyer and a seller exchanging money and goods". This rules out a sentence about someone "selling you *the idea* that you can publish. . .".

We feel confident that the dative sentences forming the raw material for our study all instantiate core meanings of the selected verbs. The data for *give* represent a possible exception. Not only is *give* highly polysemous, but its frequent use as a light verb (*I'll give you a call*), as well as its appearance in numerous idioms with dative-like structures (*give it a go, give her the benefit of the doubt,* etc.) further complicates matters. Most of the cases where we had doubts were resolved by the non-availability of one or other of the patterns under investigation: *give me a call* is common, but **give a call to me* would be aberrant. So, although a few borderline cases may have survived the cut, there are too few to compromise the overall analysis.

10.6 Data Collection and Manual Annotation

First of all, we queried the CQPweb interface of the Spoken BNC2014S data to collect all corpus concordances of each of the six verbs we selected. This step (which is described in more detail in the next section) resulted in six text files, each containing all concordance lines of one of the six verbs. Next, we identified only those concordance lines instantiating the core meaning of each verb.

In order to identify instances of the two patterns involved in the dative alternation, it was necessary to add syntactic information to the corpus data. Initially, we tried automatically parsing the concordance lines using the PCFG Stanford Parser (Klein & Manning, 2003). However, the quality of the parsed results was poor, particularly on constructions typical of the spoken register, such as *it sort of gives you a list*. For this reason, we opted for manual annotation of the patterns in each concordance line, and filtered the subset of data for each verb to retain only the dative instances of the core meanings. Each line was then manually annotated in a spreadsheet, to indicate which of the two dative patterns it represented, and to show the *recipient* and the *theme*, thus:

> *the easiest way is to sell sell the print to a big company* (BNC2014 S37Y)
> pattern: V-NP-PP; recipient: *a big company*; theme: *the print*

We further enriched the annotation to identify the *head* of the noun phrases representing the recipient and theme. So, in the sentence

> *you can just send Christmas cards . . . to people you don't see from year to year* (BNC2014 ST64)

the recipient (in full) is "people you don't see from year to year", but the head is "people". Even without further analysis, this procedure (and the spreadsheets it populated) revealed a number of unmistakeable trends. The two most striking observations (which we discuss more fully later) were: first, the V-NP-NP pattern is the dominant dative form for all the verbs except *sell*, accounting for 69.6% of all dative instances in our data; and secondly, personal pronouns dominate the recipient column when the pattern is V-NP-NP (*he showed me the letter; no-one's going to give you a job*, etc.). An interesting revelation in the dataset for *send* is that the vast majority of cases refer to sending things by electronic media. Although there are a few instances of cards or packages being sent via the postal system, the "theme" column here is mainly populated by words like *email, money, CV, link, photos*, and above all *message*. This marks a striking change from the way the verb is used in the BNC1994. The annotation process also showed up instances of a third dative pattern, in sentences like these:

> *my uncle sold it me for a fiver* (BNC2014 SWSX)
> *[she] showed it me on DVD* (BNC2014 SVFH)
> *remember not to [. . .] give it him as breakfast cereal* (BNC2014 SGY6)

This is a known British English dialectal variant of the more usual dative constructions, but as there were fewer than ten instances in the approximately 2,000 concordance lines in our sample, its presence in the data was unlikely to affect the analysis, and such instances were excluded from the final multivariate analysis.

10.7 Data Processing

In order to conduct the sociolinguistic analysis for this study, it was necessary to gather the relevant corpus data and metadata in a format that allowed further statistical processing. For this reason, we defined a pipeline to process the data automatically; this ensures future reproducibility and replicability of our results. In this section we describe the data processing pipeline.

1 Export of Concordance Lines

First of all, we queried the CQPweb interface of the Spoken BNC2014S data to collect all corpus concordances of each of the six verbs we selected. The corpus query specified the lemma and the part of speech "verb". For example, to retrieve all concordances for the target verb *give*, we used the query "{give/V}". We selected the widest context size allowed, which consists of fifty words before and fifty words after the target word (option "50 words each way"). Finally, we downloaded the concordances together with all the corpus metadata fields available (option "Method: Download all text metadata"). This step resulted in six text files, each containing all concordance lines of one of the six verbs. Figure 10.1 shows the first line of the file for *give*.

2 Export of Corpus Metadata

The concordance files contain information about the corpus text ID, the target verb, its right and left context (both as raw text and with part-of-speech tagging), the date on which the conversation was recorded, its length and its location, the number and identifiers of the speakers, their relationship, the subject and topics covered in the conversation, the URL corresponding to the concordance line, and its position in the corpus. In order to conduct the analysis, we needed to retrieve the corpus semantic annotation, which follows the definitions of the English semantic tagger of the UCREL semantic analysis system. Therefore, the second step consisted in exporting the annotation from the corpus via the CQPweb interface. Again, we queried the corpus, specifying the verb lemma and its part-of-speech; then, we selected the option "Download query as plain-text tabulation", and chose an offset of –5 and 5 for each of the following fields from the drop-down menu: "Corpus position number", "word", "semtag", "u_who" and "text_id". This allowed us to record various types of information about each of the words occurring in the concordance line for the verbs of interest, and within a window of size five, which is the widest context allowed. For each such context word, the information recorded concerns its position in the corpus, its form, its semantic tag, the identifier of the speaker uttering it, and the identifier of the text in which it occurred. Figure 10.2 shows an example of such a metadata file for the verb *give*.

3 Collecting and Cleaning the Speaker Data

Our analysis required more details about the speakers, so the next step in the data collection phase consisted in gathering and cleaning the speaker data. These were delivered to us as an Excel spreadsheet, whose rows correspond to each speaker and whose columns record the following information: identifier, exact age, age range, gender, nationality, place of birth, country of birth, native language, linguistic origin, accent/dialect, city/town of residence, country of residence, the number of years the speaker has spent living there, four different categorisations of the region of residence, highest qualification, occupation, social grade, second native language for bilingual speakers, foreign languages spoken,

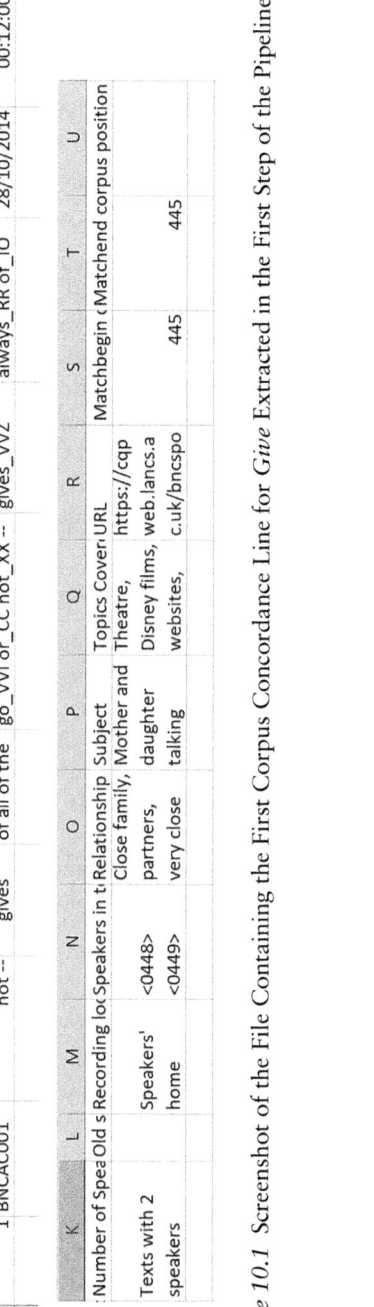

A	B	C	D	E	F	G	H	I	J
Number o	Text ID	Context before	Query item	Context after	Tagged context before	Tagged query i	Tagged context aft	Date of Reco	Length of Re
1	BNCAC001	you 're in a hurry to go or not --	gives	you a list not always of all of the	you_PPY 're_VBR in_II a_AT1 hurry_NN1 to_TO go_VVI or_CC not_XX --	gives_VVZ	you_PPY a_AT1 list_NN1 not_XX always_RR of_IO	28/10/2014	00:12:00

K	L	M	N	O	P	Q	R	S	T	U
Number of Spea	Old s	Recording loc	Speakers in t	Relationship	Subject	Topics Cover	URL	Matchbegin ¢	Matchend	corpus position
Texts with 2 speakers		Speakers' home	<0448> <0449>	Close family, partners, very close	Mother and daughter talking	Theatre, Disney films, websites,	https://cqp web.lancs.a c.uk/bncspo		445	445

Figure 10.1 Screenshot of the File Containing the First Corpus Concordance Line for *Give* Extracted in the First Step of the Pipeline

	A	B	C	D	E
1	Position of words in corpus	Concordance line	Semantic tags	Speakers	Text ID
	440 441 442 443 444 445 446	okay and it sort of gives	A5:1 Z5 Z8 Z4 Z4 A9 Z8	0448 0449 0449 0449 0449 0449	BNCAC001 BNCAC001 BNCAC001
	447 448 449 450	you a list not always	Z5 Q1:2 Z6 N6	0449 0449 0449 0449 0449	BNCAC001 BNCAC001 BNCAC001
					BNCAC001 BNCAC001 BNCAC001
2					BNCAC001 BNCAC001

Figure 10.2 Screenshot of the File Containing the Corpus Metadata for the First Concordance Line of *Give* Extracted in the Second Step of the Pipeline[1]

number of utterances and number of words uttered in the corpus. Figure 10.3 shows an example of the first speaker's data.

The speaker data display considerable variability; for example, the column "Duration living (years)" indicates the number of years that the speaker has spent living in the location indicated, and in the overall dataset it contains values such as "30 years", "30", and also "all my life" and "all her life". This is due to the fact that the data represent the responses verbatim, as originally given by the speakers. In order to enable the subsequent statistical analysis, we decided to normalise these data.

4 Combine Corpus Data With Metadata

Finally, we wrote a script that combined the details from the concordance files with the metadata files and the speaker information in one file per verb. This was followed by another script which merged the individual datasets for each verb into a single dataset and cleaned some of the variables and defined new ones. The values of the speaker's education level were mapped to a set of consistent categories, and semantic tags were mapped to their least granular class. The additional variables we defined are: length of theme/recipient, pronominality of theme/recipient, definitiveness of theme and animacy of theme/recipient.

10.8 Analysis of Corpus Data

As mentioned earlier, the V-NP-NP pattern is dominant for all the verbs except *sell* (where V-NP-PP outnumbers V-NP-NP by almost three to one). Table 10.2 shows the distribution of the two patterns for our six verbs.

Our central research question is: which factors influence a speaker to select one pattern rather than the other? There are numerous possibilities, and the Spoken BNC2014S data allow us to look at a wide range of linguistic and sociolinguistic variables. To assess the effects of these features, we conducted a multivariate analysis, and we discuss the output of this analysis in the next section.

Here, we will give an overview of the different factors considered. The dataset comprises 1,938 observations, corresponding to occurrences of

	A	B	C	D	E	F	G	H	I	J	K	L	M
1	Speaker ID	Exact Age	Age Range	Gender	Nationality	Place of Birth	Country of Bi	L1	Linguistic orig	Accent/dialec	City/Town	Country livin	Duration livir
2	1	32	30_39	F	British	Wordsley, W	England	English	England	None indicatr	Aberystwyth	Wales	14
3													

	N	O	P	Q	R	S	T	U	V	W	X	Y
	Region 1 (dial	Region 2 (dial	Region 3 (dial	Region 4 (dial	Highest quali	Occupation:t	Social Grade	NS-SEC	L2 (bilingual)	Foreign langs No. words	No. utterance	No. words
	unspecified	unspecified	unspecified	unspecified	Postgraduate	University res	A	1_2			904	10287

Figure 10.3 Screenshot of the File Containing the Data for the First Speaker Processed in the Third Step of the Pipeline

Table 10.2 Distribution of the Two Dative Patterns in the Data for the Six Verbs

Verb	Datives	V-NP-NP	V-NP-PP
give	1000	882 (88%)	118 (12%)
lend	38	27 (71%)	11 (29%)
offer	72	62 (86%)	10 (14%)
sell	103	26 (25%)	77 (75%)
send	570	436 (76%)	134 (24%)
show	276	242 (88%)	34 (12%)

the six verbs in the corpus. Each observation is characterised by a range of attributes, which we can group in the following categories:

- Syntactic, semantic, lexical features: verb lemma; syntactic realisation of the dative construction (either as V-NP-NP or V-NP-PP), lexical realisation of the recipient, lexical realisation of the theme, syntactic head of the recipient, syntactic head of the theme, semantic tag of the syntactic head of the recipient phrase, semantic tag of the syntactic head of the theme phrase, semantic tag of the verb, length of recipient, length of theme (both measured as number of characters), pronominality of recipient, pronominality of theme;
- Text metadata: number of speakers, location, relation, topics;
- Speaker metadata: exact age, age range, gender, nationality, place of birth, country of birth, L1, bilingualism; linguistic origin, accent, city of residence, country of residence, number of years they have lived in the city of residence, level 1 dialect, level 2 dialect, level 3 dialect, level 4 dialect (where a speaker's dialect is identified with varying degrees of granularity), highest qualification, occupation, foreign languages spoken, number of utterances, number of words and social grade.

We analysed the different variables in order to assess their quality and relevance to the phenomenon under study, as detailed below. As a consequence, we decided to exclude the following variables from further analysis: bilingualism (because the large majority of speakers are monolingual),[2] level 1, 2, and 3 dialect, accent, and city/town (because they were too granular and the data were too sparse), nationality (due to the overwhelming proportion of speakers categorised as British, 99% of the data points), L1 (due to the overwhelming proportion of the value "English", 97% of the data points), country (due to the overwhelming proportion of speakers from England, corresponding to 91% of the data points), number of years they have lived in the city of residence (all values are not-applicable), place of birth, country of birth, and linguistic origin (due to high variability in the values), occupation (again, due to high variability in the values), foreign languages, relation, topics and location (high variability in the values).

10.9 Exploratory Analysis

In order to answer our research questions, we conducted a preliminary exploratory analysis of the rich dataset we had collected, and this is the focus of the current section, which aims to show whether there is any correlation between an individual feature and either of the two patterns. This analysis gave us insights into the nature of the data we worked with, and informed our later investigations on the statistical models reported on in the next section.

1 Speaker's Age

Focussing on sociolinguistic variables first, the speaker's age appears to have no effect on their preference for either pattern, as confirmed by a Welch 2 sample t test ($t = -1.79$, degrees of freedom = 460.675, p-value > 0.05). If we consider another age-related metadata field, namely age range, with values 11–18, 19–29, 30–39, 40–49, 50–59, 60–69, 70–79, 80–89 and 90–99, we see no significant difference in the choice of syntactic pattern by age range category (*chi-square* = 10.9223, degrees of freedom = 8, p-value > 0.05).

2 Speaker's Level of Education

With regard to speakers' level of education, there is some evidence that speakers with postgraduate degrees are slightly more likely than others to use a V-NP-PP pattern: 24% of the instances with a speaker with postgraduate degree display this pattern, as opposed to 15% of those with a college/sixth form education, 18% for graduates, and 21% for those without post-GCSE qualifications. A Pearson's chi-square test showed a significant association between pattern and education level (*chi-square* = 14.9012, degrees of freedom = 3, p-value < 0.05), but a tiny effect (Cramér $V = 0.088$). The speakers' social grade is partly defined by their education level, so the two variables are related and we decided to use the latter.

3 Speaker's Gender

There also appears to be a small gender effect, with male speakers showing a slight preference for V-NP-PP when compared with female speakers: V-NP-PP occurs in 21% of the instances with male speakers and in 19% of the instances with female speakers. However, this difference is not statistically significant, as confirmed by a Pearson's chi-square test (*chi-square* = 0.8198, degrees of freedom = 1, p-value > 0.05).

4 Dialect

We analysed the distribution of the two patterns by the speaker's dialect, according to the level 4 of granularity, which includes the following

Table 10.3 Distribution of Dative Patterns According to Speaker's Dialect

Region	V-NP-NP	V-NP-PP
Midlands	64 (74%)	22 (26%)
Non-UK	9 (82%)	2 (18%)
North	371 (84%)	72 (16%)
Scottish	2 (100%)	0 (0%)
South	755 (78%)	210 (22%)
Unspecified	249 (82%)	54 (18%)
Welsh	18 (78%)	5 (22%)

categories: East Midlands, Eastern England, Irish, Liverpool, London, non UK, North East, North West, Scottish, South East, Unspecified, West Midlands, Welsh and Yorkshire. There does not seem to be any major difference between these different dialects in the way the two patterns are distributed. Table 10.3 shows the proportion of the two patterns by dialect and their absolute frequencies. A Pearson's chi-square test showed a significant but small association between dialect and pattern (*chi-square* = 26, degrees of freedom = 14, *p*-value < 0.05, Cramér *V* = 0.12).

5 Length of Arguments

Coming to the linguistic variables, there is strong evidence that the length of the arguments (recipient and themes) predicts the selected pattern in many cases. Broadly speaking, where the recipient is instantiated by a short NP (such as *me, my mum, the boys*, or a personal name), the V-NP-NP pattern is preferred:

> *we gave him a drink of water* (BNC2014 S7PU)
> *take you and show you our wonderful country* (BNC2014 S9RV)
> *I sent my nan a postcard from Barcelona* (BNC2014 SLDD)

The converse is also generally true: a longer recipient tends to imply the V-NP-PP pattern.

> *probably never show it to yeah any males in your life* (BNC2014 S7GJ)
> *you can just send Christmas cards . . . to people you don't see from year to year* (BNC2014 ST64)

By the same logic, a longer theme predicts V-NP-NP:

> *[name] lent me a ski jacket the helmet the skis and the poles* (BNC2014 SFLB)

but they offer me a cup of coffee and a biscuit (BNC2014 SCZV)
and sell you a picture of your house from the air (BNC2014 SC8H)

But where both recipient and theme are realised by very short words, V-NP-PP tends to be preferred. Taking account of the far higher number of V-NP-NP instances, there is a marked bias towards V-NP-PP sentences like these:

give it to him
I won't lend it to you
I'll show that to [name]

Figure 10.4 shows the relationship between the selected pattern and the length of the theme and recipient:

6 Pronominality of Arguments

It will be obvious from the previous examples that a high percentage of the short themes and recipients are pronouns. Where the pattern is V-NP-NP, the recipient is overwhelmingly likely to be a personal pronoun, with *you* and *me* being especially common. In the case of *show*, for example, a mere eighteen of the 242 V-NP-NP instances are *not* personal pronouns.

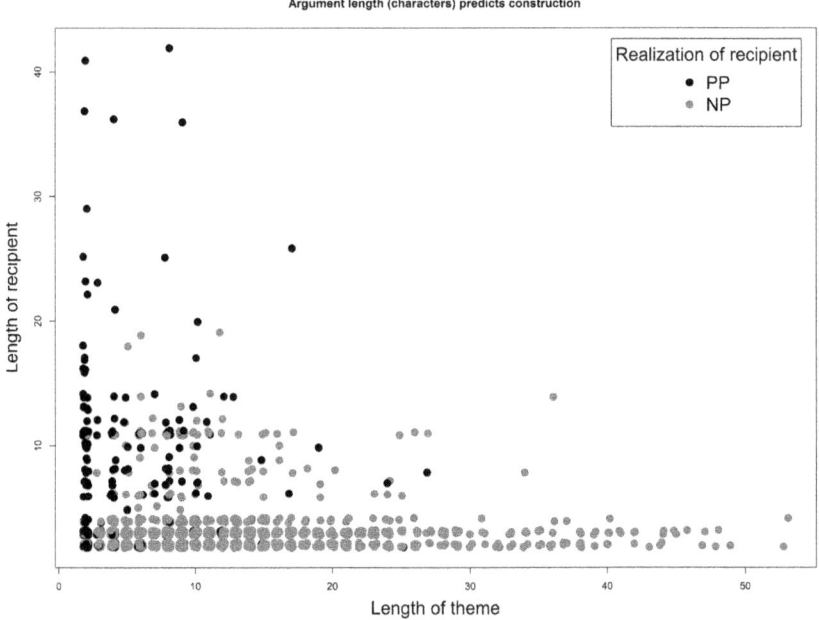

Figure 10.4 Chart Showing the Length of Theme Plotted Against Length of Recipient for the Two Patterns

In V-NP-PP sentences, the theme (which is typically inanimate), is frequently realised by the pronouns *it* or *them*, as in the following examples:

> *you sent it to a hundred and thirty people* (BNC2014 ST64)
> *sort out all our books and give them to that [name] book shop*
> (BNC2014 SPHU)

But the distribution of pronouns (personal for recipients, impersonal for themes) is not symmetric. The V-NP-NP pattern overwhelmingly prefers a personal pronoun in the recipient slot (93% of cases)—or to put it another way, the choice of a pronoun as recipient overwhelmingly predicts the V-NP-NP pattern; on the other hand, this pattern only has 9% of pronominal themes. For V-NP-PP sentences, the situation is more complicated: here, pronominal recipients account for 56% of the cases, and pronominal themes are 65% of the cases. Chi-square tests on the distribution of pronominal recipients and themes by patterns show that these differences are significant and have a medium-sized effect (pronominality of recipient: *chi-square*= 313.1513, degrees of freedom = 1, p-value < 0.05; Cramér V = 0.42; pronominality of theme: *chi-square* = 546.6041, degrees of freedom = 1, p-value < 0.05; Cramér V = 0.55).

7 Semantic Tag of Recipient and Theme

The most frequent semantic tag for recipients by a large margin is Z8, which corresponds to pronouns; the same holds for themes, although in this case the distribution of semantic tags is less skewed.

If we ask whether there is a significant difference in the way the two patterns are distributed by semantic tag of the recipient, we find that this is not the case (*chi-square* = 14.4643, degrees of freedom = 12, p-value > 0.05).

However, if we consider the semantic tag of the theme, we find a significant difference. A chi-square test shows a medium-sized statistically significant difference in the distributions of the two patterns by semantic tag (*chi-square* = 616.0445, degrees of freedom = 92, p-value < 0.05, Cramér V = 0.577); generally, the V-NP-NP pattern is more common than V-NP-PP, with the exception of the theme semantic tags "Crime, law and order" and "Pronouns, etc.", for which prepositional recipients are more common than non-prepositional ones.

10.10 Statistical Multivariate Models

For the multivariate analysis, we used a binary logistic mixed-effects model fitted in R (R Development Core Team. 2011) with the lme4 package (Bates, Maechler, & Dai, 2008). Such models are now regularly used in both corpus linguistics and sociolinguistics; see, e.g., Baayen (2008) and Tagliamonte and Baayen (2012). The response was a binary variable indicating the V-NP-NP pattern (0/False) or V-NP-PP (1/True). A binary logistic regression model attempts to model the probability of the response value (essentially switching from 0 to 1, or False to True) as a function of a series of linear combinations of predictor variables. For technical reasons, the probabilities are estimated on a logarithmic scale as odds ratios. Unlike fixed-effects regression models, mixed-effects models are generally better at dealing with specific sampling biases. The advantage of mixed-effects models over simpler fixed-effects generalised linear models is that adjustments for known biases in the data can be made explicit in the model itself. In this case, we used a random effect for verbs, thus adjusting for different overall frequencies and different rates of construction use in the verbs. Another reason for choosing a random effect for verb is that, unlike variables such as gender or social class where we have covered all relevant values, our sample only covers a subset of all verbs (Baayen, 2008, p. 241). For the multivariate regression analysis, we employed a smaller subset of the data encompassing only data points without missing information, totalling 1,602 observations.

The first step involved identifying a model that converged. In practice, this means correctly specifying the list of predictors (also variously known as fixed effects or independent variables) and the random effect(s) in a manner that correctly predicts the response, in our case the realisation of the recipient as either a PP or NP. In this step we removed a number of variables, notably semantic variables such as semantic tag or semantic field of the theme, and the sociolinguistic variables of dialect and speaker's social grade. The problem with these categorical variables was that the model did not converge due to estimated probabilities close to one or zero, a problem that can occur when a factor value is rare but when it appears it perfectly predicts the response (Venables & Ripley, 2002, pp. 198–199). Put differently, a number of rare semantic tags and sociolinguistic variable values always predicted one response value. With no variation, the model could not correctly estimate the required parameter values. Another way of viewing this is that in our dataset these variables, the semantic field of the theme or the dialect, might contain values that are good predictors of certain response values (NP or PP), but they are not good overall predictors of the variation between the two response values. In the case of the speaker's social grade, we found a large correlation with the speaker's highest qualification (*chi-square* = 844.5, degrees of freedom = 15, *p*-value < 0.05, Cramér *V* = 0.39). Hence, we decided to omit the social grade variable, since exploratory testing indicated that the highest qualification was a better predictor for the response.

Having omitted these variables, we arrived at a full model that we could use as a starting point for our analysis. The maximal converging model has the following structure:

Response: Probability of V-NP-PP
Random effect: Verb

Predictors: Gender + RecPrn + ThemePrn + log(RecLen) + log(ThemeLen) + DefTheme + AnimateRec + AnimateTheme + SpeakerHighestQual + AgeImputed + SpeakerHighestQual X AgeImputed

The numeric variables length of theme (ThemeLen) and length of recipient (RecLen) were logarithmically transformed to better adhere to the model assumption of normally distributed numerical predictors. Furthermore, we had to add an interaction term between the age and highest qualification of the speaker, since these two variables are sufficiently closely related to create problems for the model specification if no interaction term is specified. The predictor "AgeImputed" corresponds to the speaker's age, when that is available, and to the midpoint of the speaker's age range, when the exact age was not available. We also defined the variables "DefTheme" (theme expressed as a definite phrase) and "AnimateRec" (animacy of recipient). "RecPrn" and "ThemePrn" refer to the pronominality of the recipient and theme, respectively. The model's predictors are shown in Table 10.4.

The table shows the name of the predictor, the size of the effect (coefficient), the uncertainty of the effect (coefficient standard error), the z-value used to determine statistical significance, and the p-value. The coefficient represents the chance of switching from an NP recipient to a PP recipient, expressed as an odds ratio on a logarithmic scale. A positive number indicates an increase in PP recipients with the predictor, whereas a negative number indicates an increase in NP recipients; a value of zero

Table 10.4 Coefficients, Standard Errors, z-Values, and p-Values for the Selected Variables

Predictors	Coef β	SE(β)	z	p
(Intercept)	−0.63	1.08	−0.6	>0.6
GenderM	0.48	0.24	2.0	<.05
RecPrnTRUE	−2.05	0.42	−4.9	<.0001
ThemePrnTRUE	1.90	0.30	6.4	<.0001
log(RecLen)	1.39	0.30	4.7	<.0001
log(ThemeLen)	−2.11	0.22	−9.4	<.0001
DefThemeTRUE	−0.12	0.29	−0.4	>0.7
AnimateRecTRUE	0.76	0.32	2.4	<.05
AnimateThemeTRUE	1.54	1.01	1.5	>0.1
SpeakerHighestQualGraduate	1.61	0.69	2.3	<.05
SpeakerHighestQualPostgraduate	1.94	0.82	2.4	<.05
SpeakerHighestQualSecondary School	1.24	0.90	1.4	>0.2
AgeImputed	0.03	0.01	2.2	<.05
SpeakerHighestQualGraduate:AgeImputed	−0.03	0.02	−2.1	<.05
SpeakerHighestQualPostgraduate:AgeImputed	−0.03	0.02	−1.9	>0.1
SpeakerHighestQualSecondary School:AgeImputed	−0.02	0.02	−1.0	>0.3

equates to even odds. Odds ratios are not intuitively interpretable, so we proceed with discussing them as probabilities. Log odds ratios can be transformed into probabilities by taking the inverse logit function of the coefficient together with the intercept. A more convenient approach is what Gelman and Hill (2007, p. 82) call the "divide by 4 rule". To interpret the coefficients on a probability scale, where it represents the midpoint of the logistic curve, we can simply divide the coefficient by four. Based on this heuristic, we see that out of the coefficients that are statistically significant, the linguistic variables pronominality of theme, pronominality of recipient, length of theme and length of recipient stand out. Of the sociolinguistic variables, we see that a graduate or postgraduate qualification leans towards a PP recipient, as does male gender, albeit with a smaller effect. Some predictors, viz. definiteness of theme and animacy of theme, are not statistically significant.

However, this full model is not necessarily the best one. The aim is to find a model that explains the data in the simplest manner, without adding any unnecessary variables (Faraway, 2005, p. 121). A simple model for our purposes is one that, in accordance with Occam's razor, both fits the data and adequately describes the response variable (V-NP-NP vs. V-NP-PP) with as few predictors as possible. The criteria used for finding an optimal model involved using log-likelihood ratio tests to identify any significant difference between the smaller and the larger model, while at the same time maintaining a high C-index value. The C-index is a measure of how well the model predicts the data, and a C-value of 0.95 indicates an excellent fit (Baayen, 2008, p. 204). Finally, we inspected plots of the model residuals to ensure that they did not show signs of serious problems with the model structure (Faraway, 2005, pp. 53–56; Gelman & Hill, 2007, pp. 97–98).

Based on these criteria, we found that the variables definiteness of theme, animacy of theme, speaker's highest qualification and speaker age could all be eliminated. The final model has the following structure:

Response: Probability of V-NP-PP
Random effect: Verb
Predictors: Gender + RecPrn + ThemePrn + log(RecLen) + log(ThemeLen) + AnimateRec

Table 10.5 summarises the fixed effects of the model:

From Table 10.5, we see that the coefficient of gender is 0.56. Dividing it by 4, we obtain a quick estimate of the effect on a probability scale (Gelman & Hill, 2007, p. 82). Men are 14% more likely to use a V-NP-PP construction than women, after controlling for differences between verbs. The coefficient for pronominality of recipients is –1.97, meaning that pronoun recipients reduce the use of V-NP-PP constructions by about 50%. Conversely, the coefficient for pronominality of theme

Table 10.5 Coefficients, Standard Errors, z-Values, p-Values for the Selected Predictors

	Coef β	*SE(β)*	*z*	*p*
(Intercept)	0.67	0.94	0.7	>0.5
GenderM	0.56	0.22	2.5	<.05
RecPrnTRUE	–1.97	0.41	–4.8	<.0001
ThemePrnTRUE	1.99	0.29	6.9	<.0001
log(RecLen)	1.40	0.30	4.7	<.0001
log(ThemeLen)	–2.04	0.21	–9.8	<.0001
AnimateRecTRUE	0.69	0.31	2.2	<.05

is 1.99, implying an estimate of a 50% increase in the use of V-NP-PP constructions. The coefficient for the logarithmically transformed length of recipients, 1.4, is 0.35, meaning that a one-unit increase in recipient length (on a log scale) results in a 35% increase in the use of V-NP-PP. For the logarithmically transformed length of themes we see the opposite tendency. The coefficient of –2.04 suggests a 50% decrease in use of V-NP-PP for every one-unit increase. Finally, animate recipients have a 17% higher rate of use of V-NP-PP constructions compared to inanimate recipients.

Figure 10.5 visualises the fixed effects of the final model. The predictors on the right hand side of the dotted midline are associated with a higher probability of PP recipients. The horizontal bars extending from the points are 95% confidence intervals.

The random effect variable, verb, has a standard deviation of about 0.84, which translates into an average difference between verbs in their use of the V-NP-PP construction of about plus/minus 21%. In other words, although there are real differences between verbs in how often they occur with the constructions, the model takes this into account, so that the fixed effects in Table 10.5 are the effects of our predictors over and beyond the verb specific effects. Figure 10.6 above shows the random effects, with 95% confidence intervals. *Show* and *give* are notable for their preference for NP recipients, whereas *sell* (as expected from the exploratory analysis) is associated with PP recipients. *Send, offer* and *lend* do not differ greatly from the overall average, as indicated by the overlaps between the intercept and the confidence intervals.

10.11 Sociolinguistic Implications and Conclusions

Previous studies have investigated the dative alternation from a sociolinguistic perspective, and identified probabilistic differences in the dative alternation at the sociolinguistic macrolevel, e.g., between American and New Zealand English. Moreover, some of the previous research (Bresnan

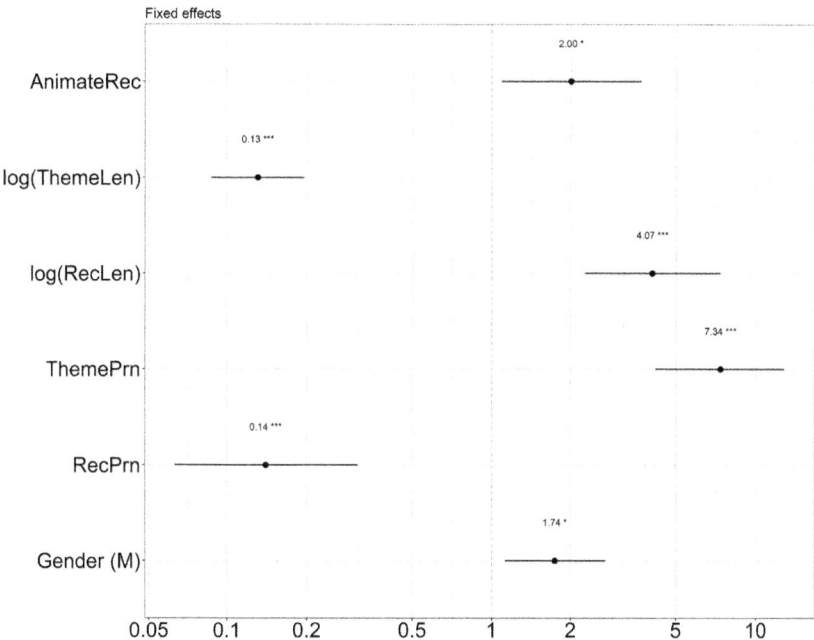

Figure 10.5 Predictors for the Minimal Model, With 95% Confidence Intervals for the Coefficient Estimates. Estimates to the Right-Hand Side of the Midline are Associated With Higher Probability of PP Recipients.

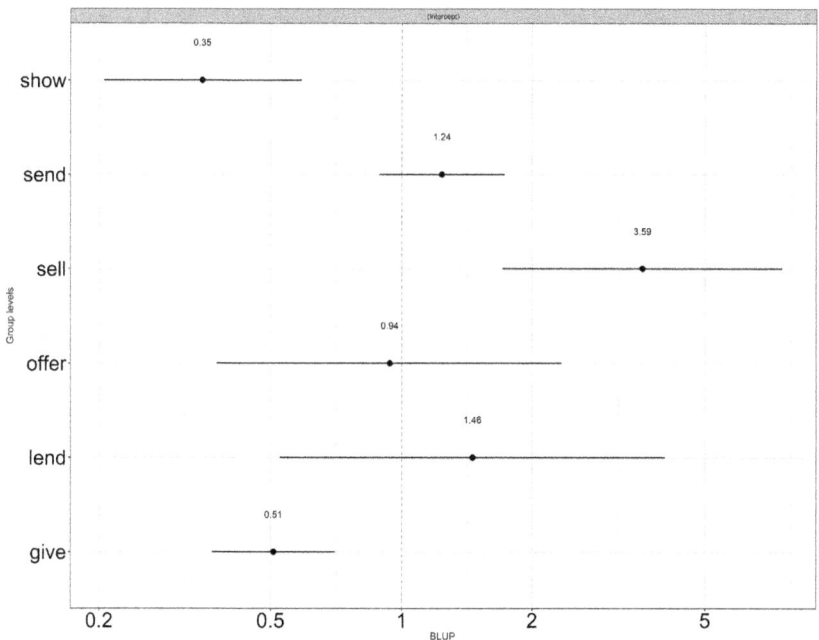

Figure 10.6 Random Effects for the Minimal Model, With 95% Confidence Intervals. *Sell* is Associated With a Higher Probability of PP Recipients, Whereas *Offer*, *Lend* and *Send* Are Not Very Different From the Overall Average.

et al., 2007; Bresnan & Hay, 2008; Bresnan & Ford, 2010) has used spoken data from recordings of phone conversations between strangers. In this study, we used spontaneous spoken data recorded from face-to-face conversations between speakers who know each other. This has given us the opportunity to test whether sociolinguistic features affected the dative alternation in the Spoken BNC2014S and whether data from this resource could confirm previous results.

Our analysis showed the effects of grammatical features on the dative alternation. Firstly, our model downplays the effect of recipient's animacy compared to the model in Bresnan et al. (2007) based on US English. Furthermore, while Bresnan et al. (2007) found a strong effect for indefiniteness of theme, this variable was omitted from our model for reasons of parsimony. What both our model and Bresnan et al.'s share are strong effects for the length of theme and argument, even though we used the log transformed number of characters as opposed to number of words used by Bresnan et al. The pronominality of the recipient also plays a large role in both models. In addition to this, we found a strong effect for the pronominality of the theme. Our results point strongly towards a construction that is modulated in accordance with Behagel's Law, with the concomitant implications for information status (Arnold et al., 2000). This result is in line with previous research showing how discourse features and processing constraints tend to play a lead role in shifting the probabilities for which variant of the construction is used (Arnold et al., 2000; Bresnan et al., 2007; Bresnan & Hay, 2008; Bresnan & Ford, 2010; Jenset & Johansson, 2013).

With regard to the effects of sociolinguistic features, our main finding is two-fold. First, as did Bresnan and Hay (2008), we identified some subtle probabilistic differences between our British data and previous results from other macro-variants of English. As Kendall et al. (2011, p. 230) point out, this does make the construction a sociolinguistic variable, since aspects of its realisation correlate with non-linguistic features. Secondly, at the level of the individual speaker, our results point to a somewhat weaker role played by sociolinguistic variables compared to the grammatical ones, also as expected based on previous studies (Bresnan & Hay, 2008; Bresnan & Ford, 2010; Kendall et al., 2011). The fact that our models found effects for variables such as gender, age and qualifications could be a feature of the previously mentioned macro-level variation, or it might be a result of the unique data based on spontaneous face-to-face conversation. Although we identified a model which indicated that speakers with graduate and postgraduate qualifications use the V-NP-PP construction more than those with lower qualifications, with a weak interaction with speaker's age, we eventually opted for a simpler model, where the only strictly sociolinguistic variable that remained is gender. We found that male speakers in the dataset tend to prefer the prepositional realisation of recipient, but further investigations would be necessary to assess whether any interaction with other factors is at play, for example conversation topics. The possibility of such confounding effects based on topic also occurs with the variables age and qualification. Unfortunately, some of the metadata such as topics or relation between speakers, which are verbatim reports from speakers, were reported at such a granular level and displayed such a high degree of variability that we were not able to incorporate them directly in the model and test their effect. We hope that future research will be able to address these points by further processing and categorising these data, and add further insights to our findings.

Notes

1 BNCAC001 was the original developmental name of corpus file BNC2014 SFLQ.
2 We also excluded the ninety-eight observations whose speaker was bilingual because they represented only 0.05% of the total, which is a number not sufficiently high to show any effect.

References

Arnold, J. E, Losongco, A., Wasow, T., & Ginstrom, R. (2000). Heaviness vs. Newness: The effects of structural complexity and discourse status on constituent ordering. *Language*, 76(1), 28–55.

Baayen, R. H. (2008). *Analyzing linguistic data: A practical introduction to statistics using R*. Cambridge: Cambridge University Press.

Bates, D., Maechler, M., & Dai, B. (2008). *lme4: Linear mixed-effects models using S4 classes*. Retrieved from http://lme4.r-forge.r-project.org/

Bayley, R. (2002). The quantitative paradigm. In J. K Chambers, P. Trudgill, & N. Schilling-Estes (Eds.), *The handbook of language variation and change* (pp. 117–141). Malden, MA: Wiley-Blackwell.

Bresnan, J., Cueni, A., Nikitina, T., & Baayen, R. H. (2007). Predicting the dative alternation. In G. Bouma, I. Kraemer, & J. Zwarts (Eds.), *Cognitive foundations of interpretation* (pp. 69–94). Amsterdam: Royal Netherlands Academy of Arts and Sciences.

Bresnan, J., & Ford, M. (2010). Predicting syntax: Processing dative constructions in American and Australian varieties of English. *Language*, 86(1), 168–213.

Bresnan, J., & Hay, J. (2008). Gradient grammar: An effect of animacy on the syntax of give in New Zealand and American English. *Lingua*, 118(2), 245–259.

Faraway, J. J. (2005). *Linear models with R*. Boca Raton, FL: Chapman & Hall/CRC.

Gelman, A., & Hill, J. (2007). *Data analysis using regression and multilevel/hierarchical models*. Cambridge: Cambridge University Press.

Godfrey, J. J., Holliman, E. C., & McDaniel, J. (1992). SWITCHBOARD: Telephone speech corpus for research and development. In *Acoustics, Speech, and Signal Processing, 1992. ICASSP-92., 1992 IEEE International Conference on, 1*, 517–520. IEEE. Retrieved from http://ieeexplore.ieee.org/xpls/abs_all.jsp?arnumber=225858

Hanks, P. (2013). *Lexical analysis: Norms and exploitations*. Cambridge, MA: MIT Press.

Jenset, G. B., & Johansson, C. (2013). Lexical fillers influence the dative alternation: Estimating constructional saliency using web document frequencies. *Journal of Quantitative Linguistics, 20*(1), 13–44. doi:10.1080/09296174.20 12.754597

Kendall, T., Bresnan, J., & Van Herk, G. (2011). The dative alternation in African American English: Researching syntactic variation and change across sociolinguistic datasets. *Corpus Linguistics and Linguistic Theory, 7*(2), 229–244.

Klein, D., & Manning, C. D. (2003). Accurate unlexicalized parsing. In *Proceedings of the 41st Annual Meeting on Association for Computational Linguistics-Volume 1*, 423–430. Sapporo, Japan: Association for Computational Linguistics.

Köhler, R. (1999). Syntactic structures: Properties and interrelations. *Journal of Quantitative Linguistics, 6*(1), 46–57. doi:10.1076/jqul.6.1.46.4137

R. Development Core Team. (2011). *R: A language and environment for statistical computing*. Vienna. Retrieved from www.r-project.org

Tagliamonte, S. A., & Baayen, R. H. (2012). Models, forests, and trees of York English: was/were variation as a case study for statistical practice. *Language Variation and Change, 24*(2), 135–178. doi:10.1017/S0954394512000129

Venables, W. N., & Ripley, B. D. (2002). *Modern applied statistics with S* (4th ed.). New York, NY: Springer.

11 *'You Still Talking to Me?'*

The Zero Auxiliary Progressive in Spoken British English Twenty Years On

Andrew Caines, Michael McCarthy and Paula Buttery

11.1 Introduction

The auxiliary verb is generally thought to be obligatory in progressive aspect constructions in English. However, we previously demonstrated that this is not always the case in spontaneous conversation, especially in certain lexico-syntactic contexts and for certain demographic groups (Caines, 2010; Caines & Buttery, 2010; Caines, McCarthy, & O'Keeffe, 2016). For instance, within the ten-million-word spoken section of the British National Corpus (Spoken BNC1994) there is a four-million-word conversational subcorpus—the so-called 'demographic' subsection—in which the auxiliary is absent for 34% of progressive aspect interrogatives with second person subjects (1).

(1) How you feeling now? [BNC1994 KBK 3474][1]

We coined the term 'zero auxiliary' to refer to such constructions, and found that it was being used in diffuse lexico-syntactic contexts[2]: not just open interrogatives (featuring a *wh*-word as in (1)) with second person subjects, but also closed interrogatives (2), other person-number subjects (3)–(4) and 'zero subject' declaratives (5).

(2) You been waiting long? [BNC1994 KDK 510]
(3) We opening them now? [BNC1994 KD0 5133]
(4) What they charging him with? [BNC1994 KDP 556]
(5) Yeah hold on just looking at something. [BNC1994 KD1 920]

We proposed that the zero auxiliary is not so much an 'error' or 'omission' but rather a variant of the progressive aspect construction in British English, deliberately selected as an alternative to the progressive with auxiliary verb (Caines, 2010). The zero auxiliary may be seen as a feature of spoken grammar, which is itself a fundamental part of people's linguistic competence (Biber, Johansson, Leech, Conrad, & Finegan, 1999; Carter & McCarthy, 2017).

These findings were based on the original British National Corpus (BNC World, 2001; 'BNC1994', henceforth), specifically the demographic section of spontaneous conversation, which features recordings collected in the early 1990s (the Spoken BNC1994DS). In this chapter, we investigate zero auxiliary use in the early-access Sample of the its successor ('the Spoken BNC2014S', henceforth)—more information about this corpus can be found in Chapter 1. Its comparable design and similar size meant we could use the Spoken BNC2014S to seek out any change in zero auxiliary use in the intervening two decades.

However, we found that the zero auxiliary has decreased in frequency in progressive interrogatives with pronominal subjects, according to our survey of the Spoken BNC2014S. Whereas in the Spoken BNC1994DS the zero auxiliary occurred in 25% of such progressive constructions, including a 34% occurrence rate for second person interrogatives, in the BNC2014 those rates drop to 6% and 9% respectively. Such a decrease in use is discussed in the context of a concurrent increase in zero auxiliary occurrence in written English, thanks to the emergence of the web domain, and the uncertainties of language sampling. Nevertheless the decrease is a pronounced one, and the sociolinguistic implication is that the age and class grading seen in the BNC1994 has flattened out in the BNC2014, such that there is no longer a strong association of younger working-class speakers with the zero auxiliary interrogative.

11.2 The Progressive Aspect in English

Cross-linguistically, auxiliary verbs "denote a closed class of verbs that are characteristically used as markers of tense, aspect, mood and voice" (Huddleston & Pullum, 2002, p. 102). The auxiliary verbs of English are distinguished from lexical verbs on account of various syntactic properties which lexical verbs do not possess. Foremost among them are the so-called NICE properties: negation, inversion, code and emphasis (for a discussion of these see Quirk, Greenbaum, Leech, & Svartvik, 1985, pp. 121–125; Huddleston & Pullum, 2002, pp. 92–102).

Within the set of auxiliary verbs, a further distinction is made between modal verbs and primary verbs (Quirk et al., 1985). Modal verbs fundamentally contribute meaning relating to concepts of mood such as "volition, probability and obligation" (Quirk et al., 1985, p. 120). Primary verbs have a range of uses including aspect (*be, have*), voice (*be*), and dummy support (*do*). We restrict our focus to the primary verbs, specifically *be* and *have*, as we study the use of progressive aspect auxiliary verbs, the paradigm for which is given in Table 11.1.

As shown in Table 11.1, the progressive aspect construction is standardly formed by periphrastic combination of auxiliary *be*, plus *have* if in the perfect aspect, and the *-ing* form of a lexical verb. Table 11.1 shows the full form auxiliary verb in declarative progressives; alternatively, the

Table 11.1 The Progressive Aspect Construction in English

	Present	Past	Present Perfect	Past Perfect
1st singular	I am being	I was being	I have been being	I had been being
2nd	You are being	You were being	You have been being	You had been being
3rd singular	She is being	She was being	She has been being	She had been being
1st plural	We are being	We were being	We have been being	We had been being
3rd plural	They are being	They were being	They have been being	They had been being

first auxiliary in all the cells may be contracted, except for the past tense column as there are typically no contracted forms for *be* in the past tense—e.g., *I'm being, you've been being, she'd been being*, etc. The progressive appears in interrogative form through inversion of the subject noun and auxiliary verb—e.g., *were we being, have they been being*. It may be negated through insertion of a negative adverbial between the auxiliary and *-ing* form—e.g., *he's not being, wasn't it being, had they not been being*.

The English progressive has been the topic of many recent publications reporting ongoing changes in its use. These relate to three broad research questions:

- The origins question: for the progressive in English, the precise answer to this issue remains a matter of debate (Denison, 1998).
- The function question: beyond a core meaning of continuousness, the progressive has developed a more complex set of meanings compared to the progressive in other languages (Dahl, 1985; Bybee, Perkins, & Pagliuca, 1994; Lee, 2007).
- The frequency question: this revolves around the progressive's "meteoric increase in frequency in the Modern English period" (Leech, Hundt, Mair, & Smith, 2009, p. 118; Hundt, 2004).

Putting aside the origins issue as a historical linguistic question beyond the scope of this study, we focus on the second and third questions, which relate to semantics and corpus linguistics. At its core, the progressive aspect refers to a happening with a limited duration which is not necessarily complete (Quirk et al., 1985). Beyond this central use the progressive has developed functions extending to future time (6)–(7) and states rather than events (8)–(10).

(6) What are you going to do? [BNC1994 KB3 491]
(7) You gonna let me have a go? [BNC1994 KBK 2676]

(8) He's being a bit sarcastic. [BNC1994 J90 109]
(9) A receptor, where G A B A is standing for gamma amino butyric acid. [BNC1994 J8K 197]
(10) We are living in a very sophisticated time. [BNC1994 KRT 807]

It has been proposed that the rapid increase in frequency of the progressive may also have facilitated its several functional extensions, especially the development of stative progressives in an aspect which was canonically reserved for non-stative use (Comrie, 1976). In addition to the increasing versatility of the progressive in terms of verb classes, the rapid change in progressive usage has allowed for experimentation with its spoken form. Notably there has been reduction of the velar nasal [ŋ] in -*ing* to variants closer to alveolar [n]. This reduction has been studied extensively in the sociolinguistic field, since it has been found to be a social marker (Campbell-Kibler, 2008). Meanwhile, contraction of the auxiliary verb has long been noted as the unmarked variant in spoken language (McElhinny, 1993). We also note that the pronoun and -*ing* form may regularly occur without auxiliary verb as a clausal complement or clausal subject (11), or may occur as an interrogative followed by a tag question which features an auxiliary verb (12).

(11) she was doing her main lessons and you maybe listening to it you'd pick up stuff [BNC2014 S32W 585]
(12) —still peeling
    —yeah
    —is she? [Spoken BNC2014 STN8 93]

We are not in a position to state which came first, but certainly the legitimate use of pronoun and -*ing* without auxiliary in other contexts may help habituate speakers to the zero auxiliary (and vice versa). Complete ellipsis may be a further consequence of the progressive being "in flux" (Comrie, 1976) and at least initially came with social marking.

11.3 The Zero Auxiliary Progressive

Here we discuss how the English progressive described in Section 11.2 has developed a zero auxiliary variant. In our previous study we found that the zero auxiliary is found throughout the progressive paradigm (Table 11.1) but occurs more frequently in certain lexico-syntactic contexts and is socially conditioned by speaker demographics (Caines, 2010).

How is this allowed to happen? Without the information carried by the auxiliary, how is it that communication is not impaired by its omission? In fact, in English, relatively little semantic information is carried by the auxiliary verb compared to the -*ing* participle in progressive constructions. The lexical content of the verb group is contained in the participle, while aspect marking is shared between the participle and auxiliary or auxiliary verb group. So if that first auxiliary is omitted, aspectual and lexical information is still borne by the participle verb. What the (first) auxiliary does do is carry tense marking (recall Table 11.1), and for that reason past tense zero auxiliaries are rare except where context unambiguously situates time reference in the past (13)–(15), while zero auxiliaries are typically interpreted as present tense.

(13) They all doing it the other day. [BNC1994 K6N 779]
(14) When we talking earlier. [BNC1994 JAD 451]
(15) That wasn't what you saying. [BNC1994 F7U 806]

In speech production the auxiliary is usually unstressed and therefore "comparatively insignificant" (Jespersen, 1933, p. 100). The manner in which it is so frequently reduced and affixed to preceding phonological material as an enclitic is one outcome of this insignificance. According to the 'principle of least effort' in speech, "if a simple articulatory gesture works just as well as a complex one, there is a natural tendency to prefer it, thus rendering the articulatory movements in speech simpler" (Wells, 1982, p. 94). Thus the principle "leads us to tend to pronounce words and sentences in a way which involves the minimum of articulatory effort consistent with the need to maintain intelligibility" (Wells, 1982, p. 94). One instantiation of this principle is auxiliary contraction, in which the reduced auxiliary clitic attaches to the preceding item—often a subject pronoun. We may think of the zero auxiliary as an extreme outcome of this principle.

Bybee observes that frequency of use often goes hand in hand with the phonetic reduction described above, terming it the 'Reducing Effect' (2007). "Oft-repeated phrases . . . tend to reduce phonetically" since "repetition of neuromotor sequences leads to greater overlap and reduction of the component articulatory gestures", and as a result, "general reductive sound change occurs earlier in high-frequency words and special reduction occurs in very high-frequency words and phrases" and "thus frequency of use is one factor in explaining sound change" (Bybee, 2007, p. 11).

It should not come as a surprise that repeated use results in physical reduction, given previously made observations in the literature. Case studies have included an investigation by Bybee (1999) into *don't*, a chunk which was found to reduce more in highly frequent contexts such as post-*I* and with verbs such as *know* (it is at its most reduced in the sequence *I don't know*). Jurafsky and colleagues (2001) show that deletion of final /t/ and /d/ strongly correlates with the relative frequency of the word in question: high-frequency *want* and *good* versus low-frequency *let* and *heard*. Since the auxiliary verbs *be* and *have* are themselves high-frequency items in English, as is the progressive construction generally, the obvious assumption to make—and it must remain an assumption since the appropriate historical speech data do not exist—is that zero auxiliary constructions emerged as a fast speech variant to the contracted or full forms. But of course frequency is not the only factor behind sound change: predictability of the word in context (Sanford, 2008) and the speaker's age and gender have also been proposed as influencing factors (Pluymaekers, Ernestus, & Baayen, 2005).

Causes of language change are difficult to identify, and very often there are multiple interacting factors. Based on the results of our previous study we proposed that the zero auxiliary emerged because of low semantic content, phonetic reduction of a high frequency form and a sociolinguistic distribution typical of patterns indicating 'covert prestige' (Trudgill, 1995). Moreover, we proposed that its frequency, lexical and sociolinguistic usage patterns and psycholinguistic processing indicated that it is a valid construction in its own right—an alternative to equivalents with a full or contracted auxiliary, which speakers select in appropriate contexts, contexts which we were able to model stochastically (Caines, 2010; Caines & Buttery, 2010; Caines, 2012).

In this way we move away from the tradition in Generative Grammar that there is an underlying logical form which may become degraded in performance in its surface realisation (Chomsky, 1965). Instead we align with the idea that speakers have a 'constructicon', or a "registry of constructions" (Fillmore, Lee-Goldman, & Rhodes, 2012), from which they make their selections according to linguistic and extra-linguistic variables (Lee, 2007; Sag, 2012). Two findings support this claim: firstly, that in a psycholinguistic study, subjects' performance measures for zero auxiliary stimuli were similar to those for other non-standard constructions often used in speech (e.g., *I wanna go*) but 'better' (faster, less errorful) than those for ungrammatical stimuli such as subject-verb agreement errors and word order transpositions (Caines, 2012). Secondly, frequency of use was conditioned by demographic variables—namely, social class and age group (not gender), such that younger working-class groups were found to use the zero auxiliary most often (Caines, 2010). This indicates to us that there is a social value attached to the zero auxiliary, which was being used in alternation with the full auxiliary form favoured by older middle-class groups. In this new study of the Spoken BNC2014S, we investigate whether the zero auxiliary has progressed, regressed or held steady in its frequency of use in spoken British English.

11.4 Corpus Studies Old and New

In this section we firstly recall our original study of auxiliary realisation in progressive constructions in the Spoken BNC1994 (Section 11.4.1), then report on our comparative study of the Spoken BNC2014S (Section 11.4.2). We found that the rate of zero auxiliary use has dramatically fallen in the two decades between the two corpora, and that the sociolinguistic contours found in the former have flattened out in the latter.

11.4.1 Corpus Study 1: The British National Corpus 1994

The BNC1994 was originally chosen for a study of progressive constructions for three reasons: (i) because it features spoken language, (ii) at the time it was the most recent large corpus of British English in existence, and (iii) because of its emphasis on balanced speaker recruitment with respect to a number of demographic variables including age, gender and social class (Crowdy, 1993).

Here we recap the results of our previous survey of auxiliary realisation in progressive aspect interrogatives in conversational British English (Caines, 2010). We comprehensively surveyed all subsections of the BNC1994 and found that the zero auxiliary occurs ubiquitously, even in writing, albeit to a lesser extent and only in transcriptions of speech and representations of dialogue in works of fiction. However, relative zero auxiliary frequencies were higher in the spoken section and so for the sake of a richer dataset we focused on that subcorpus ('the Spoken BNC1994').

In total we retrieved 93,253 progressive aspect constructions from the Spoken BNC1994 and annotated each one for a number of morphosyntactic variables—namely, person and number of subject, nominal or pronominal, clause type, *wh*-word in subject noun phrase (or not), polarity, tense, perfectivity and auxiliary form (Caines & Buttery, 2012). Our annotation variables and values are more fully presented in Table 11.2.

We found that the zero auxiliary occurred across all speech genres contained in the Spoken BNC1994, even including the more formal settings such as meetings, broadcasts and lectures. Nevertheless, the locus of the zero auxiliary was found to be the four-million-word spontaneous conversation section, and indeed, that section offers the closest comparison to the Spoken BNC2014S in size and in terms of the way it was collected and the situational contexts of the recordings.

In Table 11.3 we present the results of our previous study of progressive constructions in the conversation section of the Spoken BNC1994, and furthermore have restricted our attention to interrogatives with pronominal subjects so as to keep the new study of a manageable size. Having been the basis of a doctoral thesis, the previous study also covered declaratives and all nominal subjects—pronouns and other nouns.

As can be seen in Table 11.3, the full auxiliary form was the predominant one for interrogatives in the Spoken BNC1994. The contracted auxiliary was the minority form (partly as it is restricted to *wh*-questions only, in which the auxiliary enclitic has a token to 'attach' to) and the zero auxiliary was found throughout the person and number paradigm—above all with second person, first person plural and third person plural

Table 11.2 Progressive Aspect Construction Annotation Scheme

Variable	Value	Example
Subject type	nominal	The computer is working
	pronominal	She is working
Subject person & number	1st singular	I am working
	2nd	You are working
	3rd singular	It is working
	1st plural	We are working
	3rd plural	They are working
	zero	Just working today
Clause type	declarative	You are working
	interrogative	Are you working?
wh-word	true	When is he working?
	false	Is he working?
Tense	present	I am working
	past	I was working
Perfect aspect	present perfect	They have been working
	past perfect	They had been working
Polarity	positive	It is working
	negative	It is not working
Auxiliary	full	You are working
	contracted	You're working
	zero	You working

Table 11.3 Auxiliary Realisation for Progressive Aspect Interrogatives With Pronominal Subjects in the Conversational Section of the Spoken BNC1994

	Count	Full Aux (%)	Contracted (%)	Zero Aux (%)
1st person singular	263	258 (98.1)	2 (0.8)	3 (1.1)
2nd person sg/pl	3,553	2,285 (64.3)	55 (1.6)	1,213 (34.1)
3rd person singular	1,316	613 (46.6)	645 (49.0)	58 (4.4)
1st person plural	483	363 (75.2)	6 (1.2)	114 (23.6)
3rd person plural	287	224 (78.1)	5 (1.7)	58 (20.2)
Progressive interrogatives	5,902	3,743 (63.4)	713 (12.1)	1,446 (24.5)

pronouns. Figure 11.1 illustrates the proportional auxiliary realisations given in parentheses in Table 11.3.

Thanks to the demographic metadata collected for participants in the conversational section of the Spoken BNC1994, we could associate each progressive interrogative in the corpus with the gender of its speaker

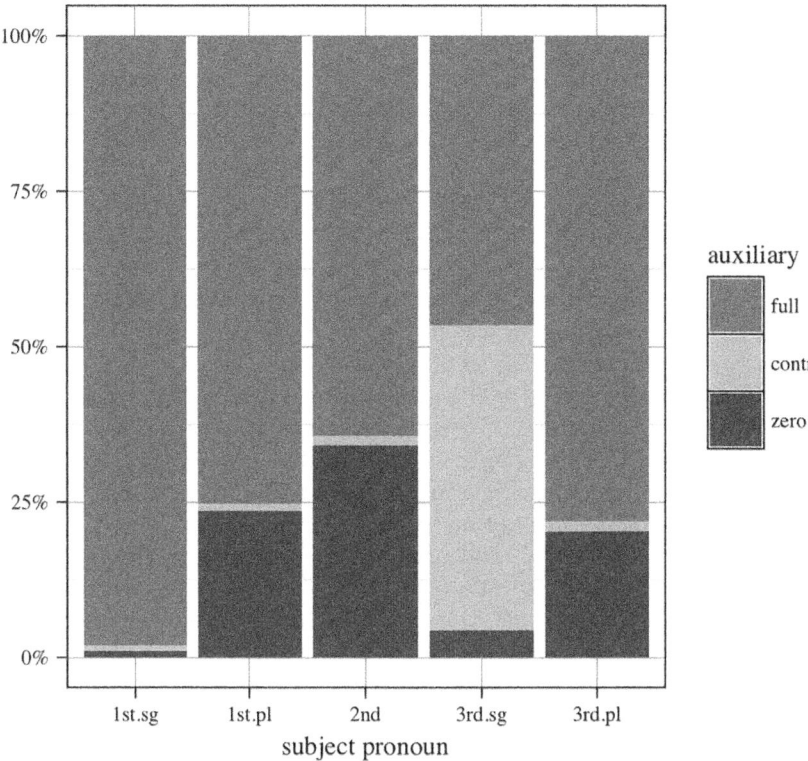

Figure 11.1 Auxiliary Realisation for Progressive Aspect Interrogatives With Pronominal Subjects in the Conversational Section of the Spoken BNC1994

Table 11.4 Gender of Speaker for Second Person Progressive Interrogatives in the Conversational Section of the Spoken BNC1994

	Count	Full Aux (%)	Contracted (%)	Zero Aux (%)
Female	2,072	1,346	30	696
(n = 560)		(65.0)	(1.4)	(33.6)
Male	1,019	674	17	328
(n = 511)		(66.1)	(1.7)	(32.2)
Unclassified	–	265	8	189
2nd person sg/pl	3,553	2,285	55	1,213
		(64.3)	(1.6)	(34.1)

(Table 11.4). We then ascertained that gender of speaker did not significantly affect zero auxiliary use in the second person progressive interrogative set, using mixed effects logistic regression[3] (Winter & Wieling, 2016) with auxiliary realisation transformed into a binary variable (zero auxiliary or not zero auxiliary), gender as fixed effect, speaker and verb as random effects. No significant improvement came from adding gender as a fixed effect in comparison with a baseline model featuring speaker and verb random effects only (AIC = –1.13; $\chi^2(1)$ = 0.87, p = 0.351).[4]

Age and social class of speaker, on the other hand, did affect zero auxiliary use. We show auxiliary realisation counts in Tables 11.5 and 11.6, and illustrate these demographic variables in Figures 11.2 and 11.3. Mixed effects logistic regression indicated that age as a fixed effect (centred values) brought significant improvement over the baseline model (random effects only): AIC = 3.26; $\chi^2(1)$ = 5.26, p = 0.022. Likewise, social class as a fixed effect constructed a significantly better model for the zero auxiliary than the baseline: AIC = 9.77; $\chi^2(3)$ = 17.8, p = 0.0014.

Social class information was provided for the Spoken BNC1994 conversation section according to the Social Grade classification, developed for British society in the 1950s by the National Readership Survey, a market research organisation. Classifications are made on a six-point scale (A, B, C1, C2, D, E) on the basis of the occupation of the chief income earner in a household, with A and B representing higher managerial or professional roles, C1 junior managerial or professional roles, C2 skilled manual workers, D semi- and unskilled workers, and E casual or lowest grade workers. The social grades in Spoken BNC1994 were actually given on a four-point scale, following the convention to merge the top two and bottom two grades, AB and DE, such that AB is taken as a proxy for middle class, C1 for lower middle class, C2 for upper working class, and DE for working class.

Table 11.5 Age Group of Speaker for Second Person Progressive Interrogatives in the Conversational Section of the Spoken BNC1994

	Count	*Full Aux (%)*	*Contracted (%)*	*Zero Aux (%)*
0–9 years	93	63	2	28
(n = 78)		(67.7)	(2.2)	(30.1)
10–19 years	684	436	9	239
(n = 251)		(63.8)	(1.3)	(34.9)
20–29 years	411	238	5	168
(n = 148)		(57.9)	(1.2)	(40.9)
30–39 years	688	426	12	250
(n = 139)		(61.9)	(1.8)	(36.3)
40–49 years	432	306	4	122
(n = 128)		(70.8)	(0.9)	(28.3)
50–59 years	380	259	8	113
(n = 85)		(68.2)	(2.1)	(29.7)
60–69 years	136	105	2	29
(n = 69)		(77.2)	(1.5)	(21.3)
70–79 years	181	134	3	44
(n = 47)		(74.0)	(1.7)	(24.3)
Unclassified	522	299	10	213
2nd person sg/pl	3,553	2,285	55	1,213
		(64.3)	(1.6)	(34.1)

Though Table 11.5 and Figure 11.2 indicate a U-shaped pattern of age group use of the zero auxiliary in Spoken BNC1994, if we group the first four age groups against the last four age groups it is apparent that the zero auxiliary is associated more with the younger speakers in the corpus than the older ones. The fact that its use is driven by speakers in their twenties and thirties above all will become important in our subsequent study of the Spoken BNC2014, as corpus statistics from the newer corpus indicate that the age group pattern we see in Figure 11.2 does not continue into the 21st century.

Similarly, Table 11.6 and Figure 11.3 indicate that the zero auxiliary is favoured by working-class rather than middle-class speakers. These are patterns typical of linguistic features with covert prestige, according to sociolinguistic theory (Trudgill, 1995). In other words, those speaker groups with less reason to identify with standard forms—generally set by older middle-class speaker groups—are those who tend to use the zero auxiliary progressive more often.

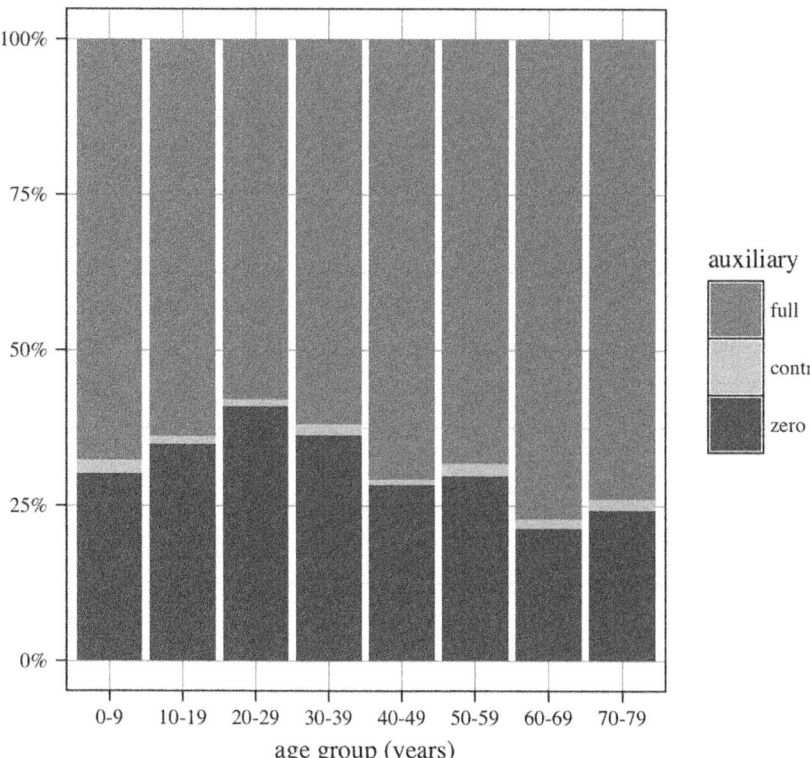

Figure 11.2 Age Group of Speaker for Second Person Progressive Interrogatives in the Conversational Section of the Spoken BNC1994

Table 11.6 Social Class of Speaker for Second Person Progressive Interrogatives in the Conversational Section of the Spoken BNC1994

	Count	Full Aux (%)	Contracted (%)	Zero Aux (%)
Middle	612	458	8	146
(AB, n = 88)		(74.8)	(1.3)	(23.9)
Lower middle	697	462	11	224
(C1, n = 116)		(66.3)	(1.6)	(32.1)
Upper working	665	401	13	251
(C2, n = 99)		(60.3)	(2.0)	(37.7)
Working	316	166	6	144
(DE, n = 60)		(52.5)	(1.9)	(45.6)
Unclassified	1,263	798	17	448
2nd person sg/pl	3,553	2,285	55	1,213
		(64.3)	(1.6)	(34.1)

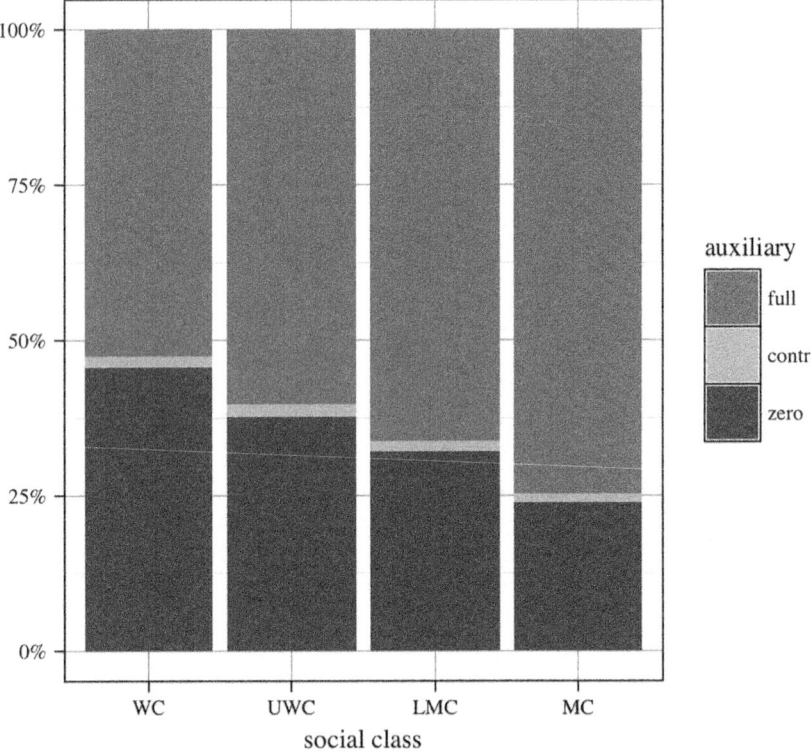

Figure 11.3 Social Class of Speaker for Second Person Progressive Interrogatives in the Conversational Section of the Spoken BNC1994

As an investigation of lexical effects on zero auxiliary use, we conducted a 'collostructional analysis' (Stefanowitsch & Gries, 2003; Gries, Hampe, & Schönefeld, 2005) to confirm whether the zero auxiliary associated strongly with any specific verbs. Specifically, we employed the collostructional technique known as 'collexeme analysis'—"the study of collocation with association measures" (Gries, 2015)—with an R program which has been made publicly available for this purpose (Gries, 2014)[5]. The program takes corpus, verb and construction frequencies as the input, and outputs a table of association strength for each verb based on the observed and expected frequencies of that verb inside and outside the target construction. Thus we are presented with the verbs ranked on a scale of attraction to the zero auxiliary progressive. The benefit of collexeme analysis is that it does not assume a normal distribution or homogeneity of variance, properties rarely encountered in language (Mandelbrot, 1966). The analysis is underpinned by the Fisher-Yates exact test and results are presented in the form, negative log to the base of ten of the one-tailed p-value computed by the test ($p_{-log,10}$).

As shown in Table 11.7, several verbs are highly attracted, and repulsed, by the second person zero auxiliary progressive interrogative. *Doing* and *going/gonna* are chief among these on the attraction side, whilst *saying, taking* and *working* are very frequent in progressive constructions but have a negative association with the zero auxiliary variant. Furthermore, if we view the zero auxiliary set on a constructional level, we find that

Table 11.7 Collexeme Analysis of Selected Verbs and Zero Auxiliary Second Person Progressive Interrogatives in the Spoken BNC1994 (* $p < 0.05$, ** $p < 0.01$, *** $p < 0.001$)

Verb	In Progressive Constructions in the Spoken BNC1994	Zero Auxiliary 2nd Person Interrogative		Relation	$p_{-log,10}$
		Expected Frequency	Observed Frequency		
doing	6,243	90	295	attraction	74.6***
going/gonna	29,161	419	553	attraction	14.7***
laughing	143	2	9	attraction	3.62***
calling	146	2	7	attraction	2.27**
having	1,691	24	34	attraction	1.47*
looking	2,424	35	41	attraction	0.79
getting	3,031	44	45	attraction	0.37
coming	2,637	38	32	repulsion	0.73
talking	3,117	45	33	repulsion	1.43*
thinking	1,257	18	8	repulsion	2.20**
trying	2,192	32	11	repulsion	4.74***
working	1,598	23	5	repulsion	5.24***
taking	1,089	16	1	repulsion	5.65***
saying	3,814	55	19	repulsion	7.97***

nine constructional schemas account for more than half the zero auxiliary second person progressive interrogatives in the Spoken BNC1994:
namely, *what you doing, how you doing, what you laughing for/at, what
you looking for/at, what you talking about, what you having, where you
going, you going/gonna* V, WH *you going/gonna* V. Such a distribution—
many contributed by the few—is not surprising given the Zipfian nature of
human languages (Zipf, 1965 [1935]), but it does remind us that the zero
auxiliary has not spread evenly through the lexicon nor the constructicon.
Instead there are prototypical high-frequency contexts for the zero auxiliary, which seemingly spreads by analogy to other contexts, albeit at lower
frequencies for now. In the next section we verify whether the zero auxiliary has diffused further across the lexicon and constructicon of English.

11.4.2 Corpus Study 2: The Early Access Sample of the Spoken BNC2014

In order to carry out a comparative study of contemporary zero auxiliary use with our previous study, we were able to query the early access
Sample of the Spoken BNC2014 ('the Spoken BNC2014S'). Access to
the Sample was granted via Lancaster University's CQPweb server (Hardie, 2012) and therefore we retrieved utterances of interest using part-of-
speech searches in CQP ('corpus query processor') syntax.

Since the zero auxiliary was more likely to be found in interrogative
rather than declarative clauses (Caines & Buttery, 2012), we opted to
retrieve only interrogatives from the Spoken BNC2014S for our comparative study with its predecessor. As an additional constraint we focused on
pronominal subjects only, again on the basis of our finding that the zero
auxiliary occurred more often with pronouns as subject than with other
noun types (Caines & Buttery, 2012). Every CQP search therefore centred around the juxtaposition of a pronoun and an *-ing* participial form,
optionally with intervening negative and adverbial items. These searches
were designed to capture progressive interrogatives with full auxiliaries
(16), contracted auxiliaries (17), and zero auxiliaries (18), negated (19),
adverbials (20), the past tense (21) and the perfect aspect (22).

(16) what time are you going back on Saturday?[6] [BNC2014 STXT 391]
(17) what's she doing? [BNC2014 S9MK 460]
(18) what time you going home? [BNC2014 SXKQ 63]
(19) why aren't I counting? [BNC2014 SHTW 623]
(20) Are you just googling it? [BNC2014 SDR9 620]
(21) why were you watching Home and Awa-? oh [BNC2014 S37E 447]
(22) has she been snorkelling? [BNC2014 SCA5 512]

With our set of CQP queries[7] we retrieved a corpus of 5,674 text
strings which were potentially progressive aspect interrogatives. We ran

a supervised annotation procedure in R (R Core Team, 2016) to confirm whether the -*ing* form indeed formed part of a progressive construction. Inevitably, our searches accumulated a bit of noise due to the syncretism of -*ing* forms in adjectival (23) and nominal (24) functions, alongside the verbal participle which features in the progressive. Plus, the -*ing* form often occurs in non-finite clause complements (25).

(23) —they're really good thank you
     —cracking
     —mm [BNC2014 SEKZ 636]
(24) is it knitting tonight? [BNC2014 S48K 926]
(25) someone else is gonna have to listen to me swearing [BNC2014 SHSL 518]

For the 3,873 hits confirmed as progressive interrogatives, we proceeded to code subject and clause properties of the construction in question using the same variables and values shown in Table 11.1. In this way our corpus was reduced to 3,674 progressive aspect interrogatives with pronominal subjects. In Table 11.8 we show auxiliary realisation patterns for these progressive interrogatives by subject person and number.

Firstly, we note that we retrieved many fewer progressive interrogatives with pronoun subjects from the Spoken BNC2014S (3,674) than from the conversation section of its predecessor (5,902), even though both corpora contain four to five million words and both feature approximately 67,000 verbal -*ing* forms. So the disparity is either due to our undertaking a less-than-comprehensive search of the Spoken BNC2014S, or because many fewer progressive interrogatives were uttered—especially with second person, third person singular and first person plural pronominal subjects (cf. Table 11.3). We cannot establish which is the

Table 11.8 Auxiliary Realisation for Progressive Aspect Interrogatives With Pronominal Subjects in the Spoken BNC2014S

	Count	Full Aux (%)	Contracted (%)	Zero Aux (%)
1st person singular	268	265 (98.8)	2 (0.8)	1 (0.4)
2nd person sg/pl	2,091	1,896 (90.7)	8 (0.4)	187 (8.9)
3rd person singular	668	477 (71.4)	181 (27.1)	10 (1.5)
1st person plural	368	352 (95.6)	1 (0.3)	15 (4.1)
3rd person plural	279	273 (97.8)	0 (0)	6 (2.2)
Progressive interrogatives	3,674	3,263 (88.8)	192 (5.2)	219 (6.0)

case without undertaking an analysis of every utterance in the Spoken BNC2014S containing a verbal *-ing* form, something which time restrictions do not allow for.

However, if we accept this as a faithful sample of progressive interrogatives in the Spoken BNC2014S, the second noticeable difference with the BNC1994 is the much lower rate of zero auxiliary occurrence: 6.0% overall, compared to 24.5% (cf. Table 11.3). Zero auxiliary frequencies are down across all persons and numbers compared to the BNC1994, but especially the second person, first person plural and third person plural pronouns. We illustrate these differences in Figure 11.4, repeating BNC1994 auxiliary realisations (Figure 11.1) alongside those for the Spoken BNC2014S, for convenience.

We now turn to our demographic variables of interest—gender, age and social class—repeating our survey of the BNC1994 in which we investigated second person progressive interrogatives only. Table 11.9 shows the gender of speaker by auxiliary realisation for second person progressive interrogatives in the Spoken BNC2014S. As in the Spoken BNC1994, gender does not affect rates of auxiliary use (cf. Table 11.4; AIC = –1.97; $\chi^2(1) = 0.026$, p = 0.871).

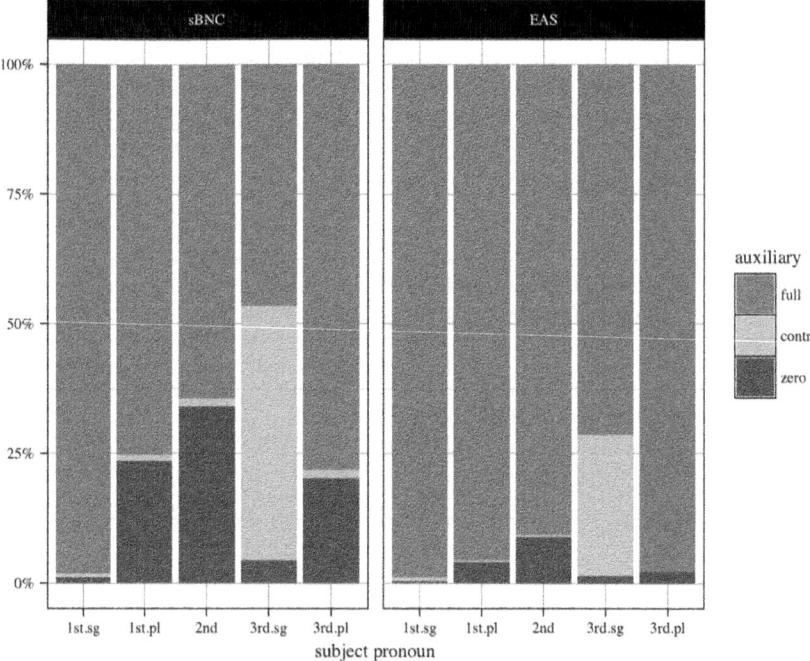

Figure 11.4 Auxiliary Realisation for Progressive Aspect Interrogatives With Pronominal Subjects in the Conversational Section of Spoken BNC2014DS (left) and the Spoken BNC2014S (right).

Table 11.9 Gender of Speaker for Second Person Progressive Interrogatives in the Spoken BNC2014S

	Count	Full Aux (%)	Contracted (%)	Zero Aux (%)
Female	1,400	1,271	5	124
(n = 207)		(90.8)	(0.4)	(8.8)
Male	691	625	3	59
(n = 171)		(90.5)	(0.4)	(9.1)
2nd person sg/pl	2,091	1,896	8	187
		(90.7)	(0.4)	(8.9)

Next, we inspect how the age group and social class[8] of speaker are found to affect zero auxiliary use in the Spoken BNC2014S, in Tables 11.10 and 11.11, starting with age group.

As we see in Table 11.10, age group does not seem to have the same effect on zero auxiliary occurrence in the Spoken BNC2014S as it did in the BNC1994 (AIC = –1.92; $\chi^2(1) = 0.08$, p = 0.777). Whereas before the younger age groups tended to use the zero auxiliary more than the older age groups, in the Spoken BNC2014S we instead find that zero auxiliary use is fairly constant across the ages of 10 to 79 years (Figure 11.5). We note also that zero auxiliary rates are lower across the board, and that while there are older age groups in the Spoken BNC2014S than there were in BNC1994 (max. 90–99 rather than 70–79), there are also far fewer speakers aged 19 and under (cf. Table 11.5). Indeed, the original Spoken BNC1994 contains a large subset of teenage speech because it features the Bergen Corpus of London Teenage Language, compiled in 1993 (COLT; Stenström, Andersen, & Kristine Hasund, 2002). COLT contains 445,000 words from thirty-one contributors aged 10–19 (with coincidental utterances by pre- and post-adolescent interlocutors) and the recordings by contributors aged 16 or under were included in the BNC1994, as recruitment for the demographic component had included speakers aged 15 upwards (Burnard, 2007).

In Table 11.11 we see less of an effect of the speaker's social class on zero auxiliary use in the Spoken BNC2014S compared to the BNC1994 (cf. Table 11.6; AIC = –1.92; $\chi^2(3) = 1.95$, p = 0.58). Figure 11.6 confirms that, whereas in the BNC1994 there was a pronounced gradient for social class, the rate of zero auxiliary use in the Spoken BNC2014S has flattened across classes. This is symptomatic of the general reduction in zero auxiliary use in the Spoken BNC2014S, and certainly suggests that the variant's covert prestige has reduced in the intervening years since the BNC1994 was collated.

As for the distribution of speakers across the social classes, it is somewhat problematic for the representativeness of the corpus that there were so few contributors to the Spoken BNC2014S from the C2 band. However, it is doubtful that this has affected our results, as the line from C1 to DE is fairly flat, and we can assume from this that even with more C2 speakers the zero auxiliary rates would be fairly similar, give or take

Table 11.10 Age Group of Speaker for Second Person Progressive Interrogatives in the Spoken BNC2014S[9]

	Count	Full Aux (%)	Contracted (%)	Zero Aux (%)
0–9 years	1	1	0	0
(n = 3)		(100)	(0)	(0)
10–19 years	100	91	0	9
(n = 21)		(91.0)	(0)	(9.0)
20–29 years	985	888	5	92
(n = 142)		(90.2)	(0.5)	(9.3)
30–39 years	413	384	1	28
(n = 54)		(93.0)	(0.2)	(6.8)
40–49 years	149	132	0	17
(n = 44)		(88.6)	(0)	(11.4)
50–59 years	166	144	0	22
(n = 41)		(86.7)	(0)	(13.3)
60–69 years	179	168	1	10
(n = 48)		(93.9)	(0.6)	(5.5)
70–79 years	64	57	0	7
(n = 13)		(89.1)	(0)	(10.9)
80–89 years	6	6	0	0
(n = 7)		(100)	(0)	(0)
90–99 years	3	3	0	0
(n = 2)		(100)	(0)	(0)
Unclassified	25	22	1	2
2nd person sg/pl	2,091	1,896	8	187
		(90.7)	(0.4)	(8.9)

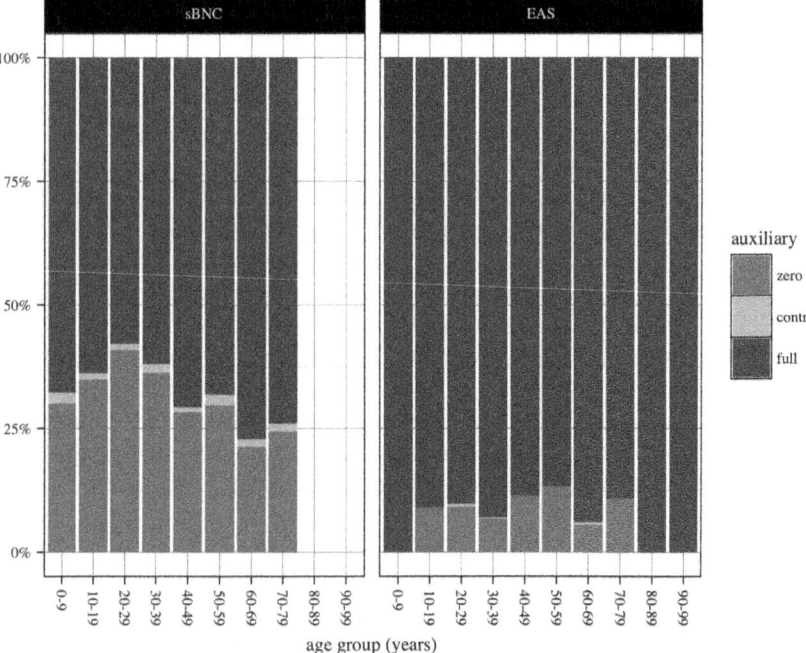

Figure 11.5 Age Group of Speaker for Second Person Progressive Interrogatives in the Conversational Section of Spoken BNC1994DS (Left) and the Spoken BNC2014S (Right)

Table 11.11 Social Class of Speaker for Second Person Progressive Interrogatives in the Spoken BNC2014S

	Count	Full Aux (%)	Contracted (%)	Zero Aux (%)
Middle	1,188	1,078	6	105
(AB, n = 145)		(90.7)	(0.5)	(8.8)
Lower middle	248	228	0	20
(C1, n = 53)		(91.9)	(0)	(8.1)
Upper working	51	49	0	2
(C2, n = 11)		(96.1)	(0)	(3.9)
Working	580	520	1	59
(DE, n = 167)		(89.6)	(0.2)	(10.2)
Unclassified	23	21	1	1
2nd person sg/pl	2,090	1,896	8	187
		(90.7)	(0.4)	(8.9)

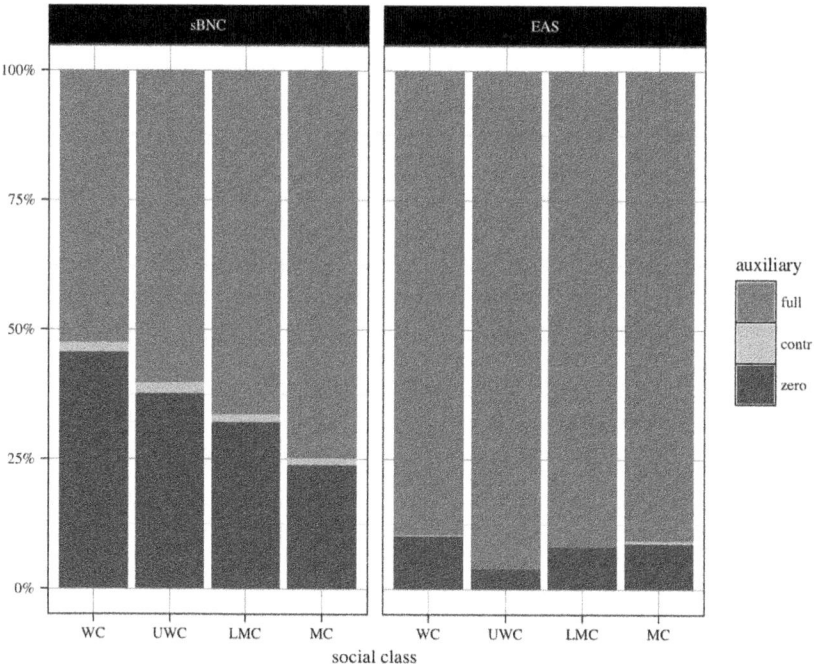

Figure 11.6 Social Class of Speaker for Second Person Progressive Interrogatives in The Conversational Section of the Spoken BNC1994 (Left) and the Spoken BNC2014S (Right)

some idiosyncrasies and other group dynamics. Moreover, the inference of social class from occupation alone is a questionable step—indeed the assignment of social class to an individual is highly fraught, full stop (Savage, 2010)—and we can be sure that a balance of genders, regions and age groups is more important to corpus representativeness than what is essentially a range of occupations. But that is the convention and data available, both in the BNC1994 and Spoken BNC2014S, and even though we are comparing 'social class' via proxy from occupation, the comparison is a fair one and certainly the BNC2014 results show that the zero auxiliary gradient previously seen has almost completely flattened out.

Now, if we introduce *corpus* as a fixed effect through mixed effects logistic regression—Spoken BNC1994 versus Spoken BNC2014S—and include progressive interrogatives from both corpora, we find that it significantly improves on a baseline model of random effects only (speaker and verb): AIC = 568; $\chi^2(1)$ = 570, $p < 0.001$. Finally, additional small improvement is brought by introducing age and social class (with interaction) to the corpus model: AIC = 2.47; $\chi^2(9)$ = 20.5, $p = 0.015$. Our regression analyses confirm that 'time' (taking the two corpora as temporal proxy) is the strongest predictor of our dependent variable, use of the zero auxiliary in progressive interrogatives.

We repeat the collexeme analysis conducted on zero auxiliary second person progressive interrogatives in the BNC1994 (Stefanowitsch & Gries, 2003; Gries, 2014). Though there are many fewer zero auxiliaries in the Spoken BNC2014S, the method is robust as it measures association based on observed and expected frequencies calculated from the total number of zero auxiliaries and the frequency of any given verb in all progressive constructions in the corpus. Recall that in the BNC1994, *doing* and *going/gonna* were the most strongly attracted verbs to the zero auxiliary construction (Table 11.7). Here we again see that the same two verbs are top-ranked with an attraction to the zero auxiliary, albeit with their order reversed (Table 11.12). In contrast, *working, looking, getting*

Table 11.12 Collexeme Analysis of Selected Verbs and Zero Auxiliary Second Person Progressive Interrogative in the Spoken BNC2014S (* $p < 0.05$, ** $p < 0.01$, *** $p < 0.001$)

Verb	In Progressive Constructions in the Spoken BNC2014S	Zero Auxiliary 2nd Person Interrogative		Relation	$p_{-log,10}$
		Expected Frequency	Observed Frequency		
going/gonna	14,386	39	77	attraction	9.65***
doing	5,089	14	36	attraction	6.96***
turning	111	0.3	2	attraction	1.43*
running	440	1	3	attraction	0.92
using	511	1.4	2	attraction	0.39
talking	1,958	5	6	attraction	0.35
coming	1,829	4.9	5	attraction	0.25
having	2,229	6	5	repulsion	0.36
getting	2,706	3.4	6	repulsion	0.41
working	1,266	3.4	2	repulsion	0.48
looking	1,828	5	3	repulsion	0.58

and *having* occur frequently in progressive constructions in the Spoken BNC2014S but are found to hold a negative association with the second person zero auxiliary. The association of the latter three has switched from 'attraction' to 'repulsion', from the Spoken BNC1994 to the Spoken BNC2014S, indicative of the general decrease in frequency of the zero auxiliary variant.

11.5 Discussion

Our comparison of auxiliary realisations in progressive constructions in the Spoken BNC2014S and Spoken BNC1994 clearly indicates a sharp fall in use of the zero auxiliary variant in the intervening two decades. Both corpora were designed and collated in a very careful manner; we take them as faithful snapshots of spoken British English in the 1990s and 2010s, and consequently conclude that the zero auxiliary has declined in general use, in progressive interrogatives with pronominal subjects at least.

Nevertheless, we must keep in mind that all corpora are samples of language as it is actually and generally used. If we consider our studies of auxiliary realisation in progressive constructions as measurements from these samples, we can consider the possibility that either reading—from the Spoken BNC1994 or the Spoken BNC2014S— might be an anomaly, since language is not normally distributed and highly idiosyncratic. For instance, just eighty-two of the 288 speakers who uttered a progressive interrogative in the Spoken BNC2014S produced the 226 zero auxiliaries we found there. Furthermore, 50% of those 226 zero auxiliaries are produced by only eleven speakers, the other seventy-one speakers producing no more than five zero auxiliaries each. A similar Zipfian distribution was found for zero auxiliaries and the speakers who uttered them in the Spoken BNC1994. Thus, even such large corpora as the conversational Spoken BNC1994 and Spoken BNC2014S are prone to the idiosyncrasies of their contributors. But still, we view them each as representative of their time, and note that zero auxiliary frequencies in the Spoken BNC1994 may have been extraordinarily high as much as those in the Spoken BNC2014S may be extraordinarily low. One further caveat is that the Spoken BNC1994 contained a large subset of teenage speech (the COLT corpus), and the Spoken BNC2014S is noticeably short of C2 speakers— not that the outdated Social Grade scale is a wholly satisfactory way to represent the complex British class system.

Nevertheless, accepting the corpora as representative and the results as a fair comparison, it is apparent that the zero auxiliary use has markedly decreased in frequency since the early 1990s. We find this outcome a little surprising as the variant has, for instance, found its way into informal genres of writing. Anecdotal examples include zero auxiliaries from Twitter (26)–(28).

230 Caines, McCarthy and Buttery

(26) How you finding our new #BBCIntroducing time slot? Which show are you listening to?
"BBC Introducing" (@bbc_introducing) 2013-01-05 20:47.[10]
(27) When we gonna have cameras behind phone screens?
"Jack Garratt" (@jackgarratt) 2016-10-30 12:05.[11]
(28) What you doing?
"Matty." (@matty_selley) 2016-10-30 09:44.[12]

Indeed, a brief survey of 5.8 million Twitter conversations—series of tweets between 'interlocutors' collected using the unsupervised method described by Ritter and colleagues (2010)—containing 59 million tokens confirms that zero auxiliary rates are higher than those found in the Spoken BNC2014S and indeed are close to what they were in the Spoken BNC1994. We searched for fourteen open interrogatives—featuring a *wh*-word—with verbs both attracted to and repulsed by the zero auxiliary[13] (Table 11.12) and retrieved 12,362 progressive interrogatives in which 62.7% had the full auxiliary form, 1.9% had a contracted form and 35.4% were zero auxiliaries. It may be, then, that the zero auxiliary, having originated in the spoken domain—as suggested by a comparison of its frequency in the Spoken BNC1994 and its written counterpart (Caines, 2010)—has more recently transitioned away from speech to the more informal genres of the written medium, primarily the digital domains in which the pressure to communicate efficiently is not only physical, as it is in speech, but also at times explicitly set. For instance, SMS texts have a per-message limit of 160 characters. In many parts of the world this matters, since 'pay as you go' usage of mobile phones remains the majority use case, even if contracted usage with limitless SMS messaging is the norm in the United Kingdom.[14] Similarly, though free of charge, Twitter users are restricted to 140 character posts at a time. In these domains, omission of semantically-light material is beneficial and potentially brings both time and cost savings.

In sociolinguistic terms, the zero auxiliary has become less of a marker of age group and social class, instead being used more equally across speaker demographics. These findings are important not only for the sake of understanding language use, language change and spoken grammar, but they also have pedagogical implications. Namely, whereas before we might have advised introducing the zero auxiliary to learners of English as an informal speech variant (Caines et al., 2016), now we would say the same while not worrying about sociolinguistic consequences for the learner. We would also encourage its use in less formal written genres such as Internet communication, particularly for collostructions with high attraction values.

Acknowledgements

This chapter reports on research supported by Cambridge English, University of Cambridge. We gratefully acknowledge the help and advice of

Jim Blevins, Anne O'Keeffe, Steve Walsh and Martijn Wieling. We thank the editors of this volume and two anonymous reviewers for their feedback which greatly improved the chapter.

Notes

1 All rights in the texts cited from the British National Corpus are reserved (Oxford University Computing Services on behalf of the BNC Consortium). Each extract is followed by 'BNC1994', a unique text identifier and a sentence number.

2 We wish to state at the outset that we accept the judgements of the trained transcribers of both corpora used here in terms of the presence or absence of auxiliary verbs. By 'zero' auxiliary we mean 'zero' or 'near-zero' presence of an auxiliary verb form. We have listened to a sample of BNC1994 recordings through the Audio BNC project (www.phon.ox.ac.uk/AudioBNC), and concurred in all cases with the transcribers that the auxiliary is not there—or at least, we cannot perceive it. We are sometimes asked whether the zero auxiliary could not in fact be an intended but barely pronounced form, especially for the English form *are*. This could well be the case, but even so would speak of the option to whittle away at auxiliary forms, and does not alter what was actually produced and perceived, whatever the speaker's intentions (the zero auxiliary and speaker intention is an issue addressed in Caines, 2012).

3 All regression analyses reported in this chapter use R (R. Core Team, 2016) and the lme4 package (Bates et al., 2015).

4 Where AIC is 'Akaike information criterion'—an information-theoretic measure of the relative quality of statistical models on the same dataset—and $\chi2(1)$ represents a chi-square test with one degree of freedom in an analysis of variance (ANOVA) between the baseline and gender regression models.

5 Even though we originally ran a collexeme analysis with a previous version of the Coll.analysis program (Coll.analysis 3.2a. A program for R for Windows 2.x.) we re-ran the analyses with the latest version of the program, as cited (www.linguistics.ucsb.edu/faculty/stgries/teaching/groningen; accessed 2017–2002–2016).

6 All rights in the texts cited from the Spoken BNC2014 Early Access Subset are reserved (Cambridge University Press). Each extract is followed by 'BNC2014', a unique text identifier and a line number.

7 Queries took one of three base forms—(1) [pos = "PP.*"] [pos = "V.G"], (2) [pos = "PP.*"] [pos = "VBN"] [pos = "V.G"], (3) [pos = "PP.*"] [word = "gon"] [word = "na"]—with variants to include all combinations of negative [pos = "XX"] and adverb tokens [pos = "R.*"].

8 Social class was coded in the Spoken BNC2014S according to the National Statistics Socio-Economic Classification (NS-SEC), used for the UK population census since 2001. NS-SEC labels were mapped back to the Social Grade classes used in the BNC1994 (Love, Dembry, Hardie, Brezina & McEnery, 2017).

9 Early contributors to the Spoken BNC2014S were asked to place themselves in age ranges which slightly differ from the ones we used for our BNC1994 study: 0–10 years, 11–18 and 19–29 rather than 0–9, 10–19 and 20–29. Later, speakers were instructed to declare their exact age in years; where they did so and were found to be aged 10 or 19 we adjusted the age group counts accordingly.

10 http://twitter.com/bbc_introducing/status/287661510598209536 (accessed 2016-11-01).

11 https://twitter.com/JackGarratt/status/792683772013600768 (accessed 2016-11-01).

12 https://twitter.com/matty_selley/status/792648472130297857 (accessed 2016-11-01).
13 Namely, *what (are) you* followed by *going, gonna, doing, talking, saying, having, getting, looking* and *taking*, plus *how (are) you doing, where (are) you going, when (are) you coming, why (are) you looking* and *where (are) you taking.*
14 Source: YouGov https://yougov.co.uk/news/2015/08/19/sim-only-march-consumers-hold-handsets-longer (accessed 2016–2010–2031).

References

Bates, D., Mächler, M., Bolker, B., & Walker, S. (2015). Fitting linear mixed-effects models using lme4. *Journal of Statistical Software*, 67(1), 1–48.

Biber, D., Johansson, S., Leech, G., Conrad, S., & Finegan, E. (1999). *Longman grammar of spoken and written English.* London: Longman.

The British National Corpus, version 2 (BNC World). (2001). Distributed by Oxford University Computing Services on behalf of the BNC Consortium. Retrieved from www.natcorp.ox.ac.uk

Burnard, L. (Ed.). (2007). *The British national corpus users reference guide.* Retrieved from www.natcorp.ox.ac.uk/docs/userManual

Bybee, J. (1999). The effect of usage on degrees of constituency: The reduction of *don't* in English. *Linguistics*, 37, 575–596.

Bybee, J. (2007). *Frequency of use and the organisation of language.* Oxford: Oxford University Press.

Bybee, J., Perkins, R. D., & Pagliuca, W. (1994). *The evolution of grammar: Tense, aspect and modality in the languages of the world.* Chicago: University of Chicago Press.

Caines, A. (2010). *You talking to me? Zero auxiliary constructions in British English.* Ph.D thesis. Cambridge: University of Cambridge.

Caines, A. (2012). You talking to me? Testing corpus data with a shadowing experiment. In S. Th. Gries & D. Divjak (Eds.), *Frequency effects in language learning and processing.* Berlin: Mouton de Gruyter.

Caines, A., & Buttery, P. (2010). You talking to me? A predictive model for zero auxiliary constructions. In *Proceedings of the 2010 Workshop on NLP and Linguistics: Finding the Common Ground, ACL 2010.* Retrieved from www.aclweb.org/anthology/W10-2107

Caines, A., & Buttery, P. (2012). Annotating progressive aspect constructions in the spoken section of the British National Corpus. In *Proceedings of the Eighth International Conference on Language Resources and Evaluation (LREC'12).* Retrieved from www.lrec-conf.org/proceedings/lrec2012/pdf/1087_Paper.pdf

Caines, A., McCarthy, M., & O'Keeffe, A. (2016). Spoken language corpora and pedagogical applications. In F. Farr & L. Murray (Eds.), *The Routledge handbook of language learning and technology.* London: Routledge.

Campbell-Kibler, K. (2008). I'll be the judge of that: Diversity in social perceptions of (ING). *Language in Society*, 37, 637–659.

Carter, R., & McCarthy, M. (2017). Spoken grammar: Where are we and where are we going? *Applied Linguistics*, 38(1), 1–20.

Chomsky, N. (1965). *Aspects of the theory of syntax.* Cambridge, MA: MIT Press.

Comrie, B. (1976). *Aspect*. Cambridge: Cambridge University Press.

Crowdy, S. (1993). Spoken corpus design. *Literary and Linguistic Computing, 8*, 259–265.

Dahl, Ö. (1985). *Tense and aspect systems*. Oxford: Wiley-Blackwell.

Denison, D. (1998). Syntax. In S. Romaine (Ed.), *The Cambridge history of the english language: Volume IV, 1776–1997*. Cambridge: Cambridge University Press.

Fillmore, C. J., Lee-Goldman, R. R., & Rhodes, R. (2012). The frameNet constructicon. In H. C. Boas & I. A. Sag (Eds.), *Sign-based construction grammar*. Stanford, CA: CSLI Publications.

Gries, S. Th. (2014). *Coll analysis 3.5: A script for R to compute perform collostructional analyses*. Retrieved from www.linguistics.ucsb.edu/faculty/stgries/teaching/groningen/index.html

Gries, S. Th. (2015). More (old and new) misunderstanding of collostructional analysis: On Schmid and Küchenhoff 2012. *Cognitive Linguistics, 26*(3), 505–536.

Gries, S. Th., Hampe, B., & Schönefeld, D. (2005). Converging evidence: Bringing together experimental and corpus data on the association of verbs and constructions. *Cognitive Linguistics, 16*, 635–676.

Hardie, A. (2012). CQPweb—combining power, flexibility and usability in a corpus analysis tool. *International Journal of Corpus Linguistics, 17*(3), 380–409.

Huddleston, R., & Pullum, G. (2002). *The Cambridge grammar of the English language*. Cambridge: Cambridge University Press.

Hundt, M. (2004). Animacy, agentivity and the spread of the progressive in Modern English. *English Language and Linguistics, 8*, 47–69.

Jespersen, O. (1933). *Essentials of English grammar*. London: George Allen and Unwin.

Jurafsky, D., Bell, A., Gregory, M., & Raymond, W. D. (2001). Probabilistic relations between words: Evidence from reduction in lexical production. In J. L. Bybee & P. Hopper (Eds.), *Frequency and the emergence of linguistic structure*. Amsterdam: John Benjamins.

Lee, S-A. (2007). Ing forms and the progressive puzzle: A construction-based approach to English progressives. *Journal of Linguistics, 43*(1), 153–195.

Leech, G., Hundt, M., Mair, C., & Smith, N. (2009). *Change in contemporary English: A grammatical study*. Cambridge: Cambridge University Press.

Love, R., Dembry, C., Hardie, A., Brezina, V., & McEnery, T. (2017). The spoken BNC2014—designing and building a spoken corpus of everyday conversations. *International Journal of Corpus Linguistics, 22*(3).

Mandelbrot, B. (1966). Information theory and psycholinguistics: A theory of word frequencies. In P. Lazarsfeld & N. Henry (Eds.), *Readings in mathematical social science*. Cambridge, MA: MIT Press.

McElhinny, B. S. (1993). Copula and auxiliary contraction in the speech of White Americans. *American Speech, 68*, 371–399.

Pluymaekers, M., Ernestus, M., & Baayen, R. H. (2005). Lexical frequency and acoustic reduction in spoken Dutch. *Journal of the Acoustical Society of America, 118*, 2561–2569.

Quirk, R., Greenbaum, S., Leech, G., & Svartvik, J. (1985). *A comprehensive grammar of the English language*. London: Longman.

R. Core Team. (2016). *R: A language and environment for statistical comput-ing*. Vienna: R Foundation for Statistical Computing. Retrieved from www.R-project.org

Ritter, A., Cherry, C., & Dolan, B. (2010). Unsupervised modeling of Twitter conversations. In R. M. Kaplan (Ed.), *Human Language Technologies: The 2010 Annual Conference of the North American Chapter of the Association for Computational Linguistics*. Los Angeles: Association for Computational Linguistics.

Sag, I. A. (2012). Sign-based Construction Grammar: An informal synopsis. In H. C. Boas & I. A. Sag (Eds.), *Sign-based construction grammar*. Stanford, CA: CSLI Publications.

Sanford, D. (2008). Metaphor and phonological reduction in English idiomatic expressions. *Cognitive Linguistics*, 19, 585–603.

Savage, M. (2010). *Identities and social change in Britain since 1940*. Oxford: Oxford University Press.

Stefanowitsch, A., & Gries, S. Th. (2003). Collostructions: Investigating the interaction between words and constructions. *International Journal of Corpus Linguistics*, 8, 209–243.

Stenström, A-B., Andersen, G., & Kristine Hasund, I. (2002). *Trends in teenage talk: Corpus compilation, analysis and findings*. Amsterdam: John Benjamins.

Trudgill, P. (1995). *Sociolinguistics: An introduction to language and society* (4th ed.). London: Penguin.

Wells, J. C. (1982). *Accents of English: Volume 1, an introduction*. Cambridge: Cambridge University Press.

Winter, B., & Wieling, M. (2016). How to analyze linguistic change using mixed models, growth curve analysis and generalized additive modeling. *Journal of Language Evolution*, 1(1), 7–18.

Zipf, G. K. (1965 [1935]). *Psycho-biology of language: An introduction to dynamic philology*. Cambridge, MA: MIT Press.

12 'You Can Just Give Those Documents to Myself'

Untriggered Reflexive Pronouns in 21st-Century Spoken British English

Laura L. Paterson

12.1 Introduction

Reflexive pronouns, such as *myself, herself* or *yourselves*, share a real-world referent with other components of the clause (or local domain) in which they occur. As such, they require a coreferent noun phrase (NP) to fulfil their syntactic criteria. In the sentence 'The cat washes herself', the NP *the cat* and the reflexive pronoun *herself* correspond to the same entity and share a syntactic bond. However, despite formal syntactic constraints, reflexive pronouns are used without coreferent NPs in (some varieties of) English (Parker, Riley, & Meyer, 1990). For example, in 'It's nearly as beautiful and slender as yourself' (an attested example from the present dataset) the reflexive *yourself* has nothing to bind with. The real-world referent of *yourself* is recoverable in discourse due to context, but is not encoded in syntax. This chapter uses the BNC2014 early access sample (Spoken BNC2014S) to investigate the use of these so-called 'untriggered' reflexive pronouns. In particular, it takes a sociolinguistic approach and investigates whether the use of untriggered forms correlates with social variables such as age, sex, social class and location.[1] The chapter also considers the syntactic distribution of untriggered reflexives, such as their use in coordinated NPs.

Existing research concerning reflexive pronouns tends to focus on their syntactic patterns, usually referring to binding theory (see Section 12.2). However, untriggered reflexives are rarely considered in their own right, and are usually discussed only as a component of a wider reflexive agreement system. The binding-focused literature does not consider sociolinguistic factors which may influence the use of untriggered reflexives, yet there is evidence that pragmatic constraints are important for pronoun choice. Section 12.2 provides an overview of existing research on reflexive pronoun use. It also foregrounds work in corpus linguistics which demonstrates the viability of this methodological approach for analysing pronouns. Section 12.3 details the data selection criteria, query terms, and data coding procedures, whilst the analysis is presented in

Section 12.4. The analysis is split into two parts, the first of which considers the syntactic distribution of untriggered reflexives, and the second of which investigates their correlation with socio-demographic variables. The results of these analyses are related back to the wider literature in Section 12.5.

12.2 Reflexive and Untriggered Reflexive Pronouns

Within syntactic theory, reflexive pronouns are separated from personal pronouns in their agreement pattern in terms of binding theory (Chomsky, 1981). Reflexive pronouns bind with their antecedent within a local domain (Principle A), whilst personal pronouns coindex with NPs outside their local domain (Principle B)—see Cunnings and Felser (2013, p. 189). Edwards and Varlokosta (2007, p. 426) cite the following illustrative examples:

1) $[_{IP}$ John$_i$ thinks that $[_{IP}$ Bill$_j$ likes himself$_{*i/j}$]]^2
2) $[_{IP}$ John$_i$ thinks that $[_{IP}$ Bill$_j$ likes him$_{i/*j}$]]

Following the principles of binding theory, example (1) is read as *himself* referring back to *Bill*, with the alternative reading (coreference between *John* and *himself*) being considered ungrammatical. Conversely, when a personal pronoun is used, as in example (2), *John* and *him* are coindexed, whilst the alternative reading, where *him* and *Bill* share a syntactic bond, is ungrammatical. Based on relatively unproblematic examples, such as these, reflexives and personal pronouns are considered to be in complementary distribution (Runner, Sussman, & Tannenhaus, 2003, p. B2), a position which cannot explain untriggered reflexives, such as (3):

3) $[_{IP}$ You$_i$ can give those documents to myself$_{*i/j}$]
4) $[_{IP}$ You$_i$ can give those documents to me$_j$]

In (3) the reflexive pronoun *myself* has nothing to bind with, as it cannot be coreferent with the subject NP *you*: they are expressions of different grammatical persons and must have different real-world referents. There is no coreferent element for *myself* and thus it is 'referentially incomplete' (Sportiche, 2013, p. 189). Such occurrences are termed untriggered reflexive pronouns (cf. Parker, Riley, & Meyer, 1990)^3 and are traditionally considered to be ungrammatical (van Gelderen, 2000). Under the rules of binding theory, one would expect a personal pronoun, as shown in (4). Whilst (3) appears to flout syntactic rules, and there is evidence to suggest that such constructions have increased processing time in the brain (cf. Cunnings & Sturt, 2014), untriggered reflexives can be understood. In (3), the first person singular *myself*, combined with an awareness of the wider discourse context, leads to an understanding that the speaker/writer of (3) is the referent of *myself*. As such, the existence of untriggered reflexive pronouns cannot be accounted for by syntactic theory alone.

Parker et al. (1990, p. 61) argue that reflexives are "fundamentally anaphoric and identify their referents as the discourse referent (i.e. the topic of the discourse)", a process which they hold distinct from pronoun/antecedent resolution. They argue that, by contrast, pronouns "are fundamentally exophoric and identify their referents as discourse participants (i.e. the speaker or the addressee)". To illustrate this distinction, they propose that a speaker who uses a pronoun in constructions such as (5) is foregrounding their "role as a discourse participant", whilst the alternative (6) would highlight their "role as the discourse referent—the topic of the discourse" (Parker et al., 1990, p. 60).

5) [$_{IP}$ This is a picture of *me*]
6) [$_{IP}$ This is a picture of *myself*]

By referring to both the wider co-text and context of such (hypothetical) utterances, Parker, Riley and Meyer move away from the syntactic constraints on reflexive pronouns and towards a consideration of pragmatics. They develop a 'hierarchy of acceptability' (1990, p. 63), which proposes that particular untriggered reflexives are more acceptable than others based on the absence of case marking, whether there is a discourse referent, and whether the untriggered form is first or second person. But the authors do not explain who gets to measure acceptability, nor do they test their example sentences on other native speakers.

As such, Parker, Riley and Meyer's explanation of untriggered reflexive pronouns is not entirely satisfactory. Furthermore, their work highlights one of the main problems with existing research on untriggered reflexives, insofar as they rely on introspective examples. As has been shown before, when corpora are analysed in response to claims based on introspection, such imagined examples are unlikely to cover all possibilities and trends in language use (for an example see McEnery and Wilson's (2001) analysis of 'to perform magic'). Furthermore, despite allusions to 'acceptability', Parker, Riley and Meyer do not consider external, social constraints on the use of reflexive pronouns, including potentially-relevant phenomena such as linguistic security (cf. Labov, 1972) or links to formality. One way to address such issues is to determine whether multiple speakers produce untriggered reflexives in similar syntactic environments and also to investigate the social context of their interactions.

In her empirical research on the discourse-pragmatic functions of what she terms '*self*-forms', Hernández (2015, p. 14) argues that "[a]lthough they are still stigmatised by unfaltering advocates of grammatical correctness, they [untriggered reflexives] are regularly found in spontaneous speech as well as writing, across multiple varieties of English". Hernández suggests that untriggered reflexives are 'unbound exophoric forms' (2015, p. 46) which are easily understood in speech because their referent is identifiable from the wider discourse and context. She follows Parker et al.'s (1990, p. 55) assertion that untriggered forms "are not anaphors at all, but, rather, alternative forms of personal pronouns". Whilst Hernández sources some of her examples from corpora, such as the original British National Corpus (the BNC1994), her paper mostly focuses on acceptability tests for untriggered forms in so-called picture NPs, such as "He thought your pictures of you/yourself were awful" (2015, p. 63), with forty-two of her sixty-seven participants showing a preference for the reflexive in this particular example.

Considering potential language-external constraints on the use of untriggered reflexives, Hernández (2015) argues that such forms are above the level of public consciousness. This assertion appears to hold true. For example, searching modern prescriptive grammar guides, such as Taggart's (2010) *Her Ladyship's Guide to the Queen's English* (a somewhat tongue-in-cheek text, which is endorsed by the National Trust) and popular prescriptive blog Grammar Girl's *Quick and Dirty Tips* (Fogarty, 2007), guidance to 'correct' what is 'wrong' with the use of untriggered reflexives is easily found. Writing in the *Chicago Tribune* Stevens (2012) argues that "If the misuse of 'I' and 'me' is an irritant, the abuse of 'myself' is nothing short of a blot on humanity" and quotes an editor of the *American Heritage Dictionary* as saying "It points to the fact that you've got anxiety about sounding correct and are going out of your way to avoid saying something wrong that isn't actually wrong". In the UK, Taggart (2010) labels untriggered reflexives "the estate agent's pronoun" explained and evaluated as "the misuse of emphatic pronouns". These statements do not allude, necessarily, to the syntactic rules flouted by untriggered reflexives, nor do they consider why their usage is (allegedly) so widespread. However, they do, as most prescriptive texts do, equate the evaluation of a particular linguistic form with its users. The conceptualisation of untriggered reflexives as something that "just sounds awful" (Stevens, 2012) for example, acts to pass judgement not on the alleged ungrammaticality of untriggered reflexives, but (implicitly) on the people using such forms.

What is significant about such prescriptive judgements is that the authors take an authoritative stance on what is 'correct'. It could be that others (speakers of different dialects, perhaps) would have a different understanding or preferred reading of untriggered reflexive pronouns. Indeed, some of the examples given by Parker et al. (1990) as 'acceptable', such as 'This is a photograph of myself about five years ago' (1990, p. 51) may be considered unacceptable by other speakers. They also argue, as noted above, that untriggered reflexives are "relatively more acceptable in the first and second person" (1990, p. 51), but give no indication as to who judges such acceptability. As such, this chapter addresses two shortcomings of existing debates about untriggered reflexive pronouns: it draws on corpus analysis of attested language data, and it makes no judgements about the social acceptability of non-standard usage.

The focus of this chapter is not to debate the relative contributions of syntactic and discourse-pragmatic constraints on untriggered reflexives, but rather, to provide a snap-shot of how untriggered reflexives are used in spoken British English in the 21st century. Through considering the syntactic environments and social distribution of untriggered reflexives, it may be possible to observe constraining factors which have, hitherto, been unanalysed. Specifically, the following research questions are addressed:

1. Do untriggered reflexives occur in particular syntactic positions?
2. Does the use of untriggered reflexives correlate with grammatical person?
3. Does the use of untriggered reflexives correlate with particular socio-demographic groups (age, sex, etc.)?

12.3 Methodology: Corpus Approaches to Pronouns

Paterson (2014) and Siemund (2010) have shown the fruitfulness of analysing pronouns using corpora. The former considered epicene (gender-neutral) pronouns in the BE06 corpus (Baker, 2009), whilst the latter used the BNC1994 to investigate the functions of the reflexive pronoun *itself*. Unfortunately, Siemund (2010) does not consider untriggered reflexives, but Lederer (2013) gets somewhat closer, using the BNC1994 to analyse occurrences of reflexives in prepositional phrases (PP).[4] She argues that some PPs appear to be able to take either a reflexive or a personal pronoun and remain grammatical. For example, she cites the sentence 'John pulled the blanket over himself/him' (from Kuno, 1987, p. 66) where it appears that either *him* or *himself* can be coreferent with the NP *John* (Lederer, 2013, p. 484). Lederer notes that current theories suggest that prepositions act as 'shielding' for the pronoun which means that usual grammatical constraints do not apply, but notes that there is, as yet, no model which explains 'what linguistic factors dictate the choice of pronoun' in such situations, especially considering that syntactic models do not account for the semantic value of prepositions (2013, p. 484).

Moving beyond a focus on reflexives occurring in PPs, Hernández (2012) analysed the distribution of (reflexive) pronouns in the Freiberg Corpus of English Dialects. In particular, her work demonstrates the usefulness of speaker metadata for highlighting patterns in pronoun choice across different social demographics. However, the Freiberg corpus contains spoken texts from the 1970s and 1980s and thus her analysis cannot shed light on present-day reflexive usage. Furthermore, the Freiberg data comprises face-to-face interviews, which could have influenced the linguistic forms used by speakers. In contrast, the Spoken BNC2014S comprises mostly informal conversation between multiple parties with existing relationships.[5]

To investigate the form and distribution of untriggered reflexive pronouns in the Spoken BNC2014S, the following tag-based query was used to extract all relevant pronouns: (_PPX1|_PPX2|_PNX1). The tag _PPX1 returned all singular reflexive pronouns, _PPX2 returned the plurals, and _PNX1 would have returned the indefinite reflexive *oneself*, but this form does not occur in the corpus. Using a tag-based query, rather than a lexical query, meant that non-standard forms of the reflexive pronouns, such as *hissen* and *meself*, were also returned in the query results. The queries returned a total of 2,825 hits and the concordance lines for all tokens were downloaded with fifty words on either side for context.

As this chapter is only concerned with untriggered reflexives, the query hits were manually coded using a five-way system: i) triggered reflexives, ii) elided/implied triggered reflexives (where the co-referent NP is recoverable, see example 8), iii) self-intensifiers, iv) untriggered reflexives, and v) unclear/other, the latter of which tended to be used when the speech was disjointed or interrupted. The 2,825 hits included triggered reflexives (7, 8), self-intensifiers (9, 10), and untriggered reflexives (11).

7) [$_{IP}$ I$_i$ find myself$_i$ at a loose hen loose end] (BNC2014 SLX6)
8) [$_{IP}$ help yourself] = [$_{IP}$ you$_i$ help yourself$_i$] (BNC2014 S2DD)
9) [$_{IP}$ he$_i$ himself$_i$ went to boarding school] (BNC2014 SP2X)
10) [$_{IP}$ you$_i$ were a child yourself$_i$] (BNC2014 S8G6)
11) [$_{IP}$ you$_i$ should not think of themselves$_{*i/j}$] (BNC2014 SVVK)

Self-intensifiers (7, 8), which have historically been labelled as 'emphatic' or 'intensive' reflexives, 'reinforcing pronouns', 'focus particles', and 'scalar adverbs' (Gast & Siemund, 2006, pp. 346–347) are a subtype of triggered reflexives. As such, they are not considered in detail here. The distribution of types of reflexives is given in Table 12.1.[6]

The spread in Table 12.1 is expected, with triggered and elided/implied triggered reflexives making up the majority (85.74%) of the query hits. Self-intensifiers account for 10.34% of the data, whilst untriggered reflexives make up 2.02%, in the form of fifty-seven raw tokens. The analysis primarily focuses on these untriggered reflexives, but briefly considers their distribution relative to the triggered forms in Section 12.4.1. Whilst the number of untriggered reflexives is quite low, this is unsurprising, as forms which obey binding theory were expected to dominate in the corpus. Further explanation for the relatively small number of tokens comes from their proscription in grammar guides (discussed above) and evidence that they are above the level of public consciousness. Nevertheless,

Table 12.1 Distribution of All Query Tokens

	Triggered	Elided/ Implied Trigger	Self-Intensifier	Untriggered	Unclear	Total Per Person
1st person						
Myself	593	53	89	30	14	913
Meself/ Mes(s)en	12	1	2			(32.32%)
Ourself	3				1	
Ourselves	102	6	4		3	
2nd person						
Yourself	514	200	27	16	15	795
Yourselves	7	9	1	3		(28.14%)
Yoursen/ Youself	3					
3rd person						
Herself	165	12	14	3	1	1,117
Himself	269	25	35	2	4	(39.54%)
Hisself	1	1				
Themself	8		3			
Theirself			1		10	
Itself	124	6	79	1		
Themselves	287	20	37	2	6	
Theirselves	1					
Total per type	2,089 (73.95%)	333 (11.79%)	292 (10.34%)	57 (2.02%)	54 (1.91%)	

the fifty-seven tokens demonstrate that untriggered reflexives occur in spontaneous spoken data, and their number facilitates close analysis of their syntactic distribution, their potential correlation with socio-demographic variables, and their use within a wider conversational context.

12.4 Analysis

The analysis of untriggered reflexive pronouns is approached bi-directionally. First, the syntactic profile and grammatical person/number preferences of untriggered reflexives are analysed, and it is established that the data presented here is similar in form and syntactic distribution to previously-examined corpora—particularly the sub-corpus analysed by Hernández (2012). Thus, despite the limited number of tokens, claims can be made about general trends in the use of untriggered reflexives. Having established that the data is viable, the analysis then takes a socio-linguistic approach to determine whether the use of untriggered reflexive pronouns correlates with socio-demographic variables, such as age, sex, and location (as provided in the speaker metadata). This second part of the analysis aims to identify whether there is evidence of social constraints on the use of untriggered reflexive pronouns.

Table 12.2 Distribution of Untriggered Reflexives

	No. (%)		Normalised Freq. pmw	No. of Speakers	No. of Texts
Myself	30	(52.63)	6.26	22	26
Yourself	16	(28.07)	3.34	15	13
Yourselves	3	(5.26)	0.63	3	3
Herself	3	(5.26)	0.63	3	3
Himself	2	(3.51)	0.42	2	2
Itself	1	(1.75)	0.21	1	1
Themselves	2	(3.51)	0.42	2	2
TOTAL	57		11.90		50

Table 12.2 shows that the untriggered reflexives in Spoken BNC2014S occur mainly in the first person singular, with second person singular forms being the next most-frequent. The former has a normalised frequency of 6.23 occurrences per million words, whilst the latter has a normalised frequency of just over half of that: 3.34 per million words for second person singular *yourself*. All the other forms are extremely rare, occurring less than once per million words. The least-frequent untriggered reflexive is the third person neutral singular *itself*, which occurs only once in the whole corpus, in the example: 'it's a soap but it has a certain [. . .] buttery uh mayonnaisy sort of element to itself' (BNC2014 S8J6). No non-standard pronouns occurred as untriggered reflexives and there is no preference for untriggered reflexives to be masculine- or feminine-marked in the third person singular (although, due to small numbers, no wider claims can be made about grammatical gender preferences).

Table 12.2 also includes information about the number of speakers using each untriggered reflexive, as well as the number of texts within which they occur. The data shows that the untriggered forms did not cluster in a small number of texts, nor were a subset of speakers responsible for extremely large token counts. Seven texts included more than one untriggered reflexive, and ten speakers produced more than one token. There are thirty-eight unique speakers in total, with some producing more than one type of untriggered reflexive: the most prolific speaker produced nine tokens, including *myself, itself* and *yourself*, demonstrating that they use such pronouns across all persons. The nuances of different speakers are considered in Section 12.4.2. But first, Section 12.4.1 focuses on syntax.

12.4.1 *Syntactic Patterns and Grammatical Persons*

Based on the data presented in Table 12.2, there is a clear preference for first person untriggered reflexive pronouns: *myself* accounts for over half (52.63%) of the untriggered reflexives in the whole corpus. This is unexpected, given that first person forms account for just 32.32% of all reflexives (see Table 12.1) and 35.02% of all pronouns (personal and reflexive) in the corpus. Close analysis of the first person untriggered forms indicates that a large portion occurred in one particular syntactic environment: thirteen of the thirty tokens of *myself* were either preceded by (eight tokens) or immediately followed by (five tokens) a coordinating conjunction, as shown in (12) and (13). There were also three cases where untriggered *myself* occurred in a list (14).

(12) he's got a long list of things he wants to know about—ANON-nameF and *myself* (BNC2014 SA69)
(13) there was a group of us er *myself* and my friends (BNC2014 SJ6L)
(14) she arranged for a personal shopping experience for herself, *myself*, and—ANONnameF (BNC2014 STQF)

Such findings are similar to those reported elsewhere. For example, Hernández (2012, p. 127) found that untriggered *myself* occurs as a subject with coordinated forms (e.g., Lisa and myself) more than any other untriggered reflexive.[7]

To investigate whether the co-occurrence of coordinating conjunctions and untriggered reflexives was specific to untriggered forms or representative of wider trends in pronoun use, the Spoken BNC2014S was queried for all personal pronouns occurring as L1/R1 to a coordinating conjunction, which was preceded or followed by another personal pronoun/proper noun. There were 2,619 hits including *me and you,—ANON-nameM and I, she and—ANONnameF*, etc. Taking an automatically-thinned set of one hundred hits showed that such constructions occur 56% of the time across clause boundaries, 19% were subjects of a clause, 4% were objects, 5% complements, 1% adjuncts, and 15% were unclear (due to disfluency, repetition, interruption, or split utterances). Comparing this to the eighteen untriggered reflexives occurring in immediate proximity to coordinating conjunctions (thirteen *myself*, three *herself* and two *yourself*), 11.11% occurred at a clause boundary, 27.78% were subjects, 22.22% were objects, 22.22% were complements, there was one adjunct (5.56%) and 11.11% were unclear. Although we are dealing with small numbers, there does seem to be a preference for untriggered reflexives to occur in object and complement positions more often than would be expected based on the thinned sample of personal pronouns, and they are also much less likely to occur at a clause boundary.

Similarly to Hernández's (2012) research, the first person untriggered forms occur as coordinated subjects more than any other untriggered form. All other reflexive forms (triggered, elided/implied triggered, and self-intensifiers) in the Spoken BNC2014S only co-occurred with coordinating conjunctions at a clause boundary.[8] In her sub-corpus of 1.5 million words of the Freiberg Corpus of English Dialects, Hernández (2012) also found twenty-four untriggered reflexives in prepositional complements and notes that "more than half" of the untriggered reflexives occurring in PPs in her data "form part of comparisons" (2012, p. 138). In the Spoken BNC2014S there are thirty-one (54.39%) untriggered reflexives occurring immediately after prepositions (in both complement and adjunct positions). They occur across all persons and numbers, most frequently occurring with *for* (six tokens) and *of* (six tokens). These include seven comparisons (*like* occurs six times and *as* occurs once), which cluster in the second person (four *yourself/selves*) alongside three tokens of *myself*. Therefore, it seems that, despite Hernández's corpus containing data from the late 20th century, there are clear parallels in the syntactic patterns found in her data and in the Spoken BNC2014S. This provides some initial evidence that the occurrence and distribution of untriggered reflexives is relatively stable in British English.

Returning to trends in grammatical persons, the second person forms accounted for a total of 33.33% of the untriggered tokens. Such preferences for first and second person forms could be seen as evidence for Parker et al.'s (1990, p. 51) claims that untriggered reflexives are more acceptable in these grammatical persons. However, one must be careful not to overstate the case. The dialogic spoken nature of the data likely increased the use of firstand second person pronouns. Whilst the analysis has shown, proportionally, that first and second person reflexives are more common, this does not equate to them being more 'acceptable'. None of the untriggered forms in the corpus are directly challenged by other conversational participants, nor are any of the speakers corrected by reiteration (where another speaker repeats an utterance containing an untriggered reflexive and replaces it with a personal pronoun). As such, the data cannot directly tell us about the (social) acceptability of such forms. However, what is apparent from the wider context of each untriggered reflexive is that their use did not cause any confusion or misunderstanding between speakers; the real-world referent of the untriggered form is understood. Therefore, a general level of 'acceptability' can be proposed, even if the use of untriggered reflexive pronouns does not conform to syntactic norms.

It is also notable in Table 12.2 that the second person untriggered reflexives are dominated by sixteen tokens of singular-marked *yourself*. This trend for the singular occurs across all persons; there are no occurrences of plurals in the first person and only two third person tokens are plural. However, singular forms represent 82.54% of all *-self* forms (triggered, implied, and self-intensifiers) and are most frequent in all grammatical persons (87.05% of first person tokens, 97.77% of second person tokens, and 68.27% of third person tokens). Thus it seems that untriggered reflexives (of which 91.21% were singular) follow a similar pattern in terms of grammatical number to all *-self* forms, and thus the preference for singular forms is not unique to untriggered forms.

Whilst the majority of the untriggered reflexives conform to established patterns, such as co-occurrence with coordinating conjunctions, use in comparisons, etc., there were ten tokens which did not fit into established categories. These included two tokens where the untriggered reflexive was a single-word utterance; *yourself* was used when two speakers were collaboratively making a list and *myself* was used as an attempt to initiate a speaker change. A further seven tokens were the object of a verb, but not part of a PP (15–17).

(15) it's providing *yourself* the best possible foundation (BNC2014 SGSY)
(16) the person who is giving *yourself* a bad you know perception (BNC2014 S6A7)
(17) little jokes that maybe make *yourself* feel better (BNC2014 SKPP)

The final token ('even *myself*') was used to frame a sentence and acts as a complex subject. Furthermore, whilst the syntactic patterns and rate of occurrence of untriggered reflexives in the present corpus is similar to that found in previous corpus-based studies, it is important to note where datasets differ. For example, there are no occurrences in the Spoken BNC2014S of the picture NPs tested by Hernández (2015) as discussed in Section 12.2. However, there are clearly common trends between the present data and those presented by Hernández (2012), which suggests that the Spoken BNC2014S is not anomalous and can, at least in a limited capacity, be taken as representative of wider syntactic trends. Having established that syntactic patterning of untriggered reflexives, the analysis now considers potential sociolinguistic constraints.

12.4.2 Demographic Groups and Language Change

One of the benefits of focusing on attested data instead of introspective examples is that analysis of untriggered reflexives can also include a detailed consideration of the wider context (and co-text) of their production. To this end, Table 12.3 shows the distribution of the fifty-seven untriggered reflexives based on the socio-demographic profiles of their speakers. Each row represents a location, the columns represent the social classes A-E, and the male/female split is given either side of the slash, i.e., 1/0 denotes one token produced by a male and zero tokens produced by a female. The social grade system of social class was used for coding and NS-SEC data was added retrospectively.[9] However, as discussed below, it was actually links to education (employment as a teacher/lecturer, or student status), not social class, that correlated with the use of untriggered reflexives.

Table 12.3 shows that there were no speakers from the East Midlands, the Southwest, Scotland or Wales who used untriggered reflexives. In

Table 12.3 Distribution of Untriggered Reflexives by Location, Social Class (A-E), & Sex (M/F): Raw Tokens

	A	B	C1	C2	D	E	ALL
East Mid							0
Eastern						0/3	3
Irish	1/0					1/0	2
Liverpool	1/0	2/0					3
London		1/0				1/0	2
Northeast	0/2					0/1	3
Northwest						1/0	1
Scottish							0
Southeast		0/1					1
Southwest							0
West Mid		2/0					2
Welsh							0
Yorkshire						2/1	3
Non-UK	4/0						4
X	9/1	2/13	3/3			0/2	33
SUM	15/3	7/14	3/3	0	0	5/7	57

fact, the majority of tokens (thirty-three) were produced by speakers who did not provide sufficient information about their location to facilitate classification at the regional level. As such, the only conclusion which can be drawn about the geographical spread of untriggered reflexives is that their use does not appear to correlate with a particular location and/ or a geographically-located dialect. Even when consulting the speaker metadata for those uncategorised by location (category X), information provided about their dialect and place of birth, suggest that location does not appear to be an important factor affecting the use of untriggered reflexives.

However, the raw figures in Table 12.3 can only tell us so much. In order to make data from different locations and relating to different social classes and sex comparable, we must acknowledge that there are different amounts of speech in the subsections of the corpus. Therefore, the figures have been normalised to tokens per 10,000 words in Table 12.4 to account for the fact that the corpus is not balanced in terms of social characteristics (such as social class, sex, or location).

Normalising the frequencies indicates that there are some geographical areas more associated with untriggered reflexives than others. In particular, Ireland shows the strongest trends towards the use of untriggered reflexives (although we must be aware that these figures were generated based on two raw tokens). Thus there is scope for future research on the use of untriggered reflexives in Irish English, but no firm conclusions can be drawn based on the Spoken BNC2014S. The normalised data for Liverpool also indicates that there could be a preference for untriggered

Table 12.4 Distribution of Untriggered Reflexives by Location/Social Class (A-E) and Sex (M/F)—Normalised

	A	B	C1	C2	D	E	ALL
East Mid							0
Eastern						0/0.47	0.079
Irish	9.82/0					11.60/0	1.604
Liverpool	7.23/0	2.27/0					0.258
London		0.54/0				0.54/0	0.106
Northeast	0/0.16					0/0.44	0.094
Northwest						0.52/0	0.064
Scottish							0
Southeast		0/0.08					0.046
Southwest							0
West Mid		0.41/0					0.340
Welsh							0
Yorkshire						0.21/0.11	0.063
Non-UK	0.85/0						0.648
X	0.18/0.03	0.18/0.18	0.20/010			0/0.08	0.123
SUM	0.308/0.046	0.055/0.110	0.118/0.081	0	0	0.080/0.115	57

reflexives, as they occurred at rates of 7.23 and 2.27 per million in social classes A and B. However, there were only two raw tokens of untriggered reflexives in Liverpool and when all the Liverpool-based speech in the corpus is taken into account, the normalised figure drops to 0.258 tokens per 10,000 words. Overall, therefore, normalisation of the tokens of untriggered reflexives demonstrates that there is no overwhelming correlation with their use and speaker geography.

The sum row of Table 12.4 also shows that there does, however, seem to be some limited correlation between the use of untriggered reflexives and sex. Men in social grade A appear to use the form the most, followed by men in the C1 category, whilst (for the grades where there is data) women in category A seem to use the form least (followed by women in C1). Thus, not only may there be a sex-based correlation, there is evidence for a corresponding social class correlation (see below). Overall, the normalised frequencies for all male and all female speakers' use of untriggered reflexives are 0.157, and 0.094 per 10,000 words respectively, which suggests that men produce the form 1.6 times as much as women. However, Table 12.4 does not account for speakers who produced multiple tokens of untriggered reflexives. There were six men and four women who produced multiple tokens, comprising a subset of the twenty-three male speakers and fifteen female speakers who used untriggered reflexives overall. Thus, there is evidence to suggest that the men in the Spoken BNC2014S were more likely to use such forms than women. Drawing loosely on historical variationist sociolinguistics (cf. Trudgill, 1974) and wide generalisations about men and women's use of language, it would therefore be predicted that untriggered reflexives are non-standard, and, indeed, this is the case.

Table 12.4 indicates that there are no speakers in social classes C and D using untriggered reflexives. However, social classes A and B, which include speakers classified as working in higher/intermediate managerial positions as well as some professional occupations, account for thirty-nine (68.42%) of the untriggered reflexives. Whilst using employment (status) as a proxy for social class is problematic, it is beyond the scope of the present chapter to address such issues in detail. However, it is noted that use of particular linguistic features (particularly prestigious variants) may correlate with educational background and, furthermore, that there is likely to be a higher proportion of people with high levels of education in social classes A and B compared with classes C and D.[10] Indeed, an analysis of speaker metadata indicates that twelve (31.58%) speakers who used untriggered reflexives work or have worked in education (two are retired teachers), including two who specifically note that they teach English language. There are a further seven (18.42%) speakers currently in education, as stated in the individual speaker metadata, who are classified in group E. These nineteen speakers are responsible for 33 (57.89%) of the untriggered reflexives in the Spoken BNC2014S.

One could interpret Tables 12.3 and 12.4 as demonstrating that untriggered reflexives are associated with higher social classes, and thus they could potentially be a prestige variant (cf. Labov, 1972). However, due to issues of grammaticality, combined with the negative evaluation of untriggered reflexives in prescriptive texts (see Section 12.2), this seems unlikely. A further potential explanation is that the use of untriggered reflexives is influenced by the relative rarity of all reflexive forms (in comparison to personal pronouns) and speakers' awareness that the (mis) use of untriggered reflexives is above the level of public consciousness.[11] Indeed, the use of untriggered reflexives can be linked to the notion of linguistic security. Based on the anecdotal evidence provided by Steve Kleinedler (*American Heritage Dictionary* editor, see Stevens (2012) in Section 12.2) that people use untriggered reflexives due to some form of social anxiety about saying the wrong thing, there is potentially a case for the role of hypercorrection here. By analogy to Meyerhoff's (2011, p. 180) example, where speakers who predominantly use [ɪn] forms encounter a dialect with [ɪŋ] forms and are "at a loss at where to put them", it can be argued that, due to their rarity, speakers may be unfamiliar with the grammar of reflexive pronouns and disregard rules of reflexive-antecedent binding.[12] In order to test whether hypercorrection is a factor in speakers' choice of untriggered reflexives, we must consider the wider context of their interactions and move beyond the immediate co-text of their use.

The most prolific user of untriggered reflexives in the corpus is a 41-year-old, British, female teacher, born in Dorchester (henceforth

S1), who describes her accent as 'South of England'. S1 produces nine untriggered reflexives in six different texts. The fact that her untriggered forms are not restricted to one conversation or one group of speakers is evidence that untriggered reflexive pronouns are part of her repertoire, and, furthermore, suggest that she was not producing such pronouns in response to a particular stimulus (such as a priming effect caused by another speaker using untriggered reflexives). A potential exception to this is S2, a 41-year-old, male entrepreneur, with dual UK/New Zealand heritage, who produces two tokens of *yourself* directed at S1. However, S1 does not reciprocate. She produces only one token of *myself* in conversation with S2 and analysis of the wider discourse indicates that this token does not occur within ten utterances either side of S2's use of untriggered reflexives. Potentially, S1's usage has influenced S2, and indeed S2 is a participant in fourteen other texts (alongside S1) where neither of them produce untriggered reflexive pronouns. However, based on the limited metadata we have about these two speakers, there are no grounds to suggest that S1's position in their relationship (they are a couple) could influence S2 any more than S2 could influence S1. It appears then that data cannot provide direct evidence for or against the argument that hypercorrection plays a role in reflexive pronoun use. Furthermore, there is no overt discussion of (reflexive) pronoun choice in the Spoken BNC2014S.

Table 12.5 demonstrates that there is a slight pattern in age preferences. Figures have been normalised to per 10,000 words in Table 12.6, which shows that rates of untriggered reflexives rise from 11–18 to 19–29, but decrease for those aged 30–39, before peaking between 40–49 and tapering off as the age of speakers increases. The peak in the age-graded data is worthy of further investigation in a larger dataset, although it is worth noting here that these figures are inflated by the speech of S1 (discussed above).

The pattern in Table 12.6 is similar (although slightly condensed) to the u-curve pattern discussed by Llamas (2007, p. 73). Llamas argues

Table 12.5 Distribution of Untriggered Reflexives by Age: Raw Tokens

	11_18	19_29	30_39	40_49	50_59	60_69	70_79	80_89	90_99	X
Myself	1	8		9	3	7		2		
Yourself		9	3	4						
Yourselves		1			1					1
Herself		2		1						
Himself		1		1						
Itself			1							
Themselves			1	1						
Tokens	1	21	5	16	4	7	0	2	0	1
Speakers	1	16	3	7	3	5	0	2	0	1

Table 12.6 Distribution of Untriggered Reflexives by Age: Normalised

	11_18	19_29	30_39	40_49	50_59	60_69	70_79	80_89	90_99	X
Myself	0.052	0.041		0.194	0.080	0.112		0.444		
Yourself		0.046	0.036	0.086						
Yourselves		0.005			0.027					0.348
Herself		0.010		0.022						
Himself		0.005		0.022						
Itself			0.012							
Themselves			0.012	0.022						
SUM	0.052	0.107	0.060	0.346	0.106	0.112	0	0.444	0	0.348

that this pattern, where non-standard forms decrease during adult working age and then rise again in older age groups, is typical of a linguistic variable which is stable and not undergoing any form of language change. Removing S1's tokens of untriggered reflexives means that the u-curve pattern discussed by Llamas maps more neatly onto Table 12.6. Furthermore, when plotting speakers, not tokens (see Table 12.5), the pattern in untriggered reflexive use is flattened, but still follows a similar trend.

Further evidence that untriggered reflexives are relatively stable is the fact that their occurrence has not dramatically increased/decreased between the 1970s/1980s data analysed by Hernández (2012) and the Spoken BNC2014S. However, the question that remains is whether there is a particular force influencing the production of untriggered reflexive pronouns. To this end, the analysis concludes by focusing on the most-used untriggered reflexive, *myself*. Of the thirty occurrences of untriggered *myself*, eight are used to emphasise that the speaker is part of a larger social group who were performing a collective action, playing roles in the same narrative, or affected by someone else's action (18, 19). S1 uses untriggered *myself* to emphasise similarity between herself and others; 'people like *myself*' and 'someone like *myself*' (which occurs twice) conveys that S1 is not alone in their opinion on a given topic.

18) he wants to know about—ANON-name-m and *myself* (BNC2014 SA69)
19) it was mum and dad aunt and unc- and *myself* (BNC2014 S6A5)
20) deposits made by *myself* (BNC2014 SC8H)
21) I think it tastes good for *myself* (BNC2014 SZQX)

There is one use of *myself* which acts as an (unsuccessful) attempt to keep the conversational floor, and two tokens are used in an attempt to take the floor, interrupting the previous speaker (only one is successful). The use of untriggered reflexives in these circumstances indicate that the speaker wishes to talk particularly about themselves; the alternative—personal pronoun *I*—does not provide such information about the topic of discourse to the addressees in the same way. Additional foregrounding of self-hood occurs in (20) where the speaker emphasises that only they could make legitimate deposits into a bank account, and (21) where the speaker is discussing how their evaluation of their own baking may be different to others' evaluations.

However, there is also some evidence that *myself* is used in its untriggered form to suggest disassociation between the speaker and the real-world referent. For example, (22) constructs one's own inner monologue as different to and separate from one's self. Despite logic dictating that the speaker and their 'inner voice' are inextricably linked, the use of *myself*, as well as the definite article (*the* inner voice, not *my* inner voice), suggests that the 'inner voice' can act somewhat independently of the speaker.

22) the internal voice that makes excuses for *myself* (BNC2014 S9EP)

Whilst there are too few tokens to make wide-reaching claims about the discourse function of the use of untriggered reflexives, it is notable that some loose patterns occurred across the 30 tokens of *myself*. This demonstrates that use of untriggered reflexives is not random, but determining the wider social constraints on their use requires further study and more examples. Finally, there are no instances in the corpus where the real-world referent of an untriggered reflexive is unclear; they are always understood by the addressees and cause no ambiguity. Thus, despite arguments that they are ungrammatical (both in a syntactic and prescriptive sense), addressees can assign referents to untriggered reflexive pronouns.

12.5 Discussion and Conclusions

The headline conclusion is that the vast majority (90%) of 380 speakers in the Spoken BNC2014S did not produce untriggered reflexive pronouns. Despite arguments that such forms appear to be above the level of public consciousness, appearing in popular prescriptive grammar guides (cf. Taggart, 2010), evidence from the present analysis, and other corpus-based work (cf. Hernández, 2012; Lederer, 2013), suggests that untriggered reflexives are extremely rare. Only ten speakers produced more than one token of such pronouns, with eight of these producing just two tokens each. The untriggered reflexives account for only 2.02% of the reflexive pronouns in the Spoken BNC2014S, and reflexive pronouns account for only 0.43% of the total number of personal and reflexive pronouns in the corpus. This means that the fifty-seven tokens of untriggered reflexive pronouns represent only 0.0086% of all 660,541 (personal and reflexive) pronouns. Nevertheless, the occurrence of fifty-seven tokens facilitated the close analysis of untriggered reflexives, which focused on their syntactic distribution and the wider context of their use.

To address the research questions, untriggered reflexives do seem to cluster in particular syntactic environments, particularly in PPs and coordinated NPs. Untriggered reflexives were rarely subjects, but this was to be expected based on the limited pre-existing corpus-based research. There was a preference for first person forms, and second person forms were more frequent than third person forms. No grammatical gender-marking trend was observed, but there were too few third person tokens to make any wider claims. The majority of the untriggered forms in the corpus were singular, but this reflected general patterns in pronoun use and was not a phenomenon restricted to untriggered reflexives. Nevertheless, a consideration of the surrounding co-text of instances of untriggered *myself* indicated that the prevalence of singular untriggered reflexives may be explained from a pragmatic perspective, insofar as they reinforce the individuality (the self-hood) of the speaker and foreground it as the topic of discourse.

In terms of socio-demographic variables, there was no strong correlation apparent in terms of location and/or dialects. There is evidence that men use untriggered reflexives more frequently than women, although the most prolific user of untriggered forms was female. (In a wider sense, however, questions can be asked about the validity of such a gender binary and the attribution of linguistic features to particular homogenised groups based on sex.) Untriggered forms appeared to cluster in higher social classes and amongst those involved with education (although it is notable that speakers ranged from high-school students to PhD students and teachers). In order to explain the fact that untriggered forms were produced by nineteen speakers with direct links to education, the notions of linguistic security and hypercorrection were introduced. However, there was not enough information in the speaker metadata, nor was there any overt discussion of reflexive pronouns, which could point to a firm conclusion about the potential role played by hypercorrection. Even reading large sections of each text, one can only assume the (socially-motivated) reasons for speakers using untriggered reflexive pronouns. Analysis of the final social variable, age, suggested that untriggered reflexives were a fairly stable linguistic phenomenon, a conclusion which is supported by the parallels between the present dataset and Hernández's (2012) work on the Freiberg Corpus of English Dialects.

Finally, the analysis turned to the discourse level in order to determine whether there were any discernible patterns in the discursive function of untriggered reflexives. Focusing on *myself*, it was encouraging that potential trends, such as the foregrounding of self-hood and the use of untriggered reflexives to emphasise a speakers' affiliation with larger social groups, were apparent. However, one caveat is that the aim of the preceding analysis was not to determine individual speakers' intent based on the pronouns they produced, but rather to establish whether there are any similarities in interactions which could explain the presence of untriggered reflexives. In order to more fully understand *why* speakers use untriggered reflexives, corpus analysis must be supplemented by alternative methods of data collection and analyses that directly involve those producing the pronouns, such as interviews with the speakers, or having them undertake grammatical acceptability tests. Such analysis is beyond the scope of this chapter, due to the anonymity of contributors to Spoken BNC2014S, but is certainly an avenue for potential future study.

What this chapter has shown, however, is that untriggered reflexive pronouns are rather rare in spontaneous speech. They have an overall normalised frequency of 11.90 per million words in the Spoken BNC2014S. As such, obtaining enough tokens for detailed close analysis or to inform statistical calculations is problematic. Thus, drawing on extremely large corpora (as opposed to other techniques such as elicitation test) seems a sensible way to collect tokens of untriggered reflexives from naturally occurring data, although the type of social interactions captured within a corpus must be taken into account. Given that untriggered reflexives are conceptualised as above the level of public consciousness, it can be posited that they may occur more frequently in situations where there is a clear power hierarchy between speakers. The informal nature of the recordings in the Spoken BNC2014S, and the apparent close relationships between speakers (S1 and S2 were a couple, for example) may mean that speakers were less concerned with apparent 'correctness' in their choice of reflexive pronouns. They may also have been less inclined to hypercorrect. To investigate the role of social power and context further, it would be useful to compare the use of untriggered reflexives across spoken corpora in which speaker relationships were different. For example, the results presented here could be contrasted with the more formal work-related talk in the Spoken BNC1994. Nevertheless, despite the limitations noted above, the analysis of the Spoken BNC2014S has demonstrated that untriggered reflexive pronouns are an (albeit rare) feature of 21st-century spoken British English, and their occurrence persists despite opposition from prescriptive sources.

Notes

1 Although it analyses correlations between social variables and linguistic variants, this analysis is not variationist per se. Variationist analysis would include not only those occurrences where untriggered reflexives occur, but all potential sites where untriggered forms could be used. Due to the sheer volume of potential sites for untriggered reflexives, plus their rarity, a full variationist analysis is beyond the scope of the present chapter.
2 Asterisks denote an ungrammatical construction (according to the principles of binding theory).

3 Hernández (2012, p. 124) notes that untriggered reflexives, are also labelled 'unbound' or 'absolute' reflexives, or 'independent self-forms'. For coherence, the term untriggered reflexives is used throughout this chapter.
4 See also Kjellmer, Aijmer, and Altenberg (2004) for an analysis of second person -*self* forms.
5 One other difference between Hernández's work and the analysis presented below is that the current chapter does not consider occasions when reflexives would be expected, but personal pronouns occur instead, as in, 'I put a rope round me' (2012, p. 123).
6 Raw frequencies are used here to provide a snapshot of the types of reflexives used across the whole corpus. Normalised frequencies are used elsewhere to make data subdivided by social characteristics comparable.
7 Parker et al. (1990, p. 54) argue that untriggered reflexives occur in NPs linked by coordinating conjunctions because case assignment (relating to the c-commanding NP) is "blocked in coordinate constructions", and thus any pronoun can occur in such constructions. They claim that "normal rules of case assignment are relaxed in coordinate structures because an intervening NP serves as a barrier to government" and, therefore, untriggered reflexives occurring in this position are "not anaphors, but, rather, personal pronouns" (1990, p. 56). However, if this were true, there would be no preference for a particular pronoun form—speakers/writers would be just as likely to use *me*, *myself*, or *I* in such constructions, which does not appear to be the case.
8 Triggered reflexives showed a tendency to occur in *by*-phrases (*by myself, by yourselves*) and elided/implied triggers occurred as the object in imperatives, such as *help yourself* and *control yourself*.
9 NS-SEC is the National Statistics Socioeconomic Classification, which uses forms of employment (typically job titles) to categorise people into different socioeconomic brackets. For the Spoken BNC2014, the NS-SEC was mapped onto the social grade (A-E) model of social class used here.
10 Class E includes people who are retired from all professions and full-time students, so claims about overall education levels cannot be made.
11 There may also be some cross-over influence from other pronoun-based prescriptions, such as uncertainty of when to use *I* or *me* in coordinated NPs: 'Thomas and I went skiing' vs. 'Me and Thomas went skiing'. However, testing such an interaction is difficult using corpus data, as there is no way to ascertain speakers' awareness of such grammatical norms.
12 Further anecdotal evidence for this claim is that performing an internet search for 'when to use myself' results in 359 million hits.

References

Baker, P. (2009). The BE06 corpus of British English and recent language change. *International Journal of Corpus Linguistics*, 14(3), 312–337.
Chomsky, N. (1981). *Lectures on government and binding*. Dordrecht, The Netherlands: Foris.
Cunnings, I., & Felser, C. (2013). The role of working memory in the processing of reflexives. *Language and Cognitive Processes*, 28(1–2), 188–219.
Cunnings, I., & Sturt, P. (2014). Coargumenthood and the processing of reflexives. *Journal of Memory and Language*, 75, 117–139.
Edwards, S., & Varlokosta, S. (2007). Pronominal and anaphoric reference in agrammatism. *Journal of Neurolinguistics*, 20, 423–444.

Fogarty, M. (2007). How to use 'myself' and other reflexive pronouns. *Grammar Girl's Quick and Dirty Tips*. Retrieved from www.quickanddirtytips.com/education/grammar/how-to-use-myself-and-other-reflexive-pronouns

Gast, V., & Siemund, P. (2006). Rethinking the relationship between self-intensifiers and reflexives. *Linguistics, 44*(2), 343–381.

Hernández, N. (2012). *Personal pronouns in the dialects of England: A corpus study of grammatical variation in spontaneous speech*. Doctoral thesis. Retrieved from www.freidok.uni-freiburg.de/volltexte/8431. Accessed 5 November 2016.

Hernández, N. (2015). Free *self*-forms in discourse-pragmatic functions: The role of viewpoint and contrast in picture NPs. In L. Gardelle & S. Sorlin (Eds.), *The pragmatics of personal pronouns* (pp. 45–67). London: John Benjamins.

Kjellmer, G., Aijmer, K., & Altenberg, B. (2004). Yourself: A general-purpose emphatic-reflexive. *Advances in Corpus Linguistics, 49*, 267–277.

Kuno, S. (1987). *Functional syntax: Anaphora, discourse and empathy*. Chicago: University of Chicago Press.

Labov, W. (1972). *Sociolinguistic patterns*. Philadelphia: University of Philadelphia Press.

Lederer, J. (2013). Understanding the *self*: How spatial parameters influence the distribution of anaphora within prepositional phrases. *Cognitive Linguistics, 24*(3), 483–529.

Llamas, C. (2007). Age. In C. Llamas, L. Mullany, & P. Stockwell (Eds.), *The Routledge companion to sociolinguistics* (pp. 69–76). Oxford: Routledge.

McEnery, T., & Wilson, A. (2001). *Corpus linguistics: An introduction* (2nd ed.). Edinburgh: Edinburgh University Press.

Meyerhoff, M. (2011). *Introducing sociolinguistics* (2nd ed.). New York, NY: Routledge.

Parker, F., Riley, K., & Meyer, C. F. (1990). Untriggered reflexive pronouns in English. *American Speech, 65*(1), 50–69.

Paterson, L. L. (2014). *British pronoun use, prescription and processing*. Basingstoke: Palgrave Macmillan.

Runner, J. T., Sussman, R. S., & Tanenhaus, M. T. (2003). Assignment of reference to reflexives and pronouns in picture noun phrases: Evidence from eye movements. *Cognition, 89*, B1–B13.

Siemund, P. (2010). Grammaticalization, lexicalization and intensification: English *itself* as a marker of middle situation types. *Linguistics, 48*(4), 797–835.

Sportiche, D. (2013). Binding theory-Structure sensitivity of referential dependencies. *Lingua, 130*, 187–208.

Stevens, H. (2012). Grammar-grouching on 'myself' issue. *Chicago Tribune*. Retrieved from http://articles.chicagotribune.com/2012-09-05/features/ct-tribu-words-work-myself-20120905_1_pronouns-grammar-girl-troublesome-words-you-ll-master

Taggart, C. (2010). *Her ladyship's guide to the queen's English*. London: National Trust Books.

Trudgill, P. (1974). *The social differentiation of English in Norwich*. Cambridge: Cambridge University Press.

van Gelderen, E. (2000). *A history of English reflexive pronouns: Person, self and interpretability*. London: John Benjamins.

Contributors

Karin Aijmer is Professor Emerita in English Linguistics at the University of Gothenburg, Sweden. Her research interests focus on pragmatics, discourse analysis, modality, corpus linguistics and contrastive analysis. Her books include *Conversational Routines in English: Convention and Creativity* (1996), *English Discourse Particles: Evidence from a Corpus* (2002), *The Semantic Field of Modal Certainty: A Study of Adverbs in English* (with co-author) (2007), and *Understanding Pragmatic Markers: A Variational Pragmatic Analysis* (2013). She is co-editor of *Pragmatics of Society* (Handbooks of Pragmatics, Mouton de Gruyter, 2011) and of *A Handbook of Corpus Pragmatics* (CUP, 2014), and co-author of *Pragmatics: An Advanced Resource Book for Students* (Routledge, 2012).

Karin Axelsson holds a permanent position as a Senior Lecturer in English Linguistics at the University of Skövde, Sweden. She is currently a Post-Doc Researcher in English linguistics at the Department of Languages and Literatures, University of Gothenburg, Sweden. She completed her PhD on tag questions in fiction dialogue in British English at the University of Gothenburg in 2011. Her main research interests are centred around tag questions in both writing and conversation, not only in English but also typologically and contrastively to Scandinavian languages. She has a general interest in corpus linguistics, in particular corpus compilation and representativeness.

Vaclav Brezina is a Lecturer at the Department of Linguistics and English Language, Lancaster University. His research interests are in the areas of corpus design & methodology, sociolinguistics and statistics. He is an author of *Statistics in Corpus Linguistics: A Practical Guide* (CUP, 2018). He also designed a number of different tools for corpus analysis such as #LancsBox, BNC64, Lancaster Vocab Tool and Lancaster Stats Tool online. He has been involved in the development of corpora such as the Spoken BNC2014, Trinity Lancaster Corpus and Guangwai-Lancaster Corpus.

Beatrix Busse is Professor of English Linguistics at Heidelberg University. Her research interests include corpus linguistics, English historical linguistics, Shakespeare studies, urban linguistics and stylistics. She is the reviews editor of the International Journal of Corpus Linguistics and member of the board of the Historical Thesaurus of the Oxford English Dictionary. Currently, she is working on the systematisation of multivariate discursive place-making strategies in Brooklyn, New York.

Paula Buttery is a Reader in Computing & Language in the Department of Computer Science & Technology at the University of Cambridge and a Fellow of Gonville & Caius College, Cambridge. Her research interests include the modelling of language acquisition, the language of individuals and technology for low-resource languages.

Andrew Caines is a Senior Research Associate at the University of Cambridge. He works for the Automated Language Teaching & Assessment Institute and his research interests are corpus linguistics, language acquisition, natural language processing of non-canonical and low-resource languages, and language change.

Jonathan Culpeper is Professor of English Language and Linguistics at Lancaster University, UK. His research spans pragmatics (especially sociopragmatics), stylistics (especially of plays) and the history of English (especially early modern English). His recent major publications include *Impoliteness: Using Language to Cause Offence* (CUP, 2011), *Pragmatics and the English Language* (Palgrave, 2014; co-authored with Michael Haugh), and *The Palgrave Handbook of (Im)politeness* (Palgrave, 2017; co-edited with Michael Haugh and Dániel Kádár).

Mathew Gillings is a PhD Student in the Department of Linguistics and English Language at Lancaster University. His research interests are in corpus, forensic, and sociolinguistics; he is currently using corpus methods to investigate verbal cues to deception. He is also a member of the research team for the AHRC-funded Encyclopaedia of Shakespeare's Language project.

Victorina González-Díaz is Senior Lecturer in English at the University of Liverpool. Her research interests cut across three main areas: historical syntax and semantics, historical stylistics and educational linguistics. She has published on the development of adjective comparison and the structure of the NP in English (see González-Díaz 2008, 2010, 2018), Jane Austen's language (see González-Díaz 2012, 2014) and has recently co-coordinated the development of a historical corpus of schoolchildren's writing and reading (APU corpus, see Yánez-Bouza and González-Díaz 2018).

Andrew Hardie is a Reader in Linguistics at Lancaster University. His main research interests are the theory and methodology of corpus linguistics; the descriptive and theoretical study of grammar using corpus data; the languages of Asia; and applications of corpus methods in the humanities and social sciences. He is one of the lead developers of the Corpus Workbench software for indexing and analysing corpus data, and the creator of its online interface, CQPweb. He is co-author, with Tony McEnery, of the book *Corpus Linguistics: Method, Theory and Practice* (2012).

Gard Jenset holds degrees in computer science and English, in addition to a PhD in English corpus linguistics from the University of Bergen (2010). After a position as Associate Professor of English Linguistics at Bergen University College, he has pursued industry work in natural language processing, computational linguistics and artificial intelligence for dialogue systems. He continues to publish research in historical linguistics, applied linguistics and corpus linguistics. With Barbara McGillivray, he is the co-author of *Quantitative Historical Linguistics* (2017) published by Oxford University Press.

Haidee Kruger is a Senior Lecturer in the Department of Linguistics at Macquarie University in Australia. She also holds a position as extraordinary professor in the research focus area Understanding and Processing Language in Complex Settings (UPSET), at the North-West University in South Africa. Haidee's current research interests are in areas of language variation and change, with a specific interest in the role of translation and editing in language-contact settings.

Robbie Love is a Research Fellow at the School of Education, University of Leeds, with research interests in applied and corpus linguistics. He completed his PhD at Lancaster University in 2017, where he was lead researcher in the development of the Spoken BNC2014. Before moving to Leeds, he held a post-doctoral position at Cambridge Assessment English, where he worked on the development of the Cambridge Learner Corpus.

Michael McCarthy is Emeritus Professor of Applied Linguistics, University of Nottingham. His interests include spoken corpora for the analysis of informal conversation and academic discourse, as well as learner spoken language.

Tony McEnery is Distinguished Professor of English Language and Linguistics at Lancaster University and Research Director of Economic and Social Research Council (ESRC). He is best known for his work on corpus linguistics. He is a former Director of a UK government-funded research centre called Corpus Approaches to Social Science (CASS) which aims to encourage the uptake of the corpus approach to the study of languages across the social sciences.

Barbara McGillivray is a Research Fellow at The Alan Turing Institute and at the University of Cambridge. Her research lies at the intersection between computational linguistics and historical linguistics. Her first book, *Methods in Latin Computational Linguistics*, was published by Brill in 2013; her second book, *Quantitative Historical Linguistics: A Corpus Framework*, co-authored with Gard Jenset, was published by Oxford University Press in 2017.

Laura L. Paterson is a Lecturer in Applied Linguistics and English Language at the Open University, UK. Her research focuses on representations of poverty, the methodological combination of geographical text analysis and discourse analysis, and discourses of marriage. She is author of *British Pronoun Use, Prescription, and Processing* (Palgrave, 2014) and co-author of *Discourses of Poverty and Place* (Palgrave, forthcoming). She is also editor of the Journal of Language and Discrimination.

Michael Rundell is Editor-in-Chief of Macmillan Dictionary and Chief Lexicographic Officer of Lexical Computing (the Sketch Engine company). He has been a lexicographer since 1980, and has worked at COBUILD (in the early 1980s), Longman (where he was involved in the development of the original BNC), and Macmillan. Together with the Sketch Engine team, he runs the Lexicom workshops, which provide training in lexicography and lexical computing all over the world. He is co-author with Sue Atkins of the *Oxford Guide to Practical Lexicography* (2008).

Tanja Säily is a Postdoctoral Researcher in the Department of Digital Humanities at the University of Helsinki. Her research interests include corpus linguistics, digital humanities, historical sociolinguistics, and English lexis and morphology. In collaboration with computer scientists, she has developed several corpus-linguistic tools and methods, such as *types*2, Text Variation Explorer, and the bootstrap test for keyword analysis. She is a member of the Research Unit for Variation, Contacts and Change in English (VARIENG) and a co-compiler of the Corpora of Early English Correspondence.

Jukka Suomela is an Assistant Professor in the Department of Computer Science at Aalto University, Finland. He works on algorithms and theory of computing, with the main focus on the foundations of distributed and parallel computing. He is a member of the council of EATCS, and he is one of the local chairs of ALGO 2018. He also participates in HELDIG, the Helsinki Centre for Digital Humanities; he is interested in algorithmic challenges arising from, e.g., linguistic research questions.

Deanna Wong is a Lecturer at the Department of Linguistics, Macquarie University. Her research interests are in the areas of corpus design and annotation, sociolinguistics and academic literacy. She is particularly interested in the spoken dimensions of human communication in face-to-face, online and academic contexts. She is currently involved in the development of the Macquarie University Student Literacy Corpus (MacLit), which is intended to establish links between pedagogical strategies and student outcomes.

Index

acceptability 237–239
adjective comparison 6, 159–161, 166–169, 172
age 4–6, 18, 28–29, 48, 61–64, 66, 72–73, 75, 77–80, 83–84, 86–87, 91, 97–99, 106–109, 111, 115–116, 121, 132–135, 139, 140, 142–143, 146–151, 159, 163, 165, 167, 174–175, 177, 186–187, 192, 196–197, 202, 203, 206, 210, 214–215, 218–219, 224–227, 230, 235, 239, 241, 249, 250, 252
analyticity 160, 179

backchannel 5, 120–131
backchannel, anchor 121, 131, 135–137, 146–152
backchannel, cluster 123, 129–131, 135–137, 146–147, 150–152
backchannel, S-structure 129, 131, 135–136, 139–140, 143, 145–152
Behagel's Law 186, 206
Bergen Corpus of London Teenage Language (COLT) 10, 62, 74, 79, 81, 86, 225, 229
binding theory 235–236, 240
BNCweb 27, 99, 106, 111
British politeness 5, 33–56
British politeness, cultural stereotype 33–36
British politeness, north-south 34–36, 51–55

Cambridge University Press 4, 11
Cancode 11, 125
C-index 203
collocation 29, 68, 72, 75–77, 88, 90, 221
collostructional analysis 221, 230

concordance 27–30, 51, 100, 106, 187, 189–194, 240
constructicon 214, 222
conversation analysis 47
coordinating conjunction 243, 245
core meaning 188–190, 211
corpus design 4, 10, 125
Corpus of English Conversation, A 103–104
corpus size 4, 63, 98, 100, 102, 111–114, 125, 151–152, 166, 169, 188, 210, 215
covert prestige 214, 219, 225
CQPweb 4–5, 27–30, 99, 101, 111–112, 127, 164, 190–192, 222

dative alternation 6, 185–186, 188, 190, 206
derivation 6, 159–163, 178–179
diachronic language change 5, 13, 66, 68, 80, 90, 97, 101–102, 105, 107, 110, 115–116, 159–160, 162–164, 166, 169–170, 172–173, 175, 177–179
discursive urban place-making 21
distribution 5, 18–22, 29, 44, 55, 66, 69, 85, 103, 106, 107, 109, 115–115, 135–137, 140, 143, 146–147, 149, 161, 170, 188, 194, 197, 199, 200, 214, 221–222, 225, 229, 235–236, 239–241, 244–252

education level, speaker's 19, 163, 166, 170, 186–187, 192, 194–197, 245, 248, 252
ellipsis 103, 105, 114, 116, 212
English, African-American 186
English, American 17, 45, 75, 78–79, 88–89, 124–125

English, Australian 44, 124, 186
English, New Zealand 80, 124, 186, 204
ethics 12, 49

gender, speaker's 5–6, 17–18, 29, 56, 61, 63–66, 72, 74, 79, 86, 90–91, 97–98, 106, 111, 115–117, 121, 132, 134–135, 139–140, 146, 150–151, 159, 163, 165, 170, 173–176, 178–179, 186–187, 192, 194, 197, 201–207, 214–217, 224–227, 239, 242, 252
generalised linear regression modelling 186
generative grammar 160, 214
grammatical person 108, 209–210, 215–229, 236–238, 241–244, 252

hypercorrection 248–252

ICE-GB 97, 102, 104–105, 112, 116
idiolect 111
indirectness 5, 33–34, 37, 54
inflection 6, 159–160, 162–163, 179
inflectional comparison 159–164, 166–170, 172–179
innit 5, 96–97, 99, 103–104, 107–108, 114, 116–117, 174
introspection 6, 185, 237

keywords 17, 30

linguistics 22
linguistics, computational 13
linguistics, corpus 3–5, 21, 200, 211, 235
linguistics, English 160–161
linguistics, historical 46
linguistics, variationist 126

metadata 3, 5, 27–30, 64, 99, 106, 112, 114, 121, 131–132, 151, 166–167, 187–188, 191–192, 194–197, 207, 216, 239, 241, 246, 248–249, 252
metrolingualism 20
mobilities 20
multivariate analysis 135, 186–187, 191, 194, 200

overlap, conversational 106, 113–114, 120, 122, 125

paralinguistics 114, 151–152
part of speech (POS) tagging 10, 51, 113–114, 117, 127, 164
Pattern Dictionary of English Verbs 189
perceptual dialectology 33, 36
periphrastic comparison 159–162, 164, 168–173, 177–179, 210
politeness 33–59, 74, 151
politeness, and class 33
politeness, and deference 37–38, 40–43, 51–55
politeness, and face 37–38
politeness, and formality 55
politeness, and solidarity 43–47, 51–55
politeness, and tentativeness 39–40, 51–55
politeness, expressions 36–48
politeness, frame-based approach 37
politeness, negative 34, 37–38
politeness, positive 37
power 17, 38, 41–44, 106, 115, 253
prepositional phrases 170–171, 185, 200, 206, 239, 244, 252
prescriptivism 20, 238, 248, 251, 253
prestige, covert 214, 219, 225
principle of least effort 213
productivity 6, 159–160, 162–166, 169–175, 177–179
progressive aspect 6, 209–211, 215–217, 222–223
prolific speakers 100–101, 111, 115–117, 242, 249, 252
pronominality 194, 199–200, 202–203, 206
punctuation 4, 111–114

reducing effect 213
register 17–18, 22, 163, 166–167, 170, 174–175, 190

selectional preferences 187, 189
semantic tag 192, 194, 196, 200–201
Sketch Engine 27
smartphone 12–13, 22
social class 64, 97–99, 106, 109–111, 114–116, 165, 167, 170, 173, 175, 179, 201, 214–215, 218, 220, 224–225, 227–228, 230, 235, 245–248, 252
socio-economic status 4–5, 7–8, 48, 121, 132, 135, 139–140, 142, 144, 148–151, 159, 163, 174, 187–188

sociolinguistics 3–6, 16–22, 60–63, 70, 74, 79, 90–91, 97–99, 103, 106, 111, 114–117, 126, 128, 131–132, 140, 146, 150, 152, 159, 162, 163, 166, 169, 177, 179, 185–197, 191, 194, 197, 200–201, 203, 206, 210, 212, 214–215, 219, 230, 235, 241, 245, 247
Stanford parser 190
s-unit 113
Switchboard Corpus 186
syntheticity 160, 179

tag questions 5, 71, 96–117, 212
tag questions, constant-polarity 104–106, 114
tag questions, imperative 108
tag questions, reversed-polarity 6, 104–105

third wave of sociolinguistic research 16–19, 177
transcriber 11, 28, 112, 128
transcription 12–13, 28, 46, 99, 116, 124, 127, 151, 215
transcription, guidelines 112–114, 128

UCREL semantic analysis system (USAS) 187, 192

variational pragmatics 19, 33

word sense disambiguation 189
w-unit 111

XML corpus markup 28, 99, 126–127

zero auxiliary 6, 209–230